Creditworthiness and 'Responsible Credit'

Comparative Law in Global Perspective

VOLUME 2

The titles published in this series are listed at *brill.com/clgp*

Creditworthiness and 'Responsible Credit'

A Comparative Study of EU and US Law

By

Noah Vardi

BRILL
NIJHOFF

LEIDEN | BOSTON

The Library of Congress Cataloging-in-Publication Data is available online at https://catalog.loc.gov
LC record available at https://lccn.loc.gov/2022026491

Typeface for the Latin, Greek, and Cyrillic scripts: "Brill". See and download: brill.com/brill-typeface.

ISSN 2772-5332
ISBN 978-90-04-52290-9 (hardback)
ISBN 978-90-04-52505-4 (e-book)

This book is printed on acid-free paper and produced in a sustainable manner.

To the memory of my father,
Moshe Vardi

∵

Contents

Acknowledgments

I would like to thank Professor Vincenzo Zeno-Zencovich for his insight and discussions on earlier drafts of the work, the General Editors of the Comparative Law in Global Perspective Series Professors Mauro Bussani and Giacinto della Cananea for hosting the book in the Series, and the Referees of the draft manuscript for their time and useful comments. I also wish to thank the many Colleagues with whom I have discussed parts of the ongoing research and the Max-Plank-Institut für ausländisches und internationales Privatrecht in Hamburg for its generous hospitality.

A special thank you, for their unwavering support, to Stefano and my family.

CHAPTER 1

Introduction: Creditworthiness and 'Responsible Credit'

Neither a borrower nor a lender be;
for loan doth oft lose both itself and friend, and
borrowing dulls the edge of husbandry
WILLIAM SHAKESPEARE, *Hamlet*, Act-I, Scene-III

∴

Introduction

An act of trust; a bet; a risk; a moral engagement and – of course – a legally binding contract: all these definitions can be used to describe a loan. Ever since money began to circulate in human communities, along with its well-known tripartite functions, it also became the object of an act of confidence (even before consolidating into a binding legal instrument): it could be lent to someone with an expectation of repayment. At the very origin of a loan there is an assumption of risk on behalf of both parties; the creditor gauges the probability of obtaining repayment and the borrower confides in the ability of doing so, whilst assuming the risk of the consequences if this becomes subjectively impossible. Excluding cases of fraud or bad faith or criminal intent – on either side –, a loan, whether for personal consumption or as a tool for investment, presupposes a 'responsible' behavior on behalf of both parties.

This comparative study is centered on the notion and problems posed by creditworthiness and 'responsible credit'. The aim of the research is to ascertain if and to what extent one can elaborate, in different legal systems, a legally enforceable duty to lend and borrow credit in a 'responsible' manner and what is the extent and meaning of the notion of 'creditworthiness' that is associated with responsible lending. More specifically, the research focuses on the functional relationship between these two notions.

The first issue concerns the substance and understanding of 'responsible credit' and whether it can be envisaged as a binding duty in existing normative frameworks. This requires first of all identifying the meaning of 'responsibility'

© KONINKLIJKE BRILL NV, LEIDEN, 2022 | DOI:10.1163/9789004525054_002

which is associated with the lending and borrowing practices, and then questioning whether there is a recognized and common normative understanding of the notion (even if it is not translated into positive norms). Responsible lending has a dual relevance, both as a duty towards the market and as a rule of conduct in the internal contractual relationship between lenders and borrowers. The study concentrates on these two interrelated aspects. Since the notion of responsibility is embedded within the deeper fundamental attitudes and values that characterize legal systems and legal traditions, a comparative study that takes into account duties arising from the breach of a 'responsibility' implies a comparison between these founding beliefs, and the interaction and influence they have over public policies and over individual fundamental rights.

It is here purported that responsible credit policies exist and can be found in the penumbra of regulation on banking risk management, consumer lending and consumer contracts, as well as in corporate borrowing, and a key instrument in existing legislation for the implementation of these policies is the 'assessment of creditworthiness' of borrowers. The research analyzes if and to what extent such a duty (of responsible credit) finds enforcement in private law.

The meaning and scope of a duty of 'responsible credit' can be outlined as a contractual (and pre-contractual) duty; such a duty can be effective both as a prudential rule at a systemic level and as one of the many duties of 'good behavior' required in contractual relationships between lenders and borrowers. The tools for ensuring the observance of this duty are supervisory in the first place and contractual in the second, and their concrete implementation depends on the legal background in which they are set; they are thus examined from a legal comparative perspective.

The second focus of the research is on the notion of 'creditworthiness': its legal meaning; whether and how the tool of creditworthiness assessment is used to implement policies of responsible lending and borrowing; and how, in this hypothesis, this affects the contractual freedom of lenders and borrowers. Furthermore, is 'creditworthiness' merely the result of a technical assessment, or does it have other implications, which require special attention? The question concerns the function of creditworthiness in ensuring access to credit, be it through a credit rating which allows firms to access the capital market, or a credit score that determines if and at which cost a consumer can borrow money or take out a mortgage (and the evident implications in terms of protection of personal and economic rights). The additional instruments that are necessary to ensure access to credit is not curtailed are therefore also examined.

The research analyzes the existence of duties of responsible credit both with reference to firms and corporate borrowers and with reference to consumer borrowers. The notion of 'creditworthiness', likewise, is examined both as a duty that derives from macro-prudential obligations (chapter 2) and in its concrete implications on individual loan contracts (chapters 3 and 4). The final part considers the impact of these duties on access to credit (chapter 5).

The study addresses these questions by analyzing topics that fall within the purport of comparative law, and more specifically, of private comparative law and of comparative law and regulation.

The first part of the research, which focuses on the macro-prudential aspects, is a comparative analysis of law and regulation; whilst the second part of the study, with its focus on the contractual implications tied to the duty of creditworthiness assessments, can be ascribed to the domain of private comparative law. The principal systems that are analyzed are the United States and European Union law, both of which have exported and contributed to the circulation of important models in this domain and have also reciprocally influenced each other, especially in the adoption of post-global financial crisis regulation.

1.1   Defining 'Responsible Credit'

The notion of 'responsible credit', as a measure to avoid insolvency and consumer over-indebtedness and comprising both a duty of 'responsible lending' and its counterpart duty of 'responsible borrowing' is neither a straightforward nor an uncontroversial notion.[1] Even defining the contours of these duties often leads to multiple and different answers.

The duty of responsible 'lending' is associated with the idea of consumer protection on the credit market and implies an assessment of the 'sustainability' of debt taken out by borrowers (not only at the precontractual stage, but also throughout the different phases of the contract).[2]

---

1   The expression 'responsible credit' is used throughout this study with this broader meaning. Where 'responsible lending' is used in the text it refers to specific obligations required only from lenders.

2   See I Ramsay, 'Consumer Credit Regulation after the Fall: International Dimensions', [2012] Journal of European Consumer and Market Law, 24, 33.

Theoretically, it may seem paradoxical and against their own self-interest for parties to engage in practices of 'irresponsible lending' and 'irresponsible borrowing'. Lenders have all interest to lend money that will be repaid, and tend to be risk-adverse; borrowers, with the exception of outright cases of fraud, have no interest in putting themselves into a position in which they are unable to repay their debts and have to face the consequences of insolvency.[3] However, as historical evidence (the most recent embodied by the 2007–2008 financial crisis triggered by the default of subprime mortgages)[4] has demonstrated, not only do financial markets allow distortions of these counter-intuitive principles, but moreover practices of 'irresponsible lending' may lead to systemic instability.

The issues surrounding responsible credit need to be framed within the wider process which has seen a growing expansion of the participation of citizens in financial and economic processes. This, however, does not mean that the effects of this participation are limited to consumers; it also affects the lending institutions, the credit market, and the stability of the system.

The growing relevance of 'responsible credit' policies is indeed due to the effects of several distinct but intertwining social and economic patterns. It can be framed as part of a process in a post-welfare state where the notion of social exclusion has emerged and where, in order to fight this phenomenon, there is an increased relevance of access to services in general, and to financial services more specifically (of which access to credit constitutes one, among other, instances).[5] Closely tied to this phenomenon are the effects of the so-called 'lending revolution' and 'democratization of credit' which took place at the beginning of the 1970's largely promoting financial liberalization, securitization, and increase in use of credit cards and other forms of credit; with the risk (and paradox) of increasing the number of low-income individuals accessing the financial market, but at the same time exposing them to the potentially negative effects of that same process of financialization (i.e. the

3   See F Ferretti, D Vandone, *Personal Debt in Europe. The EU Financial Market and Consumer Insolvency*, (Cambridge University Press 2019) 92.

4   ie SL Schwarcz, 'Understanding the Subprime Financial Crisis' (2008–2009) 60 South Carolina Law Review 549, with references to lenders' liability; O Bar-Gill, 'The Law, Economics and Psychology of Subprime Mortgage Contracts', (2009) 94 Cornell Law Review 1073.

5   See G Comparato, *The Financialisation of the Citizen* (Hart, 2018) 28 and ff. for a reconstruction of this phenomenon within the post-industrial society, also noting how "at the same time at which the state undertook a program of diminishing public indebtedness, the diffusion of financial services fostered private indebtedness" (Ibid 31).

On this, and for further bibliographical references, see *infra* Chapter 5 where the topic is analyzed with reference to access to credit and access to housing.

subprime crisis in the United States, or the effects of certain choices of bank risk management in Europe).[6]

Especially after the financial crisis, responsible credit has become a tool not only for the protection of consumers against over-indebtedness, but also a tool that is necessary for financial stability. Hence its importance, as previously highlighted, both from a systemic and prudential point of view, and from the point of view of individual credit contracts.

Irresponsible lending practices are often the result of market and regulatory failures.[7] Market failures in consumer credit markets are identified with asymmetries of information between consumers and the persons with whom they interact, and behavioral biases in consumer financial-decision making.[8] Information asymmetries exacerbate the already difficult evaluation of 'credence' goods, such as credit products, for consumers. Behavioral biases (including over-optimism, instantaneous gratification, reference dependence, myopia, and cumulative cost neglect) negatively affect consumers' ability to make rational borrowing decisions. In the absence of regulation (or where regulatory responses fail), lenders may engage in irresponsible lending practices and/or exploit consumer biases or ignorance and design credit products that profit from these asymmetries or irrational preferences. Examples include the provision of high-cost credit (including credit cards), the practice of cross-selling, and peer-to-peer lending (the latter entailing risks not only for consumer borrowers but also for consumer lenders).[9] These inefficient outcomes are made possible, as highlighted above, by several factors, that regulation should seek to correct.[10]

First of all, on the lender side, markets have devised instruments for lenders to transfer the risk of default of their debtors onto third parties, thus partly dismissing their stake in case of non-repayment. Furthermore, different studies have illustrated that 'irresponsible lending' may even prove to be a profitable model for creditors under certain conditions (i.e. the so-called 'sweatbox

---

6   See I Ramsay, 'Consumer Credit Law, Distributive Justice and the Welfare State', (1995) 15 Oxford Journal of Legal Studies 177; Comparato ibid, 27 and ff. recalling the English Turner Review (FSA Turner Review: A Regulatory Response to the Global Banking Crisis, March 2009), which highlights the effects of short-termism and risk-taking in UK bank risk management.

7   OO Cherednychenko, JM Meindertsma, 'Irresponsible Lending in the Post-Crisis Era: Is the EU Consumer Credit Directive Fit for Its Purpose?', (2019) 42 Journal of Consumer Policy 483, 490.

8   J Armour, D Awrey, P Davies, L Enriques, JN Gordon, C Mayer, J Payne, *Principles of Financial Regulation* (Oxford University Press 2016) 205–206.

9   OO Cherednychenko, JM Meindertsma (n 7) 491 and ff; 498.

10   J Armour et al (n 8) 218.

model'[11] for credit cards where revenue generation from late fees and penalties can constitute a significant source of income;[12] or where rollover and rebor-rowing practices (for example in payday loans) are highly profitable in terms of fees for lenders;[13] or where incentives for financial services providers, whose originating institutions do not eventually carry the credit risk, can lead for example to disregard for repayment ability of borrowers and failure to carry out proper creditworthiness assessments and evaluation of suitability).[14]

More generally, even without considering the – almost extreme – hypothesis of default of the borrower as a profitable event, the structure of certain credit contracts does not provide sufficient voluntary incentives for lenders to exercise responsible lending practices (i.e. the possibility of reverting to the underlying security in mortgage contracts; the growing use of insurance against default risk of the debtor; the possibility for lenders of passing on default risk through securitization; the sale of loan portfolios – see Chapter 2).

The case of the collapse of the subprime mortgage market in the United States is probably the most emblematic recent example raising issues on 'responsible credit' at point. The widespread growth of the subprime market especially during the five years prior to the crisis was due to multiple factors.[15]

---

11   RJ Mann, 'Bankruptcy Reform and the "Sweat Box" of Credit Card Debt', [2007] University of Illinois Law Review 375, 384 ff.; LM Ausubel, 'Credit Card Defaults, Credit Card Profits, and Bankruptcy' (1997) 71 American Bankruptcy Law Journal 249, 257 ff, also highlighting a tie between deregulation of the US credit card market and an increase in credit card profitability (ID at 260 ff.). On the problem of Pay-day loans see for example S Beddows, M McAteer, 'Payday lending: fixing a broken market', Association of Chartered Certified Accountants (2014) <https://inclusioncentre.co.uk/wp-content/uploads/2014/08/Payday-lending-full-report.pdf> (accessed November 2019).

12   See also World Bank, 'Global Survey on Consumer Protection and Financial Literacy: Oversight Frameworks and Practices in 114 Economies' (International Bank for Reconstruction and Development/The World Bank 2014) 24.

13   OO Cherednychenko, JM Meindertsma (n 7) 492–493.

14   World Bank (n 11) 24.

15   The subprime mortgage market rose in the 1990s, after two federal laws (the Depository Institutions Deregulation and Monetary Control Act of 1980 and the Alternative Mortgage Transaction Parity Act of 1982, followed by the Tax Reform Act of 1986 which made interest payments on mortgages and home equity loans deductible) opened the road for the adoption by lenders of risk-based pricing standards in mortgages and for the deregulation of interest rates. The growth of mortgage securitization (which began in the 1970s, with subprime securities made available in the 1990s) also played a major role in the development of the subprime market. A further stimulus to the subprime market came from specific policy regulations such as the Community Reinvestment Act ("CRA", first enacted in 1977 and updated in 2005), which aims at increasing home ownership among groups traditionally excluded from the credit market by encouraging depository institutions to help meet the credit needs of the communities in which they operate.

Subprime loans, in the jurisdictions where they are current, *per se* are not necessarily predatory loans,[16] and the creation of a 'subprime' market has to a certain extent guaranteed access to credit (and housing) to borrowers not meeting 'prime standards', furthermore allowing for the development of a more efficient lending market.[17]

However, what is particularly relevant is that whereas the higher risk for lenders issuing riskier loans was compensated by higher interest rates on the loans, this was not accompanied by sufficient awareness on behalf of borrowers of the cost – often hidden by the lenders – of those same risky loans. Subprime loans indeed are costly and 'suspect' because of, *inter alia*, cost deferrals and a high level of contractual complexity when compared to prime market mortgage contracts.[18]

In the UK, specific governmental policies aiming at promoting home ownership encouraged an increase in secured and unsecured borrowing, both by removing restrictions on bank lending and by liberalizing mortgage lending and making it possible for tenants in the social sector to purchase their dwellings (with the debt then securitized).[19] These policies contributed to the growth of a European securitization market, which in comparison to the United States was of minor dimensions and relatively heterogenous between countries. When compared to the US securitization market, driven by governmental agencies, the development of the European securitization market, starting from the late 1990's, was rather the result of an increased demand from institutional investors, technological and financial innovation and the introduction of the euro.[20]

See TJ Zywicki, JD Adamson, 'The Law and Economics of Subprime Lending', (2009) 80 University of Colorado Law Review 1, 6–8; MS Feldstein, 'Housing, Credit Markets and the Business Cycle ', Nat'l Bureau of Econ Research, (2007) Working Paper No. 13471, 2.

16   The very definition of loans as 'predatory' is uncertain; it has, for example, been summarized as a loan where there is no reasonable anticipated financial benefit to the borrower. See TJ Zywicki, JD Adamson, (n 14) 12, also recalling the definitions given by the US Federal Reserve as to what constitutes a 'predatory' loan and the criticisms that these defining attempts have raised.

17   See TJ Zywicki, JD Adamson, ibid, 6 ff.

18   O Bar-Gill, 'The Law, Economics and Psychology of Subprime Mortgage Contracts', (2009) 94 Cornell Law Review 1073, 1075–1077.

19   See the reconstruction by Comparato (n 5) 37 ff. See also JB Cullingworth, *Essays on Housing Policy* (Allen and Unwin 1979) and A De Vita, 'Diritto alla casa in diritto comparato', *Digesto delle discipline privatistiche, sez civile*, (4th ed UTET 1990), on the early emergence of housing policies in the UK and on the choice of favoring home ownership that is not common to all traditions when implementing a right to housing.

20   B Casu, A Sarkisyan, 'Securitization', in AN Berger, P Molyneux, JOS Wilson (eds), *The Oxford Handbook of Banking* (2d ed, Oxford University Press 2015), 354, 359.

1.2   Responsible Credit and the Global Financial Crisis

The global financial crisis in its origin, i.e. in the subprime crisis, has been narrated, alternatively, as the result of predatory lending behavior on behalf of creditors or as the outcome of irresponsible or fraudulent borrowers who underwrote mortgages, they knew they would not be able to repay.[21] Further theories developed a behavioral economics approach to explain subprime mortgage contracts as "the rational market response to imperfect rationality of borrowers" and as a case of both demand-side and supply-side market failures.[22] Another explanation of the subprime crisis highlights a general systematic mispricing of risk in the market.[23] Yet other evidence has demonstrated that the structure of the subprime market, in which, *inter alia*, the excessive complexity of contracts fosters inhibited competition, leads to above-cost pricing of the mortgages.[24] This higher profit margin in the subprime market contributed to inducing lenders to steer borrowers into subprime loans[25] – a phenomenon that was possible where regulatory standards were particularly "relaxed".[26]

Whereas the crisis clearly resulted from a complex combination of factors, that can only be very briefly mentioned, the outcome is what is relevant here: absent or insufficient regulation to disincentive 'irresponsible' extension of credit.

---

21   O Bar-Gill (n 18) 1079–1080, also quoting evidence found by JE Bethel, A Ferrell, G Hu, 'Legal and Economic Issues in Litigation Arising from the 2007–2008 Credit Crisis', Harvard John M. Olin Discussion Paper Series, 2/2008.

22   O Bar-Gill (n 18) 1079, ff. Myopic and optimistic borrowers respectively focus on the short-term dimension of the loan contract and underestimate the future cost of the deferred-cost contract. The market responds by offering deferred-cost contracts with low short-term prices and high long-term prices (Ibid 1119 ff.).

23   MS Feldstein (n 15) 3–4.

24   O Bar-Gill (n 18) 1131.

25   Ibid 1132.

26   Described as such by the Federal Reserve Board, which in the wake of the crisis proposed an amendment to the Truth in Lending Act: "Moreover, an atmosphere of relaxed standards, may increase the incidence of abusive lending practices by attracting less scrupulous originators into the market, while at the same time bringing more vulnerable borrowers into the market. These abuses can lead consumers to pay more for their loans than their risk profiles warrant". Truth in Lending, 73 Fed. Reg. 1672, at 1675 (proposed Jan. 9, 2008). For a reconstruction of some of the regulatory failures that were contributory causes of the crisis, see J Black, 'Paradoxes and Failures: 'New Governance' Techniques and the Financial Crisis', (2012) 75 The Modern Law Review 1037.

Other studies (again conducted on the US market) highlighted that there is a tie between increased consumer debt, specifically credit card debt, and a growth in bankruptcy filings (although with different effects on the short-term and on the long-term time horizons).[27] Bankruptcy files in turn can be seen as general externalities on the market and thus the political choice of placing or refusing liability for irresponsible lending can take into account whether these externalities are supported by subjects other than the lenders who are not repaid.[28]

Notwithstanding these structural risks and the spillover effects on the market that they may trigger, regulators have been very cautious with the idea of imposing a duty of 'responsible lending'. As is well known, the understanding of what constitutes 'responsible' conduct is historically, culturally, socially and economically differentiated both in lay terms as well as in legal terms; within the latter, the notion is further differentiated across legal systems and traditions.[29] This inevitably reflects on the subsequent framing of 'responsible

---

27   See i.e. RJ Mann, 'Credit Cards, Consumer Credit & Bankruptcy', (2006) University of Texas School of Law Law and Economics Research Paper n. 44; RM Lawless, 'The Paradox of Consumer Credit', (2007) 1 University of Illinois Law Review 347; LM Ausubel, (n 11); JAE Pottow, 'Private Liability for Reckless Consumer Lending', (2007) 1 University of Illinois Law Review 405, 409.

28   On the externality effects of bankruptcy filings see RJ Mann, *Charging Ahead. The Growth and Regulation of Payment Card Markets around the World* (Cambridge University Press, 2006) 196; RJ Mann, (n 27) 7, 23; but also B Adler, B Polak, A Schwartz, 'Regulating Consumer Bankruptcy: A theoretical Inquiry', (2000) 29 Journal of Legal Studies 585; T Sullivan, E Warren, J Westbrook, *The Fragile Middle Class: Americans in Debt* (Yale University Press 2000).

29   Even a simplified attempt at a reconstruction of the notion of 'responsibility' in comparative law is far beyond the scope of these introductory notes. May it simply be highlighted that the legal notion is tightly intertwined with the cultural dimension of tort law and the set of deep values that legal systems choose to protect (see for example, for considerations in comparative law, anthropology and tort law: R Sacco, *Antropologia giuridica. Contributo ad una macrostoria del diritto* (Il Mulino 2007); R Verdier (ed), *La Vengeance: La vengeance dans les sociétés extra-occidentales* (Cujas 1980); G Calabresi, *Ideals, Beliefs, Attitudes, and the Law. Private Law Perspectives on a Public Law Problem* (Syracuse University Press 1985); L Nader, *The Life of the Law. Anthropological Projects* (University of California Press 2002); MS Shapo, *Tort Law and Culture* (Carolina Academic Press 2003); RF Cochran, RM Ackerman, *Law and Community. The Case of Torts* (Rowman & Littlefield 2004); K Oliphant 'Culture of Tort Law in Europe' (2012) 3 Journal of European Tort Law 147; DM Engel, M McCann (eds), *Fault Lines. Tort Law as Cultural Practice* (Stanford University Press 2009); DM Engel, 'Lumping as Default in Tort Cases: The Cultural Interpretation of Injury and Causation', (2010) 44 Loyola of Los Angeles Law Review 33; M Bussani, M Infantino, 'The many cultures of tort liability' in M Bussani, AJ Sebok (eds), *Comparative Tort Law. Global Perspectives* (Elgar 2015)).

lending' or 'responsible borrowing' duties and their consequences if and when they are enforced. Indeed, since 'responsibility' encompasses a strong moral and cultural meaning, closely tied to the set of values that legal systems choose to protect and to the means and legal formants through which they are protected, it is necessary to compare both these founding legal ideals and their implementation within the systems (including the remedial and litigation apparatus that is offered in case of their infringement).[30]

As will emerge from a comparative analysis, the approach towards debt, towards creditor and/or debtor protection, towards a stronger or weaker regulation of the credit markets, and the attitude towards the promotion of public or private mechanisms for the access to welfare services and to housing (which pass through access to loans and to mortgages), are the result of different developments in national legal cultures; findings show that attitudes and policies are not necessarily convergent, on the contrary. Whilst certain major economic crises that hit globally (such as the global financial crisis of 2007–2008 and the COVID-19 crisis of 2020) have triggered coordinated responses under several aspects, especially in the immediate aftermath of the emergencies, it is on the longer run that the adoption of common policies – such as responsible credit for example – encounter obstacles. Even where notions of 'responsible credit' circulate across systems, the degree of their concrete implementation (if any) and the means through which this occurs (imposing contractual duties or rather envisaging liabilities in tort) display differing attitudes (see Chapter 4).

The notion and implementation of the idea of 'control' over lending has traditionally focused on debtors, more specifically on debtors that qualify as consumers. This perspective is justified by the need to ensure access to credit, to avoid financial exclusion and to ensure transparency of conditions. Consequently, as a remedy to cases of irresponsible lending, legislators in many systems have implemented rules on over-indebtedness, discharge, and

---

30   On the deep connections between cultural and social order and litigation systems, see for example O Chase, *Law, Culture and Ritual. Disputing Systems in Cross-Cultural Context* (New York University Press 2005); WLF Felstiner, RL Abel, A Sarat, 'The Emergence and Transformation of Disputes: Naming, Blaming, Claiming ...' (1980–1981) 15 Law & Society Review 631; RE Miller, A Sarat, 'Grievances, Claims, and Disputes: Assessing the Adversary Culture', (1980–1981) 15 Law & Society Review 525; M Galanter, 'Real World Torts: An Antidote to Anecdote', (1996) 55 Maryland Law Review1093; on the unofficial adjudication and settlement mechanisms see RC Ellickson, *Order without Law: How Neighbors Settle Disputes* (Harvard University Press 1999); RL Abel, *The Politics of Informal Justice. Vol.2: Comparative Studies* (Academic Press 1981); with reference to contractual litigation, S Maculay, 'Elegant Models, Empirical Pictures, and the Complexities of Contract', (1977) 11 Law & Society Review 507.

'consumer' bankruptcy; courts in some legal systems have recognized cases of so-called 'social force majeure',[31] and specific measures relating to consumer credit (both for the sale of consumer goods and in case of mortgages) have been approved. Less attention has been given to the responsibility of the lenders. The problem of so-called 'responsible lending' has not been tackled with the same strength as its counter-face of 'access to credit'. That is, until the aftermath of the 2007–2008 global financial crisis.

A Global Survey on Financial Consumer Protection and Financial Literacy conducted by the World Bank in 2013 for example, suggested that a vast majority – 80 out of 114 (77%) – of the countries that responded had some form of responsible lending provisions (i.e. explicit limits to lending such as loan-to-value ratios or debt service ratios, or requirements for lenders to assess the ability to repay the loan).[32]

In the European Union for example, different initiatives were undertaken in the form of public consultations, studies, opinions of the EU institutions which consider the problem of 'responsible credit', mostly under the perspective of tackling the problems of personal debt and consumer over-indebtedness

---

31   The concept of 'social *force majeure*' in the context of consumer over-indebtedness has been analyzed by T Wilhelmsson in *Critical Studies in Private Law. A Treatise on Need-Rational Principles in Modern Law* (Springer 1992) 180–216. The concept is recognized in Scandinavian law and it refers to those situations in which due to illness, unemployment or other such unforeseen changes beyond his control, a debtor is not able to repay his debt. The application of the doctrine of 'social *force majeure*' allows alleviation of interest, or other fees related to delay, and it applies to certain contractual relations that are characterized by an unequal power relationship between debtor and creditor (i.e. consumer law, labor law, apartment leases). See also J Niemi, 'Personal Insolvency' in G Howells, I Ramsay, T Wilhelmsson, D Kraft (eds), *Handbook of Research on International Consumer Law* (Elgar 2010), 409, 417–418, highlighting that the doctrine of 'social force majeure' in the context of consumer over-indebtedness is probably not bold enough and sometimes of difficult practical application, for it to be an effective instrument of relief.

32   54% of the countries with requirements for lenders to assess repayment ability have no explicit limits. The Survey highlights an increase, in the aftermath of the financial crisis, of countries with explicit limits: from 20 in 2009 to 40 in 2013. World Bank (n 11) 24. The Survey underlines how "there is very little empirical research on whether these quantitative limits work or justification for setting the value of the limits" (ID at 25). A study conducted by the UK's FSA in 2011 for example assesses the correlations between loan-to-value (LTV) limits, debt-service ratio (DSR) and probability of impairment, finding that the LTV and DSR are not strong predictors of loan impairment, based on the mortgage data available. The study resulted in a recommendation not to set any explicit limits (UK Financial Services Authority, 'Mortgage Market review: proposed package of reforms' Consultation Paper CP11/31, December 2011, 57–59 https://www.fca.org.uk/publication/consultation/fsa-cp11-31.pdf (accessed November 2019)).

that emerged alarmingly with the financial crisis.[33] The stance that this policy seems to take, is oriented towards the 'preventive' phase, aiming at delivering a 'responsible and reliable' credit market which is competitive, trustworthy, enables access to credit on fair terms and rejects irresponsible practices. The perspective adopted is thus the economic perspective of the market.[34]

According to this approach, 'responsible lending' policies should "ensure that credit products are appropriate for consumers' needs and tailored to their ability to repay their debts";[35] this means putting in place an appropriate

---

33   European Economic and Social Committee, 'Opinion of the Economic and Social Committee on 'Consumer protection and appropriate treatment of over-indebtedness to prevent social-exclusion' (Explanatory opinion)', INT/726, Brussels, 29 April 2014; Communication from the Commission to the European Parliament, the Council and the European Central Bank, the European Economic and Social Committee and the Committee of the Regions 'Consumer Financial Services Action Plan: Better Products, More Choice' COM (2017) 139 final; European Commission, 'Communication of the European Commission to the European Council of 4 March 2009 'Driving European Recovery'', COM (2009) 114; European Commission, 'Public Consultation on Responsible Lending and Borrowing', 15 June 2009. Before the crisis, starting in the 1990's, several important studies on debt relief and consumer over-indebtedness were published in the EU, often upon commission of the EU Institutions themselves; these include *inter alia* N Huls et Al, *Overindebtedness of Consumers in the EC Member States: Facts and Search for Solutions* (Story Scientia 1994); International Federation of Insolvency Professionals (INSOL), 'Consumer Debt Report: Report of Findings and Recommendations' (2001) <https://www.insol.org/_files/pdf/consdebt.pdf> (accessed November 2019); U Reifner, J Kiesiläinen, N Huls, H Springeneer, 'Consumer Overindebtedness and Consumer Law in the European Union: Final Report 16–17' (Contract Reference No. B5–1000/02/000353) (2003); European Commission, Enterprise Directorate General, *Best Project on Restructuring, Bankruptcy and a Fresh Start, Final Report of the Expert Group* (2003), (available at <https://www.iiiglobal.org/sites/default/files/EuropeanUnionProjectonRestructuringReportof Experts.pdf> (accessed November 2019)); European Council, J Niemi-Kiesiläinen, A Henrikson, Bureau of the European Committee on Legal Co-Operation (CDCJ-BU), 'Report on Legal Solutions to Debt Problems In Credit Societies' (2005) <https://rm.coe.int/16807004bd> (accessed November 2019). See JJ Kilborn, 'Expert Recommendations and the Evolution of European Best Practices for the Treatment of Overindebtedness, 1984–2010' (2010) <https://ssrn.com/abstract=1663108> (accessed November 2019).
34   See for example the Recitals of the Consumer Credit Directive (Directive 2008/48/EC of 23 April 2008 on credit agreements for consumers [2008] OJ L133/66) and of the Mortgage Credit Directive (Directive 2014/17/EU of 4 February 2014 on credit agreements for consumers relating to residential immovable property [2014] OJ L60/34). See F Ferretti, D Vandone, *Personal Debt in Europe. The EU Financial Market and Consumer Insolvency* (Cambridge University Press 2019) 88–89.
35   European Commission, 'Public Consultation on Responsible Lending and Borrowing' (n 33) 1.

framework "to ensure that all lenders and intermediaries act in a fair, honest and professional manner, before, during and after the lending transaction".[36]

As already highlighted, the counterparty to responsible lending is 'responsible borrowing', that in this context should be achieved by ensuring that in order to obtain a credit, "consumers should provide relevant, complete and accurate information on their financial conditions, and are encouraged to make informed and sustainable borrowing decisions".[37] The extent to which these policy declarations have been translated into effective and binding regulation is a matter which will be analyzed further (see Chapter 4).

1.3   Profiles of Relevance of Responsible Credit

Responsible credit has a dual profile of relevance. A general, systemic, macroprudential level, in which issues such as credit risk management, non-performing loans (NPLS), and creditworthiness assessment have a public law dimension which requires a perspective of comparative law and regulation (see Chapter 2); and a private law, individual level, which moves from the issues of ensuring access to credit down to the available remedies in contract and/or tort where the duties of 'responsible lending' have been breached, which is addressed through an analysis in private comparative law. However, as is counterintuitive, even the latter individual dimension has a series of effects on contractual parity, private autonomy, protection of entire categories of borrowers which in turn affect markets and, at a broader level still, the legal system. The comparison of the rules at the micro-level of contracts or torts yields a broader framework of the macro-policies that legal systems have embraced or wish to implement as a reaction to previous instability.

Another important dual profile that should be taken into account when considering responsible credit is its relationship with debt and insolvency procedures. 'Responsible credit' concerns the creation of a market of credit having certain characteristics mentioned above (trustworthiness, competition, absence of unfair practices); it can be considered as the 'preventive' phase if put into relation with insolvency and over-indebtedness (which, however, are beyond the scope of this study).

A systemic overview of different branches of regulation dealing with credit, banking supervision, financial instruments and prudential requirements for market operators, which fall into the changes in international financial

---

36   Ibid.
37   Ibid.

regulation adopted after the 2007–2008 crisis, reveals that a notion of 'responsible lending' can not only be identified, albeit as a hazed silhouette, rather than as a clear set of rules, but also that it is one that finds forms of positive implementation. One of the principal tools for the implementation of this policy is the practice of 'creditworthiness assessment' of borrowers.

Suffice it to recall the obligations of 'creditworthiness assessment' imposed in various degrees at the EU level by the Consumer Credit Directive;[38] the Mortgage Credit Directive;[39] the Capital Requirements Directive;[40] the Capital Requirements Regulation;[41] the Credit Rating Agencies Regulation[42] and the Credit Rating Agencies Directive;[43] the two Market in Financial Instruments Directives;[44] or the 'ability to pay rule' introduced by the Dodd-Frank Act in the United States.[45] The concrete modalities with which these assessments take place will be examined both for corporate and sovereign borrowers (Chapter 2) and for individual borrowers, with the ensuing problems tied to credit scoring (Chapter 3).

---

38   Directive 2008/48/EC, article 8 on obligation to assess the creditworthiness of the consumer, article 5(q) article 6(j) on right to be informed of result of database consultation; article 9 on database access. See also Article 18 of the Commission 'Proposal for a Directive on credit for consumers' COM(2002) 443 final.

39   Directive 2014/17/EU, article 18 and article 20(1).

40   Directive 2013/36/EU of 26 June 2013 on access to the activity of credit institutions and the prudential supervision of credit institutions and investment firms [2013] OJ L 176/338), article 77(1)(2).

41   Regulation 575/2013 of 26 June 2013 on prudential requirements for credit institutions and investment firms [2013] OJ L 176/1, article 129, article 217, article 286, article 453.

42   Regulation 462/13/EU of 21 May 2013 on credit rating agencies [2013] OJ L 146/1, preamble 9, preamble 15, preamble 30.

43   Directive 2013/14/EU of 21 May 2013 amending Directive 2003/41 on the activities and supervision of institutions for occupational retirement provision, Directive 2009/65/EU on the coordination of laws, regulations and administrative provisions relating to undertakings for collective investment in transferable securities (UCITS) and Directive 2011/61/ EU on Alternative Investment Funds Managers in respect of over-reliance on credit ratings [2013] OJ L 145/1, articles 1–3.

44   Directive 2004/39/EC of 21 April 2004, MiFID [2004] OJ L145/1 (abrogated by MiFID II), art. 19, (4)), (requiring investment firms, when providing investment advice to obtain the necessary information regarding the client's knowledge and experience in the investment field [...] so as to enable the firm to recommend to the client the investment services and financial instruments that are suitable for him); and Directive 2014/65/EU of 15 May 2014 on markets in financial instruments and amending Directive 2002/92/EC and Directive 2011/61/EU (MIFID II) [2014] OJ L173/349, article 25.

45   Dodd-Frank Wall Street Reform and Consumer Protection Act of 2010; 15 U.S.C. § 1639(c) – Dodd-Frank Act § 1411.

The fact that provisions imposing some form of prudential requirement and/or duty of assessment on lenders and financial services providers are found in regulations ranging from those on capital requirements and credit rating agencies to those on consumer credit and mortgages indicates that concern with 'responsible lending' is concrete and systemic. Furthermore, it regards not only private institutions and private consumers, but also public lenders and it is one of the tools that are invoked for the promotion of an efficient and competitive market in the banking and in the financial services sector.

1.4   Creditworthiness

The notion of "creditworthiness", expressed with this term in various languages (i.e. *merito creditizio* in Italian, *Kreditwürdigkeit* in German, *kredietwaardigheid* in Dutch, but interestingly *solvabilitè* in French and *solvencia* in Spanish) is adopted in legislative acts in various contexts and mostly associated with a test or assessment to be carried out on prospective borrowers.[46]

---

46   As previously observed regarding the notion of 'responsibility', the choice of differentiated terms is not irrelevant as it reflects different cultural and value-based meanings. Studies in law and language have long highlighted the close interconnection between law, language, and culture and the fundamental importance of language and legal translation in comparative law. See, under different disciplinary approaches, M Beaupré, I Kitamura, GR De Groot, JH Herbots, R Sacco, 'La traduction juridique', (1987) 28 Les Cahiers de droit, 734; B Bergmans, 'L'enseignement d'une terminologie juridique étrangère comme mode d'approche du droit comparé: l'exemple de l'allemand' (1987) 39 Revue internationale de droit comparé 89; multiple Authors 'Le langage du droit' (1974) 19 Archives de philosophie du droit; J-C Gémar, *Langage du droit et traduction: essais de jurilinguistique* (Linguatech 1982); R Sacco, 'Legal Formants, A Dynamic Approach to Comparative Law I' , (1991) 39 American Journal of Comparative Law 1; F Schauer, *Law and Language* (New York University Press 1993); B Bix, *Law, Language, and Legal Determinacy* (Oxford University Press, 1995); S Šarčević, *New Approach to Legal Translation* (Kluwer Law International 1997); R Sacco, 'Traduzione giuridica', in *Digesto delle discipline privatistiche, Aggiornamento*, (2000), 722; B Pozzo (ed), *Ordinary Language and Legal Language* (Giuffrè, 2005); D Cao, *Translating Law* (Multilingual Matters 2007); C Bocquet, *La traduction juridique: Fondement et méthode* (De Boeck 2008); G Dannemann, S Ferreri, M Graziadei, 'Language and terminology' in C Twigg Flessner (ed) *The Cambridge Companion to European Private Law* (Cambridge University Press 2010) 70; B Pozzo, *Lingua e diritto: oltre l'Europa* (Giuffrè 2014); B Pozzo, 'Comparative law and language' in M. Bussani, U. Mattei (eds) *The Cambridge Companion to Comparative Law* (Cambridge University Press 2012) 88; HES Mattila, *Comparative Legal Linguistics. Language of Law, Latin and Modern Lingua Francas*, (2d. ed. Routledge 2016).

In its literal meaning, 'worthy – of – credit' one finds a clear trace of a historical and social interpretation of the relationship between a creditor and a debtor, coined in terms of a tie based on trust. Hence the notion of "worthiness" that, also from an etymological point of view, implies a moral quality. The evaluation of a prospective borrower, of someone who applies for a loan, carries with it a strong subjective element: someone who is reliable, worthy of trust, who will do all it takes to pay back a loan – and who, most importantly, is willing to do so. Needless to say that the idea of one's credit history, regardless of the different notion of creditworthiness that is currently used (as this study purports to demonstrate), is a direct descendant of a subjective understanding of creditworthiness: a positive historical record vouches in favor of one's reliability (or 'worthiness') and correspondingly a negative credit history (symbolically translated into a 'low credit score', just like a low grade) becomes a background check in practice serving a function that can be assimilated to any other background check (i.e. criminal records) used by an employer, lessor, lender, to evaluate the reliability and personal qualities of a prospective employee, borrower, lessee.

This subjective understanding of 'creditworthiness' and the use that is made of one's credit history in the precontractual phase in several areas of economic exchanges, does not however sufficiently take into account that when legislative acts today require an assessment of a borrower's creditworthiness, the evaluation is much more objective than subjective.

The expression that best translates the change in the notion is that of an assessment of credit 'affordability' (an expression indeed used in statutes for example in the UK and in the United States). This study aims at highlighting precisely how this notion has evolved from a subjective to an objective understanding and how, as a consequence, it is used as one of the principal tools for the implementation of responsible credit policies. Irresponsible lending or borrowing is based on objective parameters, if it is to be used as a prudential tool of prevention of over-indebtedness. This does not entail however, that creditworthiness assessments (or rather 'affordability' assessments) should not be accompanied by additional instruments of evaluation that can take into account inclusion policies.

From a cultural point of view, it is important to recall how the transformation of the ethics of debt and the boost given by democratization of credit have altered the historical perception of creditworthiness and the notion of 'trust' surrounding lending. Credit used to be a relationship based on personal knowledge, trust and reputation within a community ("a strong belief or faith or trust in both the integrity and the duration of the community to which all creditors and debtors belonged" that "made it possible to measure the value of immediate payment against the value of payment at a later date")[47] and which helped the consolidation of the *lex mercatoria* in Europe in the late Eleventh, Twelfth, and Thirteenth centuries. In this context, breach of trust in the form of insolvency could affect the reputation of an entire community of merchants and insolvency was harshly punished;[48] under a religious conception (particularly under a Protestant ethic) frugality was a virtue, money was not to be shown off and debts (mostly coinciding with moral sin) had to be repaid as a matter of morality.[49] In the early modern market of the Sixteenth Century in England this allowed credit to be granted on trust, without specific legally binding instruments;[50] this was completely transformed in the Twentieth century with the expansion of lending on a global scale.[51]

The growth of credit markets and their territorial expansion, first with the development of consumer credit in its earlier forms, later with the phenomenon of democratization of credit, managed by complex and often transnational lending institutions and with the introduction of consumer lending and its growing impersonal nature, has altered the cultural and social perception of debt and the 'trustworthy relationship' at the basis of loans. The contemporary instruments that are used and constantly refined for 'efficient and quick and large scale' creditworthiness assessments reflect a system in which 'interpersonal trust' is replaced with "technological instruments which allow for more reliable predictions as to the likelihood of reimbursement and default of the debtor, becoming increasingly more exact, but at the same time, more intrusive" (i.e. credit scoring).[52]

1.5   Caution and Criticisms

Resistance against the introduction of 'duties of responsible lending' is multifaceted and based on numerous and different reasons. Suffice it to briefly recall the existence of measures that allow the discharge of the distressed debtor;

---

47   HJ Berman, *Law and Revolution* (Harvard University Press 1983) 351.
48   Ibid 350; C Muldrew, 'Interpreting the Market: The Ethics of Credit and Community Relations in Early Modern England', (1993) 18 Social History 163, 169. For interesting observations on the growth of public versus 'private' banking in medieval Italy, see G Todeschini 'La banca e il ghetto. Una storia italiana (secoli XIV–XVI)' (Laterza 2016).
49   See the critical reconstruction offered by Comparato (n 5) 38, moving from Max Weber's *Protestant Ethic and the Spirit of Capitalism*.
50   See Muldrew ibid.
51   Comparato (n 5) 45.
52   Comparato (n 5) 46.

the risk of financial exclusion; the increase in the cost of credit; the concern that 'creditworthiness assessment' duties and use and recording of credit history may negatively impact on personal data protection. More in general, the efficiency of a paternalist regulator can be questioned and it is accompanied by the defense of the principle of 'responsible borrowing' and the belief that this should be the tool to contrast predatory lending (a belief that is, however, disturbed by evidence of cognitive bias on behalf of optimistic borrowers).

Indeed, the risk of 'promoting' irresponsible borrowing (and a certain degree of moral hazard on behalf of debtors who expect the risk and liability of their default to fall on creditors)[53] is often invoked. Finally, some have argued that policies of responsible lending are useless in cases in which default of the borrower was unforeseeable at the moment in which the loan was being negotiated, because it is the result of an unexpected event in the life of the debtor.

Not only. Even once these resistances are outweighed by considerations based on systemic risk and more generally 'consumer' protection, the attempt of giving implementation to a duty of 'responsible lending' may clash with other economic policies relating to the market of credit (measures to ensure access to credit, to enhance competition between credit providers, ensure low-cost credit, contrast the credit crunch, promote 'democratization of credit', etc.). More generally, it may be perceived as an unacceptable interference with contractual private autonomy with possible effects on access to credit, impacting on fundamental rights (see Chapter 5). This reflects once again the profound differences in legal culture towards regulatory approaches: from admitting the legitimacy or even need of a paternalist legislator, to concern with defending contractual freedom against (unnecessary) interferences.

It should be noted however, that pursuing what may be defined as 'responsible credit' (whether through *ex ante* measures or through *ex post* liabilities) responds to general interests that transcend the single creditor-debtor relationship. As has been highlighted, first of all the systemic stability of the credit market is at stake (indeed, the impact of defaults and NPLs is all too well known). Secondly, if it is true that authoritative interventions restricting private autonomy of the parties may and should be looked upon with caution, it is neither the first nor the last instance of regulatory intervention in contractual autonomy. This intervention could be justifiable, *inter alia*, with the need to correct informational asymmetry between the parties and to supplement – substantially – the sometimes ineffective and/or insufficient simple duty of information that the lender owes the borrower. Thirdly, the

---

53   On moral hazard and consumer bankruptcy see *inter alia* Adler, Polak, Schwartz (n 28) 593 ff.

concern of avoiding the overall negative social impact of over-indebtedness is at times also brought forth as a justification for regulatory interference with party autonomy.

These issues are of course closely related to the problem of access to credit, to the extent that promoting strict policies of responsible lending may curtail access to credit for the most vulnerable categories of borrowers, who run the greatest risk of financial and social exclusion. The principal concerns are tied to the consequences that ensue from an interpretation of responsible credit solely as an instrument to implement prudential standards and respond to macro-economic and systemic policies. Under this perspective, it is feared that it is more likely to become a tool to deny credit rather than to promote access to 'suitable', 'adequate' and 'affordable' loans. Striking a balance between paternalistic and protective rules (also dictated by systemic stability concerns), which can cut off large categories of potential borrowers for 'their own sake' on the one side, and theorizing 'a right to credit' on the other, requires delicate weighing. The use of heightened transparency and the doctrines developed in regulating access to services (for example in EU law) with reference to the rules on creditworthiness assessment, in what can be termed 'a due process in access to credit', can be a valuable instrument for a more conscious balancing of parties' rights and duties (see Chapter 5).

Finally, it may be questionable whether concerns regarding 'responsible lending' should be limited to borrowers who qualify as 'consumers'. If one considers the systemic repercussions of negligent loans on the market and on global finance, it may be worthwhile to question the extension of the duty to 'borrowers' more generally, thus including for example (at least to begin with) SME's.

1.6   Methodology

When addressing responsible lending, existing literature focuses mostly on consumer over-indebtedness, on financial literacy, creditworthiness and financial exclusion. The tool of creditworthiness assessment, whilst acknowledged, is not analyzed with a comprehensive cross-sector approach. The perspective here proposed takes into account both the lender and the borrower sides and examines different sectors in which this takes place, from the assessment of issuers by credit rating agencies down to the credit scoring of individual consumers, adopting both a macro-comparative (i.e. prudential analysis and its implications) and a micro-comparative (remedies and redresses) analysis. This study thus aims at providing a wider viewpoint, but also at highlighting some recurring problematic elements such as the liability of those who carry out the evaluation in case of negligent or inaccurate rating/scoring/reporting, or the professional duties by both parties in the precontractual phase.

The research applies comparative legal methodologies and tries to identify trends, convergences and divergences between the existing models adopted in the United States and in the European Union (with subsequent transposition into European Member States). In the domain of credit and debt, of contractual, social, and also regulatory relationships, different tools prove to be useful in conducting a comparative analysis.

From a methodological point of view, one cannot proceed without engaging first of all with the functional method, even being well aware of its criticisms and of the fact that there are multiple functional approaches (so that there is not a single, but rather a multiplicity of functional methods)[54] and that "functionalism need not be divorced from the conceptual structure of various legal systems".[55] Indeed, studies in comparative law and regulation also highlight the usefulness of this methodology (along with classification and the causal theory of legal transplants).[56]

As regards functionalism, the first approach used can be defined a multi-level functional approach. The traditional principle of functionalism as developed in comparative legal studies is here applied at multiple levels that operate both horizontally (in a comparison between models of regulation adopted in different legal systems so as to ensure a form of evaluation of the

---

[54] The first reference is of course to K Zweigert and H Kötz, *An Introduction to Comparative Law* (T Weir tr, 3rd ed, Oxford University Press 1998) 32–47, first published in K Zweigert, H Kötz, *Einführung in die* Rechtsvergleichung, vol 1, (Mohr 1971) 27–48; on the further developments, analysis, and criticisms of the method, see *ex multis*, R Michaels, 'The Functional Method of Comparative Law', in M Reimann, R Zimmermann (eds), *The Oxford Handbook of Comparative Law* (Oxford University Press 2006) 339, 342–45; E Örücü 'Methodology of Comparative Law' in JM Smits (Ed), *Elgar Encyclopedia of Comparative Law* (Edward Elgar 2012) 442; J Gordley, 'The Functional Method' in PG Monateri (ed), *Methods of Comparative Law* (Edward Elgar 2012), 107; M Graziadei, 'The functionalist heritage' in P Legrand, R Munday (eds), *Comparative Legal Studies: Traditions and Transitions* (Cambridge University Press 2003) highlighting at p.125–126 how "functionalism promised to cut across municipal legal categories ... and to cast light on the relationship between law and society" as a means of escaping from legal mentalités; J Husa, 'Farewell to Functionalism or Methodological Tolerance?' (2003) 67 Rabels Zeitschrift für ausländisches und internationales Privatrecht 419.

[55] G Samuel, *An Introduction to Comparative Law Theory and Method* (Hart Publishing 2014) 76.

[56] F Bignami, 'Introduction. A new field: comparative law and regulation', in F Bignami, D Zaring (eds), *Comparative Law and Regulation. Understanding the Global Regulatory Process*, (Edward Elgar Publishing 2016) 4.

creditworthiness of potential borrowers and the responsible conduct of potential lenders) and vertically (through an analysis focusing on the relationship between supranational and national rules promoting the aims highlighted above). The scope is to identify the actors entrusted with the assessment of creditworthiness of borrowers; what type of rules impose this duty; and the nature of the duty under which this pre-contractual evaluation is carried out.

In addition to the functional approach that applies to the analysis of the different sources regulating credit contracts at multiple levels, it is necessary to also take into account two further methodologies of comparison. The first is the structuralist approach, given its importance in a systematic analysis:[57] it serves to identify the underlying 'system' of US and EU credit markets, and is especially relevant when considering the remedies in case of negligent creditworthiness assessments or irresponsible lending practices.

The second is the hermeneutical approach (the 'deep hermeneutical approach'),[58] to the extent that it allows an analysis of legal culture and the legal mentality of a system. It is not possible to analyze 'creditworthiness' without taking into account the 'culture of debt', and its meaning within society; only later can the economic models behind growth in credit markets, in consumer credit (and more generally in the financialization process of the citizen) become comprehensible.

The final methodology applied in this study falls within the comparative cultural approach,[59] which is fundamental for the comprehension of the notion of 'creditworthiness', of the tendency and frequency of recurring to forms of credit for consumption, of the social acceptance of indebtedness, and of the social stigma surrounding insolvency. The cultural approach proves particularly useful not only in the comparison between the US and European systems, but also within the different European legal traditions.

This is visible in the growing trend in EU consumer law (including in consumer credit and mortgages), where even Directives aiming at maximum harmonization contain open-textured provisions, which allow for different

---

57   See for e.g. C Valcke, "'Droit" : réflexions sur une définition aux fins de comparaison' in P Legrand, *Comparer les droits, résolument* (Presses Universitaires de France 2009) 99.

58   P Legrand, *Le droit comparé* (3rd ed Presses Universitaires de France 2009) 50–73.

59   *Ex multis*, see R Cotterrell, 'The Sociological Concept of Law' (1983) 10 Journal of Law and Society (1983), 241, ID. 'Comparative Law and Legal Culture' in Reimann, Zimmermann (eds) (n 53), 709; M van Hoecke, M Warrington, 'Legal Cultures, Legal Paradigms and Legal Doctrine: Towards a New Model for Comparative Law' (1998) 47 International & Comparative Law Quarterly 495; E Örücü, E Attwool, S Coyle, *Studies in Legal Systems: Mixed and Mixing* (Kluwer Law International 1996); PH Glenn, *Legal Traditions of the World: Sustainable Diversity in Law* (Oxford University Press 2000); Samuel (n 54) 16.

national legal and cultural interpretations[60] (and indeed, some authors have noted that maximum harmonization in the field of credit seems unjustified, given *inter alia*, its link to local traditions and cultures).[61]

The choice of a comparative methodology is grounded in a final question of policy. In a highly globalized and interconnected market such as the market of credit, the identification of the different formants that mold the ways in which the decision to grant credit is taken and the regulation of the ensuing relationship between lenders and borrowers may prove useful when supranational legislative and regulatory processes are discussed. Legal reform in this domain was undertaken in the aftermath of the global financial crisis that was triggered in 2007–2008 with the collapse of a very specific credit market: that of subprime loans. More than a decade later, an appraisal of these reforms is not only due, but can also highlight strengths and weaknesses and advance questions regarding further needs for reform. The comparison between the legal (and prudential) regulation of two credit markets (the American and the European) can perhaps yield results having a wider perspective.

1.7   Structure of the Book

The first part of the study (Chapter 2), addressing topics in comparative law and regulation, moves from the macroprudential domain of the duties that are imposed onto banking institutions, including that of assessing the creditworthiness of borrowers within credit risk management. Starting from the macro-systemic level, and then moving onto the single lending relationships, the analysis accordingly first provides an outline of the international regulatory framework on banking regulation (including the Basel Accords on Capital requirements) defining prudential duties for lending institutions. The scope is that of ascertaining whether there is a common regulatory answer to the need to ensure that borrowers at every level (both corporate and consumer) are able

60   G Howells, C Twigg-Flesner, T Wilhelmsson, *Rethinking EU Consumer Law* (Routledge 2018) 4.

61   Ibid 211–212. Studies in finance have already highlighted the importance of the cultural element; see for example R La Porta, F Lopez-de-Silanes, A Shleifer, 'The economic consequences of legal Origins' (2008) 46 Journal of Economic Literature 285; M Statman, 'Countries and culture in behavioral finance' (2008) 25 CFA Institute Conference Proceedings Quarterly, 38; JD Levinson, K Peng, 'Valuing cultural differences in behavioral economics', (2007) 4 The ICFAI Journal of Behavioural Finance 32; W Breuer, B Quinten, 'Cultural Finance', 2009 Working Paper 14 <http://ssrn.com/abstract=1282068,> (last accessed December 2020).

to repay their loans. Standards which govern credit risk management in its different phases are therefore examined; this is functional to the demonstration that lenders respond to precise duties of creditworthiness assessment of their clients at every level, and these duties are relevant not only within the bank-client relationship, but within the wider frameworks and complex regulatory mechanisms put in place to ensure stability of credit markets.

The second part of Chapter 2 analyzes the ways in which the duty of creditworthiness assessment is implemented for corporate and sovereign borrowers (consumers are considered in the following Chapter 3). This takes place through credit rating and the study thus examines the function of ratings, and the responsibilities of credit rating agencies entrusted with providing both primary and secondary markets with a public evaluation of the creditworthiness of borrowers in different moments. A broad notion of creditworthiness, such as to include a prudential function and an instrument for the implementation of responsible credit policies, requires that methodologies and procedures of assessment of potential borrowers are analyzed at every level.

As a comparative research demonstrates, not only has there been a common regulatory response to the problem of assessing borrowers within wider macroprudential mechanisms, but there has been a converging trend of outsourcing this function to credit rating agencies. The role of the rating agencies as gatekeepers, the reliance and overreliance on ratings, and the question of liability of the raters both towards their contractual counterparties and towards the markets are consequently of fundamental importance; the post 2007–2008 financial crisis approaches show an introduction and tightening of regulatory oversight towards rating agencies in the legal systems examined. It is further worth considering that a rating (which is a creditworthiness assessment) is also the gateway to accessing credit markets for issuers: an element that confirms that the assessment does not have a merely internal relevance in the lender-borrower relationship. It also highlights the need for legal mechanisms to ensure that the creditworthiness assessment is carried out accurately and diligently and that raters be held liable towards their contractual counterparties when this is not the case.

Moving from the macro-prudential to the individual level, creditworthiness assessment for consumers (who apply for consumer loans) is analyzed in Chapter 3. Focus here is on the methodology used for credit reporting and scoring. Credit data, its collection and processing (including the challenges posed by algorithmic credit scoring), and issues of data protection as well as of discrimination are examined. The initial functional perspective considers the scope and use of credit information sharing (by also referring to classic economic theories on the use of credit data) and the reasons for the development of credit scoring as the prevailing tool for the assessment of individual borrowers in expanding credit markets. The two models that are analyzed and compared are those of the United States and of the EU. The well-known diverse regulatory approach between these traditions also affects the cultural attitude towards the collection and processing of personal data so as to build personal 'credit histories': a practice that is well-embedded in US consumer culture and that can be read against the background of an early development of a market for consumer credit that required organized credit reporting for its functioning. The differences in development and structure of the reporting industry are also reflected in the regulatory responses deriving from concerns on data protection of consumers and on the need to prevent discriminatory practices in access to credit ensuing from profiling of borrowers. The principal issues that legislation on both sides of the Atlantic has sought to tackle is striking the balance between the free circulation of credit data (and regulation of credit bureaus) and the protection of data subjects (with relevant provisions contained for example in the US Federal Fair Credit Reporting Act of 1970[62] (and its amendments), the Equal Credit Opportunity Act (ECOA) of 1974[63] and in the European General Data Protection Regulation of 2016).[64] This entails devising efficient mechanisms for data revision and correction; compensating consumers in case of inaccurate or false credit reporting; and protecting consumers from discriminatory practices in access to credit (even where scoring is an automated process).

The final section of Chapter 3 analyzes the implications of credit reporting for responsible credit policies. Whereas credit reporting has served an important function in expanding the consumer credit market (and allows, with algorithmic scoring, to reach consumers who would otherwise be excluded from access to credit), enhancing consumer mobility and the choice of credit products, and according to some, helping to promote a 'responsible credit culture',[65] there are however (along with general concerns on misuse of personal data) specific considerations regarding responsible credit. These concern the need

---

62   15 U.S.C. §1681–1681x.

63   15 U.S.C. §§1691–1691f.

64   Regulation (EU) 2016/679 of the European Parliament and of the Council of 27 April 2016 on the protection of natural persons with regard to the processing of personal data and on the free movement of such data and repealing Directive 95/46/EC [2016] OJ L 119/1.

65   World Bank, 'Global Financial Development Report 2013: Rethinking the Role of State in Finance' (2012) Washington DC 131.

to avoid that through scoring and advanced profiling vulnerable consumers are targeted by predatory lending practices, and the need to ensure transparency in the scoring process both before and after it takes places. Transparency is fundamental for consumer confidence and empowerment, an increase in the negotiating power of consumers with positive records, financial literacy, and for reporting to have a 'borrower discipline' effect. Finally, it is also of fundamental importance that reporting is accurate and diligent and that efficient mechanisms are put forth to ensure that this professional standard is observed in credit reporting. This requires not only effective measures to request cancellation or correction of false data by consumers, but also systems to disincentive careless reporting and to compensate consumers (under tort or under contract) when they have been injured by erroneous reporting.

The following Chapter 4 focuses on consumer loans (consumer credit and mortgage credit contracts) and responsible credit policies. The latter are indeed part of a wider array of precontractual duties such as disclosure duties, duties of consultation, the assessment of creditworthiness of loan applicants and the regulation of certain contractual terms, that have been introduced by legislative reforms both in the United States and in the EU after the global financial crisis. The Chapter first examines these instruments as contained in US federal legislation (such as the Dodd Frank Act) and in EU directives (the Consumer Credit Directive and the Mortgage Credit Directive) and then, in the second part, their impact on contract law. For this purpose, a private comparative law analysis also considers contract law of select European Member States and the implementation of the two directives. Problems of limitation on contractual autonomy (as a tradeoff for the potential implementation of protective 'responsible lending' duties) are of particular relevance, especially as to the freedom to disregard negative outcomes of creditworthiness assessments (the question of a 'duty to deny' credit), or to conclude contracts without a prior assessment of borrowers' creditworthiness.

The last section of Chapter 4 examines enforcement issues of these provisions and tentatively assesses their effectiveness as instruments to combat irresponsible lending policies, with theories advanced in contract (including unfair terms, misrepresentation, error or fraud, abusive standards, unconscionability, breach of professional diligence, and breach of duties of good faith) and in tort (breach of a duty of care, breach of a statutory duty, negligent interference with contract, deceit, liability for dangerous products). Scholars have also accordingly suggested a wide array of remedies. A comparative overview indicates that responsible credit duties are more easily framed within contractual and pre-contractual duties rather than under tort, but the multiple theoretical foundations proposed (in the absence of binding legislation) show not only a divide across legal traditions, but also within legal systems where scholarship and courts offer differing theses.

Chapter 5 concludes the study by considering access to credit, social and financial inclusion, and the relation with responsible lending; in particular whether responsible lending duties as they are currently framed can constitute a barrier to credit for categories of vulnerable borrowers. The final analysis focuses on the interaction between responsible lending policies, financial inclusion and the protection of fundamental rights (such as housing).

The Chapter first examines the history and effects of the different policies promoting access to credit and the impact on financial inclusion of a widespread use of creditworthiness assessment.

Indeed, in the aftermath of the 2007–2008 financial crisis (where the problem of consumer over-indebtedness and its relation to policies promoting easy access to credit came to the fore), the introduction of policies on financial product regulation, on consumer over-indebtedness, on financial literacy, and on 'responsible credit' as one of the instruments to be used for a balancing of access to credit with protection from over-indebtedness, raised concerns that 'responsible credit' would provoke a contraction of credit and an increase in financial exclusion (especially if invoked during periods of economic and financial instability).[66] However, as the study purports to show, 'responsible credit' also encompasses a protective function, which can translate into the promotion of 'suitable' and 'affordable' credit, tailored onto the specific needs of borrowers.

The problems of financial and social exclusion deriving from impossibility of accessing loans are further examined and posed in relation with the question of the existence and dimension of a 'right to credit'. The research leads to the conclusion that currently, a 'right to credit' as such does not find legal recognition. However, it is purported that through other recognized rights, both at national and supranational (i.e. the EU) level, there are a series of procedural and substantive rights that have to be protected when the application for credit and its evaluation take place: a 'due process in access to credit'. These include pre-contractual duties of responsible credit, a right to non-discrimination, and the principle of consumer protection.

These conclusions also emerge with reference to the right to housing, a specific constitutionalized right that is closely tied to the access to mortgage credit. Here again it is not a 'right to a mortgage contract' that is recognized, but a right to 'due process' in application for mortgage credit; in this hypothesis

---

66   Comparato (n 5) 137.

also extending to the substantive content of the credit contract through remedies that are offered by the tool of unfair terms.

The responsible credit paradigm, even if not yet fully developed nor implemented, seems to offer a useful tool in reconciling the different needs that emerge throughout the study. In order to accomplish this function, it must be interpreted accordingly, as a flexible tool, especially when credit is the only means to access certain fundamental rights (and its denial is formally justified as being in the interest of the borrower, in a paternalist attempt to avoid future over-indebtedness). Therefore, certain personal circumstances must be taken into account to avoid that responsible lending becomes a barrier to access affordable and fair credit through supervised channels.

Creditworthiness Assessment as a Macroprudential Duty

Introduction

Any reflection on responsible credit is, naturally and logically, inherently related to the instruments through which such a scope can be pursued. A pre-eminent position is occupied by the practice of so-called 'creditworthiness assessment', that as will be outlined in this Chapter, is not simply a commercial practice carried out by lending institutions, but a legislative duty imposed by sources of different nature and importance.

This introductory part of the study, addressing topics that fall within the domain of comparative law and regulation, provides an outline of the sources and explains the relation between the obligation of evaluation of creditworthiness and the macroprudential duties imposed onto banking institutions.[1] Adopting the functional approach of comparative methodology, the introductory question is whether the concern with the ability to pay of borrowers finds a regulatory answer and whether this regulatory answer is common. The subsequent inquiry is whether there are converging instruments to ensure an assessment of the creditworthiness of borrowers; the issue naturally pertains to an examination of credit risk management by banking institutions.

The analysis necessarily moves from an outline of the international regulatory framework (starting with the Basel Accords on Capital requirements) that defined the prudential duties of banking institutions and that conditions their lending activity, especially in its development and change in the aftermath of the 2007–2008 financial crisis. The focus on the standards which govern credit risk management in its different phases and on the criteria for the

---

[1] On the object of comparative law and regulation is identified as being the law that applies to the regulatory process (intended as the "form of governance designed to address complex social, environmental, and economic problems that relies heavily on rules, enforced against market actors, and administrative authorities") but also includes the regulatory output of "legislatures, public prosecutors, courts and private bodies" and the standards (both legally binding rules and other standards such as soft law) that are implemented against civil society and public actors. See F Bignami, 'Introduction. A new field: comparative law and regulation', in F Bignami, D Zaring (eds), *Comparative Law and Regulation. Understanding the Global Regulatory Process* (Edward Elgar Publishing 2016), 3.

quantification of risk at portfolio level is functional to the demonstration that lenders have precise duties to assess the creditworthiness of their clients at every level, and this duty is not only relevant within the bank-client (lender-borrower) relationship, but rather responds to wider obligations of credit risk management and is part of a complex mechanism to ensure the stable functioning of credit markets.

In accordance with the aim of identifying the fundamental elements of the global regulatory process, both national and international institutions (i.e. in this study the European Union) are considered, and the regulatory process and law implementing it are analyzed with no distinctions as to the branch of law to which they formally belong.[2]

The research also adopts another perspective that is typical of comparative law and regulation, namely an analysis of the regulatory process that is not necessarily confined within a single jurisdiction but rather, can take place both horizontally between jurisdictions as an effect of globalization, and vertically, as an effect of the interaction between national and international institutions[3] (and not always necessarily through the adoption of binding rules of international law, for example).

This Chapter examines corporate borrowers, whereas the next Chapter examines single borrowers that qualify as consumers and that typically request credit for consumer contracts and mortgages. Ideally, the investigation begins at the macro-systemic level and then proceeds down to the single contractual relationship.

The second part of the Chapter analyzes the ways in which the duty of creditworthiness assessment is implemented for corporate and sovereign borrowers – that is through credit rating – and takes into account the role and responsibilities of the subjects (credit rating agencies) *de facto* entrusted with the function of providing both primary and secondary markets with a public evaluation of the creditworthiness of borrowers in different moments. This second part thus aims at identifying if and to what extent there are common or converging instruments to ensure and to measure the creditworthiness of borrowers.

The ratio of the focus on credit rating and credit rating agencies (and on credit reporting and credit bureaus in the next Chapter) is justified by the broad notion of creditworthiness that this study aims at analyzing: not only as the normatively recognized key to access credit at every degree, but also as the tool for the potential implementation of responsible credit policies. The

---

2 Ibid.
3 Ibid 10.

degree of reliance and the regulation of credit rating activity are examined with the scope of ascertaining, once again from a comparative and functional perspective, how creditworthiness is delegated to third parties and how their activity affects the operativity of credit markets. It therefore takes into account and compares (especially in terms of liability for their activities) the regulation of borrower assessment at every level of the market, both as internal processes for banking institutions and as activities that are outsourced to third parties.

In this context the regulatory 'gatekeeper' role played by credit rating agencies is particularly relevant, with the related problem on the one hand of their liability when the evaluation proves erroneous (whether because of negligence, misrepresentation, or intent), and on the other hand, the problem of reliance and 'over-reliance' on these ratings.

These elements allow, finally, to try and provide a more comprehensive definition of what 'assessing creditworthiness' means and to relate it with policies of 'responsible credit'.

2.1   Responsible Credit as a Macroprudential Duty: the Duty of Creditworthiness Assessment in Banking Regulation

2.1.1   *Evolution of Prudential Requirements in Banking Regulation*

Responsible credit can be pursued through different instruments, that vary not only in their nature (private law instruments and public law instruments) but also in their temporal allocation as regards the agreement on the loan. Following the temporal criterion, it may seem convenient to begin the analysis with preventive or *ex ante* tools that aim at implementing 'responsible lending'. The principal tool in this respect is the obligation of conducting a creditworthiness assessment of the borrower before extension of credit. This duty follows directly from supervision and prudential requirements (both at the macro-prudential and at the micro-prudential level) for credit institutions, where evaluation of credit risk and exposure, setting aside of capital requirements, and calculation of default probability, presuppose that some form of creditworthiness assessment has been conducted.

This is closely related to the 'delegated monitoring' role that banks carry out when they exercise their lending activity.[4] Delegated monitoring requires

---

4   Banks, as financial intermediaries, receive funds from depositors and lend them to entrepreneurs; they are delegated with the costly task of monitoring the entrepreneurs (loan contracts) on behalf of depositors. The collection of this information carried out by financial intermediaries gives them a gross cost advantage (where certain conditions are met and

screening and monitoring of prospective borrowers (both corporate and individual) and of performance of loans, and along with the other typical functions of banks and their potential systemic impacts, provides the rationale for the special attention, under form of regulation, given to their activity.

Whereas banking regulation stems from the functions these institutions have in the economy (notoriously the creation and servicing of loans, the collection of deposits and provision of cash, the creation of liquidity, the financing of trade, the processing of payments, the provision of risk management tools (i.e. financial instruments and guarantees for transactions)),[5] and the risks deriving from their fragility (for example from the maturity mismatch in their balance sheets), banking regulation has not always had the same degree of intensity. Even where some form of regulation was present, it did not necessarily comprise all of the prudential instruments conceived for the mitigation and prevention of bank failures, such as the imposition of capital requirements and requirements of liquidity; or the establishment of a 'lender of the last resort' (LOLR), or insurance against risks of losses on deposits.[6]

The tendency on behalf of regulators to leave banking activities relatively deregulated, along with the absence of 'global' standards of regulation until the early 1970's and with the effects of competition, allowed, *inter alia*, banks to extend the range of their activities to non-typical banking business (e.g. securities trading, brokerage, real estate activities, insurance activities), to expand credit risk, and to trade this credit risk through securitization.[7]

In the twenty-five years preceding the 2007–2008 financial crisis, the process of liberalization of the banking sector in most developed countries (based on the assumption that greater economic gain could be achieved through deregulation and greater competition), changed incentives for banking institutions to take risk.[8] This deregulation – especially of investment bank

---

incentive problems/delegation costs are overcome) because the alternative is either a duplication of efforts if every lender has to monitor lenders directly, or a free-rider problem, where no lender monitors. See DW Diamond, 'Financial Intermediation and Delegated Monitoring' (1984) LI Review of Economic Studies 393, 393.

5 K Sum, *Post-Crisis Banking Regulation in the European Union. Opportunities and Threats* (Palgrave Macmillan 2016) 1–2.

6 J Armour, D Awrey, P Davies, L Enriques, JN Gordon, C Mayer, J Payne, *Principles of Financial Regulation* (Oxford University Press 2016) 279 ff. Other forms of banking regulation (other than prudential rules) include entry requirements, governance rules and resolution. ID., pp. 287–288.

7 Sum (n 5) 5–6; CM McNamara, T Piontek, A Metrick, 'Basel III A: Regulatory History', (2014) Yale Program on Financial Stability Case Study 2014-1A-V1, 2.

8 Y Altunbas, S Manganelli, D Marques-Ibanez, 'Bank Risk During the Financial Crisis. Do Business Models Matter?' (2014) ECB Working Paper Series n. 1394, 10.

activities – allowed the creation and consolidation of large financial institutions exercising a wide range of activities both in the United States (where the liberalization removed barriers to the geographical expansion of banks) and in the European Union (where some of the regulations limiting certain banking activities were eliminated first with the Single Market in 1992 and then with the introduction of the single currency in 1999).[9] Furthermore, the capital regulation for these institutions (especially investment banks) which held assets in the form of marketable securities, was far less stringent than the capital regulation for traditional commercial banks whose assets were in the form of loans.[10]

The development and growth of secondary markets and the increase in the trading of derivative instruments (made possible thanks also to technological progress and financial innovation), further incentivized banks to trade and sell their loans; the change in the business models of banks is known as the move from 'originate to hold' to 'originate to distribute'.

The partial regulatory reaction to the expansion of these risks (especially after two important bank failures with global repercussions in 1974)[11] was the recognition that bank capital should have a more important role in the prudential regulatory process.[12] The previous belief, on the contrary, had been that the introduction of minimum capital requirements could be perceived as a risky constraint in a market of regulatory competition between jurisdictions. The ensuing regulatory reaction would lead to the initial Basel Accord on capital standards.

2.1.2   *The Basel Accords on Capital Standards*

A first relative move towards ensuring stability of the international financial market and promoting fair competition between major international banking institutions thus began in the mid 1970's, through the agreements reached between national supervisory authorities and central bank Governors of the Group of Ten countries, which established a Committee on Banking Regulations and Supervisory Practices, later renamed Basel Committee on Banking Supervision. The Basel Committee initially focused on the supervision

---

9   Ibid 11.

10   Armour, et al (n 6) 10.

11   The collapse of the Bankhaus Herstatt in Germany and of the Franklin National Bank in
      New York, both of which took place in 1974 and caused strong foreign exchange losses. See
      McNamara et al (n 7) 6.

12   Altunbas et al (n 8) 13.

of banks' foreign establishments,[13] whilst later (by the 1980's), moved by concerns on the stability risk posed by low capital of internationally active banks and by the competitive advantages to banking institutions ensuing from disparity in capital requirements, it began to concentrate on capital adequacy.[14]

The Committee, considered as the most powerful authority in banking regulation despite the legally non-binding nature of its rules at national level, has since issued a series of international standards for banking regulation, including the fundamental accords on capital adequacy known as Basel I (1988, amended in 1991, 1995, 1996), Basel II (2004) and Basel III (2010, integrated in 2017). These accords were applied to banking institutions worldwide, beginning, in the case of Basel I and Basel II, with those operating in the countries whose bank supervisors participated in the Committee.[15]

This allowed the affirmation of a particular form of banking regulation to emerge: capital requirements and balance sheets of most financial institutions had to conform to a global regulatory standard, laid down by a network of regulators, that was never translated into international treaties but which remained soft law, voluntarily enforced by the member regulators at the domestic level.[16] As is well known the Basel Accords introduced, among other measures, target standard ratios of capital to weighted risk assets. In Basel I the minimum capital to risk weighted asset ratio was set at 8%, of which core capital element (consisting of equity capital and disclosed reserves) set at least at 4%. In Basel II, whilst the ratio remained the same (8%), the weighted risk assets were broadened so as to include not only credit risk but also market risk and operational risk and the regulatory framework was centered around the three pillars of capital adequacy, supervisory review, and market discipline.

Basel II however did not impose a minimum common standard for capital charges and allowed large institutions to use their own internal risk assessment model to carry out risk-weighting (the so-called 'internal ratings-based' approach, IRB). According to this method, assets were assigned to categories, on which capital charges were determined according to the risk profile assigned by credit rating agencies (either directly or indirectly), with the effect

---

13   See the BCBS *Report on the supervision of banks' foreign establishments* of 1975 (also known as the "Concordat").

14   See McNamara et al (n 7) 7.

15   With some variations: for example, the United States applied Basel II only to its investment banks, allowing large commercial banks to adopt it. See D Zaring 'The emerging post-crisis paradigm for international financial regulation', in Bignami, Zaring (n 1) 500.

16   Ibid 501–502, additionally recalling examples of the affirmation of this model (albeit less successfully than Basel) also in other sectors of financial markets.

of 'rewarding' (in terms of capital requirements) those banking institutions with advanced internal risk management systems.[17]

These accords aimed at promoting international convergence on the measurement of capital adequacy and to address a series of risks. Initially (under Basel I) only credit risk was addressed; subsequently market risks (interest rate, equity position, foreign exchange and commodities risk), operational risks, and further types of risks were also taken into account.[18] Emphasis was placed on the quantitative measures (capital requirements) rather than on the qualitative aspects of loan portfolios. As a reaction to some weaknesses of Basel II that emerged during the financial crisis, such as too much leverage and inadequate liquidity buffers, Basel III revised and strengthened the three pillars.[19]

2.1.3   *The 2007–2008 Financial Crisis*

The 2007–2008 financial crisis was provoked by a combination of factors, including insufficient, inefficient or inexistent regulation. These have been summarized, *inter alia*, in the insufficiency of capital adequacy rules, the procyclicality of banking regulations, the poor regulation of over the counter (OTC) derivative transactions, and the absence of regulations on systemic risk and supervisory mechanisms at the international level.[20]

---

17   See J Atik, 'EU Implementation of Basel III in the Shadow of the Euro Crisis' (2014) 33 Review of Banking & Financial Law 287, 307–308.

18   After Basel I, when amendments to the capital accords were made as far as the measurement of market risks were concerned, banking institutions were allowed to choose between a standardized approach and a new approach based on the banks' own internal risk management models. The latter have been perceived as being incentivized by the Basel framework since the obtainable capital requirements using the internal risk model approach were lower than those attainable with standardized approaches. (McNamara et al (n 7) 9; ID., 'Basel III C: Internal Risk Models', (2014) Yale Program on Financial Stability Case Study 1C–V1; Armour et al (n 6) 301). However, the introduction of these same standards (capital regulation) incentivized 'regulatory capital arbitrage' through adoption of further financial innovations. These included for example the growing use of securitization, where the trade of securitized loans by means of special purpose entities (SPEs) allowed banks to reduce the regulatory capital requirements imposed by Basel II, whilst maintaining exposure to similar credit risk. Ibid 85–86; D Jones, 'Emerging problems with the Basel Capital Accord: Regulatory capital arbitrage and related issues' (2000) 24 Journal of Banking & Finance 35, *passim* (on securitization and other techniques of 'regulatory capital arbitrage' which involve unbundling and repackaging risks (Ibid 41 ff)).

19   Whilst maintaining the 8% ratio, it redefined the composition of total capital through a refinement of the tiered approach to the definition of capital, which distinguishes between 'going-concern' capital (Tier 1) and 'gone-concern' capital (Tier 2) and their relative composition ratios.

20   Sum (n 5) xiii.

The crisis changed the regulatory paradigm from one characterized by scarce political oversight and relative lack of comprehensive international policymaking (with goals being pursued mostly at the domestic level by national regulators on a task-specific basis), to one in which there is growing political supervision with regularized outputs and a hierarchical order, similar to the characteristics of administrative agencies, which, however, operate at a global level.[21]

As for the process that leads to the creation of legal obligations, it is characterized by a dual phase. At the international level where the policies are set, there are no binding rules; these are created in the second phase at the domestic level by the financial regulators which participate in the institutionalized international regulatory networks.[22] It is thus a model that can be better assimilated to international regulation rather than to international law.[23]

Indeed, following the crisis important supervisory and prudential provisions were adopted, first and foremost the creation of 'macroprudential authorities' (MPAS) in several jurisdictions and the establishment in 2009 of a permanent international organization, the Financial Stability Board, having the scope of promoting financial stability and of coordinating the realization and implementation of the G-20 post-crisis policy agenda.[24] The MPAS include the Financial Stability Oversight Council (FSOC) established in 2010 by the Dodd-Frank Wall Street Reform and Consumer Protection Act in the USA; the Financial Policy Committee (FPC) created in 2013 in the UK; the foundation at the EU level in 2011 of the European Systemic Risk Board having macroprudential supervisory functions; the creation of three European Supervisory Authorities with micro-prudential functions,[25] and the ensuing framework for the creation and implementation of the European Banking Union as of 2012, with its well-known strong transfer of powers from national authorities to European institutions. The Banking Union also introduced important reforms in the treatment of banking crises and bank resolutions, as well as in the treatment of non-performing loans; all of which are evidently related to the problem of risk management and sound functioning of the banking sector.

These changes in the regulatory approach highlight, as an inevitable consequence of the financial crisis, the rise of the prudential paradigm as a center-stage role in banking policy. This being the case, with credit risk as the target of

21   Zaring (n 15) 497–498.
22   Ibid.
23   Ibid 515.
24   J Armour et al (n 6) 89.
25   The European Banking Authority (EBA); the European Insurance and Occupational Pensions Authority (EIOPA); the European Securities and Markets Authority (ESMA).

these prudential policies, it follows that management of credit risk – of which creditworthiness assessment is a crucial phase – becomes the object of more stringent regulation.

As the financial crisis of 2007–2008 has demonstrated, there is a close tie between bank governance and financial risk. Indeed, the measures on banking governance adopted post-crisis both in Europe and in the USA and previously addressed by international organisms such as the Financial Stability Board and the Basel Committee for Banking Supervision,[26] include specific measures on risk and exposure for credit institutions (in some cases by strengthening existing requirements).[27]

Credit risk (i.e. the risk of counterparty failure that may be due to the inability, unwillingness or non-timeliness of the counterparty in honoring its obligation)[28] notoriously represents one of the principal risks for banking activity. Given the systemic impact of banking crises on financial systems, one of the fundamental instruments of regulation through banking governance rules focuses on credit risk and credit risk management.[29]

2.1.4 *Credit Risk Management and Creditworthiness Assessment*

It follows from the above that if banking institutions are under the duty to respect certain paradigms on their capital adequacy and balance sheets, deriving from both macro-prudential and micro-prudential requirements, then there are two fundamental processes that are affected by this obligation.

The first is the way in which credit risk is measured, and thus the importance and impact that, for example, the introduction of internal risk management models (i.e. starting with the 1996 Market Risk Amendment to Basel I) has had on banking institutions. The introduction of the internal ratings-based approach (IRB) was justified by the consideration that the standardized

---

26   Basel III was introduced in 2010 to address those issues (inadequacy in quantity and quality of capital, insufficiency of liquidity and the interconnectedness of the financial system) that were identified by the Basel Committee as the main causal factors of the 2007–2008 financial crisis.
27   E Wymeersch, 'Corporate Governance of Banks According to the CRD IV' in P Gasós (ed) *Challenges in Securities Markets Regulation: Investor Protection and Corporate Governance, SUERF Study 2015/1*, (Larcier 2015) 67.
28   Credit risk can be further subdivided into single firm credit risk or obligor credit risk (exposure of a single borrower or obligor) and portfolio credit risk where exposure is towards a group of borrowers. See C Joseph, *Advanced Credit Risk Analysis and Management*, (Wiley 2013) 37.
29   Other instruments of regulation, along with prudential rules, as seen above, are entry requirements and resolution. See Armour et al (n 6) 288.

approach did not take into account the spread of the bank's overall portfolio of assets over different classes of loans which may have uncorrelated risks.[30] The adoption of the IRB approach was quite controversial, and Basel III later sought to correct some of the deficiencies it had generated before and during the financial crisis, especially as far as the risk-weighting process and the models and quality of the internal data used by banks are concerned.

The second is the process through which credit risk is created (the origination of credit risk) which implies a decisional process on the granting of credit and presupposes some form of screening of potential borrowers (creditworthiness assessment). There seems to be a lien between regulatory capital requirements and the level of screening of borrowers (which intensifies as a response to higher levels of capital), although the analysis of the relationship between increase in capital requirements and credit risk has not always led to unanimous results in literature.[31]

The process of creditworthiness assessment is thus clearly a vital tool at the various levels ranging from implementation of macro-prudential standards (given the close tie between credit risk and systemic risk) down to the single retail 'granular' loan. It has, indeed, an inherently 'dual' function. On the one hand the respect of prudential parameters of risk exposure are relevant for the external relationship of credit institutions and credit supervising authorities. On the other hand, credit rating impacts on the internal managerial decisions of the credit institutions, affecting the way in which the decision to grant credit in single cases is taken.[32]

This duality and interconnectedness between the two functions of creditworthiness assessment is exemplified in several sources that highlight the ties between the outcomes of rating processes and the internal decisions on credit risk management (more specifically, on the decisions related to "credit approval, risk management, internal capital allocations and corporate governance functions of banks")[33] and the need to have "internal methodologies that enable the assessment of credit risk exposures to individual obligors,

---

30   See Armour et al (n 6) 301 ff.

31   See Altunbas et al (n 8) 12 and literature cited therein.

32   M Di Rienzo, *Concessione del credito e tutela degli investimenti. Regole e principi in tema di responsabilità* (Giappichelli 2013) 3 ff.

33   See Par. 444, Basel II "Use of internal ratings": "Internal ratings and default and loss estimates must play an essential role in credit approval, risk management, internal capital allocations, and corporate governance functions of banks using the IRB approach". See also Di Rienzo ibid.

securities or securitization positions and credit risk at the portfolio level" and
to ensure that "credit-granting is based on sound and well-defined criteria".[34]

The Basel III Accords, one of the first regulatory responses to the financial crisis of 2007–2008 (implemented in EU law with the so-called CRD IV
package),[35] lay down duties concerning credit risk and its calculation and

---

34   Article 79, Directive 2013/36 of the European Parliament and of the Council of 26 June
     2013 on access to the activity of credit institutions and the prudential supervision of
     credit institutions and investment firms, [2013] OJ L 176/338.

35   The so-called CRD IV package comprises Regulation 575/2013 of the European Parliament
     and of the Council of 26 June 2013 on prudential requirements for credit institutions and
     investment firms [2013] OJ L 176/1, and the Capital Requirements Directive (Directive
     2013/36).
        A 'new banking package' in the EU (including new rules approved by the Basel Com-
     mittee) was approved in May 2019 with amendments on the Capital Requirements
     Directive and the Capital Requirements Regulation (via the so-called CRD5/CRR2
     (Directive 2019/878 of the European Parliament and of the Council of 20 May 2019
     amending Directive 2013/36/EU as regards exempted entities, financial holding com-
     panies, mixed financial holding companies, remuneration, supervisory measures and
     powers and capital conservation measures [2019] OJ L 150/253 and Regulation 2019/876
     of the European Parliament and of the Council of 20 May 2019 amending Regulation
     No 575/2013 as regards the leverage ratio, the net stable funding ratio, requirements for
     own funds and eligible liabilities, counterparty credit risk, market risk, exposures to cen-
     tral counterparties, exposures to collective investment undertakings, large exposures,
     reporting and disclosure requirements, and Regulation No 648/2012 [2019] OJ L 150/1),
     on the Bank Recovery and Resolution Directive (via Directive 2019/879 of the European
     Parliament of the Council of 20 May 2019 amending Directive 2014/59/EU as regards the
     loss-absorbing and recapitalization capacity of credit institutions and investment firms
     and Directive 98/26/EC [2019] OJ L 150/296), and on the Single Resolution Mechanism
     (via Regulation 2019/877 of the European Parliament and of the Council of 20 May 2019
     amending Regulation No 806/2014 as regards the loss-absorbing and recapitalization
     capacity of credit institutions and investment firms [2019] OJ L 150/226). The entry into
     force of this package (along with that of new Basel III rules) was however suspended due
     to outbreak of the COVID-19 pandemic in 2020. Measures going in the opposite direc-
     tion (i.e. allowing exceptional uses of prudential capital buffers) were allowed (within
     the guidelines and limits set by the ECB and by the EBA) and a series of further mea-
     sures to support the lending activities of banking institutions in favor of both firms and
     households during the ensuing economic crisis were approved. These measures of for-
     bearance towards debtors translated principally in moratoriums on existing payments
     and simplified procedures – including creditworthiness assessments – for the granting
     of new loans. See A Brozzetti, E Cecchinato, E Martino, 'Supervisione bancaria e Covid-
     19', in U Malvagna, A Sciarrone Alibrandi (eds), *Sistema produttivo e finanziario post
     Covid-19: dall'efficienza alla sostenibilità. Voci dal diritto dell'economia* (Pacini giuridica
     2021) 167 and ff.; C Brescia Morra, 'Lending activity in the time of coronavirus' in WG
     Ringe, C Gortsos (eds), *Pandemic Crisis and Financial Stability* (EBI e-Book Series 2020)
     391; CV Gortsos, 'The response of the European Central Bank to current pandemic
     crisis: monetary policy and prudential banking supervision decisions', (2020) EBI

more generally aim at strengthening the regulation, supervision and risk management of banks.[36] By regulating the quality, consistency and transparency of the capital of banks, the Basel standards affect the way in which capital is allocated and how much is reserved to credit risk.[37]

It should be noted, however, more generally, that the process of credit risk management for banking institutions is not limited to creditworthiness assessment; it also includes origination, portfolio management and mitigation and transfer.[38]

As observed above, one of the principal consequences of banking deregulation (before the financial crisis originated in 2007) and of the involvement of banks in securitization activities has been a shift in the business models of

---

Working Paper Series n. 68/2020; See also ECB, "Our response to the coronavirus pandemic" <https://www.ecb.europa.eu/home/search/coronavirus/html/index.en.html> (last accessed December 2021); EBA, 'Our response to Coronavirus (Covid-19)' <https://www.eba.europa.eu/coronavirus> (last accessed December 2021) and EBA 'Guidelines on legislative and non-legislative moratoria on loan repayments applied in the light of the COVID-19 crisis' (April 2020); see also the measures adopted by the Basel Committee to alleviate the impact of COVID-19 <https://www.bis.org/press/p200403.htm> (last accessed December 2021).

36   Although Basel III constitutes one of the main reactions to the crisis at the macroprudential level, it is strongly founded on preexisting micro-prudential regulation (i.e. measures aiming at ensuring the soundness of individual banking institutions). Key elements of Basel III contained in the three pillars (already introduced by Basel II: i.e. capital adequacy, supervisory review and market discipline), include raising the quality and quantity of the capital base (reinforcing the role of common equity), strengthening the risk coverage of the capital framework, introducing leverage ratio requirements, improving bank liquidity (both through Liquidity Coverage Ratios and Net Stable Funding Rations), limiting pro-cyclicality by introducing measures to promote the build-up of capital buffers in periods of high economic growth that can be drawn upon during periods of stress, and adopting additional requirements for systemically important banks. Armour et al (n 6) 409–410.

37   The approach to credit risk measurement in Basel III has undergone some modifications in comparison to Basel II (although it is still mostly based on the model introduced with Basel II); these modifications concern mainly counterparty credit risk and its assessment, the weakness of which was highlighted during the Financial Crisis triggered in 2007. As a reaction, the Credit Value Adjustment (CVA) which adjusts the value of derivative products to account for counterparty risk, was introduced with the requirement that banks hold regulatory capital against their CVA position; as was the use of stress-testing probability of default for capital purposes. Basel III also tightened the requirements for capital against credit risks, the control on OTC derivatives, and it introduced the identification of 'wrong way risk' within counterparties (when exposure to counterparty is adversely correlated with the credit quality of that counterparty; i.e. default risk and credit exposure increase concomitantly).

38   S Bouteillé, D Coogan-Pushner, *The Handbook of Credit Risk Management. Originating, Assessing, and Managing Credit Exposures* (J. Wiley & Sons Inc 2013) xiii ff.

banks which moved from the 'originate to hold' to the 'originate to distribute' models: the loans that the bank originates are no longer held until maturity but instead are packaged into newly created securities and are sold to investors as asset-backed securities. These securities are rated by credit rating agencies, which in turn need to build on data on the underlying loans (thus typically relying on credit scores).

Before the crisis, the belief was that this new model associated with securitization had shed risk for banks, making them stronger institutions.[39] Under the Basel I regime, regulatory capital was typically much greater than the prudent capital required to hold, for example, residential mortgages. This gave banks strong incentives to convert whole mortgage loans into securities and to hold riskier mortgages, given the 'insensitivity' to credit risk of the capital regulation at the time.[40]

Also, with reference to the issue of creditworthiness, it has been argued that securitization led to a weakening of lending standards. This would derive from the fact that in the securitization process there is a misalignment of incentives between banks and investors, due to adverse selection (low quality loans are securitized while higher quality assets are retained on balance sheets, when originators exploit their information advantage over investors) and moral hazard problems (since loans can be sold, there is no/less incentive for lenders to screen and monitor borrowers). It has thus been held that the 'originate to distribute' model undermines financial stability.[41]

The tie between securitization, creditworthiness and responsible credit is visible in the EU Regulation laying down common rules on securitization, in

---

39   Armour et al (n 6) 413.

40   See G. Donadio, A Lehnert, "Residential Mortgages", in AN Berger, P Molyneux, JOS Wilson (eds), *The Oxford Handbook of Banking* (2d ed Oxford University Press 2015) 326, 343, recalling examples from the United States where starting in the mid-2000s, "private-label mortgage backed securities issuers began to account for a significant fraction of mortgage debt outstanding".

41   See B Casu, A Sarkisyan, 'Securitization', in AN Berger et al (n 40) 354, 355 and the studies cited therein, quoting, *inter alia*, A Mian, A Sufi, 'The Consequences of Mortgage Credit Expansion: Evidence from the U.S. Mortgage Default Crisis', in (2009) 124 Quarterly Journal of Economics 1449, who show a correlation between an expansion in mortgage credit to subprime ZIP codes in the US and its dissociation from income growth on one hand and the increase in securitization of subprime mortgages on the other. See also HS Shin, 'Securitisation and Financial Stability'(2009) 119 The Economic Journal 309, 312 and 325–26.

       For evidence suggesting that adverse selection is not an inevitable consequence of securitization, see Casu et al (n 41) 363 and the literature quoted.

which risk retention policies aim at preventing the recurrence (and effects) of "purely 'originate to distribute' models" where lending standards are lowered because lenders know in advance that related risks are eventually sold to third parties; in the case of securitizations where the underlying exposure are residential loans, the Regulation also refers to the need to carry out the creditworthiness assessment of borrowers according to the requirements set out in the Consumer Credit Directive and in the Mortgage Credit Directive.[42]

In the phase of origination of credit risk, there are fundamental issues that lenders take into account and that concern the potential quantification of the risk and the ensuing loss as well as the probability of default of the borrower (PD). In case of bankruptcy, the potential percentages of recovery (loss given default (LGD)[43] or recovery rate (value given default – VGD), which depend on how much the creditor is exposed at the time of default (exposure at default factor – EAD)), are also considered, as are the remedies and their costs in case of non-performance.[44]

Quantifying credit risk is the following phase in the risk management process, and it involves an assessment both at the individual transaction level and at the portfolio level (by studying credit risk behavior of homogenous groups of obligors/credit assets).

The parameters taken into account at the individual level, in order to compare credit exposures, revolve once again around exposure (the maximum potential loss in case of default, to be estimated by taking into account for example gross exposure, net exposure and adjusted exposure), probability of default, rate of recovery and tenor (amount of time in which money is out-standing).[45]

At the portfolio level, the complexity of the assessment is due to the interdependency between multiple variables (such as the dimension of the loan portfolio, the spread between rate of use and cost of its gathering, the entity of the losses deriving from the insolvency of the borrowers, the impact of fiscal

---

42 Regulation 2017/2402 of the European Parliament and of the Council of 12 December 2017 laying down a general framework for securitization and creating a specific framework for simple, transparent and standardized securitization and amending Directives 2009/65/EC, 2009/138/EC, 2011/61/EU and Regulations (EC) No 1060/2009 and (EU) No 648/2012' [2017] OJ L 347/35, Recital 28 and Article 9.

43 Loss given default (LGD) is the net loss after recovery. It is defined as one minus the recovery rate times the exposure. See Bouteillé et al (n 38) 62.

44 Ibid 4; Joseph (n 28) 270–271.

45 Bouteillé et al (n 38) 45.

pressure on the profits earned, and the administrative costs incurred in the process of granting the credit).[46]

In order to be able to quantify credit risk at the portfolio level, it is necessary to adopt not only qualitative parameters, but also quantitative ones, and this is done by using probabilistic methods. This type of provision (so-called Portfolio Theories) can only be carried out if there is knowledge of the functional relation between certain variables and if there is access to sufficient data on the historical trend of these variables.[47]

The Basel Accords are centered around portfolio approach to credit risk. Credit portfolio risk can be divided into diversifiable risk and systematic or systemic (non-diversifiable) risk. Diversifiable Risk (e.g. concentration risk, maturity risk, correlation risk, portfolio funding risk) can be reduced or eliminated through diversification of the credit portfolio. Many theories consider that systemic risks undertaken by the lender (that cannot be diversified) are returned by the reward for credit risk.[48] Both individual probability of default (PD) and portfolio probability of default are necessary for the risk management of a credit portfolio.

The calculation of the probability of default (PD) is particularly interesting in the perspective of creditworthiness assessment, as it is the outcome both of a process of rating (the probability of default being directly linked to credit risk grades), and of an observation, based on historical data, of the default frequency of entities with similar ratings. The importance of the probability of default calculation is due to its role in the three processes of credit pricing, determination of economic capital requirements, and quantification of credit risk.[49]

---

46   A Malinconico, *Il credit risk management del portafoglio prestiti. Da Basilea I a Basilea* III (Franco Angeli 2012) 85.

47   On Portfolio Theory models, ibid 86–87.

48   Joseph (n 28) 256.

49   At the individual level, the multiplication of the probability of default of an asset (PD) by the value of the loss given default (LGD), the exposure at default (EAD) and the maturity factor (M), yields the expected loss (EL) of an asset (EL = PD × EAD × LGD × M). The credit pricing will be determined in such a way so as to absorb the expected loss (higher EL leads to higher credit pricing). The Portfolio EL is the aggregation of the ELs of the portfolio components (see Joseph (n 28) 293).

      The determination of economic capital (sometimes referred to as risk capital) levels is linked to credit risks undertaken by a bank or financial intermediary and it is meant to cover both expected (EL) and unexpected loss (any loss above the expected loss) in order to avoid bankruptcy. Whereas levels of regulatory capital are determined by regulators (in implementation of the Basel Accords), economic capital is a governance choice of banks and financial institutions. A common method for the quantification of the economic capital needed is credit value at risk (CVaR), which allows to determine the amount of

For its relevance as a tool of creditworthiness assessment and for the role that is played by external subjects in standardizing and circulating rating grades, credit rating deserves further attention and will be examined in the second part of the Chapter.

Thus far it should be noted that the risk management approach is mostly a technical process whose standards can be – and to a certain extent have been – made the object of global regulatory standards.

This is not sufficient, nor does it imply, however, that the concrete evaluation of potential borrowers yields identical outcomes in all legal systems. There are, from this point of view, regulatory, legal and social factors that intervene and that impact decisions of lenders on whether or not to grant credit.

As for the regulatory factors, the financial crisis created a first important breakthrough in the regulatory approach which however, notwithstanding the changes made to the Basel Accords, remained for some time an approach still largely based on quantitative standards. This left margins of appreciation for the single banking institutions regarding the 'quality' of their loan portfolios and consequently, the application of a certain degree of discretion to their decisions. In the EU, a change only intervened in a later phase of the post-crisis regulatory scheme, in which, through the instruments of the supervisory practices (which are part of the Single Supervisory Mechanism, such as the Supervisory Review and Evaluation Process – SREP – methodology for example), important additional qualitative controls were introduced which in part constrained the independence of banking institutions in their lending choices.

Although they are beyond the scope of this study, a central aspect also concerns non-performing loans (NPLS). For example, the belated intervention at the EU level on the regulation of NPLS naturally impacted also the issue of creditworthiness at the outset.[50] The high levels of NPLS in the balance sheets of banks in the EU following the financial crisis (where the NPL ratio remains

---

losses that the firm can withstand (see Bouteillé et al (n 38) 165 ff). The exploitation of the differences between the two has allowed practices of regulatory capital arbitrage (see Jones (n 18) 40 and ff; see n 19).

50   From a supervisory perspective (i.e. for the scope of article 99(4) of Regulation 575/2013), the EBA provided a common definition of non-performing exposures that banks are encouraged to use (even if it is only binding for supervisory reporting reasons): "[...] non-performing exposures are those that satisfy either or both of the following criteria: a) material exposures which are more than 90 days past-due, b) the debtor is assessed as unlikely to pay its credit obligations in full without realization of collateral, regardless of the existence of any past-due amount or of the number of days past due". See EBA 'FINAL draft implementing Technical Standards On Supervisory reporting on forbearance and non-performing exposures under article 99(4) of Regulation (EU) No 575/2013' (EBA/ITS/2013/03/rev1, 24/07/2014).

high when compared to ratios in other advanced economies),[51] with the ensuing requirement for banks to hold higher amounts of regulatory capital and pay a risk premium on liquidity markets, urged a series of initiatives at the EU level. These include the approval of a package of measures among which a Directive on credit servicers and credit purchasers (aimed at fostering NPL secondary markets and easing collateral recovery from secured loans),[52] and a Regulation amending the capital requirement regulation (CRR)[53] and introducing common minimum coverage levels for newly originated loans that become non-performing.[54] In the auspices of EU institutions, the creation of a secondary market for distressed assets with the possibility for lending institutions to sell these loans to specialized asset management companies for example, would effectively impact the way in which banks can manage and reduce risks. By clearing NPLS from their books and 'freeing up space' in their balance sheets for new lending, they can avoid a restriction in credit supply, which is especially important in times of crisis such as for example during the COVID-19 pandemic crisis.[55]

Furthermore, these choices cannot be disjoined from other important factors, one of which (judicial enforcement mechanisms) is particularly relevant from a comparative law point of view. Indeed differences in the strength and efficiency of a country's judiciary system (for instance the length of court proceedings) will affect management choices of lending institutions, such as for

---

51   See for example the data from EBA Risk Dashboard Data in 2016 and 2018 and the annual data from the IMF Global Financial Stability Report.

52   Directive 2021/2167 of the European Parliament and of the Council of 24 November 2021 on credit servicers and credit purchasers and amending Directives 2008/48/EC and 2014/17/EU [2021] OJ L 438/1.

53   Regulation 2017/2401 of the European Parliament and of the Council of 12 December 2017 amending Regulation (EU) No 575/2013 on prudential requirements for credit institutions and investment firms' [2017] OJ L 347/1.

54   See EU Commission 'Communication on competing the Banking Union of 11 October 2017' COM (2017) 592 final.

55   See for example the explanatory memorandum of the Proposal for a directive on credit servicers COM (2018) 135 final 2018/0063(COD) and the Commission Communication 'Action plan: Tackling non-performing loans (NPLS) in the aftermath of the Covid-19 pandemic' COM/2020/822 final. See n 36 for an additional overview of banking supervision measures adopted after the outbreak of the COVID-19 pandemic.

      Also, within the wider strategy of measures adopted during the COVID-19 crisis, in which the confinement measures have had a major disruptive impact on the economy and on the credit market and consumers (especially the most vulnerable ones), there is the process of review of the 2008 Consumer Credit Directive. This has led to a Proposal for a Directive on consumer credits (on which see chapter 4) which takes into account, inter alia, the digital transformation of the lending sector, strongly accelerated during the sanitary crisis.

example the amount of provisioning made against the stock of gross NPLS (the coverage ratio).[56] These latter problems, including the effectiveness of legal frameworks for the recovery of debt and enforcement of collateral, may also lead to problems of information asymmetry and limit the demand if and when a secondary loans market is created, with significant bid-ask spread between investors purchasing loans and banks who sell them.[57]

As for the legal factors which condition the credit-granting decision-making process, and which will be further examined in this research, one of the main questions concerns the degree of freedom and discretion left to lenders in disregarding the outcomes of the assessment and the justifiable (or unjustifiable) degree of reliance on assessments that are entrusted to third parties (i.e. credit rating). The question will be analyzed in the second part of this Chapter and in Chapter 4 with reference to individual borrowers.

Ultimately, as for the social and cultural factors that are determinants of lending processes, an important distinction must be made regarding the subjects and the context in which the prudential duties are implemented. Not only are the instruments used for the 'rating' or the 'scoring' of borrowers different according to their legal status (i.e. corporations, small businesses, physical individuals), but there is also an important social factor that must be taken into account and that depends on the subjects (the lenders) called upon to make the evaluation.

From this point of view, even if it is not possible to analyze in detail the organization structure of all the types of banking institutions that are licensed to operate within different legal systems, it cannot be ignored that large commercial banks operating at a nationwide (and often international) level, coexist with smaller, often regional or even local banking or saving institutions that derive from forms of rural or mutual cooperatives (as is the case in many countries in Europe for example). The latter in many cases still maintain a 'know your customer' relationship when their activities are well – and sometimes historically – rooted in a community and it is difficult to assimilate the process of creditworthiness assessment that takes place within these smaller institutions to the one that takes place in large commercial banks, as will be examined. (On the point see Chapter 3, par. 3).

---

56   See M Lamandini, G Lusignani, DR Muñoz, 'Does Europe Have What It Takes to Finish the Banking Union? Non-Performing Loans (NPLS) and Their Hard Choices, Non-Choices and Evolving Choices', (2017) EBI Working Paper 3, with detailed data on NPL levels in countries across the EU.

57   See the EU European Parliamentary Research Service, 'Credit servicers, credit purchasers and the recovery of collateral' 2019, 3.

2.2   Credit Assessments and Credit Rating

2.2.1   *Credit Rating*

The second part of the analysis on the regulatory approach to creditworthiness assessment as a macroprudential duty focuses on its implementation for corporate and institutional borrowers, namely through credit rating. The study moves from a first inquiry on the nature and the function carried out by credit ratings and then focuses on the subjects (credit rating agencies – CRAs) that typically carry out this task. Following is the legal reconstruction of the regulatory interventions regarding both the subjects and their activity, comparing the models adopted in the United States and in the European Union.

The first issue is thus that of identifying the function of credit rating and the needs to which ratings respond in practice, first of all from an economic point of view, and then also as a response to the prudential duties examined earlier (such as those laid down in the Basel Accords for example).

Rating grades or scores assigned to borrowers are the outcome of a credit evaluation process (for example based on factors such as external, industry, internal and financial risks[58] or on the basis of quantitative credit risk default models)[59] and they indicate the degree of credit risk assigned to borrowers over a certain period of time (short or long term).

The distinguishing factors between credit rating models are multiple. They can be the outcome of automated or human evaluation processes (or both). Rating or grading models can differ *inter alia* in the weight that is assigned to single risk factors, and/or on the balance between qualitative and quantitative factors that are taken into account. Furthermore, they may be the outcome of evaluation systems that are developed by banks and financial institutions that underwrite credit risks (internal ratings) or by external agencies, often at the

---

58   A credit evaluation processes taking into account External, Industry, Internal and Financial risks impacting on the obligor is known as an "EIIF" model or study. For a detailed description of its characteristics, see Joseph (n 28) 169 and ff. Models can also be distinguished on the basis of the type of data they take into analysis (e.g. data on accounting and financial statements; data from the stock market; data from the bond market). See Malinconico (n 46) 110–111.

59   Such as the 1974 Merton Model, named after its developer Robert Merton, which estimates default of an obligor when the market value of the firm's assets reaches the default point, calculated as the equivalent to the face value of debtor. The KMV model (named after Kealhofer, McQuown and Vasicek) is another widely used model for estimating default risk that expands on the Merton model, as does the following Moody's Analytics EDF (Expected Default Frequency) indicator. The latter are sometimes referred to as alternative estimations of credit quality (alternative being to rating agency ratings). For further details see, *ex multis*, Joseph (n 28) 191 ff.; Bouteillé et al (n 38) 101–108.

request of obligors who wish to access the debt capital market, under the so-called 'issuers pay' model.[60]

Rating agencies provide ratings not only for corporate borrowers, but also for sovereign countries, supranational entities, public finance borrowers, large companies and structured finance vehicles.[61] Rating of credit for smaller entities (and for individual borrowers) is normally carried out through credit scoring techniques. In the observations above, the need to assess the creditworthiness of borrowers has been analyzed without distinction on the nature (a firm, a corporation, a single borrower, a consumer, a sovereign entity) of the borrower. Neither has this distinction been taken account of when referring to the loan portfolios of lenders. However, the process of creditworthiness evaluation is strongly conditioned by the identity and characteristics of the borrowers (as is the management of the loan portfolios).

Whereas lending portfolios can sometimes be composed of only a few 'large' borrowers (corporate entities, large firms, supranational and/or sovereign entities) for significant amounts of debt each, consumer credit portfolios will typically be extremely fragmented and will be composed of far higher numbers of borrowers for much lower amounts of debt. Not only does this impact on diversification issues in credit risk and portfolio management, but it also affects the modalities with which the creditworthiness is assessed.

In the first hypothesis, as already mentioned, the process of evaluation will generally be carried out through credit rating, with the internal rating/external rating option, and will often be based on 'objective' parameters and data, such

---

60   As previously mentioned, both systems are admitted by the Basel Accords. For example under Basel II guidelines there are certain criteria that bank regulators should take into account when permitting the ratings from a particular external credit assessment institution (ECAI) to be used, that pertain both to the nature of the credit rating agencies ("independence", "resources", and "credibility" of the ECAI), and to the methodologies of creditworthiness assessment.

The former criteria include "objectivity" of the credit assessment process (requiring a rigorous and systematic methodology, subject to ongoing review and responsive changes in financial condition); "international access/transparency" of the individual assessments; and "disclosure" of the assessment methodologies used by the ECAIs (including the definition of default, the time horizon, the meaning of each rating, the actual default rates experienced in each assessment category, the transitions of the assessments – e.g. the likelihood of a change in ratings over time). See Basel Committee on Banking Supervision, International Convergence of Capital Measurement and Capital Standards, A Revised Framework, 2004, §§91 and ff.

61   The three major rating agencies at global level (so called "Big Three") are Moody's Investors Services, Standard & Poor's, and Fitch Ratings, sharing around 95% of the market of CRAs (which comprises roughly 150 agencies). The first two (Moody's and S&P together control around 80% of the market, whilst Fitch Ratings controls an additional 15%).

as balance sheets of the firm, the external, industry, internal, and financial risks, and so forth.

In the second hypothesis, (typically consumer credit, mortgage credit), creditworthiness relies on credit scoring techniques, which face the dual challenge of having on the one hand to take into account a very relevant amount of 'subjective', personal data in determining the 'personal conditions' of creditworthiness of a potential borrower; and on the other hand, the issues and challenges posed by the fact that credit scoring is increasingly entrusted to automated, algorithm-based systems. The latter will be examined in Chapter 3, whilst the former, with the legal implications tied to fallacies in rating, is analyzed in the next sections.

Ratings are structured in such a way so as to comprise a balanced tradeoff between accuracy and stability, as the outcome of quantitative and qualitative analysis that focuses on long-term risks (whereas other market-based information focus on much shorter time spans).[62] According to the different elements to which they refer, ratings can be issuer ratings (a rating of the individual obligor as an organization); issue ratings (a rating of the creditworthiness of a specific issue or of the corporate finance obligation); structured finance obligation ratings (rating of specific issuances of a securitized pool of assets or other derivative financing transactions); and recovery ratings (a rating of the probability of recovery of unpaid principal in case of default by the issuer).

Although the legal discipline of credit rating is examined more in detail below, it is interesting to highlight in this phase if and to what extent credit rating has received legislative definition at a supranational level and in some of the legal systems that are the object of this study.

A credit rating has been defined for example in EU law as "an opinion regarding the creditworthiness of an entity, a debt or financial obligation, debt security, preferred share or other financial instrument, or of an issuer of such debt or financial obligation, debt security, preferred share or other financial instrument, issued using an established and defined ranking system of rating categories";[63] and in US law as "an assessment of the creditworthiness of an obligor as an entity, or with respect to specific securities or money markets instruments".[64]

---

62   J Manns, 'Rating Risk after the Subprime Mortgage Crisis: A User Fee Approach for Rating Agency Accountability' (2009) 87 North Carolina Law Review 1011, 1036–1037, making the comparison with credit default swaps.

63   Article 3(1)(a) Regulation (EC) 1060/2009 of the European Parliament and of the Council of 16 September 2009 on credit rating agencies, [2009] OJ L 302/1.

64   Securities Exchange Act 1934, section 3(a)60 (15 U.S.C. §§ 78a *et seq.*) as modified by the Credit Rating Agency Reform Act of 2006.

The idea that the assessment is an opinion has been contended in some judicial decisions in the United States so as to allow credit ratings to fall under the protection of the First Amendment of the US Constitution. This has allowed in earlier decisions to apply the *NY Times Co.* v. *Sullivan*[65] doctrine on erroneous statements for example, and to avoid liability for credit rating agencies.[66] Whilst the Dodd-Frank Wall Street Reform and Consumer Protection Act has introduced gatekeeper liability for credit rating agencies under Section 11 of the Securities Act (previously excluded under Rule 456(g) of the Securities Act), the relation with potential protection under the First Amendment has not been totally excluded.[67]

2.2.2   The Functional Role of Credit Rating Agencies

The strategic function of credit rating has allowed specific subjects (credit rating agencies), that have been able to exploit information asymmetries, economies of scale, and the request for external and independent certification, to acquire a dominant position on the markets for credit information. Even if not immediately, these actors have also spurred the attention of regulators. The structure of credit rating agencies and their regulation can now be analyzed so as to ascertain how the different contractual models they apply condition their position on the markets, including the type of responsibility they may owe to their contractual counterparties and/or to third parties.

Credit rating agencies, as mentioned earlier, issue ratings that serve a dual purpose. On the one hand they provide information to investors and are often requested by the issuers of debt (the development of originate-to-distribute models of banks has for example largely benefitted from, and has developed

---

65   US Supreme Court, 376 US 254 (1964).

66   See e.g. *Jefferson C. Sch. Dist. No. R-1 v. Moody's Investor's Serv. Inc.*, 175 F.3d 848 (10th Cir. 1999); *In re Enron Corp. Sec. Derivative & "ERISA" Litig.*, 511 F. Sup. 2d 742 (S.D. Tex. 2005); *Compuware Corp. v. Moody's Investors Servs. Inc.*, 499 F. 3d 520, 531, (6th Cir. 2007) applying the 'actual malice' standard of *N.Y. Times Co. v. Sullivan* to defamation and breach of contract claims brought against a rating agency. The First Amendment protection and the 'actual malice' standard applies in and so far as the published material is a matter of public concern (*Dun & Bradstreet, Inc.* v. *Greenmoss Builders, Inc.*, 472 US 749 (1985)). And indeed, *contra*, see *Abu Dhabi Commercial Bank v. Morgan Stanley & Co., Inc.* 651 F. Supp. 2d 155 (S.D.N.Y. 2009).

67   See A Tuch, 'Multiple Gatekeepers' (2010) 96 Virginia Law Review 1583, 1668; C Deats, 'Talk that isn't cheap: does the First Amendment protect credit rating agencies' faulty methodologies from regulation?', in (2010) 110 Columbia Law Review 1818, 1821–1822. On the problem of liability of CRAS see *infra*.

on the basis of, ratings of structured products).[68] On the other hand, credit ratings are employed in the regulation of institutional investors and in financial market regulation.

The regulatory use of ratings determines, *inter alia*, bank capital requirements (financial institutions can use credit ratings from approved agencies (external credit assessment institutions (ECAIS)) when calculating their capital requirements under Basel II rules).[69] Furthermore, credit ratings are also used by central banks in determining the acceptable level of collateral for financial institutions wishing to borrow from the central bank.

The independent assessment of the ability of issuers to meet their obligation is an information service that is provided by credit rating agencies and is used by the markets. Credit rating agencies also carry out a service that 'monitors' issuers after ratings have been assigned and that can induce corrective actions on behalf of those same issuers under the threat of a downgrade.[70]

Credit rating agencies can thus be qualified as information intermediaries between issuers and investors that reduce information asymmetries and, by increasing the transparency of securities, improve the efficiency of securities markets. They have also been defined as "certification" or "reputational" intermediaries.[71]

Generally, the utility of credit rating activity (and the reasons for the inelasticity of the demand of credit rating even after the strong criticisms incurred in the occasion of several crises – see *infra*) has been identified first of all in the fact that this activity responds to a demand of 'security' posed by creditors seeking a third and impartial opinion in support of their decisions to extend

---

68   J de Haan, F Amtenbrink, 'Credit Rating Agencies', 2011 DNB Working Paper, n. 278, 1. Assets that are selected to be part of a pool in a securitization process are scrutinized by rating agencies and underwriters so as to evaluate the expected performance of the pool. See Casu et al (n 41) 363.

69   A joint forum in 2009 of the Basel Committee on Banking Supervision, the International Organization of Securities Commissions (IOSCO) and the International Association of Insurance Supervisors conducted a stocktaking on the use of credit ratings, identifying five main forms of use in its member jurisdictions: a) determination of capital requirements; b) identification or classification of assets (usually in the context of eligible investments or permissible asset concentrations; c) provision of a credible evaluation of the credit risk associated with assets purchased as part of a securitization offering or a covered bond offering; d) determination of disclosure requirements; and e) determination of prospectus liability (See Joint Forum Basel Committee on Banking Supervision, the International Organisation of Securities Commissions (IOSCO) and the International Association of Insurance Supervisors, 'Stocktaking on the use of credit ratings' June 2009).

70   de Haan et al (n 68) ibid.

71   See S Choi, 'Market Lessons for Gatekeepers' (1997–1998) 92 Northwestern University Law Review 916 for the qualification of CRAS as certification intermediaries.

credit to their debtors.[72] Economies of scale can be achieved by a relatively small number of rating agencies that can make the creditworthiness assessment on behalf of many investors (especially considering the high costs that individual investors face in assessing an issuer's securities).[73]

Secondly, credit rating is a form of cognitive simplification, as it translates a complex assessment into a simple, synthetic, and easily recognizable judgment and thus facilitates the circulation of information on issuers in the market.[74]

Thirdly, users of credit ratings seem to attribute an additional utility in having recourse to ratings, as these are perceived as the outcome of complex and costly analysis (based on data that is not always publicly available) and that is made possible thanks to (the trust in) the professional capacity of the credit rating agencies.[75] Additionally, there are of course the 'external' advantages of credit rating (i.e. the information) that benefit the market generally as a third party in the issuer-credit rating agency relation.

2.2.2.1   Contractual Models

Another important aspect, as highlighted earlier, is the contractual model that is at the basis of the activity of credit rating and the impact that this (or rather, these) contractual models have on the credibility and position of credit rating agencies on the market. Equally relevant is the logically subsequent issue of their responsibility both towards their contractual counterparties and/or towards third parties (i.e. investors).

It should be noted first of all that the existence of two contractual and business models (the investors pay/unsolicited ratings model and the issuers pay/ solicited model) at the basis of the rating activity impacts differently both on the ratings, as far as their neutrality and possible accuracy are concerned, and on the rating market. Whereas the above considerations on the utility and the demand for credit rating are perfectly valid under the investors pay model, where what is being sold is information and where the most important asset for credit rating agencies – allowing them to compete in the ratings market – is their reputation (exemplified by the accuracy of their ratings), under the later and now prevailing issuers pay model the incentives are somewhat inverted.

---

72   See M Lubrano di Scorpaniello, *Società di rating. Innovazioni di governance e tutela dell'affidamento* (Giuffrè 2016) 38 ff.

73   SL Schwarcz, 'Private Ordering of Public Markets: the Rating Agency Paradox' (2002) 2 University of Illinois Law Review 1,12.

74   M. Lubrano di Scorpaniello (n 72) ibid.

75   Ibid.

Whilst the issuers are willing to pay the fees for the rating, their interest is clearly not neutral (as the pricing of their credit will depend on the rating) and the rating agencies often face conflicts of interest between pleasing their clients with positive or overly generous ratings (with the downside effect of generating a market for the highest ratings), and maintaining their reputation through the integrity of their judgments.

The relative difficulty in proving the inaccuracy of a rating (only possible *ex post* and indirectly through the default rate of the debt-instruments that are rated)[76] and the slower reaction of the investors' market as opposed to the issuers' one in sanctioning shortcomings of credit rating agencies, can further exacerbate the conflict.[77]

Furthermore, there may be a certain risk of so-called 'downward bias' of unsolicited ratings, which would result in lower ratings when they are unsolicited. This may be the result of different factors, such as, under the so-called 'self-selection hypothesis', the phenomenon of self-selection of high-quality companies into the solicited rating status, reflecting strategic behavior on the part of the borrowers and a 'strategic conservatism' of rating agencies.[78]

Other hypotheses attempting to explain the tendency of unsolicited ratings to be lower all else being equal, include the theory that this practice on behalf of credit rating agencies would act as an incentive for issuers who would otherwise not purchase ratings to do so (in order to avoid the lower grade). Furthermore, unsolicited ratings are based only on information that is publicly available and thus would tend to be more prudent.[79]

Finally, the regulatory incorporation of ratings has impacted not only the rating market, but also the role of credit rating agencies. According to some

---

76   S Rousseau, 'Regulating Credit Rating Agencies After the Financial Crisis: the Long and Winding Road Toward Accountability' (2009) Capital Markets Institute. Rotman School of Management, University of Toronto, 43.

77   A Castaldo, L Palla, *L'informazione nei mercati finanziari: il ruolo delle agenzie di rating* (Giappichelli 2016) 107–108.

78   A Miglionico, *Enhancing the regulation of credit rating agencies, in search of a method*, Centre for Financial & Management Studies, SOAS (London 2012), 39–40; CE Bannier, P Behr, A Güttler, 'Rating opaque borrowers: why are unsolicited ratings lower?' (2009) Frankfurt School-Working Paper Series, n. 133, Frankfurt School of Finance & Management, 6 ff.

79   This would lead to the "public disclosure hypothesis" according to which, *inter alia*, issuers who do not request a rating but disclose a sufficient amount of public information do not receive lower ratings compared to those issuers who have solicited a rating. See P Van Roy, 'Is there a difference between solicited and unsolicited bank ratings and if so, why?', National Bank of Belgium, (2006) *Working Paper Research Series* No. 79, 2 and *passim.*, also providing an overview of the literature and research comparing the outcomes of solicited with unsolicited ratings.

scholars, what is being "sold" no longer has informational value but has great market value because of the regulatory recognition that it is accorded (in what has been defined as a market of "regulatory licenses").[80]

2.2.2.2 Relevance of Credit Rating and Credit Rating Agencies for Creditworthiness Assessments and Regulatory Reform in the Wake of the Financial Crisis

The dual economic relevance of the activity of credit rating (and credit rating agencies) and its impact both on the issuer-rater relationship and on the rater-market relationship is highly emblematic of the problems posed when considering responsible credit and creditworthiness assessments. The regulation of the activity both *ex ante*, through for example rules on methodology of rating and access to the activity (regulation/authorization of the subjects) and through rules *ex post* (the liability of credit rating agencies for erroneous ratings) is indicative of the relevance of promoting (or ensuring?) a correct process of creditworthiness assessment in the general interest of the market. It could be said that the systemic importance of the process is a direct consequence of the macro-prudential duties highlighted earlier. It is thus appropriate to examine more in detail the regulatory approach of credit rating activity and its changes in the United States and in the European Union.

The strong criticisms on the role of credit rating agencies in the 2008 financial crisis (which included an underestimation of credit risk for structured credit products; the rating failures for private residential mortgage backed securities in the USA; the loss and lack of information on the risk characteristics of assets underlying the securities; an untimely reaction, in terms of rating adjustments, to the financial crisis; and the failures in some of the sovereign ratings),[81] but also in previous sovereign (e.g. Asian crisis of 1997) and corporation failures (e.g. Enron in 2000–2001, WorldCom in 2002, Parmalat in 2003), led to regulatory responses on the activities of credit rating agencies worldwide, including in the United States and in the European Union (and later to the adoption of provisions having the scope of a progressive reduction in the over-reliance on credit ratings and of the regulatory value of the ratings).[82]

---

80   F Partnoy, 'The Paradox of Credit Ratings', in RM Levich, G Majnoni, C Reinhart, (eds), *Ratings, Rating Agencies and the Global Financial System* (Springer Science+Business Media 2002) 65–66.

81   de Haan et al (n 68) 2–3; for a detailed analysis see for example JC Coffee Jr, 'Ratings Reform: The Good, the Bad, and the Ugly' (2011) 1 Harvard Business Law Review 231, 236–246.

82   See for example the recitals n. 2, 6, 8, 9 of EU Regulation n. 462/2013 on credit rating agencies. See Lubrano di Scorpaniello (n 72) 25 ff.

The main criticisms and scopes for legislation concerned, *inter alia*, the management of potential (and actual) conflicts of interest in the issuer-pays model; the improvement of the quality of the rating process; the differentiation of ratings on structured finance from those on bonds and expanded information on structured products; and the enhancement of credit rating agency assessment of data quality received from issuers.[83]

Proposals of reform in this area have generally revolved around either adoption of greater or more stringent regulation on credit rating agencies (especially as a means to avoid conflicts of interest in the rating process), or of deregulation by downsizing the role of credit ratings.[84]

The regulation of credit rating agencies has taken different forms and contents, both in the relatively scarce legislation adopted in the decades preceding the 2008 financial crisis (mostly based on self-regulatory regime) and in its aftermath. The most relevant – albeit pre-2008 crisis – provision in the US relating to credit rating agencies was the Credit Rating Agency Reform Act (CRARA) of 2006, which established a registration system for rating agencies seeking 'nationally recognized statistical rating organizations' (NRSRO) status.[85] The CRARA aimed at promoting competition in the rating industry and at enhancing transparency in order to avoid conflicts of interest and abusive practices; it endowed the SEC with regulatory authority (whereas previously regulation of credit rating agencies was left to industry self-regulation, such as the standards set by the International Organization of Securities Commissions (IOSCO) in its 'Code for Conduct Fundamentals for Credit Rating Agencies').[86]

The main issues on the agenda of legislators in the wake of the financial crisis concerned, as previously highlighted, multiple aspects. On the one hand, the oligopolistic structure of the credit rating sector and the conflicts of interest; on the other hand, the problem of overreliance on credit ratings and the civil liability of credit rating agencies. The two latter aspects are of particular relevance for the scope of this study and require further examination.

---

83 Such were the recommendations issued by the Financial Stability Forum in its 'Report of the Financial Stability Forum on Enhancing Market and Institutional Resilience', 2008, pp. 32–36.

84 Coffee Jr. (n. 81) 246.

85 The status of NRSROs is mentioned as early as 1975 in Rule 15c3–1 (Net Capital Rule) released by the SEC (Concept Release Nationally Recognized Statistical Rating Organizations), although the requisites needed to obtain this status were not clarified at the time (this only occurred in 2006 with the adoption of the Credit Rating Agency Reform Act). See Coffee Jr. (n 81) 247; M Marchesi, *Rating e trasparenza. Esperienze europee e nordamericane a confronto* (Giappichelli 2015) 22–28.

86 See ANR Sy, 'Systemic Regulation of Credit Rating Agencies and Rated Markets', 2009 IMF Working Paper 6; de Haan et al (n 68) 17.

Starting with the United States, the financial crisis triggered and hastened a proposed reform of the CRARA and of credit rating activity which arrived under the 2010 Dodd-Frank Act, introducing supervisory rules on credit rating activity, organizational and governance requisites for credit rating agencies, and rules on methods and criteria with which the latter are to carry out their creditworthiness assessments.

Particularly interesting from a comparative point of view, was also the introduction of a form of gatekeeper liability, by abolishing the exemption from Rule 15E(m) of the SEC regulation for credit rating agencies (on which see *infra*) and subjecting them to the same standards of expert liability and oversight as apply to auditors, securities analysts and investment bankers (§931(3) creating liability where an agency "knowingly or recklessly failed a) to conduct a reasonable investigation of the rated security with respect to the factual elements relied upon by its own methodology for evaluating credit risk; or b) to obtain reasonable verification of such factual elements [...] from other sources that the credit rating agency considered to be competent and that were independent of the issuer and underwriter").[87]

In Europe, before the shortcomings of credit rating agencies' ratings and their role in the 2008 financial crisis were highlighted, the Enron and Parmalat scandals in 2002 and 2003 had urged interventions on behalf of the EU so as to assess the main regulatory issues of concern with regard to rating agencies. However, no specific regulation centered on rating agencies was adopted as the scattered provisions referring to credit rating agencies inserted in legislative measures that were part of the Commission's Financial Services Action Plan were deemed sufficient. These included first of all the Directive on Market Abuse,[88] whose duties of confidentiality were intended as applicable to credit rating agencies who have access to inside information, including the prohibition to disseminate false or misleading information constituting market manipulation and whose provisions in the field of conflicts of interest, fair presentation of investment recommendations and the access to inside information constitute "a comprehensive legal framework for credit rating agencies while, at the same time, acknowledging their specific role and the differences between credit ratings and investment recommendations".[89]

---

87   Dodd-Frank Wall Street Reform and Consumer Protection Act Section 933(b).

88   Directive 2003/6/EC of the European Parliament and of the Council of 28 January 2003 on insider dealing and market manipulation, [2003] *OJ* L 96/16, and its implementing Directives.

89   Communication from the Commission on Credit Ratings Agencies (2006/C 59/02), 3.1.

Provisions referring to credit rating agencies were also found in the 2006 Capital Requirements Directive, where the criteria that rating agencies must satisfy in order to obtain the status of External Credit Assessment Institutions (ECAIS) for the purposes of determination of capital requirements are laid;[90] and in the Market on Financial Instruments Directive (MiFID), whose provisions on authorization, conduct of business and organizational requirements apply for credit rating agencies undertaking investment services and activities besides credit rating activities.[91] The general approach here as elsewhere was that of relying on self-regulation of the credit rating industry, exemplified by the IOSCO Code and its 'comply or explain' basis. An approach that was still upheld in the initial discussion on the measures to be adopted as a first reaction to the outbreak of the crisis,[92] and only subsequently discarded in favor of more stringent forms of regulation.

Indeed, it was only in 2009, in the midst of the financial turmoil and the strong debate and criticism on the role of credit rating agencies in exacerbating the crisis especially through frequent downgrading of sovereign ratings of European states, that the first specific Regulation on Credit Agencies (Regulation 1060/2009) was approved, and almost immediately put up for amendments (in 2011 and in 2013).[93] The regulatory approach of the EU on credit rating agencies was centered on three levels: competition, governance and public supervision.

The reform of the credit rating sector fell within the wider scheme of reform of the European financial sector, with the establishment of a European Systemic Risk Board (ESRB) with duties of macroprudential supervision, and of a new European System of Financial Supervision with duties of microprudential supervision (the establishment of the European Securities and

90　Articles 80 and 81, Directive 2006/48/EC of 14 June 2006 relating to the taking up and pursuit of the business of credit institutions (recast) [2006] OJ L 177/1 (later repealed by Directive 2013/36/EU of 26 June 2013 on access to the activity of credit institutions and the prudential supervision of credit institutions and investment firms [2013] OJ L 176/338).

91　Directive 2004/39/EC of 21 April 2004, on markets in financial instruments [2004] OJ L 145/1.

92　See for example the reports issued by the European Securities Markets Expert Group (ESME) and the Committee of European Securities Regulators (CESR) in 2008. For a reconstruction of the various phases of the regulatory debate see de Haan et al (n 68) 18.

93　Regulation 1060/2009 was amended by Regulation EU 513/2011 of 11 May 2011 amending Regulation 1060/2009 [2009] OJ L145/30; by Directive 2011/61/EU of 8 June 2011 on Alternative Investment Fund Managers [2011] OJ L174/1; and by Regulation EU 462/2013 of 21 May 2013 amending Regulation 1060/2009 [2013] OJ L146/1.

Markets Authority (ESMA) in 2011,[94] having supervisory powers on credit rating agencies, is to be read in this context).[95]

The European regulatory approach to credit rating agencies is based on a regime of registration[96] (as a condition for their recognition as ECAIs) and supervision; on the management of conflicts of interest and the improvement of rating methodologies; on the increase of information duties for rating agencies and an increase in transparency (even if it is not clear to what extent a full disclosure of rating methodologies can be expected and whether this would not constitute a disincentive to research and development of new rating methodologies); and on the adoption of rules of conduct (largely based on the IOSCO code) for registered credit rating agencies (including, for example, differentiated credit rating categories for structured finance instruments and traditional corporate bond or sovereign bond ratings).[97]

Before examining the problem of liability of credit rating agencies, it may be useful to observe how the financial crisis of 2007–2008 hastened and urged regulatory reforms concerning the legal status and the activity of rating agencies, which were made the object of specific legislation in multiple jurisdictions. In the wake of the crisis and of the emerging responsibilities of these subjects, the regulatory responses that were triggered tended to subtract credit rating activity from a domain based on industry self-regulation and left entirely to private autonomy on the basis of contractual relationships between the rated and the rater, and to introduce forms of public oversight. The other path of reform was centered on a downsizing of the role of credit ratings, by reducing both the regulatory value of ratings and the so-called 'over-reliance' on them.

2.2.3 Credit Rating in a Perspective of Responsible Credit: Liability of Credit Rating Agencies and Over-Reliance on Ratings

2.2.3.1 Liability of Credit Rating Agencies

In the analysis of creditworthiness assessments on which this work is focused, it is interesting to note that the shortcomings of credit rating agencies before and during the 2007–2008 global financial crisis led to the challenging of two

---

94   Regulation EU 1095/2010 of 24 November 2010 establishing a European Supervisory Authority (European Securities and Markets Authority), [2010] OJ L 331/84.

95   The other two European Supervisory Authorities part of the ESFS are the European Banking Authority (EBA) and the European Insurance and Occupational Pensions Authority (EIOPA).

96   Article 14 Regulation 1060/2009.

97   de Haan et al (n 68) 20–23 ff.; M Bussani, 'Le agenzie di *rating* fra immunità e responsabilità', (2014) 60 Rivista di diritto civile 1337, 1340.

closely tied issues, which more generally fall within the idea of responsible credit: the reduction of over-reliance on credit ratings, and the establishment of some form of liability for credit rating agencies. Both issues were tackled at a global level, in some cases with an interconnected link.

Such is the case of the EU Regulation on Credit Rating Agencies, that whilst recognizing possible claims for damages for investors and issuers from credit rating agencies in case the latter have infringed a series of duties intentionally or with gross negligence, simultaneously requires the proof by the investors that they have "reasonably relied, in accordance with Article 5a(1) or otherwise with due care, on a credit rating for a decision to invest into, hold onto or divest from a financial instrument covered by that credit rating ".[98]

The very nature of credit ratings (i.e. information) makes them bound to circulate and be used and relied on beyond strict national borders. This inherent characteristic of information and the function that it achieves thus requires and justifies harmonized rules for their regulation.

One of the main problems of this legislation, that can be comparatively observed in jurisdictions that have reformed their regulation of credit rating activity, seems to pertain to the formulation of an effective array of sanctions and tools of deterrence for intentionally or negligently inaccurate or erroneous credit ratings or rating outlooks.

Potential plaintiffs fall into two categories: investors who rely on negligent or inaccurate ratings, and issuers who are injured by negligent or inaccurate initial rating or subsequent negligent or inaccurate downgrading of their debt instruments (with a common claim of amplifying or accelerating an ongoing crisis: e.g. the case of European sovereign debts crisis set off in 2009).

As with any other case of liability deriving from false or inaccurate statements in financial markets, the effects of negligent or erroneous ratings should be distinguished according to their impact on primary or secondary markets. On primary markets, inaccurate ratings will interfere with the allocation of goods and investments, by favoring non-worthy issuers; on the secondary market, the interference operates between investors, in the distribution of benefits.[99]

The sphere of liability for false information towards the investor will accordingly differ, pertaining to a form of pre-contractual liability in the first hypothesis of the primary market and to a form of potential extra-contractual liability in the hypothesis of the secondary market.[100]

---

98   Article 35a, Regulation EU 462/2013. See also further in the text.
99   P Giudici, *La responsabilità civile nel diritto dei mercati finanziari* (Giuffrè 2008) 27.
100   Ibid 215.

2.2.3.1.1   *Liability Towards Issuers (or Subscribers)*
Theorizing and imposing forms of liability for credit rating requires a preliminary inquiry into the nature of the relation that is at the basis of a credit rating.
There is first of all a contractual relation, which in the issuer-pays/solicited
rating model is between the issuer and the rater (whereas in the currently
much less common subscribers-pay/unsolicited rating model the contract is
between the credit rating agency and the purchasers-subscribers of the rating
reports).

US scholarship has highlighted how the relationship initially was one of
agency between the rating agencies and prospective purchasers and own-
ers of debt (under the subscriber-pays model). With the introduction of the
NRSRO system in 1975 the US federal government and the SEC inverted the
scheme and rapidly imposed issuer-purchased ratings as the prevailing and
necessary model, with those who were once targets of rating agencies now acting as their clients, and the once customers now transformed into targets of
information.[101]

The contractual relationship has been alternatively defined, *inter alia*,
as an agency agreement, as a contract for the performance of a professional
service/contract for work, or as an 'innominate' contract, and it is under contractual rules that not only the obligations between the parties but also breach
of duties will be assessed and governed.

The consequence of this is that in the absence of specific legislation governing contracts between issuers and rating agencies, parties tend to include
clauses in their contracts excluding liability in favor of agencies, thus making it
necessary to find contractual remedies able to circumvent these limitations.[102]

However, under the EU regime of civil liability of credit rating agencies
outlined in Regulation n. 462/2013, any exclusion of liability for credit rating
agencies that is not "reasonable and proportionate or allowed by applicable
national law" shall be deprived of any legal effect, as is any limitation for gross
negligence or intention.[103]

The European model also adopts a contractual perspective. Indeed, the performance of the credit rating agencies and their standard of care will be, in
most cases, evaluated according to the parameter of professional standards and

---

101   Manns (n 62) 1056.
102   See B Haar, 'Civil Liability of Credit Rating Agencies after CRA3 – Regulatory All-or-Nothing
        Approaches between Immunity and Over-Deterrence', (2014) 25 European Business Law
        Review 315, 316; A Scarso, 'The Liability of Credit Rating Agencies in a Comparative
        Perspective' (2013) 4 Journal of European Tort Law 163, 166 ff for a reconstruction of
        German and Italian scholarship on the classification of the ratings agreement.
103   Article 35a(3), Regulation EU 462/2013.

diligence set in legislation and/or in codes of conduct.[104] In some instances, such as the French legislation transposing the first European CRA Regulation in 2010, injured issuers ("the clients") could also invoke the "delictual and quasi-delictual" liability of the agencies, thus admitting a form of extracontractual liability even if the parties were bound by a contractual obligation.[105] This regime was later modified in 2018 in order to align the French discipline to the European liability rules laid down in the third version of the CRA Regulation (Regulation EU n. 513/2011), moving from a very wide and general clause of liability to the typified hypotheses of negligent conduct contained in Annex III of the European Regulation.

Elements to be kept in mind in the relationship between the issuer and the rater are first of all that most (though not all) of the information used for elaborating the rating (the evaluation process) are supplied by the issuer to the rater on a voluntary basis. A second important element is that the methodology of the rating is determined by the rater, and notwithstanding an enhanced quest on behalf of regulators for a disclosure of these methodologies,[106] it is clearly also necessary to strike a balance between transparency on the one side and protection of evaluation procedures that have been researched and developed by the raters on the other side. It is interesting to note that similar concerns are expressed as regards the development of credit scoring methodologies, which are often protected as trade secrets (see Chapter 3). The latter consideration will rarely lead to a full disclosure of the details of the process. These and any other elements that may be inserted into the rating agreement will determine assessments on possible breach or negligent performance of the contract.

As for the type of injury suffered, the typical hypotheses are those of provoking an increase in the cost of credit for the issuers (initial or subsequent, as in the case of a supervening downgrading that can even activate 'rating trigger' clauses allowing creditors to demand immediate restitution of capitals

---

104   Scarso (n 102) 168.
105   Article L.544–5, alinèa 1er, of the *Code monétarie et financier*, introduced by the *loi* n. 2010–1249 provided that *"Les agences de notation de crédt mentionnées à l'article L.544–4 engagent leur responsabilité délictuelle et quasi délictuelle, tant à l'égard de leurs clients que des tiers, des conséquences dommageable des fautes et manquements par elles commis dans la mise en oeuvre des obligations définies dans le règlement (CE) n. 1060/2009 du Parlement européen et du Conseil, du 16 septembre 2009, précité"*. This article was abrogated in 2018. See also M Audit, 'Aspects internationaux de la responsabilité des agences de notation', (2011) 100 Revue critique de droit international privé 581, 597.
106   See article 8, c.1, Reg. 1060/2009 and Annex I/En.5.

lent).[107] In the more serious cases, there may be an acceleration or aggravation of a default of the issuer (both corporate and/or sovereign).

However, this very contractual relation is functional to the output of a product – the rating – that has an important utility not only for the contractual counterparty (issuer), but also for third parties (the market). Clearly the utility for the former and the latter is different.

It is not irrelevant that third parties do not pay (directly) for this use and that the sole legal and financial relationship of credit rating agencies is with the issuers of debt.[108] It should also be kept in mind that the contractual relationship between the issuer and the rater is not simply a private relationship that 'can' also have external effects (as it almost always has, even if theoretically the issuer may relinquish the publication of a rating that he finds may damage him): the normative relevance and incorporation of ratings in laws and standards in some cases may impose the publication of the rating (its diffusion to the market) as a condition for making investment choices.[109]

The activity of issuance of a rating may also be defined as an instance of 'private ordering', especially because of the normative effect that is recognized to the rating. This leads to a recognition on both sides of the Atlantic of the role of credit rating agencies as gatekeepers, with important consequences on the liability of rating agencies as compared to the liability of other private actors.[110]

Furthermore, the practice of monitoring and updating ratings periodically after their publication that in some cases is codified by law (e.g. in the EU, article 8, c.5 Regulation 1060/2009) or in codes of conduct (e.g. IOSCO code), seems to strengthen the impression that the public utility of ratings can outlive the initial contractual relationship by keeping the obligation of creditworthiness evaluation 'alive' even after the contract is terminated. The monitoring can lead to a confirmation, an upgrading or a downgrading of the initial rating. Some have identified the need to protect the reputation of credit rating agencies (their most valuable asset on the market) as the interest that underlies

---

107   Audit (n 105) 597.

108   Manns (n 62) 1015.

109   Lubrano di Scorpaniello (n 72) 127.

110   Manns (n 62) 1014; on the specific characteristics of CRAS as gatekeepers, see F Partnoy, 'How and Why Credit Rating Agencies Are Not Like Other Gatekeepers', in Y Fuchita, RE Litan (eds), *Financial Gatekeepers: Can they Protect Investors?* (Brookings Institution Press and the Nomura Institute of Capital Markets Research 2006), highlighting, *inter alia*, the conflicts of interest, the oligopoly market structure in which they operate, the (historical) exemption from liability, their role in structured finance, and the benefit of "regulatory licenses" which are recognized to CRAS.

such a unilateral obligation.[111] An additional ratio for such a duty has been identified in the fact that the interests of the market constitute a sufficient foundation for the rating activity *per se*, once the rating has been published and has become a 'public good'[112] with the normative recognition already highlighted. The interest in maintaining a consolidated position as a 'licensed regulator'[113] may justify the expense of this unilateral undertaking.

2.2.3.1.2   *Liability Towards Third Parties*

The nature of this second relationship (between credit rating agencies and the public/the market) is more difficult to define especially as far as the reliance of the third party is concerned, but there is a prevailing tendency to confine it outside the boundaries of contract. Indeed, one of the main difficulties of a thesis arguing a contractual relationship between the agencies and the general public that uses the ratings lies in the absence of a valid consideration and of a mutual interest relationship between the credit rating agency and users of its ratings.[114]

However, there have been some doctrinal attempts to qualify it as quasi-contractual, or (for example in Germany), as an instance of precontractual liability (and on the basis of the intermediary function of credit rating agencies in the capital market).[115] Others have qualified it as contractual and have thus tried to extend the regime of contractual liability to third parties under the theory of the protective effect of contract to third parties. The potential existence of an implicit agreement between the issuer and the rating agency so as to protect third parties (investors) has been theorized by German doctrine, with however, a series of requirements so as to avoid an unreasonable extension of the potential liability in contract. These requirements include the need for the claimant to be in a "creditor like position" and that the third party (the investor) has a specific vulnerability (i.e. that there is no other potentially

---

111   Lubrano di Scorpaniello (n 72) 140; on the effects of reputation as a bonding mechanism in the market for intermediary services see SJ Choi, 'A Framework for the Regulation of Securities Market Intermediaries' (2004) 1 Berkeley Business Law Journal 45, 51–52.

112   See Manns (n 62) 1035, according to whom the federal government in the USA "effectively made ratings a public good by issuing numerous regulations that required issuers to secure ratings concerning their creditworthiness in order to participate in financial markets". See also SJ Choi (n 111) 49–50 on the financing problems of intermediaries commensurate to the service of information (as public goods) they provide.

113   See Partnoy (n 110) ibid.

114   See Lubrano di Scorpaniello (n 72) 164–165.

115   See for a reconstruction, Haar (n 102) 317–318.

liable party); the latter requirement would be hard to meet if the third party has a claim not only against the insolvent issuer but also against the rating agency.[116]

The theory of liability arising from qualified 'social contact' has also been advanced by Italian doctrine, which has for example theorized its applicability to liability of credit rating agencies based on the contention that the qualification of rating agencies as experts and the reliance of third parties on this expertise (and on the correctness of ratings deriving therefrom) imposes 'duties of protection' of the former towards the latter; the breach of such duties in case of negligent conduct gives rise to a liability that is assimilated to contractual liability (pursuant to articles 1173 and 1218 of the Italian Civil Code). Courts, however, have rejected this reconstruction proposed by plaintiffs in proceedings against credit rating agencies.[117]

The nature of this relationship becomes particularly relevant in the definition of liability of rating agencies and of what constitutes 'reliance' on ratings. There are different hypothesis concerning the relationship between credit rating agencies and third parties (e.g. the market) that rely on the ratings. First of all, there is a distinction to be made within the category of 'third parties': third

---

116   See Haar (n 102) 317. See however the ruling by the Court of Appeal of Düsseldorf of February 8th, 2018, I-6 U 50/17, (2018) Neuen Juristichen Wochenschrift 1615, excluding liability of a CRA both under Article 35a of Regulation 1060/2009 and under the German legal rules on contracts with protective effect towards third parties (where the rating concerned not the specific bond purchased by the investor, but only the issuer of the bond). The Court thus differentiates between corporate rating and financial product rating and further highlights that in case of a corporate rating it would not be possible to identify the group of potentially protected "third parties".

117   See Tribunale di Catanzaro, 2/3/2012, n. 685, (2013) Giurisprudenza commerciale II 462; Tribunale di Roma 17/1/2012, n. 835, (2013) Danno e responsabilità 183). The theory of liability from "social contact" is grounded on the work of L Mengoni, 'Sulla natura della responsabilità precontrattuale', (1956) 54 Rivista del diritto commerciale, 9–10, 360 and the further developments carried out, *inter alia*, by C Castronovo, *La nuova responsabilità civile* (Giuffrè 2006); C Scognamiglio, 'Il danno al patrimonio tra contratto e torto', (2007) 72 Responsabilità civile e previdenza, 1255; A Di Majo, 'Il problema del danno al patrimonio', in (1984) 2 Rivista critica di diritto privato, 322; L Lambo, 'Responsabilità civile e obblighi di protezione', (2008) 13 Danno e responsabilità, 129; S Faillace, *La responsabilità da contatto sociale* (Cedam 2004). With reference to the issue of liability of CRAS towards third parties, see G Facci, 'Le agenzie di rating e la responsabilità per informazioni inesatte' (2008) 24 Contratto e impresa 164; A Sacco Ginevri, 'Le società di rating nel regolamento CE n. 1060/2009: profili organizzativi dell'attività' (2010) 33 *Nuove leggi civili commentate* 291; C Scaroni, 'La responsabilità delle agenzie di rating nei confronti degli investitori' (2011) 27 Contratto e impresa 764; P Sanna, *La responsabilità civile delle agenzie di rating nei confronti degli investitori* (Edizioni scientifiche italiane 2011); L Di Donna, *La responsabilità civile delle agenzie di rating* (Cedam 2012).

parties who are clients of subscribers to credit rating agency publications (e.g. clients of banks that have subscribed to publications of CRAs) and third parties who are part of the 'general public'.[118]

Another distinction (adopted for example by US Courts in a distinction between ratings as 'opinions' given heightened protection the First Amendment and ratings as 'commercial speech') is the one between professional or qualified investors (or more generally, ratings directed at a 'restricted' or prequalified group of investors, such as for example in a process of securitization), and 'investors' as general (and non-professional) public.[119]

It should be noted that when ratings are treated as commercial speech (as in the US model), credit rating agencies may be held liable when there is proof of intention to deceive or mislead investors with inaccurate and faulty ratings, but not where there is mere negligence. Ratings treated as 'commercial speech' receive weaker protection than ratings treated as 'opinions' that are assimilated to journalistic information and thus are given the heightened constitutional protection reserved for the press.[120]

Another *revirement* of the common law protection under freedom of expression to ratings as 'opinions' was expressed by the Federal Court of Australia, allowing the Court to examine misrepresentation claims against a credit rating agency.[121]

The regime of this extra-contractual liability can be further distinguished according to whether it falls within the hypotheses laid down in the specific sector legislation (e.g. in the EU, the Credit Rating Regulation), or whether it can be assigned to other instances of extra-contractual liability.[122]

---

118 Scarso (n 102) 165.

119 See *Abu Dhabi Commercial Bank v. Morgan Stanley & Co., et al* (2009); *Dun & Bradstreet Inc v Greenmoss Builders* (1985).; *In re National Century Fin. Enters., Inc., Inv. Litig.*, 580 F. Supp. 2d 630 (District Court, S.D. Ohio 2008).

120 See, also on the questionability of qualifying ratings as media information, A Miglionico, *The Governance of Credit Rating Agencies. Regulatory Regimes and Liability Issues* (Elgar 2019) 206 ff; Deats (n 67) 1850 ff, advocating in favor of the treatment of ratings as commercial speech.

121 *Bathurst Regional Council v. Local Government Financial Services Pty Ltd (No.5)*[2012] FCA 1200), subjecting the expression of opinions to certain conditions (the carrying of a representation) under certain circumstances (knowledge that another may act in reliance on the opinion and where the person expressing the opinion professes to have an expertise in forming and giving opinions of the kind in question) (see *ID* at 2416 and ff.).

122 Audit (n 105) 593, who highlights the potential difficulties of this second hypothesis, which in the case of the EU would be disciplined by the Rome II Regulation (Regulation EC n. 864/2007) for the determination of the applicable law.

The qualification of the 'rating' is also decisive for the determination of the type of liability. Suffice it to consider that the obligation undertaken by raters is that of providing an 'opinion', an 'estimate' regarding the creditworthiness of an issuer or of an issued asset; the opinion is not a scientific measurement, nor an audit, nor a disclosure of information related for example to the issuing of a financial instrument onto the market, nor any other factual verification. The latter are all hypotheses in which the boundaries of liability and violation of the professional duties of the accountants or supervising authorities can be more clearly defined.

In continental systems for example, the nature of ratings as 'economic information' (and not, for example, as 'economic products') has been identified as a key for the determination of the regime of liability. Whereas an 'economic product' could entail somewhat strict liability in analogy with a defective product, the nature of 'information' restricts liability to cases of intentional diffusion of erroneous or inaccurate news.[123]

As mentioned earlier, the debate in the United States has focused on the nature and extent of the constitutional protection (and exemption from liability) accorded to ratings as 'opinions' – or, as they have been emblematically defined: "the world's shortest editorials".[124]

The nature of the liability can be roughly classified as deriving either from a violation of professional duties on behalf of the rater (e.g. inaccurate or negligent rating) or from the detrimental reliance caused in the public. The issue in this case is widely debated in other common law traditions as well.

The thesis of detrimental reliance is derived for example from the duties laid down by regulation aiming at disciplining the publication of information regarding financial markets (e.g. publication of prospectuses when securities are offered to the public or admitted to trading; liability of accountants for the publication of reports (thus made available for the general public-market, and no longer confined in the client-professional relationship)). English courts have

---

123 G Alpa, 'La responsabilità civile delle agenzie di rating. Alcuni rilievi sistematici' (2013) Rivista trimestrale di diritto dell'economia, n 2, 71, 79–80; see also, contesting the nature of information of ratings, F Lukacs, 'La responsabilità delle società di *rating* nei confronti dei soggetti valutati (per l'emissione di *solicited* o *unsolicited rating*) e nei confronti dei terzi' in A Principe (ed), *Le agenzie di rating* (Giuffrè 2014) 223. On a potential parallel between ratings and defective products (in judicial interpretation), see Haar (n 102) 324 commenting an important judgement establishing liability of a CRA (*Bathurst Regional Council v. Local Government Financial Services Pty Ltd (No.5)*).

124 G Husisian, 'What Standard of Care Should Govern the World's Shortest Editorials?: An Analysis of Bond Rating Agency Liability', in (1990) 75 Cornell Law Review 411.

traditionally applied the doctrines of *Hedley Byrne*[125] and *Caparo Industries*[126] to exclude the existence of a duty of care towards a claimant for the economic loss following negligent statements where there is no direct contractual relationship between the claimant and the defendant (privity of contract), unless the claimant can prove that the defendant was aware of the circulation of the statement and the detrimental reliance upon it by the claimant.[127]

An interesting departure from these principles was established in the above mentioned 2012 Australian case of *Bathurst Regional Council v. Local Government Financial Services Pty Ltd*[128] which found a duty of care of the credit rating agency towards the end investor (in one of the first cases dealing with financial instruments involved in the 2007–2008 crisis).

Liability for negligent misstatement or information under both common law and civil law requires reliance as the causal link between conduct and injury (although in the United States, the Fraud-on-the market theory (FOTM) has also been used to solve the problem of the causal link between the circulation of false or misleading information on the market in violation of section 10(b) of the Securities and Exchange Act of 1934, and the detrimental reliance ensuing therefrom).[129]

In the civilian tradition, for example in Germany and in Italy (even if not unanimously), this type of liability (for negligent misstatement on financial markets) is construed as a form of extracontractual liability, with the injury considered as an instance of pure economic loss.[130]

---

125   *Hedley Byrne & Co. Ltd v. Heller & Partners Ltd*, [1964] AC 465.

126   *Caparo Industries plc v. Dickman*, [1990] 2 AC 605.

127   For a detailed reconstruction of the tests laid down by the UK House of Lords for the establishment of a duty of care in these cases, see K Alexander, 'Tort Liability for Ratings of Structured Securities under English Law', (2015) University of Oslo Faculty of Law Legal Studies Research Paper Series No. 2015-06.

128   [2012] FCA 1200 (on which see *supra*).

129   According to the FOTM theory (a presumption of reliance), it is not necessary to prove specific reliance on the false information, given the presumption that in an "efficient capital markets hypothesis" this information was already reflected in the price of the security during the transaction. The FOTM theory (adopted by the Supreme Court in *Basic Inc. v. Levinson*, (485 US 224, (1988)) greatly expanded the potential reach of liability for false or misleading information on the market (favored by the use of securities class actions) and provoked an exponential increase in the civil sanctions for false information; the reform later introduced in 1995 with the Private Securities Litigation Reform Act re-dimensioned the entity of this litigation by reducing the number of securities class actions. On this reconstruction, see Giudici (n 99) 254–257 and the literature quoted; DR Fischel, 'Use of Modern Finance Theory in Securities Fraud Cases Involving Actively Traded Securities' in (1982) 38 Business Lawyer 1.

130   See Giudici (n 99) 272–275.

However, the framing of a wide regime of liability of credit rating agencies towards the public (not towards the issuers) entails the risk of lifting the floodgate of lawsuits against rating agencies on behalf of any investor who can prove that his or her – pure economic – loss derives from reliance on an inaccurate rating. Aside from the widespread caution that traditionally is associated in many legal systems when recognizing compensation for pure economic losses,[131] the risk of upsetting the market of ratings by making them too costly (as a consequence of the need to spread the costs of potential liability) has also been frequently highlighted.

It would seem however appropriate, in analyzing such hypotheses of liability of CRAS towards investors (i.e. the public, the market) to distinguish between intentional (infringement of duties) or grossly negligent ratings on the one side, and 'erroneous' or simply 'negligent' ratings on the other.

The EU regime of liability for credit rating agencies enacted in 2013 seems to move in this direction, with the further distinctive element of the 'over-reliance' on credit ratings.

2.2.3.2   The Problem of Over-Reliance on Credit Ratings
The two typical hypotheses in which reliance on credit ratings is found include reliance laid down in standards, laws and regulations, and reliance by the market; the relation between the two is closely intertwined as the first (reliance in standards and laws) increases the second.[132]

The first hypothesis has also been defined as regulatory incorporation of credit ratings. Examples include, naturally, the Basel II regime. Previously, one can consider also the exemption in the United States under Rule 3a-7 of the Investment Company Act of 1940 of certain financings from registration and compliance with the Act if the securities, among other requirements, were rated "investment grade" by a NRSRO rating agency.[133]

Another example can be found in many federal and provincial regulations in Canada that refer to ratings issued by credit rating agencies to distinguish investment-grade from speculative securities and to base prudential regulation in the banking and investment industries on this distinction (in some instances allowing exemptions from authorization for institutional investors

---

131   See for an overview M Bussani, VV Palmer (eds), *Pure Economic Loss in Europe* (Cambridge University Press 2011) and WH van Boom, H Koziol, CA Witting (eds), *Pure Economic Loss* (Springer 2004).

132   G Deipenbrock, 'Trying or Failing Better Next Time? – The European Legal Framework for Credit Rating Agencies after Its Second Reform' (2014) 25 European Business Law Review 207, 215.

133   See Schwarcz (n 73) 4.

or other reductions in the regulatory burdens for issuers of investment-grade securities).[134]

The phenomenon of over-reliance originates from a mechanical reliance on (external) credit ratings and a reduction on behalf of market participants in the use of their own credit risk assessment mechanisms. Scope of the various policies aimed at reducing the over-reliance on credit ratings in the aftermath of the financial crisis was to reduce the stability-threatening herding effects (when regulations require or incentivize large numbers of market participants to act similarly) and cliff effects (CRA rating downgrades can amplify pro-cyclicality and cause systemic disruptions) due to the fact that CRA rating thresholds were hard-wired into laws, regulations and market practice.[135]

The removal of references to CRA ratings in standards, laws and regulation and their replacement wherever possible with suitable alternative standards of creditworthiness is one strategy in this direction,[136] and indeed this is the approach laid down in article 5c of EU Regulation 462/2013 (going so far as setting a deadline, 2020, for the deletion of all references to credit ratings in EU law), but under the condition that "appropriate alternatives to credit risk assessment have been identified and implemented".[137] The same approach was taken in the United States by the Dodd-Frank Act, that imposed the removal of references in statutes and regulations to NRSROs.[138]

At a more general level, it should be noted that the reduction of an excessive reliance on credit ratings and rating outlooks as one of the measures to restore financial stability was one of the goals promoted at the EU level by the establishment of the Banking Union (thus explaining for example the provisions contained in Regulation 462/2013 on credit rating agencies, which in articles 5a through 5c address over-reliance on credit ratings by financial institutions, by the European Supervisory Authorities and the European Systemic Risk Board, and in Union law),[139] and article 77 of the CRD IV which encourages institu-

---

134 See Rousseau (n 76) 17, citing the Money Market Mutual Fund Conditions Regulations SORS/2001-475, S.2 a) (ii), 2.c), 2 d) (ii), (iii); the Investment Dealers Association Rule Book, s. 100.4E f), g); and the National Instrument 44–101, Short Form Prospectus Distributions.

135 FSB, *Principles for Reducing Reliance on CRA Ratings*, 27 October 2010.

136 Ibid (1).

137 Article 5c, Regulation EU n. 463/2013.

138 See Sections 939 and 939A, Dodd-Frank Wall Street Reform and Consumer Protection Act.

139 Regulation EU n. 463/2013, Article 5a: "The entities referred to in the first subparagraph of Article 4(1) shall make their own credit risk assessment and shall not solely or mechanically rely on credit ratings for assessing the creditworthiness of an entity or financial instrument".

tions "that are significant in terms of their size, internal organization, and the nature, scale and complexity of their activities to develop internal credit risk assessment capacity and to increase use of the internal ratings based approach" and makes sure that they "do not solely or mechanistically rely on external credit ratings for assessing the creditworthiness of an entity or financial instrument".[140]

In relation to the issue of liability of credit rating agencies, some of the strongest criticisms, especially after the global financial crisis, on the failures and/or shortcomings of rating agencies underlies the fact that their liability towards investors can be envisaged to the extent that there has not been an 'over-reliance' on credit ratings.

EU legislation seems to support this approach. Whereas article 35a (1) of Regulation 1060/2009 as amended in 2013, allows an investor or issuer to claim damages from a credit rating agency in case it has committed intentionally or with gross negligence any of the infringements listed in the Annex III of the Regulation having an impact on a credit rating, an investor can claim damages where the decision to invest into, hold onto or divest from a financial instrument depended on a credit rating of that instrument; and an issuer may claim damages where it establishes that it or its financial instruments are covered by that credit rating and the infringement was not caused by misleading and inaccurate information provided by the issuer to the credit rating agency, directly or through information publicly available.[141] However, the same article imposes on the plaintiffs (investors) the burden of proof of having relied "reasonably" or otherwise "with due care" on the credit rating evaluation in taking the decision on the investment.

The difficulties in meeting this dual burden of proof (infringement of duties by the credit rating agency and proof that the reliance of the investor was not unreasonable) seem to indicate the concerns of the legislator to avoid a floodgate of litigation deriving from the recognition of a widespread form of liability and the ensuing risks of a market freeze as a result of over-deterrence

---

140 Directive 2013/36/EU, article 77(1)(2). See also articles 1–3 of Directive 2013/14/EU of the European Parliament and of the Council of 21 May 2013 amending Directive 2003/41/EC on the activities and supervision of institutions for occupational retirement provision, Directive 2009/65/EC on the coordination of laws, regulations and administrative provisions relating to undertakings for collective investment in transferable securities (UCITS) and Directive 2011/61/EU on Alternative Investment Funds Managers in respect of over-reliance on credit ratings, [2013] OJ L145/1.

141 Article 35a(1), EU Regulation 462/2013.

and/or an excessively conservative approach on ratings on behalf of rating agencies.[142]

The type of injury suffered is also extremely meaningful when taking into account the concerns surrounding a broad regime of liability for credit rating agencies. This would entail a widespread recognition of recoverability of pure economic loss (with the issue of the allocation of costs of mistaken investments on behalf of investors).[143] And indeed, concerns have been raised when analyzing the potentially recoverable damages. The risks of awarding excessive damages (without for example taking into account the absence of costs borne by those injured (e.g. investors) under the issuer-pays model; or the different impact that erroneous ratings have on the primary and on the secondary market) have led to different considerations on the opportunity of introducing liability caps (once again to avoid affecting the rating market with excessive costs of liability).[144]

Causation, furthermore, may also add toil to the burden of proof imposed on plaintiffs. Suffice it to consider the difficulty in proving that the rating was the sole and direct cause of the investment decision and not simply one of its multiple causes (with potential cases of multiple tortfeasors, as in the hypothesis of negligent certification on behalf of accountants, negligent or inaccurate publication of prospectuses on behalf of the issuers, negligent activities of financial intermediaries and so forth).[145] Whereas privity of con-

---

142   See MB Cane, A Shamir, T Jodar, 'Below Investment Grade and Above the Law: A Past, Present and Future Look at the Accountability of Credit Rating Agencies' (2012) 27 Fordham Journal of Corporate & Financial Law 1063,1067–1071, recalling the effects on the US market in the immediate aftermath of the approval of the Dodd-Frank Act and the tensions between CRAs and the SEC. See also Haar (n 102) 330–333; Alpa (n 123) 74.

143   For a reconstruction of the debate see for example Bussani (n 97) 1350–1351.

144   Article 36a(4) of the EU Regulation 1060/2009 as modified in 2013 poses a limit to fines on CRAs that "shall not exceed 20% of the annual turnover of the credit rating agency concerned in the preceding business year and, where the credit rating agency has directly or indirectly benefitted financially from the infringement, the fine shall be at least equal to that financial benefit".

       See Haar (n 102) 331 ff, summarizing different proposals for liability caps and advocating a criterion based on disgorgement of profits of rating agencies.

       See also AM Pacces, A Romano, 'A Strict Liability Regime for Rating Agencies', 2014 European Corporate Governance Institute Law Working Paper n. 245/2014, who propose the introduction of a capped strict liability rule for CRAs with: a) damage compensation capped at a multiplier of the CRA's income; b) a contractual component (allowing CRAs, in the absence of regulatory benefits, to determine at what level they want to commit their prediction); and c) an expiration date (so as to shield CRAs from systemic risk whenever defaults are largely uncorrelated in the short term).

145   See Di Donna (n 117) 289.

tract is one of the main obstacles for claims based in contract brought forth by investors/third parties, causation is one of the main hurdles for claims brought under tort.[146]

Even the scope of harmonization is somewhat re-dimensioned given the remand to the applicable national laws according to the relevant rules of private international law for the definition of terms such as "damage", "intention", "gross negligence", "reasonably relied", "due care", "impact", "reasonable" and "proportionate", and for other matters of civil liability not covered by the Regulation. Furthermore, advance limitation of the civil liability of rating agencies is admitted, as long as the limitation is reasonable and proportionate and allowed by the applicable national law.[147]

The problem of liability of credit rating agencies represents the most notorious attempt at finding a judicial remedy to those seeking compensation for an erroneous reliance on the creditworthiness of a debtor. In this hypothesis, the two interests seeking protection are in the first place the reliance of creditors on the rating as a basis for extending credit *latu sensu* (investing in securities wrongly rated); in the second place, the interest in the correct functioning of the market *per se*, with the further consideration that the use of credit ratings as an instrument guiding investment decisions is to a certain extent a result of what has been defined a "regulatory incorporation" of ratings operated by Basel II.

2.3 A Few Final Observations: Inferences from the Comparison of Regulatory Choices and Issues Surrounding a Hypothetical 'Right to a Creditworthiness Assessment'

At this point it is possible to draw a few inferences from the issues examined, before advancing some final considerations.

The comparative analysis on whether the problem of the creditworthiness of borrowers is first of all a problem of macroprudential nature finds a positive answer, as demonstrated by the regulatory interventions examined above on credit risk management. As a comparative regulatory approach has shown, the supranational and formally non-binding sources containing prudential standards for credit risk management (namely the Basel Accords) have received wide implementation.

---

146   Haar (n 102) 333.
147   Article 35a(3–4), EU Regulation 462/2013.

The functional answer to the problem of how to ensure proper credit risk management is in part conferred to the activity of credit rating – which in turn was long entrusted to credit rating agencies. This is a converging and common solution that has affirmed itself in practice before receiving comprehensive legal discipline. The experiences in the two main systems that have been analyzed, namely the United States and the EU, have shown a trend in which the activity of credit rating agencies was left to self-regulation and private autonomy, with the different contractual models examined, up to the financial crisis of 2007–2008. What followed was a change in the regulatory paradigm, as part of the overall regulatory reaction of the financial sector, which for credit rating activity entailed new forms of public oversight, the recognition of forms of liability, and attempts at reducing the regulatory role of credit rating and rating agencies.

As for the liability of credit rating agencies, that many see as due to their role as gatekeepers, an important distinction is necessary when comparing the legal reforms enacted after 2007. Whereas there seems to be a convergence on hypotheses of liability for contractual duties (i.e. in the relationship between the rater and the rated), a finding of responsibility is less straightforward in the case of liability towards the public.

Here difficulties arise from different considerations, that may be the recognition of protected constitutional status to information (even if only as commercial speech), as is the case for example in US case law, or the traditional restraint in recognizing damages for pure economic loss (in many European jurisdictions). In both instances the divide is between recognizing breach for contractual duties and the limits for third party injuries.

In the second case, beyond the sometimes-formal arguments, there are evident reasons for caution. These can roughly, albeit with the risk of oversimplification, be reconducted to a floodgate argument and to the nature of the injury. However, so as to avoid abuses even without imposing widespread tortious liability, on the one hand intentional behavior can still be pursued; on the other hand, as previously highlighted, the reforms in legislation have introduced forms of regulatory supervision and have aimed at regulating credit rating activity more in detail, whilst at the same time aiming at reducing the regulatory role of credit rating.

All of the considerations above, from the macroprudential duties down to the relationship between the issuer and the rater, can lead to a few further final considerations.

Is there a 'right to a creditworthiness assessment' for borrowers that is specular to the 'duty of creditworthiness assessment' imposed on lenders? Is such a hypothetical 'right to a creditworthiness assessment' a right not only for issuers but a wider expectation on behalf of the market? The two issues have to distinguished.

With regard to issuers, once the prevailing model of the relationship between issuers and credit rating agencies is the issuer-pays model, the right is undoubtedly a contractual right which finds its source and its limits (as seen above) in private autonomy.[148] It would seem that issuers have a strong interest in continuing the implementation of this model, given, for example, data that highlight lower outcomes for un-solicited ratings.[149] This same right can be defended using contractual remedies, including, for example, request of termination and damages in case of breach or non-performance of the obligation to elaborate a rating.

Such a right, however, seems to be relevant beyond the boundaries of contract, as already seen. This depends first of all on the regulatory incorporation of ratings which vests the right to an assessment with a license value: the assessment constitutes the condition to access the market. In the second place, and in partial response to the second question posed regarding the expectations of the market, the quality of public good that ratings or scores carry also justifies the extra-contractual relevance of the rating contract.

For both reasons, a hypothetical 'right to a creditworthiness assessment' would necessarily encompass that the assessment be also as accurate and truthful as possible. The observation that the latter condition, as emerges from the current regime of liability towards investors of credit rating agencies, still encounters a series of strong limitations on the one hand, and the concerns regarding the market freeze on the other, would seem to give a first, negative response, to envisaging a 'right to a truthful assessment' recognized to the market as such.

It should furthermore be noted, that whereas absence of rating (whether truthful or not) would constitute a barrier to access the capitals market for issuers, given their regulatory relevance, the absence of rating does not prevent investors from making their decisions on the market. It does make the process more uncertain and more costly given the information asymmetry, but it does not hinder access *per se*.

If a 'right to a rating' as a condition for accessing or maintaining a position on the market is possibly envisaged, it would however seem that with it issuers do not really have an interest in a widespread liability of rating agencies because of the freeze it would cause and the risk of excessively conservative ratings. The only hypothesis in which there could be such an interest is where

---

148   Tribunale di Milano, 1.7.2011, Parmalat v. The McGraw Hills Companies.
149   The problem of so-called 'downward bias' highlighted above (*sub* 1.6).

there was a fraudulent issue and/or subsequent bankruptcy of the issuer and the latter has an interest in discharging liability onto the credit rating agency.[150] The other party that has an interest in proving a liability of the rating agency is the third-party investor, which, however as seen, has to prove that it did not solely rely on the rating for the decision to invest and is not a direct counterparty in the rating contract nor does it pay for the rating (given the issuer-pays model that is today dominant). This may reduce the incentive for suing (as is demonstrated by the relatively scarce litigation even after the Dodd-Frank Act in the United States and the European 2013 reform to the CRA Regulation).

A final consideration should also be made. In the light of the elements examined above, what exactly does the 'assessment of creditworthiness' mean? The evaluation of creditworthiness of a borrower does not only entail a 'default/not default' judgement. It encompasses something more that has to do, for example, with the 'ability and *will* to pay' (emphasis added). Indeed, the very definition that is found for example in documents of credit rating agencies define credit rating as an opinion reflecting the CRA's "... view of the obligor's capacity and willingness to meet its financial commitments as they come due ..."[151] or "the issuer's ability to obtain cash sufficient to service the obligation, and its willingness to pay".[152] The judgement is thus more complex and has to do with an overall evaluation of the position of the borrower.

This wider assessment can probably be directly linked to the circumstance that *de facto* a rating constitutes the gateway to access the market. This explains on the one hand the power of credit rating agencies and their survival notwithstanding questionability of the accurateness of the ratings and the interest that issuers have in obtaining an assessment from those agencies that enjoy credibility because of reputation. At the same time, the actual 'certificational' value that ratings have is inevitably re-dimensioned given that all issuers want a rating (and the related phenomena of rating shopping and rating inflation must also be taken into account); that there are conflicts of interest; and that liability of credit rating agencies seems to be more theoretical than practical notwithstanding the reforms undertaken after 2008.

---

150   Such was, for example, the case with the Parmalat bankruptcy and the suit against Standard& Poor's in 2005 (Trib di Milano, 1 luglio 2011, Parmalat v. The McGraw Hills Companies), settled in 2015.

151   See S&Ps document containing "Global Ratings Definitions" <https://www.standard andpoors.com/en_US/web/guest/article/-/view/sourceId/504352> (accessed November 2019).

152   See "Moody's Rating Symobols and Definitions Publication" <https://www.moodys.com/researchdocumentcontentpage.aspx?docid=PBC_79004> (accessed November 2019).

The very final remarks turn to the issue of responsible credit and its relationship with creditworthiness assessment. The case of credit rating agencies and their liability is, as previously noted, highly emblematic of the duality inherent in the concept of responsible credit. There is on the one hand a multitude of hard-wired provisions deriving from duties of a macro-prudential nature, that impose assessing the creditworthiness of borrowers and that regulate credit risk management for financial institutions. For a long time, especially before the upheaval of the financial crisis, the duties of creditworthiness assessment could be fulfilled by 'outsourcing' the assessment to external actors – credit rating agencies/external credit assessment institutions – and this outsourcing was even encouraged to a certain extent by its codification in rules and standards. Thus, on the one hand, it seems only logic that if this external creditworthiness assessment is performed negligently, those subjects who professionally undertake the duty to perform this assessment should – and are – called to respond through different forms of liability.

However, the second aspect to be considered (that the more recent regulatory approaches seem to have indeed embraced), and that highlights the 'duality' of the issue, is that of the 'reliance' on this assessment and its potential role in inverting the burden of proof in the case of liability. Indeed, if the professional credit rater can prove that the lender mechanically or automatically 'over-relied' on the rating, then the liability for an 'irresponsible' extension of credit can be allocated onto the ultimate decision maker (the lender). Whether such a form of liability, i.e. for 'irresponsible lending' can be envisioned and if so, under which form, is however another issue to be analyzed in the following chapters.

Creditworthiness for Individuals: Methodologies and Legal Issues

Introduction

In the previous Chapter the relation between a notion of 'responsible lending' and the duty of creditworthiness assessment has been analyzed under a macro-prudential approach, by examining the role that lenders have on the credit market and the rules and obligations by which they must abide. Under this perspective the assessment of creditworthiness is of relevance as part of the systemic and prudential duties that lending institutions have, and the evaluation of borrowers is delegated to specific actors such as credit rating agencies. Following are important issues relating to the role of the raters, their position on the market, the value attributed to their ratings, the reliance (often regulatory) on these ratings and, finally, the liability in case of erroneous, negligent, or intentionally misstated ratings.

The systemic relevance of conducting creditworthiness assessments is, however, also appreciable at a 'micro-prudential' level, where loans to individuals (i.e. consumers) and loans to small business firms are considered. As already observed, these loans also weigh when they are taken into account in their aggregate form, as overall loan portfolios of banks, and they become particularly relevant when they are distributed through securitization (and graded by credit rating agencies) and/or if they become non-performing loans (NPLs). Their genesis thus deserves to be examined as the first moment in which assessments on the creditworthiness of borrowers is carried out.

The typical cases for 'consumer loans' are those of personal loans, consumer credit contracts, credit card contracts, mortgages. For small business firms the loans are commercial and industrial loans. Moreover, the connection with consumer over-indebtedness as a failure to meet payments of precisely these loans, has led scholars to speak of 'responsible lending' in this sector more than in any other sector of the credit market.

This Chapter examines the methodology with which creditworthiness is assessed at the individual and retail level with a focus on credit data, its collection and processing through credit reporting, and on some of the problematic issues related to this activity. Implications for responsible credit are also taken into consideration; as seen previously, these policies are often associated to

© KONINKLIJKE BRILL NV, LEIDEN, 2022 | DOI:10.1163/9789004525054_004 the practice of creditworthiness assessment, which for individuals typically (but not mandatorily) entails collection, processing and circulation of personal data.

According to some theories, the sharing and circulation of credit data could contribute to implementation of responsible credit both as regards increased competition on the lender side (i.e. borrowers with 'positive' credit files can more easily switch credit or other service providers and the latter are incentivized to offer credit at better rates and wider ranges of products, increasingly tailored onto the profile of potential clients); and through forms of 'borrower discipline' (which would lead to responsible behavior on the borrower side). In addition, the affirmation on the markets of credit profiling that derives from non-financial data and uses machine learning (ML) techniques can allow subjects with no or very thin credit history to access credit.

The flip side of the coin however, as intuitive, is no less relevant. There are also important problematic aspects tied to credit data collection and sharing, which can revert the same wide availability of information into an instrument to target vulnerable subjects, to practice discrimination, and to exclude consumers with episodes of bad credit history from future access to credit and other services (leading to social and financial exclusion).

As in the case of credit rating, the starting point here is once again a functional perspective aiming at highlighting the scope and use of credit information sharing, the development of credit scoring and the reasons for its practical affirmation as a response to the needs of lenders for efficient and quick methods for assessing the creditworthiness of potential borrowers in expanding markets of consumer credit. In this part reference is made to the classic economic theories on the use of credit data.

In order to screen loan applicants and evaluate their creditworthiness, lenders need to obtain information on potential borrowers. This can be done either by referring to information that the bank already has, when the applicant is already a client; or by a direct interview or other direct interaction with the applicant (information that can then be processed by the bank's risk management techniques); or by turning to other lenders who have previously had relations with the applicants. In the latter case, the information exchange will generally imply reciprocal obligations to exchange information in the future, and when this occurs on a voluntary basis it is carried out by 'information brokers' (i.e. credit bureaus or credit reporting agencies); when the exchange is mandated by law, the information will be collected by public credit registers.[1]

---

1 T Jappelli, M Pagano, 'Information Sharing in Credit Markets: The European Experience' (2000) CSEF Working Paper n. 35, 7.

The following section of the Chapter overviews the subjects who create and manage the databases accessed by lenders to obtain information on borrowers, and the regulatory framework within which they operate. This second part of the inquiry is centered on the processing of data, including the practice of credit scoring, and the issues concerning rights of the 'rated' subjects (namely rights arising under data protection and antidiscrimination legislation).

The two models that are analyzed and compared are those of the United States and of the EU. The latter still has important areas of regulation that are not harmonized and fall within the scope of national law of the Member States; the framework of credit data collection and processing is still fragmented at the EU level and there are attempts by the European Central Bank at introducing standardized rules and practices for data infrastructure (see *infra* 3.1.2). The US market on the contrary is consolidated and relatively 'concentrated' in the hands of a few private actors, with an absence of any form of public credit registers (whereas these are found in many EU countries which contemplate both public and private credit reporting activity).

The first part of the inquiry, in comparative law and regulation, examines the interaction between the structure of the market (number and types of actors) and the existing regulatory framework, with the scope of identifying the impact of the latter in consolidating or altering the characteristics of the former.

The second part comparatively examines the regulatory framework for credit reporting activity that can be traced not only from the legislative sources but also from judicial and scholarly formants, especially in the reactions to highly criticized practices which first emerged in the United States in the late 1960's and more recently sparked renewed global attention with the development of forms of 'alternative' and algorithmic credit scoring.

In this reconstruction, the methodology comprises a cultural approach to issues of constitutional and fundamental rights' relevance such as self-determination and equality. These considerations must naturally also be inserted in the social and economic context in which the activity of credit reporting first began.

It should be briefly recalled at point, as an economic background, that the US consumer credit market is traditionally very developed with large numbers of consumers who access the market. In the case of consumer credit, these markets are characterized by large volumes of loans for relatively modest sums when taken singularly. Historically, the need for lenders to assess whether their potential clients could repay the (usually unsecured) loans before granting them credit, could be satisfied by acquiring background information on the borrowers; this under the assumption that past behavior could serve to predict future behavior.

With the expansion of the market for consumer credit and housing, the practice of turning to specialized intermediaries on credit information increased greatly and these information brokers refined their techniques of data processing. Forms of credit reporting existed already in the nineteenth century[2] (and according to some studies, credit bureaus emerged as early as the 1920's because of their competitive advantage when operating in local segmented markets, protected by rules on branching between the different States).[3] However, it was the technological development in the 1960's of the industry of credit reporting, as a tool at the service of the growing consumer credit market, that first provoked the attention of the public opinion with concerns on transparency and rights of individuals and then the intervention of the federal legislator in the early 1970's.

In Europe the process of specialization and consolidation of credit reporting activity, especially of the private sector, took place later (with the exception of Germany and Sweden in which credit bureaus have existed for almost a century, concomitantly with the development in the United States). In other European countries such as France, Italy and Spain, private credit bureaus only developed in the 1990's, whilst earlier credit information collection and sharing was conveyed through public credit registers.

Regulation of credit reporting in both cases typically involves the interests of three subjects. Lenders, who voluntarily (or mandatorily, when such obligations are laid down in legislative provisions, mainly for prudential reasons) convey information on their clients to information brokers or intermediaries; information intermediaries, who can be private, for profit, or public entities (i.e. credit bureaus or credit registers) and whose activity can be subject to obligations of various nature, from authorization to exercise their activity to duties on the way in which data is collected, processed and shared; and consumer-borrowers (i.e. the data subjects, who typically have rights of access to – and correction of – erroneous information regarding them and often have a right to give preventive consent before transmission of their personal data (see *infra*)).

---

2   For a history of their development in the US, with special reference to mercantile credit, see R Olegario, *A Culture of Credit. Embedding Trust and Transparency in American Business*, Cambridge (Harvard University Press 2006).

3   Jappelli et al (n 1) 19; according to the Authors, "lenders' incentives to pool information are greatest when local credit markets are segmented by regulation"; in Europe, conversely, "where banks are free to compete nationwide, credit bureaus developed later and on a smaller scale".

3.1   Creditworthiness Assessment and Credit Reporting

This section examines some of the principal methodologies through which lenders assess the creditworthiness of borrowers.[4] The compliance of these methods with regulatory duties and antidiscrimination provisions are analyzed in the following paragraphs.

It should be noted first of all that the collection and exchange of information between lenders responds, as previously highlighted, to reasons of financial prudential supervision. The type of information serving this purpose is diverse and credit risk management requires not only data asset quality, capital adequacy, liquidity, internal systems of control and so forth, but also data on past due loans and non-performing loans.[5] As seen previously, the data on the latter are used when credit rating agencies have to evaluate issuers (see Chapter 2).

The sharing of consumer credit data (often ensured by centralized databases, sometimes managed by public authorities) responds, according to classical economic theory, to the need to reduce the problems of asymmetrical information between borrowers and lenders, and those of adverse selection of borrowers (thus reducing the risk of economic loss deriving from non-performance).[6]

Given that the risk of non-repayment can depend not only on inability, but also on unwillingness to repay (moral hazard), the exchange of information between lenders would also serve as a means to disincentive moral hazard and to strengthen borrower discipline, if through this exchange of information the debtor's reputation comes into play (the so-called 'reputation collateral' element).[7] This latter assumption can however be criticized under two different profiles. The first lies on the assumption that consumers (and economic actors, more generally), behave in an economically rational way; an assumption that has been widely questioned and criticized by behavioral studies. With reference to the credit sector more specifically, these studies have highlighted

---

4   See generally LC Thomas, *Consumer Credit Models: Pricing, Profit and Portfolios* (Oxford University Press 2009).

5   F Ferretti, 'Credit Bureaus Between Risk-Management, Creditworthiness Assessment and Prudential Supervision', (2015) EUI Working Papers Law 2015/20, 4.

6   JE Stiglitz, A Weiss, 'Credit Rationing in Markets with Imperfect Information', in (1981) 71 The American Economic Review 393, arguing that in equilibrium a loan market may be characterized by credit rationing in which interest rates a bank charges may either have an adverse selection effect or have an incentive effect; and "both effects derive directly from the residual imperfect information which is present in loan markets after banks have evaluated loan applications" (ID. at p. 393).

7   Ferretti (n 5) 7.

cognitive bias in borrower behavior both in past events, (such as the US sub-prime crisis, on which see Chapter 1), and in criticizing the effectiveness of tools, such as disclosure, identified by regulators as a safeguard against irresponsible behavior (see Chapter 4). The second criticism derives from the empirical finding of the difficulties or unawareness that most borrowers have in checking their credit report and understanding its construction; hence the additional problem of opacity on behalf of credit bureaus.

Finally, according to classic economic theory, the exchange of credit information on borrowers also enhances competition, by reducing the information monopoly of larger established lenders, by allowing more lenders on the market to identify prospective 'good' borrowers and offer them credit products at more advantageous terms, and by facilitating the circulation of borrowers who have verifiable credit history (also known as 'established reputation collateral') (see 3.1.2).

In implementing their role of screening and monitoring of borrowers, banks use information that is both 'soft' and 'hard'. In finance literature, this distinction concerns the ways in which lenders organize their activity (with application not only to banks, but also to a variety of financial markets) and the impact that information availability and collection has on the organizational structure of the institutions.

More specifically, 'soft' information is information that is not easily summarized in a score and requires a wider knowledge of the context to make it fully intelligible; 'hard' information is information that is easily reduced to numbers, and because of its quantitative quality it is advanced by the development of new communication technologies that transmit and process information proficiently.[8]

A lending technique based on soft information for small business lending is for example 'relationship lending', which uses information that is gathered over time by the loan officer based on a direct relationship (contact) with the borrowing firm, its owner, the local community and so forth. Lending techniques for small businesses based on hard information, that is more easily available at the time of the loan origination, include financial statement lending, asset-based lending, and credit scoring (techniques that are also known as 'transactions-based lending').[9]

---

8 JM Liberti, MA Peterson, 'Information: Hard and Soft' (2019) 8 Review of Corporate Finance Studies 1, 2.

9 AN Berger, GF Udell, 'Small Business Credit Availability and Relationship Lending: The Importance of Bank Organisational Structure', (2001) FEDS Working Paper n. 36, 5.

The increasing availability of information and communication technology has led to the growth in use of lending technologies that rely on hard information. One of the most important examples is the increase in use of credit scoring, which standardizes information (in a credit score) and can be defined as a "hardening of soft information". The adoption of credit scoring also received regulatory backing in both Basel II and Basel III, which have encouraged banks to develop and improve their credit scoring techniques. Credit scoring has of course evolved over time both in its scope and in its methodologies.

The assessment of creditworthiness for individual consumer credit is carried out through different techniques of credit reporting and scoring, which – unlike credit rating – have (mostly) internal relevance for lenders. Indeed, the legislation on credit rating and credit rating agencies does not apply to credit scoring and credit bureaus. Nonetheless, both practices raise recurring issues, such as reconciling the important economic functions of data sharing (e.g. reducing information asymmetries and preventing moral hazard of borrowers) with the protection of the rights and autonomy of the 'rated'/'evaluated'/'scored' subjects.

The interest and issues related to credit scoring methodologies concern the pre-contractual and later contractual relation between lenders and borrowers; however, as discussed further, they also impact on the credit market both in terms of its functioning and in terms of conforming to prudential requirements.

Moving from a functional analysis, credit reporting and scoring provides lenders with models that assist them in decisions on granting consumer credit. They serve to predict the probability of default of borrowers or applicants over a fixed time horizon.[10] Credit scoring is – and has been – central in the development of consumer credit, allowing for an automation of the risk assessment tool and a lowering in transaction costs, and consequently enabling an increase in the volume of decisions relating to the granting of credit; it represents one of the first tools for the management of financial risk.

The lowering of costs associated with the growth in the use of hard information such as credit scoring in the decision-making process on the granting

---

10   Currently most banks adopt the definition of default given by the Basel II Capital Accord, according to which default occurs when either or both events occur: 1) the bank considers that the obligor is unlikely to pay its credit obligations in full without the bank recurring to actions such as realizing security (if held); 2) the obligor is past due more than 90 days on any material credit obligation to the banking group. (Basel Committee on Banking Supervision, International Convergence of Capital Measurement and Capital Standards – revised framework-comprehensive version (2006) [hereinafter Basel II Capital Accord], 7, par. 452).

of loans is due to several factors. These are often associated with the fact that easier automation of the information means delegation to computers or lower-skilled and cheaper labor; standardization of the information creates economies of scale if additional applications have to be added to the system; lower transaction costs become very relevant for small loans that have fixed costs; and more durable and easily stored information entail lower costs in maintaining the information for future decisions.[11]

The use of standardized (hard) information has also affected the size and competitiveness of financial markets. Indeed, standardization of information has increased the number of suppliers of loans on the market and has allowed the circulation of information from a local to a global level. Not only has this made information easier to communicate, but also progressively more difficult to contain.[12]

Clearly there are also downsides of various nature in the use of hard information. Suffice it to highlight at this stage, that standardization of information implies an inevitable loss of some information in the 'simplification' process, with the ensuing issue of how this lost information could have led to different outcomes in the decision concerning the grant or denial of a loan, especially for small businesses and individuals whose creditworthiness would often be assessed differently if based on 'soft' information.

Furthermore, if analyzed from the perspective of potential borrowers, the use of standardized information whose relevance for the lender in the decision-making process is known, can induce behavioral responses from loan applicants (i.e. attempts at gaming the system). The continuity of the system will depend on whether the cost of manipulating the numbers is high enough when compared to the benefit deriving from the maneuver, and if the relative weight and function of the informational inputs in the decision is unknown to the potential borrower.[13]

Following the approval of the Basel Capital Accords (Basel II and Basel III) and the legitimation of internal rating models (the so-called Internal Ratings-based Approach) for the evaluation of credit risk, credit scoring has become a key instrument used by banking institutions to comply with prudential requirements, and the development of new and more accurate scoring models has received a strong incentive. When taken in its aggregate form (known as 'consumer loan portfolio' or 'retail claims portfolio'), credit risk becomes

---

11   Liberti et al (n 8) 8–9.

12   Ibid, recalling the cases of the credit card market in the 1950's and of the early development of credit reporting agencies.

13   Ibid 11.

relevant for prudential issues.[14] Under this perspective the model and methodology of credit scoring adopted by banks clearly becomes of crucial importance.[15]

For borrowers who qualify as corporations, financial institutions or public sector, rating models which have a longer term of reference are used. Scoring models (quantitative in nature) are used for the assessment of individual, retail consumers and small business firms, often alongside other qualitative models (including borrower-specific and market-specific factors).

Another difference between retail or corporate and commercial loans related to creditworthiness assessment and lending decisions also naturally concerns the control of the credit risk of a financial institution. In the first case, credit rationing (restriction of the quantity of loans made available to individual borrowers) is typically used, and loan decisions tend to be 'accept' or 'reject' decisions, with little or no difference in the range of interest rates or prices. In the case of commercial loans, credit risk is controlled by using both interest rates and credit quantity (and consequently borrowers will be charged

---

14 According to the Basel II framework, claims that are included in the regulatory retail portfolios are those that meet the following four criteria: 1) exposure to an individual person or persons or to a small business (orientation criterion); 2) exposure takes the form of any of the following: revolving credit and lines of credit (including credit cards and overdrafts), personal term loans and leases (e.g. installment loans, auto loans and leases, student and educational loans, personal finance) and small business facilities and commitments (product criterion); 3) the regulatory retail portfolio is sufficiently diversified to a degree that reduces the risk in the portfolio, warranting 75% risk weight (granularity criterion); 4) the maximum aggregated retail exposure to one counterpart cannot exceed an absolute threshold of 1 million euros (low value of individual exposures). See Basel II Capital Accord, 2, par. 69–70. (See also Chapter 2).

15 The Basel II Capital Accord as previously mentioned permits banks to choose between two methodologies for the calculation of their capital requirements for credit risk: either the Standardized Approach which is supported by external credit assessments, or the Internal Ratings-based Approach (IRB) which allows banks (under approval of the bank's supervisor) to use their internal rating systems for credit risk (Basel Committee on Banking Supervision, International Convergence of Capital Measurement and Capital Standards (2006),cit., II, par. 50). IRB is further broken down into two types. The first is the IRB Foundation (IRB-F), in which only the probability of default (PD) is provided by internal estimates of the bank, with the other factors (loss given default (LGD) and exposure at default (EAD)) calculated using regulatory inputs. The second type is the IRB advanced (IRB-A), where all the inputs to the calculation of the risk weighted assets are estimated internally, under regulatory supervision. The IRB, fully recognized at the international level, gave banks a strong incentive to improve and develop credit scoring methodologies.

different rates of interest and credit risk premiums according to their level of riskiness).[16]

In the following sections, consumer credit scoring, including so-called algorithmic credit scoring, are analyzed first, followed by an analysis of the legal issues (i.e. data protection and antidiscrimination) raised by credit reporting activity. The last section gives a brief overview of credit scoring for small businesses before the final considerations on the implications of credit reporting for responsible credit policies.

3.1.1 *Consumer Credit Scoring*

Credit scoring began in the 1950's and has since developed around different models. Scoring is used both to calculate a score that represents the probability of default of a borrower, and/or for the classification of borrowers into different classes of default risk.

Traditional models are based on the use of statistical techniques and include linear probability models, logit models, probits and linear discriminant analysis.[17] The first three models are based on historical data on credit performance and characteristics of the borrower that are used to estimate the probability of default and to calculate the predicted probability of default of new applicants; the last model is based on a division of borrowers into high and low default-risk classes.[18]

The growth in the use of this technique in the lending decision process in substitution (or sometimes alongside) traditional relationship lending was enhanced by important changes in the banking practice and industry that took place starting in the 1980's.[19] These changes included a gradual shift in focus of lenders from corporate borrowers to individual ones. For this type of lending, maximization of profits passed through an increase in the consumer lending book, inevitably accompanied by accepting the risk of a certain controlled level of bad debts (whereas corporate lending has traditionally focused on avoidance of losses). As a consequence, lending products began to

---

16   A Saunders, M Millon Cornett, *Financial Institutions Management. A risk management approach* (6th ed McGraw-Hill/Irwin 2008) 310.

17   Ibid 316.

18   S Bridges, R Disney, 'Modelling Consumer Credit and Default: The Research Agenda', Experian Centre for Economic Modelling (ExCEM), University of Nottingham, 2001, 6, further noting that newer methods include options-pricing theory and neural networks.

19   Relationship lending, in which creditworthiness was assessed by individual loan officers, was known in the industry as being based on the "five 'Cs' of lending: character (of borrowers), their capacity, capital, collateral, and conditions (largely economic conditions)". See TA Durkin, G Elliehausen, 'Consumer Lending' in AN Berger, P Molyneux, JOS Wilson, (eds) *The Oxford Handbook of Banking* (2nd ed. Oxford University Press 2015) 320.

be marketed and the increase in the number of applications required a faster method of loan application processing that could potentially also take place at a distance and that would not require higher costs (such as an increase in personnel charged with the evaluation of the applications).[20]

Depending on the phase of the credit cycle in which they are used (and thus the available set of variables for evaluating a borrower's creditworthiness), credit scoring models can be divided into 'application scoring' models (used to aid in the decision whether or not to extend credit to an applicant) and 'behavioral scoring' models (used to aid in the decision on how to deal with existing clients, including decisions on whether to increase their credit limit).[21]

Initially credit scoring adopted statistical methods of classification to the categorization of good and bad loans[22] and was centered on the issue of whether or not credit should be granted to a new applicant ('application scoring').[23] This method was based on the pragmatic need to predict whether or not a borrower would default and, on the assumption that creditworthiness was determined by relatively stable factors (over low time intervals, i.e. a few years).[24] These factors were used to create a model that was based on past applicants' data and their subsequent credit history to classify and rank current applicants and their risk of defaulting.[25]

Data taken into account would typically include application data (taken from the application form, such as length of relationship with the bank, age of the applicant, income and so forth); past behavior (e.g. performance on loans in the past over a determined time interval); repayment performance; information from credit bureaus (including default percentages in the applicants area).

---

20   See LC Thomas, DB Edelman, J Crook, *Credit scoring and its applications*, (2nd ed SIAM 2017) 12.

21   Ibid 1.

22   Reference for this was R.A. Fisher's work on statistics (RA Fischer, 'The Use of Multiple Measurements in Taxonomic Problems', in (1936) 7 Annals of Eugenics, 179). See Thomas, *Consumer Credit Models* (n 4) 5.

23   The first statistical models of credit scoring were based on a simple univariate analysis, replaced in the 1960s by a multivariate discriminant analysis (MDA). See G Sabato, 'Credit Risk Scoring Models', 2010, 4 <https://ssrn.com/abstract=1546347> (accessed September 2019).

24   See Thomas, *Consumer Credit Models* (n 4) 5.

25   The default risk taken into account by this model is the specific risk that a borrower will go 90 days overdue on his payments in the next year – without however taking into account the probability that this default will take place, as long as there is a correct "ordering" of the applicants. Using this model, lenders then decide what percentage of applicants to accept (based on different business evaluations of the most efficient cut-off score). Ibid 6.

The development of credit bureaus which collected and crossed data on performance of borrowers with other official information (i.e. electoral rolls and bankruptcy proceedings – with problems on data protection that can be easily inferred) contributed greatly to the affirmation of this type of credit scoring. Applicant scoring today also uses alternative sources of data (such as psychometric data or online social data), especially after the potentialities of Big Data have affirmed themselves (see *infra*).

A subsequent model, developed in the 1980s and known as 'behavioral scoring', introduced a new approach to credit scoring, based on recent past behavior regarding payments and purchases of current customers of the lender. The data collected during this 'observation period' is used to 'forecast' the default risk of customers in the next future/over a fixed time period. This method however, remains a method that whilst taking into account a wider number of factors compared to application scoring, is still based on past data in order to predict future default risk (in order to decide, for example, whether to extend the credit line, advance further credit etc.).

A significant change in credit scoring methodology took place with a modification in perspective: the need for lenders to customize credit scoring to their lending strategies, meaning business objectives of profitability, market share and so forth to be met. Credit must be offered (and tailored) to borrowers so as to maximize the profitability of the consumer for the lender: hence this model is known as that of 'profit scoring systems'.[26] The original scope of estimating risk of default has been enhanced through the use of scorecards that estimate response, usage and retention of a new product, attrition (the probability of a shift towards another lender), and debt management (the success of different approaches to prevent default in case of loan delinquency).[27] As a counterpart, the expansion (and almost saturation) of certain credit markets (i.e. credit cards), entailed corresponding expectations on the side of borrowers: an expectation of customization of lending products, tailored to their needs, and the possibility to compare and to evaluate whether it is more convenient to switch to another lender who is offering better conditions.

Several issues have been highlighted regarding the construction of score cards and have led to criticisms. These include for example the introduction of new biases and the adoption of assumptions that are not universally accepted or that may work for large numbers but prove fallacious for single cases.[28]

---

26   Ibid 7.
27   LC Thomas, 'A survey of credit risk and behavioural scoring: forecasting financial risk of lending to consumers' (2000) 16 International Journal of Forecasting 149, 152.
28   Ferretti (n 5) 9 and literature cited therein.

One of the critical observations lies in the fact that score cards are constructed on data taken from individuals who have already been granted credit and will thus be biased when compared to the overall population of applicants; hence the risk of excluding from access to credit those applicants that have characteristics similar to the 'rejected' applicants who were considered to be 'bad risk' individuals when the sample was constructed,[29] but on whose potential performance there is no knowledge.[30]

Another problematic aspect is due to the so-called 'population drift'; the fact that the sample of population used to build a score card may be very different from the population that the score card will be used on, given the tendency for the distribution of the population to change over time.[31]

A further issue that is central in every scoring model that is developed concerns the use (and misuse) of data on borrowers. The problem of data protection is analyzed further below, however at this point suffice it to highlight that this issue is strongly tied to the fact that the methodology applied by different credit scoring techniques is not disclosed and is often protected by trade secrecy laws (see for example the famous "SCHUFA judgements" in Germany).[32] Some authors have however argued, especially under the European General Data Protection Regulation (GDPR) framework (which

---

29   Bridges et al (n 18) 6–7, further describing 'reject inference' and the phenomenon of 'statistical discrimination'.

30   Thomas 'A survey of credit risk' (n 27) 150.

31   Bridges et al (n 18) 7.

32   These refer to the judgment by the German Supreme Court (*Bundesgerichtshof*, VI ZR 156/13, 28th January 2014), that whilst recognizing that credit scoring qualifies under data protection legislation also recognizes that the underlying methodology (calculation) used can be protected as a trade secret. (See Ferretti (n 5) 10; and also S Wachter, B Mittelstadt, L Floridi, 'Why a Right to Explanation of Automated Decision-Making Does Not Exist in the General Data Protection Regulation' (2017) 7 International Data Privacy Law 76, 87). See also *LG Gießen* 6th March 2013-1 S 301/12. Under the German Federal Data Protection Act (BDSG), as amended in 2009 so as to include specific provisions on credit scoring, it is however required (pursuant to §28b BDSG) that the calculations are demonstrable in terms of a scientifically recognized mathematical-statistical procedure for the determination of the probability of particular conduct (see R Metz, 'Scoring: New Legislation in Germany' (2012) 35 Journal of Consumer Policy 297, 301).

On US law, see B Reddix-Smalls, 'Credit Scoring and Trade Secrecy: An Algorithmic Quagmire or How the Lack of Transparency in Complex Financial Models Scuttled the Finance Market' (2011) 12 U.C. Davis Business Law Journal 87, 91–94 recalling case law on trade secrecy and credit scoring, and 117 ff; F Pasquale, 'Restoring Transparency to Automated Authority' (2011) 9 Journal on Telecommunications & High Technology Law 235, 237–238, highlighting that "trade secrecy effectively creates a property right in many algorithms whose creators do not want to disclose them in patent applications".

only mentions intellectual property rights as an exception to notification and access requirements in a Recital (63) of the GDPR and not in the text of the Regulation), that fundamental rights (i.e. data protection) should take precedence over trade secrecy.[33]

The question of the lack of transparency in the scoring process is one of the recurring issues when viewed from the consumer-borrower-data subject perspective. The issue, which is not new, has received renovated attention with the development of algorithmic scoring and its complex intelligibility.

Whilst remanding once again to the problems of data protection and non-discrimination, it is nonetheless important to recall some of the basic requirements and characteristics that data must have in order to effectively fulfill the function of information input in the elaboration of a credit report. The latter typically results from the processing of two macro categories of data: identity data and credit data. These need to be first of all available, taking into account different rules on length of data retention, on the frequency with which databases – i.e. credit bureaus – are updated, on the completeness of data, on the timeliness with which they are made available. Data must also be accurate (i.e. correct, truthful, complete, up to date, sufficient, adequate and relevant) and reliable.

These characteristics explain in part why lenders often turn to credit bureaus or credit reference agencies (third-party party providers), who can develop, thanks also to their size and economies of scale, different techniques to try and reduce inaccuracy and unreliability (for example through cross-checking, and so forth) at lower cost compared to single lenders.

In the second place, development of credit scoring models must comply with data protection provisions and legislative and regulatory restrictions on the use of certain data in credit scoring.

The role of credit registers and credit bureaus is examined first, followed by an overview of data protection and antidiscrimination issues raised.

---

33   See ME Kaminski, 'The Right to Explanation, Explained' (2019) 34 Berkeley Technology Law Journal 189, 200; G Malgieri, G Comandé, 'Why a Right to Legibility of Automated Decision-Making Exists in the General Data Protection Regulation' (2017) 7 International Data Privacy Law 243, 262 ff. See also, with reference to the applicability to algorithms (protecting them as trade secrets) of EU Directive 2016/943 on the protection of undisclosed know how and business information (trade secrets) against their unlawful acquisition, used and disclosure, M Maggiolino, 'EU trade secrets law and algorithmic transparency' (2018) 27 AIDA Annali italiani del diritto d'autore, della cultura e dello spettacolo 199.

3.1.2   Credit Registers and Credit Bureaus

The expansion and consolidation of credit scoring was facilitated by the development of centralized credit reporting. This enables lenders to purchase data on credit and financial accounts from credit bureaus or credit reference agencies and use this data along with the information that consumers provide in their credit applications.[34] As was also the case with credit rating, a determinant role in the affirmation of credit scoring was played by specialized subjects, both public and private, who were either institutionally charged with (in the former case), or who privately offered (in the latter case), credit reporting.

Functions, regulatory regimes, type of collectible and collected data, and ownership structures of credit bureaus are regulated at national levels with often significant differences. This is still true even within the EU.

As far as the subjects are concerned, the types of credit reporting systems vary and are not necessarily all present in different legal systems; they include both public credit registers (PCRs) and private credit bureaus (CBs) (or credit reference agencies/credit reporting agencies (CRAs)).

Public Credit Registers are generally operated by Central Banks and impose mandatory collection of credit information (reporting is compulsory for certain institutions defined by national laws, which also determine the type of information that must be reported, typically loans above a certain threshold; public registers also exist for real estate collateral and bankruptcy). The information thus collected must be shared in the public interest of financial stability and supervision (hence justifying the entrusting of such data collection and storage with public authorities, usually the ones in charge of banking supervision).

In the EU there is no single pan-European retail credit register (neither in the Mortgage Credit Directive nor in other instruments in which there is a duty to assess creditworthiness (i.e. Credit Rating Agencies package)), in accordance with the recommendations made by the Study Group on Credit Histories and based on arguments of efficiency. Public credit registers exist in many – but not all – Member States,[35] with differences as to the type of information collected, the reporting threshold and the features of the memory system (i.e. how long negative information is kept in databases).[36] Given however the need to promote the integration of the cross-border retail credit market,

---

34   N Aggarwal, 'The Norms of Algorithmic Credit Scoring' (2020), 3 <https://ssrn.com/abstract=3569083 or http://dx.doi.org/10.2139/ssrn.3569083> (accessed July 2020).

35   PCRs exist in Austria, Belgium, Bulgaria, Czech Republic, France, Germany, Italy, Latvia, Lithuania, Slovakia, Slovenia, Spain, Portugal, and Romania, in some cases dating back several decades, as in Germany (1934), Finland (1961), and Italy (1964).

36   Jappelli et al (n 1) 13–14.

and given the differences in data content, definitions and registration criteria in national credit reporting systems, the alternative to the creation of a single European Register is then, consequently, that of ensuring access to all creditors on a non-discriminatory basis, and as a further step, that of harmonizing the content of the databases – a step which however has not been implemented accordingly.[37]

In the United States there is no public credit register and credit reporting is left to the private industry with few (three), large, national credit bureaus[38] (which starting in the early 1990s also began to expand in Europe, acquiring many national credit bureaus).[39] This concentration reflects a tendency in the market of credit information due to economies of scale: the larger the credit bureau, the more complete and accurate its information.[40] The different structure of the market and characteristics of the actors have naturally impacted regulatory concerns differently, as will be seen *infra*.

Credit bureaus or credit reference agencies are privately owned institutions (according to different ownership schemes, including those in which creditors are majority or minority shareholders) which generally operate for profit and have an economic incentive to increase the number of reports issued for the creditors that are their clients.[41] They are not accountable to public bodies or regulators nor to lenders for credit decisions that the latter make.[42] They collect various financial data on transactions between credit providers and consumers (and in some cases also between other providers of services such as utilities, etc., that are not financial institutions but that advance services to consumers) and pool these data in databases that are shared among lenders.

---

37   Report of the Expert Group on Credit Histories, DG Internal Market and Services (2009), Recommendations 1, 2, and 19. The EGCH suggested giving creditors a free choice between all access models available to them, (i.e. direct access, indirect access, report portability, right of access), but considered that indirect access may be the most suitable as a first step in generating a cross-border market. The Directive does not adopt/provide for a particular model. In 2003 a 'Memorandum of Understanding on the exchange of information among national central credit registers for the purpose of passing it on to reporting institutions' was signed (and amended in 2010) by the public credit registries of 9 Member States (Austria, Belgium, Czech Republic, France, Germany, Italy, Portugal, Romania and Spain).

38   The three national credit bureaus in the U.S. are Experian, Equifax and TransUnion.

39   Experian, Equifax and TransUnion have acquired national credit bureaus in Britain, Spain, Portugal, Germany and Italy.

40   Jappelli et al (n 1) 19.

41   See Report of the Expert Group on Credit Histories, DG Internal Market and Services, 8–10.

42   Ferretti (n 5) 17.

The operative principle in this model is the principle of reciprocity (lenders who provide information to credit bureaus are also guaranteed access to the databases); this principle is guaranteed by the contractual relationships between the lenders or other providers and the credit bureaus and is enforced by sanctions (to prevent lenders from utilizing the information in the databases without conveying their own).[43]

Consumer data sharing is the most widespread instrument used by lenders both to assess creditworthiness of consumers and as a tool for credit-risk management of lending institutions.[44] There are however also other non-lending businesses that may turn to credit bureaus to obtain information before providing services or advancing goods that will be paid for at a later stage.[45]

Credit reference agencies license automated scoring methodologies and develop scores used to grade individual consumers on the basis of the information contained in credit reports. In the United States for example, the standard model was developed by Fair Isaac and Company starting in the 1950's and is known as the FICO score (which was introduced officially as a score in the 1980's); it is a relative score between 300 and 850, which represents the consumer's creditworthiness. This score has become a standard across many markets in the United States.

In Germany, as another example, the SCHUFA Score has become a standard (to the extent that the clause imposed by data protection legislation requiring consent on behalf of consumers before their data is communicated to credit reporting agencies is commonly known as the "SCHUFA clause").

Credit reports are drawn from various sources ('credit information furnishers') using technologies in statistics and artificial intelligence.[46] Traditionally these furnishers included credit-card companies, mortgage lenders, and other credit providers; with the development of Big Data or alternative or algorithmic credit scoring, new scoring agencies and companies have emerged who use machine-learning algorithms to design credit scores using Big Data from multiple and not only credit-related or financial-related sources.[47]

---

43 Jappelli et al (n 1) 8.
44 Ferretti (n 5) 1.
45 Ibid 17.
46 M Hurley, J Adebayo, 'Credit Scoring in the Era of Big Data' (2016) 18 Yale Journal of Law & Technology 148, 154; F Ferretti, 'The 'Credit Scoring Pandemic' and the European Vaccine: Making Sense of EU Data Protection Legislation', (2009) *Journal of Information, Law & Technology*, 1, 2.
47 Examples include ZestFinance and LENNDO, but also traditional credit scoring companies like FICO and Experian use non traditional data to develop alternative models of credit scoring. See Hurley et al (n 46) 157–158.

As for the content of the databases, since the data collected originate from very different sources (i.e. the borrower, other databases, credit registers, public registers) and they depend on the legislative framework of national systems, one of the main distinctions is between databases containing only 'negative data' (i.e. defaults, delays, bankruptcies and the non-payment leading to the position of default) and those also including 'positive data' (i.e. borrower's payments, other credit commitments and details which do not constitute defaults; more generally facts of contractually compliant behavior, including outstanding credit, amount of loans, repayment patterns, assets, liabilities, guarantees, collateral).

Some authors have argued that systems of only negative reporting (i.e. which only report payment delinquencies) are more likely to constitute incentives for repayment by borrowers than systems which also report positive information (in the latter case the report on the overall financial position of the borrower may 'mitigate' the negative impression deriving from a default on a payment). Only negative reporting would also lead, according to the same study, to lower default rates and interest rates and to induce banks to lend in situations where they would not under complete information sharing.[48]

Other studies have on the contrary highlighted, especially in the aftermath of the financial crisis, that positive reporting helped preserve the access to institutional credit of creditworthy borrowers who would otherwise have been excluded.[49] The General Principles for Credit Reporting prepared by the World Bank in 2011 for example recommend including positive data in credit reporting systems.[50] The European Parliament has also expressed favor towards access to both positive and negative credit data as a fundamental tool in "helping consumers obtain access to credit and fight financial exclusion".[51] Extensive credit reporting more in general is identified as one of the tools that by allowing more accurate and thorough assessments of creditworthiness of borrowers can contribute to the identification of credit products that meet the financial capacity of the latter (i.e. the idea of 'affordable credit') and help

48 JA Padilla, M Pagano, 'Sharing Default Information as a Borrower Discipline Device' (1999) CSEF Working Paper n. 21, 2 ff.).

49 See World Bank, 'Global Financial Development Report 2013: Rethinking the Role of State in Finance' (2012) Washington DC 131, quoting studies on different markets and the value of positive reporting (as a form of more detailed information) in relationship lending, where it can help profitable lending to informationally opaque borrowers.

50 World Bank, 'General Principles for Credit Reporting' (2011) Financial Infrastructure Series, Credit Reporting Policy and Research n. 1. The Principles are intended as an international agreed framework in the form of international standards for credit reporting systems' policy and oversight.

51 European Parliament resolution on financial services policy (2005–2010) – White Paper (2006/2270(INI), n. 33 [P6_TA(2007)0338].

reduce consumer over-indebtedness.[52] It would thus qualify as an instrument for the promotion of responsible lending policies (see also *infra*).

According to studies conducted in Europe in the aftermath of the financial crisis, in which the over-emphasis on real estate prices had played a crucial role, extensive credit reporting would also help move the focus for creditors from collateral-based lending policies, to increasingly information-based policies (with reliance on credit exposure, repayment history and potential).[53]

The lack of uniformity results in different types of data collected even across Member States within the EU. These include both positive and negative, or only negative data (in France for example the collection of positive data was ruled unconstitutional by the *Conseil Constitutionnel* in 2014 as a disproportionate intrusion on the right to privacy)[54] and the inclusion or non-inclusion of additional 'non-credit' data.

Another important difference that can be observed between public credit registers, as previously noted, is the design of the memory system, which can be related to so-called 'second chance' policies: when public credit registers eventually 'forget' default of borrowers this could be justified both on grounds of equity and on grounds of economic efficiency. Public credit registers with perpetual and indelible memory would constitute a disincentive for defaulted borrowers to undertake new projects and, more generally for borrowers to apply for credit, under fear of default.[55]

Surveys conducted by the Association of Consumer Credit Information Suppliers in Europe have for example classified four distinct types of credit registers according to the depth and breadth of data held (with a scale ranging from the 'advanced credit registers', to the 'negative-only providers', with 'high positive providers' and 'low positive providers' in intermediate positions).[56]

The absence of a uniform standard at the EU level has been highlighted as an obstacle to promote cross-border supply of credit and an integration of credit markets for consumers, and an obstacle to the creation of fair competition between providers of credit. More generally, it has for example been noted

---

52   CEPS-ECRI Task Force Report 'Towards Better Use of Credit Reporting in Europe' (2013) 18.

53   Ibid; see also MA Turner, PD Walker, S Chaudhuri, J Duncan, R Varghese, 'Credit Impacts of More Comprehensive Credit Reporting in Australia and New Zealand', (2012) Policy & Economic Research Council 9–12.

54   Décision n. 2014-690 DC du 13 mars 2014. See Ferretti (n 5) 14.

55   Jappelli et al (n 1) 15, recalling the example of the household PCR in Belgium.

56   See CEPS-ECRI Task Force Report (n 52) 28; and ACCIS, '2017 Survey of Members. Analysis of Credit Reporting in Europe' (2018), summarizing results from previous surveys conducted in 2010, 2012 and 2015.

that the exchange of credit information allows customers to build reputational collateral and seek access to credit outside consolidated lending relationships (a factor that enhances consumer mobility): this reduces the information monopoly of established lenders which may thus be hesitant to share (especially positive) credit information.[57]

It should be recalled at point that credit data is also fundamental for statistical purposes and economic analysis that are used to implement the economic policy of the European Union.[58] The fragmented regulation of credit databases, and even of some key definitions such as those concerning 'default' or 'arrears', on which for example neither the Consumer Credit Directive nor the Mortgage Credit Directive have found a common definition, is also problematic in view of the Banking Union and the role of the European Central Bank in the prudential supervision of credit institutions (a task that is carried out within the Single Supervisory Mechanism),[59] in consideration also of the scope and role of credit risk data in credit risk management for financial institutions and in the prudential supervision of banks.

The importance of collecting data on credit risk and exposure for purposes of market stability and governance has induced the European Central Bank and the ESCB Task Force on Analytical Credit Datasets to elaborate a system that allows the standardization of household credit risk, so as to be able to measure indebtedness and over-indebtedness. This led to the launch of the AnaCredit project.[60] The focus on granular credit and credit risk data credit reporting systems derives from the consideration of the high relevance within the ESCB of this type of credit for monetary policy, financial stability and research analysis and for micro-prudential supervisory purposes (as emerged during the financial crisis).[61]

57　See World Bank, Global Financial Development Report 2013, 132; see also CEPS-ECRI Task Force Report (n 52) 12–13.
58　Article 3 TEU; Article 119 and Article 127 TFEU.
59　See Article 127(6) of the TFUE and Regulation (EU) N. 1024/2013 of 15/10/2013 conferring specific tasks on the European Central Bank concerning policies relating to the prudential supervision of credit institutions [2013] OJ L 287/63. See Ferretti (n 5) 25–26.
60　AnaCredit stands for Analytical Credit Dataset; the legal basis of the project lies in the Decision of the ECB n. 6/2014 of 24 February 2014 on the organization of preparatory measures for the collection of granular credit data by the European System of Central Banks.
61　See V Damia and JM Israël, 'Standardised granular credit and credit risk data', (2014) Seventh IFC Conference on Indicators to support Monetary and Financial Stability Analysis: Data Sources and Statistical Methodologies 3. Granular data are collected in granular-credit datasets such as central credit registers or similar granular (loan-by-loan or borrower-by-borrower).

Other meaningful examples of differences in the regulation of credit reference agencies can be found between the EU and the US regimes. It is important to observe first of all, that credit reporting in the United States has developed as a private industry, whilst in many Member States in the EU the activity of credit reporting was initially tied to public supervision and prudential duties, and therefore entrusted with public entities.

Studies comparing credit institutions across 129 countries have for example highlighted that in the comparison between creditor power theories and information theories (which are not necessarily mutually exclusive), as the two determinants developed by economic theory which would explain how much private credit would be extended by a financial system to firms and individuals, legal origin has a fundamental effect. Indeed, common law countries tend to have higher creditor rights scores than civil law ones (especially deriving from the French tradition); whilst the latter have a much higher incidence of public registries than the former.[62]

The cultural and social approach towards sharing of credit data cannot be ignored in this context (see *infra*); legal traditions that show historical concern with the circulation of financial data may adopt more restrictive regulation on credit data and credit reporting, at the 'expense' of enhancing the growth of their consumer credit markets.

The project, implemented by ECB Regulation 2016/867 which sets out reporting requirements, aims at creating a dataset containing detailed information on bank loans (above the threshold of 25000 euros) made out to legal entities and corporations in the euro area (Article 5 (1), ECB Regulation 2016/867 of 18 May 2016 on the collection of granular credit and credit risk data). The scope of the project is to harmonize statistical reporting requirements on the collection of granular credit and credit risk data (given the insufficiency of aggregate data for an adequate understanding of credit exposures and associated credit risks since a number of economic and financial factors diverge across different sectors of the economy) and thus support the ECB in its central banking and supervision functions. AnaCredit will also help in assessing the sustainability and vulnerability of the non-financial corporations' debt positions; a function that will be important in identifying potential early indicators of crises, considering that the largest exposure of banks' credit is to the non-financial sector (A Perrella, J Catz, 'Interconnecting multiple granular datasets to evaluate credit risks. The ESCB experience', ECB, 17th International Conference on Credit Risk Evaluation Designed for Institutional Targeting in finance (2018) 7 <http://www.greta.it/credit/credit2018/PAPERS/Friday/poster/10_Perrella_Catz .pdf> (accessed July 2020)). In the first phase of implementation, the project excludes loans made to private persons; however, should the ECB decide to extend the dataset to physical debtors in the future, the data will be collected anonymously and data protection safeguards shall be respected (Recital 12, ECB Regulation 2016/867).

62   See S Djankov, C McLiesh, A Shleifer, 'Private credit in 129 countries', (2007) 84 Journal of Financial Economics 299, 301.

This may be one of the elements that can in part help explain the different regulatory concerns that emerged with regard to credit reporting; for example the protection of an industry as counterbalanced with the protection of individual rights of consumers on the one side, and the counterbalancing of the 'general economic interest' of financial stability with the protection of 'fundamental' individual rights on the other. Naturally there are also different traditional approaches towards data protection that according to some observers entail sometimes opposed initial perspectives, such as for example the need to ensure data protection *versus* the protection of freedom of information and data flow.[63]

3.1.3   *Algorithmic Scoring and Big Data*
One of the developments of credit scoring that has recalled interest and attention from different domains and from observers working outside the field of the banking and loans industry has been the application of so-called algorithmic decision-making to credit scoring (also known as 'algorithmic credit scoring').[64] This entails that human decision making is augmented or substituted by using machine-learning (ML) algorithms.[65]

The traditional reliance of credit scoring on linear statistical methods and a limited number of fixed variables is due both to demonstrated statistical correlation between a borrower's credit history (the variable that traditionally receives the highest weight) and their likely credit risk, and to the limited access on behalf of lenders to non-financial and non-credit data on consumers.[66] Possibilities opened up in the mid 2000s, when the growth in

---

63   The example is brought by Thomas et al (n 20) 20 who refer to the English Data Protection Act and the US Freedom of Information Act respectively as starting points that govern the activity of Credit Bureaus and that roughly speaking determine opposite approaches: in the UK information is restricted/protected unless there is a good reason to disclose it, while in the US the information is available unless there is a good reason to restrict it. The English example can be extended to EU policy on privacy protection. See PM Schwartz, 'The EU-U.S. Privacy Collision: a Turn to Institutions and Procedures', (2013) 126 Harvard Law Review 1966, 1976 ff.

64   The widespread use of algorithmic scoring can be traced to the introduction by Fair, Isaac and Company of their "FICO" score in 1989; even if the exact details of the FICO score remain undisclosed, they are the result of an algorithmic output. See MA Bruckner, 'The Promise and Perils of Algorithmic Lenders' Use of Big Data' (2018) 93 Chicago – Kent Law Review 3, 11.

65   Aggarwal (n 34) 1.

66   Ibid 3.

volume of available personal limits and advances in ML methods allowed the development of 'algorithmic' (or 'big data' or 'alternative data') credit scoring, which processes a much larger volume and variety of data (including 'alternative' data) and uses more complex ML techniques to analyze them.[67]

Furthermore, the association of algorithmic lending with Big Data led to the appearance of new lenders on the market, known as "fintech" lenders or "marketplace lenders" and who are usually non-bank financial companies. These lenders operate online and use financial technology to evaluate borrower creditworthiness (often through the use of 'non-traditional' methods, i.e. Big Data), and to match prospective borrowers with sources of credit.[68]

It has been observed that credit scoring (the most recent models especially), makes use of the same techniques that have proved most successful in data mining: data summary (for which standard descriptive statistics like frequencies, means, variances and cross-tabulations are used); variable reduction, observation clustering (clustering customers into groups so as to target them differently and so as to build different scorecards for each group); predication (on response to promotion for new financial products for example) and explanation.[69]

As for the data that is used for algorithmic or alternative credit scoring, these include, as observed earlier, both non-credit financial data and non-credit non-financial data, to the extent that it is commonly affirmed that today "all data is credit data".[70] Non-credit financial data are for example those of rental and mobile phone payment data; examples of non-credit non-financial data are those related to education, employment, social and behavioral data (e.g. social media activity, online browsing data, mobile phone usage and so

---

67   Ibid; Hurley et al (n 46).

68   Bruckner (n 64) 12–13.

69   Thomas et al (n 20) 9, calling credit scoring the "grandmother" of data mining. Non-parametric statistical and AI modelling approaches that have been developed (alongside the statistical and operational research methods used traditionally) include the ubiquitous neural networks, expert systems, genetic algorithms and nearest neighbor methods. See Thomas, 'A survey of credit risk' (n 27) 152.

70   The expression ("All data is credit data. We just don't know how to use it yet.") was famously used by Douglas Merrill, ZestCash C.E.O., in an interview to the *New York Times* in 2012 <https://archive.nytimes.com/query.nytimes.itcom/gst/fullpage-9A0CE7DD153C F936A15750C0A9649D8B63.html> (accessed July 2020).

forth).[71] These data can more generally be classified into four categories: borrower's data; proprietary data; public data; and social network data.[72]

The development of algorithmic credit scoring can expand and has to comply with the existing regulations, which pertain not only to consumer credit or consumer loans or mortgage lending but include also the normative provisions on antidiscrimination and on data protection. The latter are particularly relevant where they lay down provisions on automated decisions and when they impose duties or guarantee rights where data is collected from third parties.

Whereas in traditional models of credit scoring (i.e. application or behavioral) the third parties involved in the process of data collection are principally credit bureaus or credit reference agencies, in the case of Big data/alternative/algorithmic scoring the data is collected from multiple subjects, including social media platforms, telecommunication companies and so forth.[73]

---

71   See Aggarwal (n 34) 4. On this point, see the amendment proposals made by the EU Parliament in January 2022 (2021/0171(COD)) to the Proposal for a Directive of the European Parliament and of the Council on consumer credits (COM(2021)0347) extending and introducing limits to the type of data that can be collected for creditworthiness assessments (Amendment to Proposal Recital 49 and Proposal for a new Directive Article 18, par. 2.1, par.2.2., Amendment to Proposal for a Directive Article 19, par.3), including a specific prohibition against taking into account the medical history of people affected by cancer (Proposal for a new Directive Recital 49a), or for credit offers (Proposal for a new Directive Recital 40a) or for personalized advertising of credit agreements (Amendment to Proposal for a Directive Article 7, par. 1 and for a new Article 8, par. 3b) or personalized offers (Proposal for a new Article 13, par.1,1.).

72   Hurley et al (n 46) 17, recalling the example of the thousands of data points collected by ZestFinance.

73   In the EU for example, the European Banking Authority released an opinion in 2015 on lending-based crowdfunding in which in the absence of *ad hoc* legislation, and given the need to promote safety and soundness of markets and a convergence of practices across the EU and a possible application of existing EU directives and regulation already in force, it considers the Payment Services Directive (Directive 2007/64/EU of the European Parliament and of the Council of 13 November 2007 on payment services in the internal market, later repealed by Directive (EU) 2015/2366 of the European Parliament and of the Council of 25 November 2015 (PSD II) as the most feasibly applicable to lending-based crowdfunding (for the payments-related aspects of crowdfunding activities), therefore putting these subjects on par with payment institutions (Opinion of the European Banking Authority on lending-based crowdfunding, EBA/Op/2015/03, 26 February 2015). On this aspect see G Biferali, 'Il social lending. Problemi di regolamentazione', (2017) Rivista trimestrale di diritto dell'economia, 4/2017, 443. The Proposal for a new Directive on consumer credits published in 2021 instead includes crowdfunding credit services within its sphere of application (where those services are not provided by a creditor or by a credit intermediary) (COM(2021) 347 final), Article 2.

Furthermore, it is important to note that credit scoring is expressly taken into account by the 2021 EU Proposal for a Regulation on Artificial Intelligence[74] according to which "AI systems intended to be used to evaluate the creditworthiness of natural persons or establish their credit score", (with the exception of AI systems used by small scale providers for their own use) are classified as 'high risk' AI Systems (under Annex III of the Proposal which identifies standalone AI systems with mainly fundamental rights implications).

Adopting a risk-based approach, the Regulation proposal allows these 'high-risk' AI systems to operate on the European market subject to compliance with certain mandatory requirements and an *ex ante* conformity assessment. Recital 37 of the Regulation proposal, in signaling that AI systems used to evaluate the credit score or creditworthiness of natural persons should be classified as high risk, further highlights the relationship between these systems and the possibility of accessing financial resources or essential services such as housing, electricity, and telecommunication services and the risk that AI systems "may lead to discrimination of persons or groups and perpetuate historical patterns of discrimination, for example based on racial or ethnic origins, disabilities, age, sexual orientation, or create new forms of discriminatory impacts". (On the problem of discrimination and access to fundamental services see *infra*).

The use of this technology has naturally led to enthusiasts and to critics, who raise objections that are not limited only to its application to credit scoring. It is beyond the scope of this chapter to analyze the multiplicity of positions that have emerged on the topic; however, with regard to credit scoring, it may be useful to recall some frequent observations.

The most recurrent arguments in favor of the use of algorithmic scoring are couched first of all in terms of efficiency. A more accurate creditworthiness assessment, possibly resulting from an increase in the revealed amount of information about borrowers, could mitigate the inefficiencies due to adverse selection effects before credit is granted and help monitor borrowers after credit is granted, thus helping reduce moral hazard.[75] These 'efficient'

---

74 Commission 'Proposal for a Regulation of the European Parliament and of the Council Laying down Harmonised Rules on Artificial Intelligence (Artificial Intelligence Act) and Amending Certain Union Legislative Acts' COM (2021) 206 final.

75 Aggarwal (n 34) 8. This could also include more accurate assessments on the affordability of credit for a borrower "by revealing non-linearities in data that could more accurately predict a borrower's expenditure and disposable income during the repayment term". Ibid quoting also FCA, 'Preventing Financial Distress by Predicting Unaffordable Consumer Credit Agreements: An Applied Framework', (2017) FCA Occasional Paper 28. See also JE Stiglitz (n 6).

outcomes naturally depend on the degree of accuracy that algorithmic scoring actually achieves; an outcome that in turn depends on the quality, completeness and accuracy of the data as well as on the ML models that are used.[76]

There are indeed concerns that the use of extremely large data sets may not reduce, but rather exacerbate inaccuracy.[77] Furthermore, the high analytical costs in cleaning, collating and interpreting vast amounts of data, so as to find statistical connections within large datasets should not be underestimated.[78] It should additionally be noted that high informational costs are also imposed on regulators and policy makers who wish to develop measures to control the risks tied to the use of complex AI and ML techniques.[79]

Secondly, the same ML techniques, especially when they are so-called 'black box' ML techniques (i.e. the conversion of inputs to outputs without revealing how this is done),[80] entail the risk of being excessively opaque.[81] Theoretically this also makes it more difficult to provide explanations *ex post* on the decisional process, such as postulated for example under the GDPR in Europe (on which see *infra*), and of being potential sources of 'algorithmic discrimination', which would, in turn, lead to distributional unfairness.[82]

Another common and fundamental argument in favor of algorithmic scoring lies instead with the alleged distributional fairness that it would enhance, especially for those consumers who due to 'thin' or 'non-existent' records would otherwise be excluded from access to credit. The innovative use of Big Data and creditworthiness algorithms would allow faster, cheaper and more

---

76   Aggarwal (n 34) 9.

77   Hurley et al (n 46) 178, quoting studies by the National Consumer Law Center, Yu et al, 'Big Data: A Big Disappointment for Scoring Consumer Credit Risk' (2014) 14<https://www .nclc.org/images/pdf/pr-reports/report-big-data.pdf> (accessed July 2020), and by the Electronic Privacy Information Center, 'Credit Scoring' (2016) https://epic.org/privacy/ creditscoring/ (accessed July 2020).

78   C Brummer, Y Yadav, 'Fintech and the Innovation Trilemma' (2019) 107 The Georgetown Law Journal 235, 268.

79   Ibid 275; see also more generally, J Burrell, 'How the machine 'thinks': Understanding opacity in machine learning algorithms' (2016) 3 Big Data & Society 1.

80   D Keats Citron, F Pasquale, 'The Scored Society: Due Process for Automated Predictions' (2014) 89 Washington Law Review 1, 6.

81   ML algorithms are programmed in such a way that they can reprogram themselves in response to new data and to the external validation of their performance, without the need for real-time human intervention. See Brummer et al (n 78) 271 and literature cited therein. See also F Pasquale (n 32) 237 and 248–249. For an articulated discussion on how transparency should be understood and constructed in automated decision-making processes and on the existing US regulatory framework that could be applied, see TZ Zarsky, 'Transparent Predictions', (2013) University of Illinois Law Review 1503.

82   Aggarwal (n 34) 10.

predictive credit determinations and not only eliminate the discriminatory effects of credit-score-based determinations but would also allow the so-called 'Credit Invisible' borrowers, traditionally the most adversely affected by the discrimination of traditional lenders, to have access to credit.[83]

The risk of discrimination however is not overcome with algorithmic scoring.[84] On the contrary, first of all certain methodologies allegedly used by alternative or fintech scoring companies (such as so-called 'creditworthiness by association') may lead to a *de facto* reintroduction of prohibited (digital) redlining practices.[85]

Furthermore, whereas discrimination can be reduced (if bias is more easily detected) when compared to face-to-face/human decision making, the risk remains high especially when there is bias in the data (statistical discrimination) used to develop the ML scoring model and the algorithms inherit the prejudices of previous decision makers or reproduce existing patterns of discrimination.[86] According to some, this may occur even if the algorithms have not been manually programmed to do so (i.e. by assigning inappropriate weight to certain factors).[87] It may depend on errors, or failure to recognize or address statistical biases, or reproduction of past prejudice, or an insufficient set of factors that are taken into account, that can occur in any of the different phases through which data mining is used to solve a problem.[88]

This can be all the more evident when the definition of the target variable (the outcome of interest in the process of data mining) involves a notion which is not a 'self-evident' notion but rather a function of how the lending industry has constructed the system (i.e. the predicted likelihood of missing a certain number of repayments of an outstanding debt).[89]

---

83   Bruckner (n 64) 268–269.
84   See for example K Crawford, 'The Hidden Biases in Big Data', in (April 1, 2013) Harvard Business Review, calling "the notion that correlation always indicates causation, and that massive data sets and predictive analytics always reflect objective truth" a form of "data fundamentalism".
85   Hurley et al (n 46) 151, 167.
86   S Barocas, AD Selbst, 'Big Data's Disparate Impact' (2016) 104 California Law Review 671, 674; Aggarwal (n 34) 11; see also, more generally, B Friedman, H Nissenbaum, 'Bias in Computer Systems' (1996) 14 ACM Transactions on Information Systems 330.
87   Barocas et al (n 86) 674; Hurley et al (n 46) 182–183; see also the Report released by the White House in 2014 'Big Data: Seizing Opportunities, Preserving Values' 64 <https://obamawhitehouse.archives.gov/sites/default/files/docs/big_data_privacy_report_may_1_2014.pdf>.
88   Barocas et al (n 86) 675; 677 ff.
89   Ibid 679.

Others highlight that even trying to build fair or non-discriminatory ML systems, by, for example, avoiding to feed the system data that is considered socially unacceptable, may still result in unfair systems as these excluded variables are likely related to some of the included variables and by allowing a prediction of the omitted variable, may let unwanted discrimination to sneak back in.[90] Whereas according to others, bias is the common consequence of the process of translation by programmers of policy into code, and the distortion of the policy that often takes place during the process.[91]

Distributional fairness could be also undermined by algorithmic scoring when it allows price differentiation and discriminatory loan pricing in consumer lending markets.[92] There is also the risk that 'alternative' credit scoring tools are not used to assess creditworthiness, but rather to single out and target the most vulnerable consumers with high-cost loan products.[93]

This naturally raises an important issue when considering responsible lending policies. Indeed, not only does scoring, as a form of 'generalized classification' risk losing some of the potentially more prudent individualized assessment which a responsible lending standard would contemplate,[94] but it also facilitates the singling out of vulnerable subjects to forms of predatory lending. The safeguards against solely automated decisions laid down by the European GDPR for example may in certain cases extend to automated online advertising which relies on automated tools for targeted advertising based on profiling: this may further trigger antidiscrimination issues where certain groups are regularly targeted for payday or other forms of high interest loans.[95]

---

90   L Edwards, M Veale, 'Slave to the Algorithm? Why A 'Right to an Explanation' Is Probably Not the Remedy You Are Looking For' (2017) 16 Duke Law & Technology Review 18, 29. The Authors also note that in the EU there have been much fewer "scare revelations of 'racially biased' algorithms than in the US". (ID p.30).

91   D Keats Citron, 'Technological Due Process', (2008) 85 Washington University Law Review 1249, 1260–1262; D Keats Citron et al (n 80) 4.

92   R Bartlett, A Morse, R Stanton, N Wallace, 'Consumer lending discrimination in the Fintech era' (2019) UC Berkeley Public Law Research Paper <https://ssrn.com/abstract =3063448> (accessed July 2020) analyzing the presence and level of discrimination in Government Sponsored Enterprises mortgage markets in the U.S. See also B Reddix-Smalls (n 32) 118–119.

93   Hurley et al (46) 167, 190.

94   See I Ramsay, 'From Truth in Lending to Responsible Lending', in G Howells, A Janssen, R Schulze (eds) Information Rights and Obligations (Ashgate 2005) 59–60.

95   See Article 29 Data Protection Working Party 'Guidelines on Automated individual decision-making and profiling for the purposes of Regulation 2016/679' (3 October 2017) 22.

Additional issues depend on the way in which data – especially 'alternative' data – are processed (often with an 'opaque' or 'black box' methodology) and on the weight that different data have on the final score that is elaborated. Whereas this problem was already present with traditional credit scoring, in which consumers were not aware of exactly how their score was calculated, nor did they have full access to the data records on them used by credit bureaus or credit reference agencies, the lack of disclosure becomes even more relevant when, as in algorithmic scoring, there is a multitude of data (often non-credit related and non-financial), collected from a multitude of sources and consumers are not aware of the way in which their profiling affects their creditworthiness.[96]

This naturally poses problems not only of privacy and data protection, but also of self-determination for consumers, to the extent that they are not conscious nor informed of how their actions (especially non-credit and non-financially related) are processed and how this may determine the way in which they are assessed (with a resulting credit score). The fact that the core of regulation on so-called 'privacy self-management' is centered around consent given by subjects to the collection, use and disclosure of personal data does not ensure that there is actual knowledge nor control over their data, especially with the 'aggregation effect' deriving from Big Data analytics.[97]

3.2 Data Protection and Antidiscrimination: Comparative Legal Issues

Credit reporting, regardless of the model, must comply not only with the regulation on consumer credit and mortgage credit, but also with antidiscrimination laws and with norms regulating privacy and more specifically, data protection. As previously observed, the relevance of data protection and antidiscrimination norms in credit reporting is related to the impact that this activity has on the fundamental rights of the physical individuals who apply for loans throughout the different phases of the application process, the decision-making and the performance (if the credit is granted) of the loan contract. Several studies have tried to identify the effects of data protection

---

96   F Pasquale, Black Box Society (Harvard University Press 2015); Hurley et al (n 46) 182, 189; see also, in partial dissent, quoting examples of algorithmic transparency, Bruckner (n 64) 40, 45; and more generally, Zarsky (n 81) 1541 ff.

97   DJ Solove, 'Introduction: Privacy Self-Management and the Consent Dilemma' (2013) 126 Harvard Law Review 1880, 1889.

on information distribution, access to credit, consumer indebtedness and consumer credit risk.[98]

One of the methods, based on the development of a 'Financial Privacy Index' (a quantitative measure that rates countries according to the protection of personal information that passes through credit bureaus) examines four different factors: supervisory authority, the rights of data subjects, the obligations of credit bureaus, and judicial remedies and enforcement.[99] A comparison between the US and the EU regulation (and more specifically in Germany, France and the UK) and credit markets would seem to indicate a correlation between higher data protection and lower information allocation and higher credit risk (because financial service providers have less information on consumers to evaluate their risk and this may lead to misinformed credit decisions).[100] Lower information allocation is thought to result in thinner credit markets and lower consumer indebtedness; the hypothesis is that "the more credit reports are sold the higher is the access to credit. This is associated with greater consumer indebtedness and higher consumer credit risk".[101]

3.2.1   Data Protection

When considering collection and processing of data for credit reporting, data protection legislation is relevant from a dual and opposite perspective. It not only requires that the collection and transmission of data does not infringe rights of individual subjects, but it also aims at ensuring, once collected, a free circulation and non-discriminatory access to the data within the market. The need to strike a balance between these opposing rights and interests is common to most legal systems; the experience on both sides of the Atlantic provides a paradigmatic illustration. The point in which the equilibrium between these tensions is found diverges in the two systems.

---

98   See for example, *ex multis*, Jappelli et al (n 1); and more generally, C Bennett, *Regulating Privacy-Data Protection and Public Policy in Europe and the United States* (Cornell University Press 1992); LB Pincus, R Johns, 'Private Parts: A Global Analysis of Privacy Protection Schemes and a Proposed Innovation for Their Comparative Evaluation' (1997) 16 Journal of Business Ethics 1237; JR Reidenberg, PM Schwartz, *Data Privacy Law – A Study of United States Data Protection* (Michie 1996).

99   N Jentzsch, 'The Regulation of Financial Privacy: The United States vs. Europe' (2003) ECRI Research Report No.5.

100   Ibid 22 ff.

101   Ibid i, 28, further noting that greater consumer indebtedness and higher consumer credit risk are due, among other factors, "to the fact that access is broadened and marginally less creditworthy households are entering the market".

It may be useful to very briefly recall (albeit with the risk of over-simplification),[102] some of the characteristics of the US and European models of data protection (notoriously described as constituting a regulatory divide) that are commonly highlighted when comparing the approach to privacy in the two traditions, especially in the information society.

The right to privacy and to personal data protection are rights that are deeply embedded in the legal traditions under observation as a result of a growing process which took place mainly in the 20th Century of recognition of their relevance as fundamental rights, albeit with different theorizations.[103]

---

[102] The analysis of the history of the right to privacy and its affirmation, as also of the specific aspect of data protection is beyond the scope of this study. The sparse references to some of the regulatory features of the European and US models of data protection presuppose the voluminous literature and scholarly debates and only serve as a background reference for the specific issue of the processing of credit data.

[103] The multiplicity of theories at the basis of the right of privacy have led many scholars to highlight first of all the difficulty in defining it and the ambiguity that often surrounds the notion. With no claim at exhaustivity, the interpretations of privacy in the American debate range from the seminal 'right to be let alone' (SD Warren, LD Brandeis, 'The Right to Privacy' (1890) 4 Harvard Law Review 195), to the 'dignity' approach (EJ Bloustein, 'Privacy as an Aspect of Human Dignity: An Answer to Dean Prosser' (1964) 39 New York University Law Review 962), to the 'identity' approach (M Hildebrandt, 'Privacy and Identity', in E Claes, E Duff, S Gutwirth (eds), *Privacy and the Criminal Law* (Intersentia 2006) 43), to narrower visions of protection of the intimate sphere (e.g. R Wacks, 'The Poverty of Privacy', (1980) 96 Law Quarterly Review 73; JC Inness, *Privacy, Intimacy, and Isolation* (Oxford University Press 1992)), to freedom and self-determination approaches (A Westin, *Privacy and Freedom* (Atheneum 1967); S Gutwirth, *Privacy and the information age* (R Casert tr, Rowman & Littlefield 2002)), to privacy as 'limited accessibility' (R Gavison, 'Privacy and the Limits of the Law', (1980) 89 Yale Law Journal 421), to a social value of privacy approach, (P Regan, *Legislating Privacy*, (University of North Carolina Press 1995)), to 'reductionist' approaches (J. Thomson, 'The Right to Privacy' (1975) 4 Philosophy and Public Affairs 295); to economic analysis approaches (RA Posner, 'The Right of Privacy' (9178) 12 Georgia Law Review 393); to the European respect and personal dignity approaches, (EJ Eberle, *Dignity and Liberty: Constitutional Visions in Germany and the United States* (Praeger 2002); F Rigaux, *La protection de la vie privée et des autres biens de la personnalité* (Bruylant 1990)); rights to one's image, name and reputation (V Zeno-Zencovich, *Onore e reputazione nel sistema del diritto civile. Uno studio comparato* (Jovene 1985); A Bertrand, *Droit à la vie privée et droit à l'image* (LexisNexis-Litec 1999)), and personality right and right to informational self-determination (C Ahrens, *Persönlichkeitsrecht und Freiheit der Medienberichterstattung: Konfliktsituationene, Schutzansprüche, Verfahrensfragen* (Schmidt 2002); H-U Erichsen et al (eds.), *Recht der Persönlichkeit* (Duncker & Humblot 1996); G Resta, *Autonomia privata e diritti della personalità* (Jovene 2005)).

The notion and scope of protection of personal data, as also its relation to the right to privacy, have received multiple interpretations.[104] A widely accepted tenet is that data protection concerns the procedures for the processing of personal data, that is, the conditions under which processing is legitimate. It does not prohibit the processing but attempts to reconcile fundamental but potentially conflicting values such as privacy, free flow of information, the need for government surveillance and so forth.[105]

The status of data protection within the system, its recognition and hierarchical position in the scale of values, and the regulatory models to which it is subject respond to differences in legal and cultural tradition.

In the European model, personal data is considered as a personality right, a notion that dates back to the developments of German and Italian

---

104 Several of the theories on the foundation of the right to privacy have also been transposed to data protection, identified as protecting, once again *inter alia*, informational control, interests of autonomy, self-determination, democracy and pluralism (Westin (n 103); S Rodotà, *Elaboratori elettronici e controllo sociale* (Il Mulino 1973); S Rodotà, *Tecnologie e diritti* (Il Mulino 1995); L Bygrave, *Data Protection Law: Approaching Its Rationale, Logic and Limits* (Kluwer Law International 2002); E Brouwer, *Digital Borders and Real Rights* (Brill 2007); A Rouvroy – Y Poullet, 'The Right to Informational Self-Determination and the Values of Self-Development: Reassessing the Value of Privacy for Democracy' in S. Gutwirth (ed), *Reinventing Data Protection* (Springer 2009) 45. The relationship between data protection and privacy has also received numerous interpretations, in some cases considering the two rights as almost interchangeable, in other cases highlighting the specificity of data protection within the wider notion of privacy (as demonstrated for example by its separate recognition in fundamental Charters and Conventions in Europe-see *infra*) (see also, more generally, LA Bygrave, 'The Place of Privacy in Data Protection Law' (2001) 24 University of New South Wales Law Journal 277); its wider and more specific scope of application, since it also relates to other fundamental rights and freedoms of individuals such as equality and due process but only with reference to the processing of personal data (P De Hert, S Gutwirth, 'Data Protection in the Case Law of Strasbourg and Luxembourg: Constitutionalisation in Action', in S Gutwirth et al (eds), *Reinventing Data Protection* (Springer 2009) 6); its different foundation within constitutional law traditions (for example within Europe, there are legal systems in which the foundation for the recognition of data protection was found in rights other than privacy (not explicitly recognized in their constitutions), such as the right to liberty in France or the right to human dignity in Germany or as a personality right (further protected by other fundamental rights of freedom) in Italy; whereas in the Netherlands and in Belgium it was directly linked to the right to privacy explicitly recognized by their constitutions) (Ibid 10); A Levin, MJ Nicholson, 'Privacy Law in the United States, the EU and Canada: The Allure of the Middle Ground' (2005) 2 University of Ottawa Law & Technology Journal 357; G Alpa, M Bessone, *Banche dati, telematica e diritti della persona* (Cedam 1984); V Zeno-Zencovich (ed), *Le banche dati in Italia. Realtà normative e progetti di regolamentazione* (Jovene 1985).

105 De Hert et al (n 104) 3–4; A Rouvroy et al (n 104).

doctrine in the 1970's and 80's and to fundamental judgements of the German Constitutional Court on the right of 'informational self-determination'.[106] This notion influenced the European framework on privacy and data protection, by shaping both the ECJ and the ECtHR case law (and the interpretation given to Article 8 of the European Convention on Human Rights, interpreted so as to cover personal data collected by public and private subjects and as requiring that the protection of this right finds a basis in law, clearly defined legitimate purposes, and proportionality), and future regulation.[107] The right to privacy recognized in the ECHR, began to be presented in the 1970's with growing challenges deriving from technological developments, which not always easily fell easily within the scope of 'private life' and 'protection against interference by public authorities' laid down in Article 8. This led the Council of Europe to promote the adoption in 1981 of a separate Convention on Data Protection.[108] Protection of personal data was also later enshrined (as an autonomous right, under article 8) in the European Charter of Human Rights, now incorporated in the Treaty of Lisbon; while it is recognized as a 'provision of general application' with other fundamental rights in the TFEU, (article 16).

Under the European model, data protection finds detailed definition in legislative instruments and these are shaped around the 'rights framework'. Indeed, the EU Data Protection Directive of 1995 was envisioned as a measure to improve the protection of the fundamental right to privacy, even if it was grounded on the basis of market harmonization with the scope of facilitating data flows and trade in Europe.[109]

It has been noted that a different concern on the vertical or also horizontal application of data protection rules is one of the traditional differences between the US and the European approaches which also relates to a conceptual foundation of privacy as liberty (a political value) in the first case and as dignity (a social value) in the second.[110] US law tends to characterize 'personal information' more narrowly than in the European model (that has

---

106   See the German Constitutional Court, Microcensus Act Case (27 BVerfGE 1,1969) and the Census Act Case, (65 BVerfGE 1, Dec.15 1983).
107   See F Bignami, G Resta, 'Transatlantic Privacy Regulation: Conflict and Cooperation', (2015) 78 Law and Contemporary Problems 231, 232–233; V Zeno-Zencovich, G Giannone Codiglione, 'Ten legal perspectives on the "big data revolution"' (2016) 23 *Big Data e Concorrenza, Concorrenza e mercato numero speciale*, F. Di Porto (ed), 33.
108   Council of Europe, Convention for the Protection of Individuals with regard to automatic processing of personal data, 28 January 1981, ETS No.108. See De Hert et al (n 104) 6.
109   Bignami et al (n 107) 234; Zeno-Zencovich et al (n 107) ibid.
110   JQ Whitman, 'The Two Western Cultures of Privacy: Dignity versus Liberty' (2004) 113 Yale Law Journal 1151, 1160–61; see also Eberle (n 103); RC Post, 'Three Concepts of Privacy' (2001) 89 Georgetown Law Journal 2087.

largely influenced legal systems outside the EU as well) and this consequently places a limit on public intervention to regulate information privacy. The US model has also adopted a sector-by-sector regulation as opposed to omnibus legislation.

Some have also famously theorized a different governance function of privacy rules adopted in the US and the EU; a liberal, market-based governance versus a socially-protective, rights-based governance and an approach that relies on self-regulation of the industry as opposed to state-sponsored regulation.[111] The market-based approach helps explain the focus of regulation on the market and thus on transparency (i.e. access to data) rather than substantive regulation of information privacy; a policy that is related to First Amendment (and Fourth and Fifth Amendment) jurisprudence and the everlasting tension between freedom of information and protection of privacy.[112] Even if important fundamental rights which shape US data protection law were recognized in the Code of Fair Information Practices published in 1973[113] (such as transparency in the use and processing of data; an individual right of access to personal data; a limitation on the uses to purposes for which the personal information was originally collected; a right to correction of personal data; the duty to ensure the accuracy of personal data; the obligation to adopt security measures to prevent fraudulent uses of data) and later transposed in the US Privacy Act of 1974 and in other sector-specific statutes, data privacy has not been recognized as a constitutional right.[114]

With reference more specifically to data used in credit reporting, according to the US Supreme Court consumer reports have a 'reduced constitutional value of speech' as they do not involve 'matters of public concern' and are thus not considered protected speech under the First Amendment (and do not for example require a showing of 'actual malice' to recover presumed and punitive damages in defamation cases),[115] nor receive protection against injunctions (which, as will be seen, is a fundamental tool in case of data

---

111   See JR Reidenberg, 'Resolving Conflicting International Data Privacy Rules in Cyberspace' (1999–2000) 52 Stanford Law Review 1315, 1341–1343 ff; Schwartz, 'The EU-U.S. Privacy Collision' (n 63) 1974; see also F. Ferretti, 'The 'Credit Scoring Pandemic' and the European Vaccine' (n 46) 11–12.

112   Reidenberg (n 111) 1343; FH Cate, *Privacy in the Information Age* (Brookings Institution Press 1997) 78–79.

113   U.S. Dep't of Health, Education and Welfare, Secretary's Advisory Committee on Automated Personal Data Systems, Records, computers, and the Rights of Citizens (1973).

114   Bignami et al (n 107) 235–236 and cases cited therein.

115   US Supreme Court, *Dun & Bradstreet, Inc. v. Greenmoss Builders*, 472 US 749 (1985), 759, 761–762.

breaches and requests of correction of inaccurate or false data processed in a credit report).[116]

It has been observed, even when taking into consideration fundamental federal statutes such as the Freedom of Information Act and the Privacy Act, that "Privacy laws in the US most often prohibit certain disclosures, rather than collection, use or storage of personal information. When those protections extend to the use of personal information, it is often as a by-product of legislative commitment to another goal, such as eliminating discrimination."[117] When compared to EU data protection, US law contains fewer restrictions on the quantity of personal data that may be collected and used and for how long, and even under the Privacy Act there are relatively few substantive limits on the use of personal information.[118]

The market-based approach also accounts for the central importance given to notice, consent and accuracy in information privacy and the fact that sectorial statutes tend to address accuracy of information, but do not yield broad access to personal information held by others; they interpret purpose limitations on the use of information strictly (in the Fair Credit Reporting Act for example purposes compatible with the rationale receive broad interpretation and include the use of credit reports for certain marketing purposes).[119] Also, enforcement is mostly in the hands of private litigants in courts, rather than in those of administrative agencies (i.e. data protection authorities as in Europe).[120]

As will be seen further, these differing models are reflected also in the regulation of credit reporting and credit scoring, even though it is important to note that the sectorial legislation on credit reporting in the United States contains some characteristics that are not recurrent in data protection legislation in force in other sectors (especially after the 1996 Credit Reporting Reform Act corrected important loopholes in the previous Fair Credit Reporting Act and strengthened the protection for information privacy).[121] Strong criticisms have however been raised on the efficacy of these provisions and especially as regards the remedies in case of violation of the norms (see 3.2.1.1).

---

116   See M Schramm-Strosser, 'The 'Not So' Fair Credit Reporting Act: Federal Preemption, Injunctive Relief, and the Need to Return Remedies for Common Law Defamation to the States' (2012) 14 Duquesne Business Law Journal 165 212 ff; see also US Court of Appeals, Fifth Circuit, *Hood v. Dun Bradstreet Inc.*, 486 F.2d 25 (5th Cir. 1973).

117   Cate (n 112) 98–99 (and 77–78).

118   Bignami et al (n 107) 236–237.

119   (15 U.S.C. §1681b(c)1) Reidenberg (n 111) 1344–1345.

120   Bignami et al (n 107) 236.

121   Cate (n 112) 82–83.

Similar problems on data protection in credit reporting arose also during the drafting of sectorial laws in the EU. Concerns on the collection, use, and circulation of personal data employed in credit scoring (both in the older traditional models and in the new 'big data' or 'alternative' scoring models) were issues which the European legislator was well aware of when drafting legislation on consumer loans. This is evident *prima facie* when considering the various safeguard clauses on data protection contained in the Consumer Credit Directive (Article 9 CCD) and in the Mortgage Credit Directive (Article 21 MCD).

The European authorities were called upon, during the drafting of the Mortgage Credit Directive, to express their opinion on the counterbalancing between the needs of an efficient and secure credit market in which there is free movement of data, and the protection of privacy and personal data of consumers. The European Central Bank for example issued an opinion in 2011 on the Draft proposal for the Credit Mortgage Directive, in which referring to access to databases it declared that it understood that "the uniform credit registration criteria should be understood as *minimum standards* [emphasis added], allowing private credit bureaus or credit reference agencies and public credit registers, against the background of their purposes and business models, to collect additional information on these credits where appropriate".[122] The European Data Protection Supervisor, in its Opinion of a few weeks later instead held that it was necessary to specify in a more detailed way the sources from which information on the creditor's creditworthiness can be obtained and the need to "communicate the data subjects' rights before any access to the database, thereby ensuring concrete and effective possibilities for data subjects to exercise their rights" (i.e. right to access, rectify, block or erase the data contained in the database).[123]

At a more general level, the drafting process in the EU is indicative of the rights and interests that need to be counterbalanced in crafting regulation which implies or acknowledges credit scoring, and which often respond to juxtaposed needs.

On the one hand, there are data protection issues, which include the definition (and limitation) of sources from which information on the prospective borrower can be collected; the possible restriction of subjects who can access the databases (i.e. should 'only creditors or intermediaries who concluded a

---

122   European Central Bank, 'Opinion of 5 July 2011 on a proposal for a directive of the European Parliament and of the Council on credit agreements relating to residential property' (CON/2011/58) 3.2.2.

123   European Data Protection Supervisor, Opinion on the proposal for a Directive of the European Parliament and of the Council on Credit agreements relating to residential property, 25 July 2011, n. 14–16, (pgs. 4–5).

contract with a consumer or are required by the consumer to take steps to conclude a contractual relationship with him' access the data?);[124] the storage of the information; the right of the consumer to view, modify and cancel the information (including the problem of 'updating' the information: suffice it to consider the negative effect that one episode of 'bad credit' can have on a consumer's credit record and how it can affect future access to credit for years).[125]

On the other hand, there is the need to ensure that widespread access to the databases responds to the needs of the market (stability) and of the efficiency of the banking sector, by proposing adequate credit/financial products and ensuring fair competition between banks, including cross-border institutions. As previously observed, credit reporting is also a response on the creditor's side to the problem of asymmetric information between borrowers and creditors (mitigating adverse selection and moral hazard problems)[126] and it is an important tool used for prudential requirements, recognized by banking regulation. Circulation of credit data (especially cross-border) also allows consumer mobility.

Some of the rules and practices on the admissible collection and circulation of personal data on borrowers is emblematic of the attempt at counterbalancing public interest and individual rights. An interesting example can be taken from the Italian experience, where the Data Protection Authority has ruled that given that the transmission of information from credit intermediaries (private entities) to the Public Credit Register (the *Centrale dei Rischi* of the Bank of Italy – a public entity) during the phase of "input" of data is laid down in legislative provisions,[127] the transmission of the information does not require previous consent by the data subjects nor does it entitle them to the removal of the data (except in the case of ascertained unlawfulness of the data collection and processing).[128] This position was later confirmed with the Personal Data Protection Code[129] and its amendments introduced by

---

124   See EDPS Opinion, *cit.*, at n. 14.
125   See also, generally, the European Data Protection Supervisor Guidelines 2014 on data protection in EU financial services regulation.
126   (n 6); see also Jappelli et al (n 1).
127   See Articles 51 and 53 of the Italian *Testo Unico Bancario* (Banking Law) (having the public and private aim of signaling positions of credit risk) and article 27(2) of the Italian Data Privacy Law (675/1996 repealed by D.lgs. 196/2003, later amended by D.lgs. 101/2018).
128   *Autorità Garante per la protezione dei dati personali*, 17th October 2001, [40907]; see also Autorità Garante per la protezione dei dati personali 6th February 2001, [40879]; 10th April 2001 [31015]; 25th February 2000 [39248]. On a different position, see G Alpa, 'Aspetti della disciplina sui dati personali riguardanti gli enti e l'attività economica' (1998) *Rivista trimestrale di diritto e procedura civile*, 713, 726 ff.
129   D.lgs. 196/2003, article 18.

the GDPR[130] that affirmed the lawfulness of data processing by public subjects solely for public scopes (which in the case of management of credit risk lies with the Bank of Italy – as provided by article 53 of the Banking Law).[131] As prescribed by the Personal Data Protection Code,[132] and with the scope of promoting the proper functioning of the financial and credit market, Italy has also adopted in 2005 (and amended in 2019) a "Code of conduct for credit reporting systems operated by private entities regarding consumer credit, creditworthiness and punctuality in payments" that allows records to be processed without the data subjects' consent by companies that participate in the credit reporting systems (i.e. private entities) on the basis of the so-called legitimate interest of the companies (i.e. the correct measurement of creditworthiness and credit risk; the correct assessment of the reliability and timeliness of payments; the prevention of risks of fraud, including identity theft). The rights laid down in the GDPR must be guaranteed and only data relevant for the purpose of credit risk assessment may be processed.[133]

Some differences in the approach to data protection between the United States and the European Union have been highlighted above. According to some observers, the cultural background against which privacy is set cannot be ignored when analyzing the case of credit reporting; in this area the traditional reluctancy found in continental cultures and etiquette to discuss one's financial matters, which should remain one's own affairs, would be visible in the regulatory protection accorded to credit data.[134]

As seen above, the debate whether credit reporting should include only negative or both negative and positive data is resolved somewhat strictly in the French legal system for example; this could be read as the modern translation of the historical evolution of privacy, and of the notion that financial information "is information 'of a personal character' over which one must have control just as one must have control over one's image".[135] Also, in the case of German credit reporting, not only is consumer consent for sharing information

---

130   Article 2-ter of d.lgs. 196/2003, as modified by d.lgs. 101/2018.
131   G Biferali, '*Big Data* e valutazione del merito creditizio' (2018) 34 Diritto dell'informazione e dell'informatica n3, 487, 496–497.
132   Articles 12 and 117, D.lgs. 196/2003.
133   See, with reference to the problem of 'economic data' and consent, V Zeno-Zencovich, 'Privacy e informazioni a contenuto economico' in F Cardarelli, S Sica, V Zeno-Zencovich (eds) *Il codice dei dati personali. Temi e problemi* (Giuffrè 2004) 445; see also A Sciarrone Alibrandi 'Centrali dei rischi creditizi e normativa di privacy: informazione e controlli dell'interessato' (2003) 49 Rivista di diritto civile 423, 428 ff, (arguing that consent is not necessary).
134   Whitman (n 110) 1190–1191.
135   Ibid.

required through the signature of "SCHUFA clauses", but for the scope of credit scoring data is anonymized and statistically aggregated so as to avoid violations of privacy rights of individual consumers.[136] A cultural reading of these different approaches can lead to affirm that credit reporting is Europe is associated directly with the law of bankruptcy, which "stigmatizes the dishonorable failure to pay one's debts", whilst in the American practice it is read as the law that "allows merchants to pry into the buying habits of honorable, solvent, persons".[137]

The way in which these different approaches to privacy and data protection are translated into the sectorial or general laws applicable to credit reporting both in the United States and in EU legislation deserves further attention.

3.2.1.1   Data Protection and Credit Reporting in US Legislation

Starting with the United States, two specific regulations on credit reporting were passed in the 1970's (the Federal Fair Credit Reporting Act (FCRA) enacted in 1970[138] and the Equal Credit Opportunity Act (ECOA) enacted in 1974)[139] prohibiting collection of certain types of information and discrimination in access to credit following from these data.[140] The FCRA and its amendments (including the Consumer Credit Reporting Reform Act of 1996, the Fair Credit Reporting Act of 1999, the Gramm-Leach-Bliley Act of 1999, the Fair and Accurate Credit Transactions Act of 2003) still constitute the basis of consumer credit information regulation.

The FCRA is part of the sectorial laws on financial transactions, which include the protection of personal information in banking, consumer credit and mortgage financing. It "sets forth rights for individuals and responsibilities for consumer credit reporting agencies in connection with the preparation and dissemination of personal information in a consumer report bearing on the individual's creditworthiness, credit standing, credit capacity, character,

---

136   U Wuermeling, 'Scoring von Kreditrisiken' (2002) Neue Juristische Wochenschrift, 3508, 3509; Whitman (n 110) 1191.

137   Whitman (n 110) 1191–1192.

138   15 U.S.C. §1681–1681x. For a detailed reconstruction of the circumstances and phases which led to the approval of the statute, including the release of reports and publication of literature on abuses in credit reporting, see RM McNamara, 'The Fair Credit Reporting Act: A Legislative Overview', (1973) 22 Journal of Public Law 67 and *ex multis*, RE Smith, *Ben Franklin's Web Site. Privacy and Curiosity from Plymouth Rock to the Internet* (Privacy Journal Publisher 2004) 311 ff.

139   15 U.S.C. §§1691–1691f.

140   Following the Dodd-Frank Act, the Consumer Financial Protection Bureau (CFPB) as the main regulator under the ECOA and the FCRA has issued regulation (known as Regulation B) which provides the substantive and procedural framework for fair lending.

general reputation, personal characteristics or mode of living."[141] The Fair Debt Collection Practices Act of 1977 should also be recalled as it limits debt collectors' disclosures of a debtor's financial situation to some third parties – but not to credit reporting agencies.[142]

Given the 'empiricism' of credit scoring, any characteristic of the borrower which is useful in predicting his/her default/non-default can be used in the scoring system.[143] This naturally raises conflicts with regulation on data protection and has led to enaction of specific measures prohibiting the collection of certain types of data for the scope of credit scoring. When the Fair Credit Reporting Act was passed in the 1970's, the practice of credit reporting (and later credit scoring – that is the development of a score on the basis of the data and the variables contained in credit reports) was already widespread. The practice of collecting and organizing data regarding repayment abilities of consumers is associated with the expansion of purchase on credit made in department stores, starting in the 1920's; over the following decades a few major credit reporting agencies consolidated their position in the US market.[144]

The FCRA intervened to regulate (and prevent abuses on)[145] data that was already being shared, although it was not computerized; until then the consumer reporting industry operated almost entirely outside state or federal regulators' scrutiny.[146] Scope of the federal law was to regulate the collection, sharing, transmission (i.e. from creditors (lenders) to credit reporting agencies) and sale of these data (i.e. vice-versa: from credit reporting agencies to creditors or other subjects who have a permissible purpose).[147] It aimed at promoting accuracy, fairness, impartiality and privacy of information in the files of consumer reporting agencies.[148] As will be further recalled, the statute that

---

141 J Reidenberg 'Privacy in the Information Economy: A Fortress or Frontier for Individual Rights?'(1992) 44 Federal Communications Law Journal 195, 210.

142 Cate (n 112) 84.

143 Thomas et al (n 20) 7.

144 Equifax, TransUnion and Experian (previously TRW) were the major agencies at the time the FCRA was adopted, in the 1970's.

145 Awareness in the public opinion on abuses in credit reporting was raised following the publication of literature and reports on the subject in the early 1970's, such as for example McNamara (n 138).

146 S Feldman, 'The Fair Credit Reporting Act – From the Regulators Vantage Point' (1971) 14 Santa Clara Lawyer 459, 461.

147 See E Rosenblatt, *Credit Data and Scoring: The First Triumph of Big Data and Big Algorithms* (Elsevier 2020) 1–2.

148 15 U.S.C. §1681a. The FCRA was amended by the Consumer Credit Reform Act of 1996 to improve the accuracy of consumer reports and by the Fair and Accurate Credit

was finally adopted did not prove as effective in protecting consumer rights as initially anticipated and there are strong indicators that the necessary compromise with the credit reporting industry tipped the scale of the balance in its favor, in particular when considering remedies for injured consumers.[149]

In line with the approach on privacy regulation in the US, it should be noted first of all that the relevant regulations for credit reporting and scoring are specific, sectorial regulations which tend to address activities rather than subjects. Indeed, the FCRA defines applicability with reference to 'consumer reports' rather than with reference to individuals.[150] As will be seen later, this is a first important distinction with the European model, that entrusts the regulation of credit scoring to the General Regulation on Data Protection (GDPR) and chooses to center regulation around the issues related with the protection of data of the individuals (rather than on – or also on – the activity of credit reporting, which as already highlighted, is also relevant for a more efficient credit market and requires a delicate counterbalancing of interests).

Under other aspects, the FCRA contains provisions that are otherwise 'uncommon' in the US model of data protection. Whereas US law does not generally lay down a duty to inform individuals that data about them is collected, this is the case for credit reports for non-statutorily permitted purposes.[151] Furthermore, the FCRA exceptionally contains a general obligation to notify the public of the treatment of personal information (to be carried out through newspaper advertisements and for the sole case of the use of credit report information for junk mail solicitations).[152]

The FCRA imposes several obligations onto consumer reporting agencies, including the duty to follow reasonable procedures to ensure maximum possible accuracy of the report on the individual;[153] duties of disclosure to consumers on the information, sources and recipients of their credit files;[154] and the duty to give notice of adverse credit determinations and of the lenders' use

Transaction Act of 2003 that gave consumers the right to obtain disclosure of credit scores.

149 See for example ED De Armond, 'A Dearth of Remedies' (2008) 113 Penn State Law Review 1, 5 ff who speaks of "a modern trend of remediless federal privacy rights" referred not only to the FCRA, but also to other federal privacy statutes such as the Health Insurance Portability and Accountability Act of 1996 and the 1999 Gramm-Leach Bliley Act.
150 15 U.S.C. §1681a(d)(1). See Reidenberg (n 111) 1333.
151 15 U.S.C. §1681b(a)(2).
152 15 U.S.C. §1681b(e)(5). Reidenberg (n 111) 1334–1335.
153 15 U.S.C. §1681e(b).
154 15 U.S.C. §1681g.

of the consumer report information[155] (i.e. the nature and substance of most of the information in the file).

It also recognizes rights for the consumers, such as the right to dispute inaccurate information and request their correction or deletion.[156] Although the law does allow individuals to dispute items on their credit history, this does not mean that credit bureaus are obliged to reveal the way in which history is transformed into a score: as highlighted earlier, this process is protected as a trade secret.[157]

Even later *ad hoc* legislation (i.e. the Fair and Accurate Credit Transactions Act (FACTA) of 2003) did not improve the possibility for individuals to understand the way in which their credit scores were developed (and act accordingly): the FACTA requires credit bureaus to disclose credit scores to consumers in exchange for a fee but only with reference to four key factors involved in credit decisions and with no requirement for "any information concerning credit scores or any other risk scores or predictors relating to the consumer".[158]

To the extent that they qualify as 'Consumer Reporting Agencies'[159] (which includes bank-affiliated algorithmic lenders but may exclude direct lenders if they assemble and evaluate information about borrowers for their own use and do not furnish them to third parties), the obligations in the FCRA also apply to algorithmic lenders; with, however, some operational difficulties due to the fact that the FCRA and the ECOA were designed before the new models of algorithmic lending existed.[160] This is one of the reasons for which existing laws are mostly insufficient to respond to the challenges posed by Big Data scoring.[161]

It should also be noted that when Big Data processes are used predictively (combining the use of data sets with predictive analytics and yielding results that may be considered personal sensitive information) they may fall beyond the scope of privacy regulation given that the personally identifiable information (PII) was not collected directly from any first or third party but

---

155   15 U.S.C. §1681m.
156   15 U.S.C. §1681i.
157   Keats Citron et al (n 80) 17.
158   15 U.S.C. – § 1681g(a)(1)(B); 15 U.S.C. §1681g (f)(C); see Keats Citron et al (n 80) 17.
159   15 U.S.C. § 1681f: "Any person which, for monetary fees, dues, or on a cooperative nonprofit basis, regularly engages in whole or in part in the practice of assembling or evaluating consumer credit information or other information on consumers for the purpose of furnishing consumer reports to third parties, and which uses any means or facility of interstate commerce for the purpose of preparing or furnishing consumer reports".
160   Bruckner (n 64) 50–51; 52–55 providing an overview of the main difficulties that the compliance with the FCRA poses for algorithmic lenders. See also Hurley (n 46) 185–186.
161   Hurley (n 46) 183 ff.

predicted.[162] As it has been observed, "Privacy law is primarily concerned with causality, whereas Big Data is generally a tool of correlation" making traditional approaches to privacy protection difficult with respect to Big Data.[163]

An important issue, that recalls the problems on liability of credit rating agencies previously examined, concerns the profiles of responsibility tied to credit reporting. In the first place, it is worth noting that the main hypothesis of responsibility is tied to the personality rights involved when a physical individual borrower is 'evaluated' or 'scored', and pertains to the injury of the individual's reputation (as a payer who is 'unreliable' or a credit applicant who is 'unworthy' of credit). Thus, defamation is the typical tort that comes into play, if and when it is recognized.

In the case of the FCRA, it should be noted that consumer reporting agencies are protected from defamation law. Indeed, the FCRA preempted previous State law of defamation[164] which applied before the approval of the FRCA and treated the injury as defamation (even if it was difficult to succeed since consumer reporting agencies operate in secrecy and most States had adopted a qualified privilege for credit reporting agencies in defamation suits).

The Federal law created a general statutory cause of action in negligence for failure to "follow reasonable procedures to assure maximum possible accuracy of information".[165] The FCRA provides that any person who is negligent in failing to comply with any requirement imposed on it shall be liable for any actual damages sustained by the consumer as a result of the failure, for the costs of the action and for reasonable attorney's fees.[166] If the failure to comply is willful, the court in addition may allow punitive damages.[167] Criminal sanctions are imposed for "Any person who knowingly and willfully obtains information on a consumer from a consumer reporting agency under false pretenses"[168] and

---

162   See K Crawford, J Schultz, 'Big Data and Due Process: Towards a Framework to Redress Predictive Privacy Harms', (2014) 55 Boston College Law Review 93, 98 and literature cited; see also in general P Schwartz, D Solove, 'The PII Problem: Privacy and a New Concept of Personally Identifiable Information', (2001) 86 New York University Law Review 1814.

163   Crawford et al (n 162) 108.

164   See 15 U.S.C. §1681t(b)(1)(F) and15 U.S.C. §1681h(e).

165   15 U.S.C. §1681e(b). See RD Blair, V Maurer, 'Statute Law and Common Law: The Fair Credit Reporting Act' (1984) 49 Missouri Law Review 289, 291; on the development in common law of the qualified privilege for malice for those who report financial information of others see ED De Armond, 'Frothy Chaos: Modern Data Warehousing and Old-Fashioned Defamation' (2007) 41 Valparaiso University Law Review 1059, 1119 ff.

166   15 U.S.C. §1681o.

167   15 U.S.C. § 1681n.

168   15 U.S.C. §1681q.

for "Any officer or employee of a consumer reporting agency who knowingly and willfully provides information concerning an individual from the agency's files to a person not authorized to receive that information".[169]

However, it has been observed *inter alia* that the reduction of possible penalties for reputation injuries "allows tactics of stalling, obstinacy and obfuscation by the credit industry".[170] Secondly, even though the FCRA explicitly allows common-law defamation actions (if the consumer can prove malice or willful intent on behalf of the consumer reporting agency and disclosure in one of the listed methods),[171] "courts have interpreted the FCRA's preemption provisions as forbidding courts from granting injunctive relief for the violation of a state common law action for defamation".[172] Furthermore, if for example a consumer seeks the removal or modification of erroneous information from his credit report, the procedure (a "reasonable investigation" by the CRA into the alleged erroneous information and removal where appropriate) requires that the administrative remedies must be exhausted before filing suit for damages (and even then, if the investigation is negligent or incorrect, the erroneous information may not actually be removed from the consumer report).[173] Not only; the civil liability provisions contained in the FCRA (15 U.S.C. §1681n and §1681o) have been judged as inadequate surrogates for traditional state tort law actions,[174] and they do not provide sufficient incentives for (and adequate enforcement of) accuracy in consumer reports (as also the rules on deterrence to noncompliance, personal investigation, notice by users, and access by consumers).[175]

---

169   15 U.S.C. § 1681r. The FCRA also provides for administrative remedies that were initially entrusted to the FTC for enforcement, and later, with the Dodd-Frank Act partially transferred to the Consumer Financial Protection Bureau (CFPB). As seen in Chapter 1, the problem of inaccurate statements on creditworthiness is not limited to injuries on the reputation of mistreated individuals but can also affect, in the case of credit ratings of corporations or institutional issuers, investors on the market.

170   Keats Citron et al (n 80) 17.

171   15 U.S.C. §1681h(e).

172   Schramm-Strosser (n 116) 171 and cases cited therein; and 190. See especially *Washington v. CSC Credit Services Inc.*, 199 F.3d 263 (5th Cir. 2000).

173   15 U.S.C. §1681i. See Schramm-Strosser (n 116) 185–187, quoting judicial cases and arguing in favor of the injunctive relief that a common law defamation action could provide for consumers in cases of this type.

174   De Armond (n 149) 8.

175   Feldman (n 146) 468–469, and 484, noting (even if in 1974) that the amount of monetary damages is generally small or nonexistent and that "placing the burden of proof of negligence on the consumer seriously weakens the provisions attaching liability to negligent noncompliance" (ibid 483); see also AP Everhart Sickler, 'The (Un)Fair Credit Reporting Act', (2016) 28 Loyola Consumer Law Review 238, 241.

These modifications and interpretations of the FCRA have led many to high-light how the original intent of improving the position of consumers in credit reporting has turned into a regulatory scheme that protects the credit report-ing industry and is largely the result of a compromise (i.e. allowing individuals access to credit reports in exchange for qualified privilege for certain torts).[176]

These issues are typically associated with the negative impacts and injury – first of all to one's reputation, and in the second place to one's finance – that derive from inaccurate or erroneous credit reporting. There is vast literature – and case law (and statistical reports)[177] – recounting the devastating impact that a drop in one's credit score has on one's ability to access credit, obtain insurance, a mortgage, market interest rates on loans, employment, and so forth. Many of the criticisms highlighted against the main piece of legislation regulating this activity in the United States (the FRCA) is that it is inadequate precisely in protecting this right to an accurate 'financial reputation'. The prob-lem is closely associated with the object of this study, namely, creditworthiness and 'responsible credit'. The point is analyzed more in detail *infra*, in a com-parison between US and EU regulation, which is now examined.

3.2.1.2   Data Protection and Credit Reporting in EU Legislation
In Europe the current normative reference (comprehensive and applica-ble both to the public and the private sector, as opposed to the US sectorial approach), is embodied in the General Data Protection Regulation (GDPR)[178] which repealed the previous 1995 Data Protection Directive (DPD).[179] The first data protection regulation at EU level (and first binding international instrument for the protection against abuses in the collection and processing

---

176   See Keats Citron et al (n 80) 16–17; Schramm-Strosser (n 116) 170 and 195, on the nature of the political compromise; De Armond (n 149) 1097 ff; VG Maurer, RE Thomas, 'Getting Credit Where Credit Is Due: Proposed Changes in the Fair Credit Reporting Act' (1997) 34 American Business Law Journal 607, 624–625 highlighting the costs of error-reduction and error correction in false negative reports and the disincentives for credit reporting agencies in removing false-negative reports; and more generally, 637 and ff on the short-comings of the FCRA.

177   For an overview on mismatched data in credit files see for examples the reports analyzed by De Armond (n 149) 1074 ff.

178   Regulation (EU) 2016/679 of the European Parliament and of the Council of 27 April 2016 on the protection of natural persons with regard to the processing of personal data and on the free movement of such data and repealing Directive 95/46/EC [2016] OJ L 119/1.

179   Directive 95/46/EC of the European Parliament and of the Council of 24 October 1995 on the protection of individuals with regard to the processing of personal data and on the free movement of such data, [1995] OJ L281/31. On the relevant provisions for credit scor-ing in the 1995 Data Protection Directive see the overview by Ferretti 'The 'Credit Scoring Pandemic' and the European Vaccine' (n 46) 9 ff.

of personal data and for the regulation of the cross-border flow of personal data) dates back, as mentioned, to 1981 and is embodied in the Council of Europe Convention for the Protection of Individuals with regard to Automatic Processing of Personal Data (Treaty 108/81).[180]

The impact of data protection policies on the activity of credit bureaus (both public credit registers and private bureaus) entailed important changes in perspective and in regulation that led to take into account not only the strategic function of credit reporting for lenders and for the credit market, but also the consequences from the point of view of the rights and position of reported subjects. As already previously in the United States, concerns with the impact of negative reporting on the reputation and access to credit of individuals initially brought about attempts at lifting the secrecy from the procedures surrounding credit reporting (data collection, construction of credit reports, notification of negative records).[181]

As for the General Data Protection Regulation, it contains duties for data controllers and processors (such as data minimization, accuracy and purpose limitation[182] and the processing of data only for lawful purposes),[183] but also rights for data subjects (right to access data and to object to processing),[184] along with regulatory enforcement powers.[185] These principles govern the use of data that is used to conduct creditworthiness assessments.

An analysis of the GDPR is beyond the scope of this study. However, amongst the relevant provisions applying to the processing of credit data, it is necessary first of all to recall that processing can only occur on a lawful basis, which according to article 6 GDPR requires at least one of the following: a) consent of the data subject to the processing; b) processing is necessary for the performance or for the entering into a contract in which the data subject is party;

---

180 See also the Communication of the European Commission of 2017 'Building A European Data Economy' (Communication from the Commission to the European Parliament, the Council, the European Economic and Social Committee and the Committee of the Regions, 10.1.2017, COM (2017)9 final)) on the need to integrate data protection within a wider framework of a data economy based on the free flow of data and the development of new technologies and related issues.

181 In Italy for example until the early 1990's there was professional secrecy covering data reported to the Public Credit Register made inaccessible even to the data subjects involved. See C Frigeni, 'Segnalazioni presso le centrali rischi creditizi e tutela dell'interessato: profili evolutivi' (2013) 66 Banca, borsa e titoli di credito 365, 372 recalling article 3 of the CICR resolution of 16th May 1962 which created the Public Credit Register.

182 Article 5(1) GDPR.

183 Articles 4(11) and 6 GDPR.

184 Articles 16 and 17 GDPR.

185 Aggarwal (n 34) 6.

c) processing is imposed by a legal obligation to which the data controller is subject; d) processing is necessary in order to protect the vital interests of the data subject or of another natural person; e) processing is necessary for the performance of a task of public interest or in the exercise of official authority vested in the controller; f) processing is necessary for the purposes of the legitimate interests pursued by the controller or by a third party except where such interests are overridden by the interests or fundamental rights and freedoms of the data subject which require protection of personal data, in particular where the data subject is a child (the last condition does not apply to processing carried out by public authorities in the performance of their tasks). The basis on which credit intermediaries collect and process data for credit reporting are typically the first and the last (consent and legitimate interest of data controllers). The legitimate interest, also known as the 'balance of interest clause', allows a relatively more flexible area (when compared with the other bases of legitimation) within which data controllers can process data lawfully.[186] In a case dealing with credit data under the regime of the DPD (which contained in its article 7(f) a legitimate interest basis whose implementation was left to Member States), the ECJ excluded that the balance of interest criterion could be limited only to data in public sources and that a national rule that precluded, in the absence of a data subject's consent, "in a categorical and generalized way" the processing of data not appearing in public sources was incompatible with the legitimate interest requirement (which, according to the same ruling, had a direct effect).[187] This 'liberal' reading of processing of data guaranteed the credit industry access to and processing of negative financial data (as the national law under examination of the Court only referred to negative and not positive data).[188] It has also been noted that the Court missed the opportunity of specifying the meaning of balance of interest when considering the legitimate interests of the data controllers versus the infringement of the data subject's rights which occurs when data controllers access and process data that does not appear in public sources.[189]

Under the GDPR the legitimate interest basis is supposed to receive a harmonized implementation (which was not achieved under the DPD with differing national standards).[190] To this end, given that the text of Article 6(f) GDPR

---

186   F Ferretti, 'The Never-Ending European Credit Data Mess', Report for The European Consumer Organization (2017) 46.

187   ECJ, Joined Cases C-468/10 and 469/10, *ASNEF FECEMD v Administración del Estado* [2011] ECLI:EU:C:2011:777.

188   Ferretti, 'The Never-Ending European Credit Data Mess' (n 186) 48.

189   Ibid.

190   The grounds for processing data varies between countries in the EU and according to a 2018 survey, whereas under the previous Data Protection Directive the majority of States

maintains the substance of the previous norm, clues derive from Recital 47, which exemplifies that a legitimate interest of a controller "may provide a legal basis for processing, provided that the interests or the fundamental rights and freedoms of the data subject are not overriding" when there is for example a "relevant and appropriate relationship between the data subject and the controller in situations such as where the data subject is a client or in the service of the controller" (e.g. such as a lending relationship); in any case the existence of a legitimate interest would "need careful assessment including whether a data subject can reasonably expect at the time and in the context of the collection of the personal data that processing for that purpose may take place" (and could be thus excluded where "personal data are processed in circumstances where data subjects do not reasonably expect further processing"). The legitimate interest basis should not apply to the processing for public authorities in the performance of their tasks. Two further examples of legitimate interests of data controllers are identified in the processing for the prevention of fraud, and in the processing for direct marketing purposes.[191]

Other important provisions in the GDPR that are relevant for credit reporting include the duty for lenders to inform consumers when the personal data concerning them are obtained from third parties (such as credit bureaus or credit reporting agencies).[192] There may also be a right for borrowers to receive a preventive notice of an imminent negative reporting (a late or defaulted payment) on their file respectively to the credit register and to private credit bureaus.[193] Consumer applicants have the right to access[194] and rectify any errors in their credit files.[195]

Of particular relevance when taking into account credit scoring and automated decisions, are the provisions which grant consumers not only the right not to be subject to a decision that is taken solely on the basis of 'automated processing', including profiling, (unless it is necessary for entering into

---

obtained data on the basis of 'legitimate interest' *ex* Article 7 of the DPD, the subsequent approval of 'specific laws' for the processing of negative data changed the basis of legitimation and a majority of CRAs use these specific laws as a basis for processing negative data (ACCIS, 2017 Survey (n 56) 21).

191 Recital 47 GDPR.
192 Article 14 GDPR.
193 See for example under Italian law, the "Code of conduct for credit reporting systems operated by private entities regarding consumer credit, creditworthiness and punctuality in payments", article 4, 7th comma and Article 125, c.3, *T.U.B.* (Banking Law) which applies to data transmitted both to the public credit register and to private credit bureaus in case of consumer credit; whereas for other loans the preventive notice applies only when the reporting is made to the public credit register.
194 Article 15 GDPR.
195 Article 16 GDPR.

or performing a contract or the data subject has given explicit consent or if the decision is authorized by Union or Member State law), but also to safeguard in the latter hypotheses "the right to obtain human intervention on the part of the controller, to express his or her point of view and to contest the decision".[196]

A right of access granting data subjects some explanations on automated decisions was already laid down in the 1995 Data Protection Directive, as was a right not to be subject to a decision based solely on automated processing (article 15 of the DPD). The latter provision, due to a formulation considered to be ambiguous, has been interpreted both as a prohibition or as a right to object.[197]

When compared to US regulation, the EU model generally adopts a cautious approach towards computer data processing, which is visible in this provision. Indeed, the FCRA, whilst requiring so-called adverse impact notices, does not however lay down a provision restricting automated processing; it should be noted that the US regulator tends to allow especially new businesses, often free of regulation under a sectorial regime, more leeway to test innovative practices of data processing.[198]

The rationale for the more restrictive European provision (dating back to the DPD) has been identified with a concern over the gradual weakening of the ability of individuals to influence the decision making processes in which they are involved with the contextual growth of automated decision making and profiling processes that are accepted as valid and objective.[199]

It is first of all important to observe that the general prohibition laid down by article 22 of the GDPR concerns decisions that are based *solely* on automated processing (i.e. a decision that is the outcome of an automated processing and is not in any way further assessed before its formalization, even if it is formally ascribed to a human being).[200] Whereas for decision-making

196   Article 22 GDPR.

197   Wachter et al (n. 32) 94, quoting examples from the practice of different Member States. See also I Mendoza, LA Bygrave, 'The Right not to be Subject to Automated Decisions based on Profiling' in T Synodinou, P Jougleux, C Markou, T Prastitou (eds), *EU Internet Law: Regulation and Enforcement* (Springer 2017) 9–10, also noting that with few exceptions (i.e. Germany), there has been scarce litigation in front of national or European courts for the enforcement of Article 15 of the DPD (Ibid 4).

198   Schwartz, 'The EU-US Privacy Collision' (n 63) 1978–79.

199   See Mendoza et al (n 197) 7, quoting the Proposal for a Council Directive concerning the protection of individuals in relation to the processing of personal data, COM (90) 314 final – Syn 287).

200   See Mendoza et al (n 197) 11 recalling, as an example of what does *not* constitute a solely automated decision, the evaluation made by the German Federal Court of Justice in the

processes that are not solely automated – but may include profiling–, the GDPR allows them as long as certain requirements of data protection and its process-ing (lawfulness, fairness, transparency; purpose limitation; data minimization; accuracy; storage limitation) are met.[201]

With regard to solely automated decisions, a first issue, as already under the DPD, is whether Article 22 GDPR should be read as a "right to object" to, or as a "prohibition" of solely automated decisions, which applies whether or not the data subject takes action regarding the processing of their personal data.[202]

In the second place, the 'prohibition' only applies when the decision solely based on automated processing "produces legal effects" concerning the data subject or "similarly significantly affects him or her". Even if there is no further definition of what is intended by 'legal effects' or 'similarly significant' effects for the scope of Article 22, there seems to be agreement that the decision affects someone's legal rights, including under a contract.[203] For the object of this study, the applicability to credit contracts seems confirmed by Recital 71 of the GDPR which expressly makes the typical example of "an automatic refusal of an online credit application".

In the third place, if the exceptions laid down in Article 22(2) GDPR apply (and thus a solely automated decision is allowed), then certain safeguard mea-sures have to be adopted for the protection of the rights and freedoms and legitimate interest of the data subjects, including the right to be informed and the right to obtain human intervention and to challenge the decision.

In this case the consumer must not only be informed, but must also be provided by the data controller with "meaningful information about the logic involved, as well as the significance and the envisaged consequences of such

---

so-called 'Schufa Judgement' of 2014 (n 32), in which the credit-scoring system was held to fall outside the scope of the German Federal Data Protection Act of 1990 (transposing the DPD) because the actual decision was made by a person, *based* on automated elements which prepared evidence for it (emphasis added). An example of a contrary approach is the one taken by the UK Data Protection Authority in an Opinion released in 2017, inter-preting Article 22 as applicable when irrelevant human intervention is involved in the decision process. See Malgieri (n 33) 250.

201   Articles 5(1) and 6 GDPR.

202   The latter is the interpretation found for example in the Article 29 Data Protection Working Party Guidelines (n 95) 19–20 and Annex 2. The topic has been widely debated. In favor of this reading, see also *ex multis* M Brkan, 'Do Algorithms Rule the World? Algorithmic Decision-Making in the Framework of the GDPR and Beyond' (2019) 27 International Journal of Law and Information Technology 91, 98–99 arguing that this interpretation is the result of a systematic interpretation of Article 22 GDPR.

203   Article 29 Data Protection Working Party Guidelines (n 95) 21.

processing for the data subject"[204] including where the personal data have not been obtained from the data subject.[205]

The scope and meaning of the provisions laid down in Article 22 GDPR have received different interpretations. According to some there is no right to "explanation" *ex* article 22 GDPR but rather a "limited right to be informed", and only an *ex ante* explanation is required, regarding the functioning of the system, not the way in which a specific decision was made.[206] Another interpretation holds that a right to explanation *ex post* of automated decisions could be implicit in the right to 'contest' a decision ex Article 22 (3) GDPR.[207] Yet others have for example proposed the adoption of a 'legibility test' (i.e. an assessment of the 'architecture' and of the 'implementation' of the system) as a means for complying with the duty to provide meaningful information about the logic involved in an automated decision-making process (thus overcoming the distinction between an *ex ante* and an *ex post* explanation).[208] The 'right to explanation' arises where the automated decision-making is based solely on automated processes; thus, where there is any involvement (even nominal) of a human decision-making the right of access and information can be avoided.[209]

It has also been highlighted, as already observed, that the right to an explanation even where provided encounters the limits of understanding big data analytics – the problem of "opacity as technical illiteracy".[210] Yet others note that a right to explanation (with the restrictions and ambiguities in form with which it has been couched) may not be the appropriate or feasible solution that matches user needs (transparency does not necessarily secure substantive justice or effective remedies).[211]

---

204   Article 13(2)(f) GDPR.
205   Article 14 (2)(g) GDPR and with reference to the right of access, Article 15(1)(h) GDPR.
206   Wachter et al (n 32) 79–83.
207   Mendoza et al (n 197) 16–17.
208   Malgieri et al (n 33) 244, 245 ff; 259 ff.
209   Wachter et al (n 32) 88.
210   Burrell (n 79) 1. The other two forms of opacity in algorithmic classifications (with the ensuing problems for socially consequential mechanisms of classification and ranking) are 1) opacity as intentional corporate or state secrecy and 2) opacity that derives from the characteristics of machine learning algorithms and the scale required to apply them usefully (ibid 1–2).
211   Edwards et al (n 90) 21–23, who however also highlight that explanations may be useful for scopes other than subject rights, such as helping users trust and make better use of ML systems and allowing, through pedagogical explanations, to avoid the disclosure of protected IP or trade secrets used in models.
        It is interesting to note that with reference to credit data, these rights (laid down by articles 15–22 of the GDPR) may be limited if the data processing is carried out by public

As for the right to obtain human intervention, (by a reviewer who has appropriate authority and capability to change the decision) and the right to challenge the decision, they are closely related to the right to transparency (the right to obtain an explanation as a *de facto* pre-condition for the exercise of the right to obtain human intervention, to express the data subject's point of view and to challenge the decision), as is also highlighted by Recital 71 GDPR.[212]

As previously noted, both US and EU law provide that in certain instances (negative decisions under the FCRA, automated decisions under the GDPR) there is a right to receive information or the highly debated "explanations", as provided in the GDPR for automated decisions and qualified under the wider umbrella of "rights of access" by the data subject. The effectiveness of this type of remedy has been thoroughly questioned and has given rise to scholarship that propounds a right to "technological due process",[213] or that requests "algorithmic accountability" (e.g. laws that govern decision-making by complex algorithms).[214]

The scope of these appeals naturally extends beyond the domain of credit scoring and would apply for all cases of attributions resulting from automated decisions (and in some cases even go as far as proposing that scoring systems should be subject to licensing and audit requirements when they are used

---

entities on the basis of express legislative provisions (such as those tied to goals of monetary and currency policy, payment systems, control over intermediaries in the financial and credit markets and of their stability) – as is the case in the Italian data protection law (article 2-undecies, comma 1 letter d) of the Privacy Code).

212   See Article 29 Data Protection Working Party Guidelines (n 95) 27.

213   Notoriously Keats Citron, 'Technological Due Process' (n 91); Keats Citron et al (n 80) 19; Crawford et al (n 162); NM Richards, JH King, 'Three Paradoxes of Big Data' (2013) 66 Stanford Law Review Online 41, 43 ff; on the role of due process in predicting processes automated by data mining, DJ Steinbock, 'Data Matching, Data Mining, and Due Process' (2005) 40 Georgia Law Review 1.

214   ME Kaminiski, 'The Right to Explanation, Explained' (2019) 34 Berkeley Technology Law Journal 189, 190; M Ananny, K Crawford, 'Seeing Without Knowing: Limitations of the Transparency Ideal and Its Application to Algorithmic Accountability' (2016) 20 New Media & Society 973 who critically interrogate the efficacy of transparency for understanding and governing algorithmic systems and propose an alternative typology of algorithmic accountability; DR Deasai, JA Kroll, 'Trust But Verify: A Guide to Algorithms and the Law' (2017) 31 Harvard Journal of Law & Technology 1; JA Kroll, J Huey, S Barocas, EW Felten, JR Reidenberg, DG Robinson, H Yu, 'Accountable Algorithms' (2017) 165 University of Pennsylvania Law Review 633 also critically assessing transparency as the tool for accountability and proposing other technological tools to ensure 'procedural regularity'; PT Kim, 'Auditing Algorithms for Discrimination'(2017) 166 University of Pennsylvania Law Review Online 189; see also Brkan (n 202) 110, specifying that logically speaking, "algorithmic transparency" should precede "algorithmic accountability".

in critical areas such as employment, insurance and health care).[215] Current regulation according to many is inadequate to ensure this type of right; some authors have noted however that the GDPR provisions on a right to explanation come close to guaranteeing a form of "technical due process" or of "qualified transparency".[216]

Finally, as observed above when examining the FCRA and the questions regarding its effectiveness as a tool for ensuring accuracy of data reporting, the issue of liability in case of erroneous or inaccurate reporting is fundamental.

The GDPR currently states in its Article 82 a right to compensation for "any person who has suffered material or non-material damage as a result of an infringement" of the Regulation. Previously, under article 23 of the DPD, Member States had to provide that compensation would be awarded to any person who had suffered damage as a result of an unlawful processing operation or of any act incompatible with the national provisions adopted pursuant to the DPD (basically laying down a hypothesis of tortious liability).

There were relevant differences in the implementation of this provision in the DPD by Member States.[217] These included *inter alia* whether there was a presumption of fault against the data controller in case of data breach (*ex* article 23(2) of the DPD – a presumption held for example in the Belgian, Portuguese and Italian transposition, but refused by Finland, France and Luxemburg) and whether the damage included not only material but also immaterial or moral damage (with for example the German and the UK case law initially oriented towards recognizing moral damage only where there was also material damage; a trend overturned in the UK by the Vidal-Hall case).[218] With regards not only to the type of damages that can be recovered but also to the nature of the injury, under Italian law for example, where actions under tort do not exclude actions under contract, there is case law recognizing incorrect or inaccurate reporting of a missed or delayed payment both as a tort, for which material (such as higher costs of credit and loss of a chance of

---

215 Keats Citron et al (n 80) 21–22.
216 See Kaminiski (n 214) 198 and 210 borrowing from Frank Pasquale's definition in *The Black Box Society* who defines 'qualified transparency' as a system of targeted revelations of different degrees of depth and scope aimed at different recipients.
217 For an overview see for example E Truli, 'The General Data Protection Regulation and Civil Liability', in M Bakhoum, M Conde Gallego, B Mackenrodt, et al, *Personal Data in Competition, Consumer Protection and Intellectual Property Law* (Springer 2018) 303; see also the Report by the European Union Agency for Fundamental Rights, 'Access to data protection remedies in EU Member States' (2013).
218 *Vidal-Hall v Google Inc* [2014] EWHC 13 (QB), 16 January 2014. See Truli (n 217) 317 ff and references therein.

timely access to credit) and moral compensation (i.e. injury to the borrower's reputation) can be awarded, and as a breach of contractual duties of good faith between the borrower and the lender (who reports inaccurate data to third parties).[219]

With the entry into force of the GDPR in 2018 and the repeal of the DPD (and the national provisions transposing it which were in conflict with the new regulation), the reference for data protection liability became article 82 of the GDPR. The harmonized system of liability laid down by article 82 GDPR is more comprehensive when compared with the provisions in the DPD and according to some it directly addresses several of the difficulties arising from what had been the DPD's divergent implementation by Member States,[220] such as clarifying the recoverability of both material and immaterial damages;[221] making the data processor potentially liable along with the data controller and in such a case laying down a hypothesis of joint liability;[222] and confirming a presumption of fault now extended both to the controller or the processor.[223]

In addition to compensation, data breaches may also require specific remedies (such as injunctive reliefs to stop an infringement, correct or erase inaccurate or false data and so forth) as already recognized by legislative provisions of Member States under the DPD, and as expressly recognized by Article 79(1) of the GDPR which speaks of a right to "an effective judicial remedy" (against a controller or a processor). Finally, it should be recalled that the GDPR (Article 83) also lays down a detailed system of administrative fines to be implemented by Data Protection Authorities.[224]

---

219   The tort was expressly classified by the Italian Privacy Code as a tort for the exercise of hazardous activities under article 2050 of the Civil Code (see Article 15(1) of the d.lgs. 196/2003, later abrogated with the entry into force of the GDPR). For a reconstruction and for references to case law of the Court of Cassation and of the Italian Banking and Financial Ombdudsman (ABF), see Frigeni (n 181) 376 ff; U Minneci, 'Erronea segnalazione alla centrale rischi: profili rimediali', (2004) 22 Rivista critica di diritto privato 89; F Mezzanotte, 'Centrali rischi private e 'diritto di preavviso' della segnalazione' (2017) 33 La nuova giurisprudenza civile commentata n 2, 303, 307–308; see also A Sciarrone Alibrandi, 'Trasmissione dei dati alle centrali rischi: consenso e informazione dell'interessato', in A Sciarrone Alibrandi (ed) *Centrale dei rischi. Profili civilistici* (Giuffrè 2005) 61 ff.

220   See Truli (n 217) 325 ff.

221   Article 82(1) GDPR.

222   Article 82(2) and 82(4) GDPR.

223   Article 82(3) GDPR.

224   See, for an overview of the interaction between Article 82 and Article 83 GDPR, J Chamberlain, J Reichel, 'The Relationship Between Damages and Administrative Fines in the EU General Data Protection Regulation' (2020) Stockholm Faculty of Law Research Paper Series n. 72.

With reference to the type of injuries that can arise for individuals from data breaches, Recital 85 of the GDPR expressly lists among others "financial loss" and "damage to reputation", thus recalling fundamental hypothesis of material and immaterial injury that can arise from erroneous or inaccurate credit reporting. In such instances, the right to also obtain injunctive relief (or specific performance if considered from the perspective of the contractual relationship between the borrower and the lender) is crucial to ensuring an effective protection of the interests of the data subject.[225]

3.2.2   *Antidiscrimination*

As highlighted previously, along with data protection issues, the development of credit scoring also immediately triggered questions of antidiscrimination. The risks of discriminatory outcomes are now analyzed with reference to data processing, whilst their impact on access to credit are considered in Chapter 5. Some of the issues have been examined when considering the developments of algorithmic credit scoring; however, even before these more recent technological advancements rekindled antidiscrimination concerns, the practice of credit scoring had long caught the attention of scholars, practitioners and legislators. One of the first issues was whether the practice of credit reporting would require *ad hoc* regulation or whether existing antidiscrimination laws could be applied efficiently (a question that is now being re-proposed with regards to automated decision-making processes and the expansion of algorithmic credit scoring).

In the United States, Congress chose to enact a specific federal statute, the Equal Credit Opportunity Act (ECOA) in 1974. Scope of the ECOA is the prevention of discriminatory lending practices and the increase of credit availability for all creditworthy applicants. The Act, formally Title VII of the Consumer Credit Protection Act, prohibits discrimination on the basis of race, color, religion, national origin, sex, marital status, age, receipt of public assistance or good faith exercise of any rights under the Consumer Credit Protection Act.[226] The Act also requires creditors to provide applicants, upon request, with the reasons underlying decisions to deny or revoke credit (so-called adverse impact notices)[227] and a copy of the appraisal report used in connection with the applicant's application for a loan that is or would have been secured by

---

225   On Italian law see for example Frigeni (n 181) 398 ff.; on Germany and the UK, see Truli (n 217) 18–19 and 28–29.
226   15 U.S.C. § 1691(a).
227   15 U.S.C. §1691(d).

a lien on residential real property.[228] The scarcity of litigation (and enforce-ment) does not allow an appraisal of the effectiveness of the ECOA.[229]

The ECOA can also apply to algorithmic traders.[230] Indeed, some authors have observed that the use of algorithmic profiling for the allocation of resources "is, in a certain sense, inherently discriminatory: profiling takes place when data subjects are grouped in categories according to variables, and deci-sions are made on the basis of subjects falling within so-defined groups".[231]

A violation of the ECOA usually translates into two types of conduct; dis-parate treatment, banning intentionally different treatment of potential borrowers, and disparate impact, prohibiting the use of apparently neutral criteria that however result in disparate treatment of applicants without a 'legitimate business need'.[232] The 'legitimate business need' defense requires proof of a demonstrable relationship between the challenged policy and creditworthiness.[233] Some authors have noted that it will be easier for algo-rithmic lenders to establish a business necessity defense, unless plaintiffs can offer a non-discriminatory alternative option to model creditworthiness; this assuming that plaintiffs could pinpoint policies that led to discriminatory out-comes even absent access to the models and data (protected by trade secrecy), and understand how big-data credit-scoring works.[234]

Others, (i.e. the National Consumer Law Center (NCLC)) believe that it will be harder for algorithmic lenders than for traditional lenders to establish the 'demonstrable relationship' given that the data used by traditional models

228   15 U.S.C. §1691(e).

229   Keats Citron et al (n 80) 15. In case of discrimination in home mortgage loans or home improvement loans, see also the Fair Housing Act (Sec. 800 [42 U.S.C. 3601 note] Short Title). See also JH Matheson, 'The Equal Credit Opportunity Act: A Functional Failure' (1984) 21 Harvard Journal on Legislation 371 arguing that due to several flaws, especially its (private and public) enforcement mechanisms, the structure of the ECOA has proved fallacious in combating credit discrimination.

230   See definition of 'creditors' under ECOA (15 U.S.C. §1691a(e) 2015). See also Bruckner (n 64) 32; Hurley et al (n 46) 191.

231   B Goodman, S Flaxman, 'European Union regulations on algorithmic decision-making and a 'right to explanation'' (2017) 38 AI Magazine n. 3, 3. On the specific hypothesis of discrimination tied to Big Data see infra.

232   Bruckner (n 64) 33 and literature cited therein. However, according to some the latter may be difficult; see for example Hurley et al (n 46) 193 according to whom it is not certain that disparate-impact claims are available under ECOA as the statutory text makes no mention of disparate impact analysis (even if ECOA's implementing regulations do).

233   Bruckner (n 64) 35; also citing 12 C.F.R. pt.202 supp. I § 2020.6(a)-2 (2013) Official Staff Interpretations.

234   Hurley et al (n 46) 195.

have a more understandable relation with the past and future probability of timely repayment of obligations.[235]

In the European Union, the principle of antidiscrimination – which is laid down in the Charter of Fundamental Rights (under Article 21 prohibiting discrimination on any ground and Article 23 imposing equality between men and women in all areas) and in the ECHR (in Article 14 and Protocol n. 12), other than in the Treaty (Articles 8, 10, and 19 TFEU) – is in practice construed as a principle which governs market interactions, as a result of an ensemble of sectorial legislation that identifies legally protected groups and prohibits discrimination in specific types of market interactions.[236]

The framework of reference for credit is not constituted by a specific piece of regulation, as is the case with the ECOA in the United States but is rather designed by the combined provisions of several general directives which establish minimum standards.[237] Only very recently, with the new Proposal for a Directive on consumer credits[238] an express reference to antidiscrimination is found in specific regulation of credit contracts: article 6 of the Directive proposal requires Member States to ensure that consumers legally resident in the Union are not discriminated on ground of their nationality or place of residence on an any ground as referred to in Article 21 of the Charter of Fundamental Rights of the European Union, when those consumers request,

---

235   Bruckner (n 64) 36.

236   P Hacker, 'Teaching fairness to artificial intelligence: Existing and novel strategies against algorithmic discrimination under EU law' (2018) 55 Common Market Law Review 1143, 1151; see P Craig, G de Búrca, *EU Law. Text, Cases and Materials* (6th ed Oxford University Press 2015) 892; see also E Ellis, P Watson, *EU Anti-Discrimination Law* (2nd ed Oxford University Press 2012).

237   These include the Racial Equality Directive (Council Directive 2000/43/EC of 29 June 2000 implementing the principle of equal treatment between persons irrespective of racial or ethnic origin, [2000] OJ L180/22) which lays down the principle of equal treatment between persons irrespective of racial or ethnic origin in several areas; the Framework Employment Directive (Council Directive 2000/78/EC of 27 November 2000 establishing a general framework for equal treatment in employment and occupation [2000] OJ L 303/16) which protects against discrimination based on religion or belief, disability, age or sexual orientation in employment matters; the Goods and Services Directive (Council Directive 2004/113/EC of 13 December 2004 implementing the principle of equal treatment between men and women in the access to supply of goods and services [2004] OJ L373/37) which guards against gender discrimination outside of the employment context (i.e. in access to publicly available goods and services); and the Gender Equality Directive recast (Directive 2006/54/EC of the European Parliament and of the Council of 5 July 2006 on the implementation of the principle of equal opportunities and equal treatment of men and women in matters of employment and occupation (recast)[2006] OJ L 204/23) against discrimination in employment.

238   COM (2021) 347 final.

conclude or hold a credit agreement or crowdfunding credit services within the Union.

Especially relevant for access to credit and consumer credit contracts are Directive 2004/43 implementing the principle of equal treatment between persons irrespective of racial or ethnic origin, and Directive 2004/113 implementing the principle of equal treatment between men and women in the access to supply of goods and services (which must also be interpreted in conformity with the principles laid down in the European Charter on Fundamental Rights).[239] In a famous judgment relating to insurance and related financial services, the *Test-Achats* case,[240] the ECJ interpreted Directive 2004/113 in the light of the CFREU (striking down Article 5(2) of the Directive which allowed, without temporal limitation and against the so-called rule of unisex premiums and benefits, proportionate differences in individuals' premiums based on sex as the relevant factor in the assessment of risk based on relevant and accurate actuarial and statistical data). The judgement laid down an absolute prohibition of discrimination on the ground of sex in the access to financial services (becoming an important precedent for cases related to payment protection insurances (PPI's) for instance).[241]

Historically, this piecemeal framework was due to the initial scope of antidiscrimination laws, that is to facilitate mobility and the functioning of the internal market (i.e. combating discrimination based on nationality between EU-citizens or combating gender discrimination in employment). Only later did antidiscrimination laws develop into tools protecting fundamental rights in and of themselves.[242] Secondary EU law has turned the antidiscrimination principle (initially originated and limited to labor law and antidiscrimination law (as equal treatment of men and women)) into a general principle of private

---

239   See OO Cherednychenko, 'The EU Charter of Fundamental Rights and Consumer Credit: Towards Responsible Lending?', in H Collins (Ed), *European Contract Law and the Charter of Fundamental Rights* (Intersentia 2017) 147–148, recalling the *Test-Achats* case; and I Benhör, *EU Consumer Law and Human Rights* (Oxford University Press 2013) 130 ff.

240   ECJ Case C-236/09, *Association belge des Consommateurs Test-Achats ASBL v Conseil des ministres*, [2011] ECLI:EU:C:2011:100.

241   OO Cherednychenko (n 239) ibid, questioning whether this absolute prohibition of discrimination may not, under certain circumstances, be to the detriment of women, who on average live longer. See also N Reich, 'Non-Discrimination and the Many Faces of Private Law in the Union – Some Thoughts After the "Test-Achats" Judgement' (2011) 2 European Journal of Risk Regulation 283.

242   R Gellert, K De Vries, P De Hert, S Gutwirth, 'A comparative analysis of antidiscrimination and data protection legislations' in B Custers et al (eds) *Discrimination and privacy in the information society. Data mining and profiling in large databases* (Springer 2021) 61, 67.

law (whilst maintaining however its character of "a market-bound rule directed at fair access first, to labor, and later, to the consumer market").[243] (On the effects of antidiscrimination more generally on access to credit see Chapter 5).

Just as in US antidiscrimination doctrine (whose model, more in general, strongly influenced the European one),[244] EU doctrine also distinguishes between direct (or disparate treatment) and indirect discrimination, which respond to different instances.[245] This legislation however does not apply to all market interactions, but only to specific areas.

In the second place, it was enacted mostly before the widespread use of automated and machine-learning decision applications, and its extension to the latter (so as to cover so-called algorithmic discrimination) is neither straightforward nor easy, for reasons already highlighted earlier when examining the US model. These include the fact that algorithmic processes may bypass the material and personal scope of existing antidiscrimination legislation; that the implied predictive accuracy of ML models provides an easy justification for many effects of indirect discrimination; and that the proof that the model is wrong (in order to refute the latter claims) is almost impossible for the victims who lack knowledge, access to training data and to model specifications.[246]

According to some authors, certain discriminatory outcomes deriving from ML techniques of data processing could however also fall within the protective scope of data protection law, more specifically under the GDPR in the EU context; this could include the requirement of fair data processing, (laid down in Article 5(1)(a) GDPR), and the requirement of accuracy (Article 5(1)(d) GDPR which would be infringed where biased training data typically have low

---

243   H-W Micklitz, 'The Visible Hand of European Regulatory Private Law. The Transformation of European Private Law from Autonomy to Functionalism in Competition and Regulation', (2008) EUI Working Papers Law 2008/14, 16, further questioning whether "these new values have to made compatible with the different patterns of justice, with social (distributive justice) and with corrective justice" and whether it is linked to 'access justice' "or whether it reaches beyond and implies distributive effects". See on the point *infra* chapter 5.

244   See for example G de Búrca, 'The Trajectories of European and American Antidiscrimination Law', (2012) 60 American Journal of Comparative Law 1, 4–5.

245   Direct discrimination occurs where one person is treated less favorably than another is or would be treated in a comparable situation on grounds of membership in a protected class. Indirect discrimination occurs where an apparently neutral provision, criterion or practice would put persons of one protected group at a particular disadvantage compared with others unless that provision is objectively justified by a legitimate aim and the means of achieving it are appropriate and necessary. (See e.g. Art. 2(2)(a) and Art. 2(2)(b) Directive 2000/43/EC; Art.2(a) and Art. 2(b) Directive 2004/113/EC).

246   Hacker (n 236) 1154 ff.

predictive accuracy).[247] In addition, a violation of Article 22(3) GDPR could be envisaged where there is a lack of bias detection and of minimization strategies (which should be included within the procedural safeguards of the interests of data subjects required by Recital 71 GDPR).[248]

3.3 Small Business Lending and Credit Scoring

Before drawing some conclusive considerations on the relationship between credit scoring and policies of responsible credit, a few final remarks can be reserved to the practice of creditworthiness assessment for small businesses, that share some – but not all – of the issues highlighted for individual consumer credit scoring.

For small and medium-sized corporate borrowers, the activity of screening and monitoring of borrowers is typically carried out by the banks themselves and requires the analysis of additional factors compared to those taken into account in individual credit scoring. The difficulties, and subsequent costs, in evaluating this category of borrowers is furthermore given by the fact that there is limited information on these borrowers in the public domain (compared, for example, to large corporate borrowers that are monitored by credit rating agencies). Studies have highlighted that the opacity in information between insiders and outsiders makes small firms particularly vulnerable in terms of credit availability; perceived problems of adverse selection and moral hazard on behalf of potential providers of credit, are exacerbated by the difficulties in accessing information on the small firms. These small firms on the other hand, are further crippled by the fact that they do not have access to public capital markets and are strongly dependent on financial institutions for funding.[249]

As mentioned earlier, small business lending technologies include both transactions-based lending that uses hard information (financial statement lending based on the strength of balance sheet and income statements of the

---

247   Ibid 1171–1172 ff; Gellert et al (n 242) 80–81. See also Recital 71 GDPR.

248   Hacker (n 236) 1177; Art.29 Working Party Guidelines (n 95) 16. See also Mendoza et al (n 197) 12. On the need to minimize algorithmic discrimination when processing big data (which may result not only in "infringements of the fundamental rights of individuals, but also in differential treatment of and indirect discrimination against groups of people with similar characteristics") see also the Resolution of the European Parliament of 14 March 2017 on fundamental rights implications of big data: privacy, data protection, non-discrimination, security and law-enforcement, n. 19–22 (2016/2225(INI), [2018] OJ C 263/82).

249   Berger et al (n 9) 1.

firm (quantitative financial ratios); asset-based lending that takes account of the quality of available collateral (collateral ratios); small-business credit scoring, that uses an adaptation of the statistical techniques used in consumer lending), and so-called relationship lending, based on soft information of different nature deriving from ongoing direct contact with the firm over time (such as loans, provision of other financial services and products, analysis of the business environment of the firm, and so forth) that often help overcome the informational opacity problem.[250] This last consideration can find additional support in socio-cultural factors which highlight not only the status of borrowers, but also the type and role of lenders in a certain territory.

Many banking institutions were born as rural, artisanal or other small-scale production savings institutions, often as forms of mutual or cooperative banks – a form that many institutions maintain to this day.[251] The structure, governance and mission of these banking institutions has always entailed a personal relationship between the bank and its clients, often direct stakeholders in the institution (as members/owners and customers) and a strong tie with the local communities in which the banks operate. The tie between cooperative banks and SMEs is also very strong, with cooperative banks often representing an important channel through which SMEs obtain access to credit.[252] It is only consequential that creditworthiness assessment for these

---

250   Ibid 6.

251   In Europe for example, statistics from 2019 elaborated by the European Association of Cooperative Banks, report that in the European Union cooperative banks hold on average 20% of the market share for deposits and 30% of market share for SMEs financing (European Association of Cooperative Banks, Facts and Figures 2019); the European Economic and Social Committee reports respectively 26% share of the market for deposits and 27% of loans to SMEs (European Economic and Social Committee, 'Europe's cooperative banking models study', Revised edition 2018, 15). (The percentages within the with Member States however differ greatly. See for a detailed analysis F Lang, S Signore, S Gvetadze, 'The role of cooperative banks and smaller institutions for the financing of SMEs and small midcaps in Europe' (2016) European Investment Fund Research & Market Analysis Working Paper 2016/36, 28 ff).
       In the United States Community banks, having similar scopes, in 2019 held around 13% of all domestic deposits of banks and credit unions (FDIC 2019 Summary of Deposits Highlights, FDIC Quarterly Vol 14, (2020) p. 31), whilst Community banks (as defined in a 2012 FDIC Community Banking Study) in 2012 represented 95% of US banking organizations (see FDIC Community Banking Study, 2012); in 2020 the estimate was 97%.

252   An important factor that characterizes and distinguishes the EU and the US economies should be recalled: according to the ECB, whilst in the Euro area financial intermediaries (especially banks) are the main channel of funding for borrowers in the economy (counting for more than 70% of the external financing of the non-financial corporate sector, whilst less than 30% derives from financial markets and other funding), in the United States the percentages are inverted. See Lang et al (n 251) 5.

particular clients of these banking institutions is often still based on relation-ship lending, which is also perceived as one of the points of strength of this type of banking model. Here the social and cultural factors that tie these insti-tutions to their local communities (along with the structure and mission of cooperative banking), are an important determinant of the modalities with which lending and creditworthiness assessment are carried out for small businesses.

When compared with consumer lending, the growth in the use of credit scoring for small business firms consolidated itself later in time. Some empiri-cal studies seem to indicate that the use of credit scoring for small businesses facilitates (and reduces the costs of) both the decision process on grant-ing credit and the monitoring process of creditworthiness of borrowers for banks.[253]

Several of the economies of scale highlighted earlier when comparing the usage of 'hard information' versus 'soft information' as the input for lending decisions has allowed small business borrowers to access an enlarged lend-ing market. Indeed, standardized information and a gradual replacement of 'relationship' lending with other lending technologies has entailed that large banks have expanded small-business lending activity and this activity no lon-ger necessarily occurs only at the local level. The easier circulation of infor-mation on borrowers has also enhanced the securitization of small business loans. Consequently, the potential credit market for this category of borrowers has widened alongside the development of technologies that facilitated the growth in the usage of credit scoring models.

A widely used system of credit scoring for small and medium sized cor-porate borrowers is the so-called 'CAMEL' classification, which takes into

Regarding the United States, see the Small Business Lending Survey published by the FDIC in 2018, according to which notwithstanding a decrease of almost one third in the number of small banks (i.e. banks with under $10 billion in assets) between 2009 and 2017, at the end of 2017 small banks held nearly 53% of small loans to businesses, although holding only 17% of banking assets. (FDIC, Small Business Lending Survey 2018, p.5). On the impact of the Dodd-Frank Act on the activities of community banking, see TD Marsh, JW Norman, 'The Impact of Dodd-Frank on Community Banks' (2013) American Enterprise Institute, Wake Forest University Legal Studies Paper No.2302392. On the EU see *supra* and F Lang et al (n 251) 28 ff.

253 G Albareto, R Felici, E Sette, 'Does credit scoring improve the selection of borrowers and credit quality?'(2016) Banca d'Italia Working Papers, n. 1090, 5 and 17–19 who also high-light, as a result of an empirical study on loans to small firms in Italy, an increase in the quality of loans that are granted using credit scoring techniques with an overall positive impact on the performance of banks (ibid 22–23).

account different factors (Capital, Asset quality, Management, Earning, and Liquidity).[254] Evaluation of borrowers, however, is not only an initial assessment (as already seen in the case of loans to single individuals and in the case of large corporate borrowers), but also requires the subsequent monitoring on the performance of loans, for which loan officers are responsible.

The outcome of the monitoring activity of small and medium sized corporate borrowers can lead, unlike what occurs for individual consumer loans, to the triggering of a series of remedial actions that borrowers agree to beforehand by signing detailed covenants at the moment in which the loan contract is concluded. Whilst these covenants may bind borrowers to maintain their assets or certain levels of leverage, or the payment of dividends, or to avoid additional loans, they also confer onto lenders the power to adopt remedial actions when signals of non-performance result from the monitoring activity. The remedial actions may imply an intervention in the financial structure of the borrower-company, including restrictions on certain activities and requirements of modifications on the company's management.[255]

3.4   Comparative Overview and Conclusive Remarks on Credit Scoring and Responsible Lending

It is now possible to draw a few conclusive comparative remarks on the problems posed by credit reporting and on the relevance that credit scoring has for policies of responsible credit.

A first common feature of the systems that have been examined is the emergence, as a phenomenon triggered by the growth of markets for consumer credit, and then as a factor for its further affirmation, of complex forms for the reduction of information asymmetries between lenders and borrowers regarding the creditworthiness of the latter; for the prevention of moral hazard of borrowers through 'reputation collateral'; and for efficient screening of credit applications. These forms have translated (relatively early in the United States, later in European countries) into an industry of credit reporting. Whereas this industry has remained mostly private in the United States, in European States

---

254   See J Armour et al, *Principles of Financial Regulation* (Oxford University Press 2016) 284–285. The CAMEL procedure analyzes the different factors recalled so as to assess if there is sufficient equity available to afford protection against fluctuations of performance; the nature and the condition in which the assets of the company are; the quality of management; the projected earnings of the firm; the relation between project earnings and cash flow in order to allow repayment of loans and interest. Ibid.

255   Ibid 286.

it has frequently been consolidated within supervisory activity of financial regulations and has been made the object of prudential regulations (often with the establishment of specific organisms such as public credit registers, having the specific scope of collecting credit reports); European States only later also registered the arrival and affirmation of private credit bureaus. Given the sensitive nature of the personal information that these subjects collected and processed and then sold, the earliest regulatory interventions were motivated by data protection concerns.

In consideration of the different regulatory background regarding privacy and data protection (a fundamental right in the EU tradition, enshrined in articles 7 and 8 of the Charter of fundamental rights of the EU and Article 16 of the TFEU), the tools at the disposal of regulators were different; from this point of view it has been observed how the US federal legislator forged an *ad hoc* instrument for the activity of credit reporting (the FCRA and later the ECOA) with the scope of striking a balance between the interests of free circulation of the industry and the protection issues of data subjects; a balance which according to many observers, tips the scale towards the industry given the inefficiency of the corrective measures at the disposal of data subjects and the reduction of the actions (in tort) at their disposal in case of injury to their reputation.

In the EU, the activity of credit reporting fell more readily within the scope of the general data protection legislation (starting with the DPD and later with the GDPR). The latter Regulation also strengthened an instrument much debated and invoked with the affirmation of ML techniques used in decision making, namely specific safeguard rules for solely automated decisions. However, it should also be mentioned that within the EU (and thus within Member States) there is no univocal dataset nor uniform standard for credit reporting and the picture remains fragmented. On the other side, whilst it would be reasonable to assume that a specific regulation, such as the one approved in the United States, would envisage and discipline all the various aspects and issues involved in credit reporting, it has been observed that the most recent applications of algorithmic and big data credit scoring fall beyond the scope of the existing regulation.

With regards to the interaction between credit data collection and sharing and responsible credit, there are multiple considerations to be made.

First of all, it has been held that credit sharing can help promote a 'responsible credit culture' by "discouraging excessive debt and rewarding responsible borrowing and repayment".[256]

More information could be associated with the goal of 'affordability' of loans under a dual perspective. The first is tied to enhanced consumer mobility. A system of credit reporting that allows access to information to all lenders can help open the market to additional actors and potentially provide consumers with more choice (including products that better respond to consumers' needs and financial capacity) and more transparent pricing of credit products.

The second is tied to the duty of assessing creditworthiness of borrowers. When more information is available the assessment potentially can be more thorough and help avoid consumer over-indebtedness.[257] Under the condition, however, that the information gathered and processed is accurate; studies have highlighted the risk that more information accumulated by a credit reporting agency can also mean more erroneous information, with growing costs to maintain accuracy.[258]

As previously observed, these potentially positive effects for the implementation of responsible lending policies can conflict with data protection concerns. These arise especially from misuse of data, from the consequences of inaccurate data processing and from the financial exclusion that may follow negative reporting.

There are however further problematic aspects tied to responsible credit that can be taken into account and that have already in part been highlighted above.

There is, as previously noted, a potential 'tension' between the use of techniques of credit scoring, based on generalizations, and the practice of 'individualized' creditworthiness assessment that policies of responsible lending would seem to indicate as more appropriate to avoid over-indebtedness.[259] However, given the alleged efficiency of scoring as a tool for the expansion of credit markets and its potential (especially with the development of algorithmic scoring) in reaching consumers who would otherwise be excluded from access to credit, it seems that turning back to old techniques of traditional creditworthiness assessment would not only be unrealistic but also

---

256   World Bank, Global Financial Development Report (n 49) 131; see also A de Janvry, C McIntosh, E Sadoulet, 'The Supply and Demand Side Impacts of Credit Market Information' (2010) 93 Journal of Development Economics 173; Padilla et al, 'Sharing Default Information as a Borrower Discipline Device' (n 48).
257   See CEPS-ECRI Task Force Report (n 52) 1, 5.
258   Maurer et al (n 176) 619–620.
259   Ramsay, 'From Truth in Lending to Responsible Lending' (n 94) 59.

counter-productive even for responsible credit policies. Indeed, as effectively affirmed, "If credit scoring has the potential to democratize access to credit then one benefit of the responsible lending standard is to focus attention on credit scoring systems and ensure greater transparency in their operation".[260] Additional aspects come into play and require attention.

First of all, avoiding that credit scoring is used to single vulnerable borrowers and make them the target of predatory lending practices. The issue has been deemed to fall within the scope of data protection, such as the GDPR in the EU for example. As previously highlighted, the GDPR lays safeguards against solely automated decisions; these safeguards may also extend to automated online advertising relying on automated tools for target advertising based on profiling.[261]

In the second place, the need to allow a major degree of transparency in credit scoring: this is relevant both *before* a decision to grant or deny credit is taken (i.e. the need for consumers and potential borrowers to understand and 'manage' the way their credit reports and credit scoring are built) and *after*, as part of a more general right of 'access' represented by what is defined as 'technological due process'.

Transparency serves as a fundamental instrument for consumer confidence (and for financial planning and consumer empowerment),[262] and for financial literacy. Access to the consumer's credit file on transparent terms ultimately allows the consumer with positive records to have more negotiating power with lenders over the terms of the credit product.[263] All this contributes, as a further and mirrored consequence, to make transparency a device for 'borrower discipline', which is of strategic importance from the perspective of lenders.[264]

Finally, responsible credit also requires accuracy, not only on behalf of the information that borrowers provide when applying for a loan ('responsible borrowing'), but also on behalf of those who elaborate data and transform it into credit scores.

Given the key role that creditworthiness/affordability assessment in its various forms has in implementing policies of responsible credit, and given that this assessment is delegated to specialized third parties (credit reporting/reference agencies or credit rating agencies for corporations) it is evident that an

---

260   Ibid 60.
261   See Article 29 Data Protection Working Party Guidelines (n 95) 22.
262   CEPS-ECRI Task Force Report (n 52) 14.
263   Ibid.
264   The term naturally is borrowed from Padilla et al 'Sharing Default Information as a Borrower Discipline Device' (n 48).

efficient instrument that allows an effective and timely correction of errors and contains incentives for a diligent construction of credit reports is crucial.

The issue is not only tied to protection and transparency regarding one's data, nor is it only tied to an *ex post* possible access to the factors that were taken into account during the decision-making process, whether human or automated. The issue is also tied to a possibility of 'control' (through request of correction): where this remains a nominal right that is burdensome, costly and inefficient as regards the result, then the right of access and the issue of transparency run the risk of remaining blunt weapons, which leave the subject/consumer aware but helpless in front of a mistreatment of his data or an identity theft and a consequent injury to his reputation and to his financial interests.

From a theoretical point of view the instruments, it seems, should thus be threefold. An effective right to intervene and request correction or erasure of false or inaccurate data; a system of disincentive for careless reporting (a preventive measure to avoid the costs of lengthy procedures of *ex post* correction and the – quantifiable – damages in terms of loss of a chance that affect consumers in the meantime, also in consideration of the effects that breaches of privacy have in the digital age);[265] a form of compensation for the measurable loss deriving from an injury to one's reputation and creditworthiness.

Another way of putting it is that creditworthiness can be envisioned as a right, with an economically measurable value, and whose injury requires compensation. Creditworthiness is a tool of individual 'market identity' which allows individuals to 'define themselves by their interactions and integrity in the marketplace'.[266] An impairment of one's ability to obtain credit because of injury (i.e. theft, mistreatment) to one's personal data affects the conditions with which an individual can engage on the market in a way that according to some is analogous to deprivation of property (theft of personal information);[267] or more generally to injury to one's personality right (through false or inaccurate data which infringe reputation). The duty of care of this right can be left with the tools of an extracontractual liability (as envisaged for example under the FCRA and the GDPR) or (additionally, in systems where concurrence between actions is permitted) with the tools of contract, where

---

265   For an overview of the different possible liability regimes and their analysis from a law and economics perspective, see Blair et al (n 165) 292–296; and Maurer et al (n 176) 617 ff, building an economic model to examine the tradeoff between accuracy (desirable but costly) and competing interests.

266   See D Keats Citron, 'Reservoirs of Danger: The Evolution of Public and Private Law at the Dawn of the Information Age', (2007) 80 South California Law Review 24, 295.

267   Ibid.

negligent reporting is construed as a violation of duties of contractual good faith between the lender and the borrower.

The issue is not distant from the problems raised by negligent credit rating for undertakings examined in the previous chapter, where the rating is the translation into a circulating 'grade' of the creditworthiness assessment of an issuer and it *de facto* constitutes the precondition to access the capital markets.

Having examined in the previous and current Chapters the origin of the legal duties of conducting creditworthiness assessments and the concrete techniques with which this assessment is carried out for corporate and institutional borrowers, and for individuals and small businesses, the analysis can now turn in the next Chapter to the role of creditworthiness as a tool for the implementation of responsible credit policies.

Creditworthiness Assessment and Other Contractual Duties as Tools of 'Responsible Credit': the Case of Consumer Loans

Introduction

When responsible credit is considered in its most commonly interpreted meaning, it relates to the conclusion of 'responsible' credit agreements between lenders and consumers. It is around this interpretation of the notion that legislation containing references to 'responsible lending' has been introduced in several legal systems. Indeed, the type of agreements that were first targeted for reform after the 2007–2008 global financial crisis included consumer credit and mortgage credit. Within the wider framework of these contracts, there are some common recurring instruments (adopted for example by the two EU directives concerning these contracts and by the reform of existing federal and state legislation in the United States) aiming at the implementation of 'responsible credit' policies. These include several precontractual duties that can be reconducted under the wider umbrella of disclosure duties, duties of consultation, the assessment of the creditworthiness of potential borrowers, and the regulation of certain economic parameters within these contracts.[1]

This Chapter first examines these instruments as they have been laid down in federal law in the United States (especially in the 2010 Dodd-Frank Act and the 1968 Truth in Lending Act) and in EU legislation (in the Consumer Credit Directive[2] and the Proposal for its amendment[3] and in the Mortgage Credit

---

1 See World Bank, 'Responsible Lending. Overview of Regulatory Tools'(2013) The World Bank, Washington D.C. listing at paragraph 23 some of the recurring measures adopted by regulators to define rules of responsible lending which include those mentioned in the text. See also para. 25 for recommendations of the World Bank on the point.

  In the case of mortgage contracts, the EU Mortgage Credit Directive (Directive 2014/17/EU of 4 February 2014 on credit agreements for consumers relating to residential immovable property [2014] OJ L60/34, Recital 55) indicates Loan-to-value (LTV) and Loan-to-Income (LTI) ratios as possible instruments to be used in the creditworthiness assessment and further encourages Member States to implement the Financial Stability Board's Principles for Sound Residential Mortgage Underwriting Practices (on which see *infra*).

2 Directive 2008/48/EC of 23 April 2008 on credit agreements for consumers [2008] OJ L133/66.

3 In 2021, after a process of evaluation (REFIT) of the 2008 Consumer Credit Directive and of its implementation, the European Commission published a 'Proposal for a Directive on

Directive[4]), and then how they impact the relevant contract law, by also taking into account some examples of their transposition in national laws of European Member States (part 2).

It also examines what type of enforcement is accorded to these measures and it tentatively assesses the efficacity of these provisions in contrasting irresponsible lending practices (part 3). The analysis begins with the duty of creditworthiness assessment (or 'ability to pay' under US law) and then examines the other measures aiming at 'preventive' responsible lending policies.

It should be noted that achieving 'responsible credit' as a preventive policy requires not only duties of conduct on behalf of lenders and borrowers; there is also the need to ensure that credit products have certain characteristics. More specifically, for the scope of responsible credit, consumer credit products should be designed in the best interests of consumers to whom they are marketed, so as to avoid that 'toxic' products are put into circulation.[5] At the

---

Consumer Credits' (COM(2021)347 final) with the scope of tackling some of the areas in consumer credit characterized by a strong fragmentation as well as to integrate some unclear or incomplete provisions in the 2008 Directive and to take into account the growing digitalization of the credit sector and its impact on the market for credit and on consumers. The review process was undertaken within a wider framework of reform measures in the banking and financial services sector as well as under the EU Commission's New Consumer Agenda. An additional impulse derived from the effects of the COVID-19 crisis: not only during this emergency were consumer credit and mortgage loan repayments granted specific moratoria so as to combat further determinantal effects of the economic downturn onto consumers (especially the most vulnerable ones), but the COVID-19 also gave a strong acceleration to the process of digital transformation of the lending sector (i.e. in terms of the decision-making processes for consumers and lenders, of the role of new market players such as peer-to-peer lenders, of the offer of new credit products, of the way in which information is disclosed and the way in which the creditworthiness of consumers is assessed). Indeed, several of the developments due to digitalization were not foreseen when the 2008 Directive was adopted.

The Directive proposal (whose provisions will be recalled at point further in the text when they introduce changes to the existing discipline) has opted for an extensive amendment of the existing Directive to include new provisions in line with existing EU law and so as to extend its scope to credit agreements concluded through peer-to-peer lending platforms (crowdfunding services). As highlighted further (*infra*), the Proposal brings consumer credit contracts closer to the provisions adopted under the Mortgage Credit Directive.

4   Directive 2014/17/EU.
5   OO Cherednychenko, JM Meindertsma, 'Irresponsible Lending in the Post-Crisis Era: Is the EU Consumer Credit Directive Fit for Its Purpose?' (2019) 42 Journal of Consumer Policy 483, 487, also quoting the European Coalition for Responsible Credit, Principles of Responsible Credit, P.1 "Responsible and affordable credit must be provided for all". The features of credit products that would be in contrast with 'responsible lending' policies include, *inter alia*, "denominating a loan in a currency other than that in which consumers receive income, charging consumers excessively high interest rates, encouraging consumers to make only minimum repayments on a non-instalment loan for an indefinite period, or allowing

EU level, whereas regulation of product design has found some application for financial instruments, the adoption of substantive rules implementing these aims in the field of loans (such as for example limitation of high-cost credit, regulation of pay-day loans and of credit card debt, regulation of cross-selling practices) has been less widespread or even absent.[6] In the United States on the other hand, in the aftermath of the financial crisis, the regulation (and elimination) of certain products of the mortgage market was one of the goals of the Dodd-Frank Wall Street Reform and Consumer Protection Act of 2010 (including restrictions on interest-only loans, balloon payments and negative amortization).[7]

4.1 Creditworthiness Assessment in Consumer Credit Contracts and Mortgage Loan Contracts

The duty to conduct an assessment of the creditworthiness of the borrower, as a 'responsible lending' policy is found in legislation regulating consumer loans both at the national level in several legal systems (sometimes enacted or reformed before the financial crisis) and at the supranational level, such as in the case of EU law. In the words of the EU Commission, the creditworthiness

---

consumers to endlessly renew an instalment loan where they cannot afford to repay it on due dates".

6 See OO Cherednychenko, 'Freedom of contract in the post-crisis era: Quo Vadis?' (2014) 10 European Review of Contract Law 390; Cherednychenko et al 'Irresponsible Lending in the Post-Crisis Era' (n 5) 503 ff with reference to the Consumer Credit Directive.

Regulation of product design at the EU level for financial products can be found in provisions contained in the MiFID II (Directive 2014/65/EU of 15 May 2014 on markets in financial instruments and amending Directive 2002/92/EC and 2011/61/EU (recast), [2014] OJ L 173/349), that has for example imposed a process of mandatory product approval (MiFID II, articles 9(3)(b), 16(3), 24(2)) and has introduced a system of 'product intervention' (MiFID II, article 69(2)(s)(t) and MiFIR (Regulation EU/600/2014 of 15 May 2014 on markets in financial instruments and amending Regulation EU/648/2012, [2014] OJ L173/84), articles 39–43) giving national competent authorities, the ESMA and the EBA the power to remove harmful products from the market. 'Know your merchandise' rules for manufacturers and distributors of financial products have also been introduced, so as to ensure that bank staff understand and have sufficient expertise for the products they recommend or place. (See D Busch, C Van Dam, 'A Bank's Duty of Care. Perspectives from European and Comparative Law Part II', (2019) 30 European Business Law Review 367, 409–410).

7 15 U.S.C. §1639(c) (Dodd-Frank Act, Title IX, Mortgage Reform and Anti-Predatory Lending Act, Section 1411).

assessments envisaged in both the Consumer Credit Directive and the Mortgage Credit Directive "seek to prevent irresponsible lending and borrowing".[8] The expression 'consumer loans' is here intended so as to include consumer credit agreements (agreements through which a creditor grants or promises to grant credit to a consumer in the form of a deferred payment, loan or other financial accommodation) and mortgage credit loans (credit agreements covering credit for consumers secured by a mortgage or otherwise relating to residential immovable property).

Financial crises historically tend to be the result *inter alia* of credit-fueled asset booms which provoke damage to the financial system when they fall; a typical instance is the one tied to residential real estate (as was notoriously the case with the 2007–2008 global financial crisis).[9] This explains why some of the most relevant prudential measures adopted after the financial crisis refer to residential mortgages and introduce important innovations in the preconditions for access to credit for residential purposes, including not only the duty to assess the creditworthiness of borrowers, but also the adoption of loan-to-income ratios, the issuance of guidance on procedural and substantive standards for origination of leveraged loans,[10] the requirement of tests on the 'affordability' of mortgages.[11]

Provisions on creditworthiness assessment of potential consumer-borrowers are contained both in binding legislative measures (such as the Consumer Credit and Mortgage Credit Directives in the EU, and in different legislative provisions on consumer lending and mortgages in the United States) and in guiding principles prepared by supervision authorities (i.e. the FSB Principles for Sound Residential Mortgage Underwriting Practices published in 2012; the European Banking Authority guidelines on creditworthiness assessment

---

8   See the EU Commission 2017 Financial Services Action Plan: Better Products, More Choice (COM)2017 139 final, 6.2 (p.9).

9   See J Armour et al, *Principles of Financial Regulation* (Oxford University Press 2016) 414. The real estate boom of the early 2000s that led to the 2007–2008 crisis was aggravated by financial innovation; the increase in the supply of credit (and an expansion of securitization especially in the US market, with the creation of mortgage-backed securities) fueled the already large boom. Ibid.

10   See in the United States the OCC/FRB/FDIC 'Interagency Guidance on Leveraged Lending', (22 March 2013) 78 Federal Register 56.

11   Required for UK mortgage lenders under the Financial Conduct Authority's conduct of business rules (FCA Handbook, MCOB 11.6 'Responsible lending and financing').

published in 2015 and largely based on the FSB principles,[12] integrated and substituted by the 2020 Guidelines on loan origination and monitoring).[13]

The FSB principles contain in a nutshell the key issues and problems involved when creditworthiness must be assessed at the individual level, such as the need to collect data, keep tracks of credit history, respect data protection measures, and collect 'other' financial information (beyond income verification). Interestingly, a distinction is made between 'ability to pay' and 'propensity to pay' of the debtor (corresponding to a verification of income and of other financial information),[14] as is also the need to properly assess borrowers' ability to fully repay the loans without suffering 'undue hardship and over-indebtedness'.[15]

With regard to these parameters, the assessment can be qualified either as a 'creditor-focused' test or as a 'borrower-focused' test. In the first case, the assessment aims at determining credit risk and is centered on whether or not the borrower is able to meet his payments (without taking into account how the obligations are met); in a borrower-focused test the assessment aims at determining whether or not the credit is affordable for the borrower, and thus it should verify if repayments can be met in a sustainable manner and within a reasonable time (an example is found in UK legislation).[16] The 'affordability' test implies a delicate counterbalancing between the need to ensure that borrowers are protected from unsustainable credit agreements on the one hand, and the need to avoid that excessively strict inquiry obligations imposed on lenders may burden not only the precontractual phase of the credit relationship, but also allocate all future risk on the creditors in case of unforeseeable future events, and further still, allow borrowers to be discharged from their contractual obligations without there being a corresponding duty to 'borrow

---

12   The EBA guidelines were enacted to ensure consistent implementation of the principles on 'responsible lending' set out in the EU Mortgage Credit Directive. See also the Communication from the Commission to the European Parliament, the Council and the European Central Bank, the European Economic and Social Committee and the Committee of the Regions – Consumer Financial Services Action Plan: Better Products, More Choice (23.3.2017 COM(2017) 139 final, p. 8–9) referring to the need to mitigate the risk of irresponsible lending and borrowing causing over-indebtedness and referring to creditworthiness assessment as seeking to prevent these phenomena.
13   EBA Guidelines on loan origination and monitoring of 29 May 2020.
14   FSB Principles for Sound Residential Mortgage Underwriting Practices, n. 1.
15   FSB Principles for Sound Residential Mortgage Underwriting Practices, n. 2.1.
16   Cherednychenko et al (n 5) 488–489.

responsibly' (for example by providing truthful statements on their financial situation during the precontractual assessment).[17]

The US Dodd-Frank Act lays down an 'Ability-to-Pay' Rule (on which see *infra* 4.1.1) which requires a "reasonable and good faith determination based on verified and documented information" on behalf of the lender that the consumer has "reasonable ability to repay the loan" (a rule in part already introduced in 2008). However, there are also a series of presumption mechanisms in favor of lenders where the mortgage loan at issue meets certain requirements ("qualified mortgages"), that seem to differentiate the actual scope of the notion of 'affordable loan' in English and in US legislation.

It has been highlighted that traditionally the concept of 'creditworthiness' comprises both a subjective and an objective element. The subjective element is the 'willingness to pay'; its evaluation presupposes that there is also an assessment of the debtor's personal qualities and character. The objective element is the 'ability to pay', and its evaluation consists in the assessment of economic parameters at different levels.[18]

Whereas the traditional assessment of a potential borrower used to encompass both aspects, the expansion of the credit industry to a wider public of borrowers (for sometimes small amounts, as can be the case with consumer credit loans) has required an acceleration of the process of loan approvals and thus a growing automation of the whole creditworthiness assessment phase, with the surrender of the 'subjective' elements in favor of the 'objective' ones.

This trend is also encouraged by the fact that as mentioned, when compared to business loans, consumer credit loan portfolios are made up of large numbers of highly fragmented loans for relatively small amounts, that taken singularly do not expose lenders to excessive risks (nor excessive profits); they are standard mass loan contracts. This induces lenders to make their profit margins by standardizing the whole lending process, including the moment of creditworthiness assessment whose automation reduces the costs of multiple single subjective evaluations (and allows lenders to concentrate their costs on the creditworthiness assessment of 'larger' borrowers such as firms).[19]

---

17   See K Fairweather, 'The development of responsible lending in the UK consumer credit regime', in J Devenney, M Kenny (eds) *Consumer Credit, Debt and Investment in Europe* (Cambridge University Press 2012) 96–98, recalling OFT consultation with the banking industry.

18   See D Legeais, *Les Opérations de crédit* (LexisNexis 2015) 254.

19   See Chapter 2.1. See also G Piepoli, 'Sovraindebitamento e credito responsabile' (2013) 66 Banca borsa e titoli di credito 38, 39.

From the point of view of the lending institutions, the 'quality' of a mortgage loan results from the combination of the borrower's ability to repay (the ratio between the loan amount to the borrower's income (LTI) or 'debt-service-to-income' (DTI)), and the ability of the bank to obtain repayment through repossession and sale of the mortgaged property (the ratio of the loan amount to the value of the house 'LTV').[20] Regulation can target 'marginal' or 'risky' lending, identified using these ratios, through tools aimed at the lender side such as imposition of higher risk-weighted capital requirements; restriction on the proportion of 'marginal real estate loans' in the overall assets of banks; and prohibition of lending for 'marginal real estate loans'.[21]

As useful as LTV ratios and other mathematical indicators may be, it seems that if it is read as a tool for the implementation of a policy of 'responsible lending', the process of creditworthiness assessment should not be exclusively automated but rather require a cross-examination of different factors (the FSB includes, *inter alia*, the need to discount temporarily high incomes,[22] to make reasonable allowances for committed and other non-discretionary expenditures,[23] to make prudent allowances for future negative outcomes;[24] to adopt property appraisal standards that lead to realistic appraisals)[25] and should be carried out by "checking individually the creditworthiness of the consumer".[26] The costs of implementation of this duty are evident.[27]

4.1.1   *Assessing the 'Ability to Pay' of Borrowers in US Law*
In the United States the financial crisis naturally spurred debate and reform in the domain of consumer credit, credit cards and especially mortgage loans; the latter was particularly affected by a comprehensive reform of the entire financial services sector, implemented with the approval of the Dodd-Frank Act in 2010. Focus here is limited to those provisions that directly concern the origination of mortgage loan contracts and more specifically the relationship

---

20   See Armour et al (n 9) 414.
21   Ibid 421.
22   FSB Principles for Sound Residential Mortgage Underwriting Practices, n. 2.1.
23   FSB Principles for Sound Residential Mortgage Underwriting Practices, n. 2.2.
24   FSB Principles for Sound Residential Mortgage Underwriting Practices, n. 2.3.
25   FSB Principles for Sound Residential Mortgage Underwriting Practices, n. 4.2.
26   See Recital 26 of Directive 2008/48/EC. On this see G Falcone, '"Prestito responsabile" e valutazione del merito creditizio', (2017) 44 Giurisprudenza commerciale 147, 149.
27   The Final Report on Guidelines on Creditworthiness Assessment issued by the EBA in 2015 indeed examines the costs of implementation for Creditors of its 6 Guidelines in the 28 Member States to whom the Guidelines are addressed, given (or absent) national requirements that already meet those laid out by the EBA.

between lenders and borrowers with a view to identifying potential duties of 'responsible lending'. As already highlighted above, one of the principal obligations that are deemed as falling under the umbrella of 'responsible credit' is the one related to the assessment of the borrower's creditworthiness or ability to repay his debt.

Indeed, such a duty was not germane to regulation before the crisis; it did, however, prove its insufficiency with the collapse of the subprime market and the ensuing crisis that derived therefrom. Without analyzing the process that led to the crisis nor the different weaknesses of the system, this paragraph briefly surveys the principal provisions adopted in the aftermath of the crisis which relate to the assessment of borrowers' repayment capacity.[28] Duties of disclosure and legal theories providing basis for the prohibition or sanctioning of unfair or 'abusive' lending practices are examined *infra* (see par. 4.3.2).

Federal Consumer Protection in US law consists of an articulated (and often described as highly unorganized *et similia*)[29] series of different statues that have been adopted and often amended by Congress over the last fifty years and whose enforcement is left with a variety of federal regulatory agencies, including (principally, but not only) the Federal Reserve.

Among the most relevant statutes in the domain of consumer financial protection (often dating back to the 1960's and 70's), it may be useful to recall (without purporting to be exhaustive) the Truth in Lending Act of 1968 (TILA),[30] mandating a uniform method for the disclosure of the costs and terms of consumer credit transactions; the Equal Credit Opportunity Act of 1974 (ECOA),[31] prohibiting discrimination in the granting of credit; the Real Estate Settlement Procedures Act of 1974 (RESPA),[32] regulating settlement services provided in connection with residential real estate transactions; the Home Mortgage Disclosure Act of 1975 (HMDA)[33] (requiring the disclosure by financial institutions of mortgage related data); the Electronic Fund Transfer Act of 1978 (EFTA),[34] containing a structure for electronic transfers of consumer funds and some rules against loss for consumers; the Fair Debt Collection Practices

---

28 For a detailed reconstruction of how the 'ability to pay' rule made its way into legislation on loan mortgages, see JAE Pottow, 'Ability to Pay' (2011) 8 Berkeley Business Law Journal, 176.

29 See CL Peterson, 'Truth, Understanding, and High-Cost Consumer Credit: The Historical Context of the Truth in Lending Act' (2003) 55 Florida Law Review 808, 815 ff.

30 15 U.S.C. § 1601 ff.

31 15 U.S.C. §1691 ff.

32 12 U.S.C. 2601 ff.

33 12 U.S.C. 2801 ff.

34 15 U.S.C. §1693 ff.

Act of 1978 (FDCPA),[35] providing consumer protections against over-aggressive debt collectors; and the Fair Credit Reporting Act of 1970 (FCRA),[36] establishing consumer protection standards in the gathering, compiling and delivery of personal information. Emerging problems or practices tied to some of these markets led to the adoption of further statutes, including the Interstate Land Sales Full Disclosure Act of 1968 (ILSA); the Truth in Savings Act of 1991 (TISA); the Home Ownership and Equity Protection Act of 1994 (HOEPA); the Credit Card Accountability Responsibility and Disclosure Act of 2009 (CARD); the Military Lending Act of 2006 (MLA), and the Secure and Fair Enforcement for Mortgage Licensing Act of 2008 (SAFE). Over the years, the Federal Trade Commission Act (1938) also declared unlawful any "unfair or deceptive acts or practices in or affecting commerce".[37]

The 1994 Home Ownership and Equity Protection Act (approved as an amendment to the Truth in Lending Act) for example was passed as a measure to address predatory mortgage lending and prevent abusive lending practices in certain segments of the residential mortgage market. This was done by singling out and prohibiting the use of certain terms for high-rate mortgage loans, without however arriving to an actual prohibition of the practice of abusive high-rate mortgage lending. The HOEPA *inter alia* restricted 'improvident lending' (where the loan is made on the basis of the availability of the asset and not on the ability of the borrower to repay the loan).[38]

Most provisions on consumer credit were traditionally enacted at the State level, including several anti-predatory lending laws (sometimes referred to as 'mini-HOEPA' laws), adopted before the financial crisis (during the credit boom); this State legislation was however often preempted, not without criticisms, by federal regulators, in particular by the Office of the Comptroller of the Currency and the Office of Thrift Supervision.[39]

Policies aiming at imposing duties able to contrast predatory lending made their appearance not only with the signaled attempts contained in the HOEPA, but further in 2008, immediately after the collapse of the subprime market. A new regulation was adopted by the Federal Reserve under the Truth in

---

35   15 U.S.C. §1692 ff.

36   15 U.S.C. §1681 ff.

37   15 U.S.C. §45 (a)(1).

38   See M Saunders, A Cohen, 'Federal Regulation of Consumer Credit: The Cause or the Cure for Predatory Lending?' (2004) Joint Center for Housing Studies, Harvard University, BABC 04-21, 10.

39   See AE Wilmarth, Jr., 'The Dodd-Frank Act's Expansion of State Authority to Protect Consumers of Financial Services' (2011) 36 Journal of Corporation Law 893, 896–898; 909–910; M Saunders et al (n 38) 6 ff.

Lending Act imposing that lenders verify borrowers' ability to repay higher-priced loans, with a presumption that the creditor had complied with the ability-to-repay requirements if the creditor had followed certain specified underwriting practices. The rule however was deemed as arriving too late to stop and avoid the effects of the practices of predatory lending which had led to the financial crisis. It is interesting to note that a similar duty to verify the consumer's ability to repay was also imposed in one of the provisions aiming at the reform of the credit card market (the Credit Card Accountability Responsibility and Disclosure Act of 2009 – CARD Act).[40]

As is well known, the crisis led to a major reform of the system, largely embodied in the Dodd-Frank Act, which addresses issues of the mortgage market in several of its Titles (IX, X and XIV). Title XIV, also known as the Mortgage Reform and Anti-Predatory Lending Act, and containing a series of amendments to the Truth in Lending Act, is particularly relevant.[41] The reform *inter alia* enlarges the role of the States in disciplining and enforcing measures on consumer financial protection[42] and it introduces, with the Consumer Financial Protection Act (CFPA, Title X of the Dodd-Frank Act), the first federal agency having exclusive focus on consumer financial protection. The Consumer Financial Protection Bureau (CFPB) was indeed created as an independent bureau within the Federal Reserve System in order to implement and enforce the provisions on consumer protection inserted in the Dodd-Frank Act.

With reference to contrasting predatory lending and introducing protective measures for consumer-borrowers in mortgage loans, Title XIV of the Dodd-Frank Act introduces a prohibition of loan originator compensation

---

40   According to CARD Act §109 "A card issuer may not open any credit card account for any consumer under an open end consumer credit plan, or increase any credit limit applicable to such account, unless the card issuer considers the ability of the consumer to make the required payments under the terms of such account".

41   For an interesting analysis of the macroprudential measures adopted (or hoped for) in mortgage regulation, see SL Schwarcz, 'Macroprudential Regulation of Mortgage Lending', (2016) 69 South Methodist University Law Review 595.

42   The anti-predatory lending statues of North Carolina of 1999 (among the first to be enacted) served somewhat as a model for the substantive provisions of Title XIV of the Dodd-Frank Act. For the scope of this analysis, only some of most relevant regulatory modifications on the process of creditworthiness assessment will be examined. All of the plans, reforms, and economic programs adopted after 2008 by the US Government with the scope of avoiding foreclosure, renegotiating and modifying mortgage loans, reforming consumer loans and credit cards, and more generally tackling the effects of the subprime crisis will not be reviewed here. For a detailed reconstruction of this process, see, *ex multis*, KC Engel, PA McCoy, *The Subprime Virus: Reckless Credit, Regulatory Failure and Next Steps* (Oxford University Press 2011) 124 ff.

tied to terms other than the size of a loan and minimum standards for mort-gages, including a provision that creditors shall not make a home mortgage loan unless they can make "a reasonable and good faith determination based on verified and documented information that, at the time the loan is consum-mated, the consumer has a reasonable ability to repay the loan according to its terms, and all applicable taxes, insurance (including mortgage guarantee insurance) and assessments".

The basis for determination of the ability to pay "shall include consideration of the consumer's credit history, current income, expected income the con-sumer is reasonably assured of receiving, current obligations, debt-to income ratio or the residual income the consumer will have after paying non-mortgage debt and mortgage-related obligations, employment status, and other finan-cial resources other than the consumer's equity in the dwelling or real property that secures repayments of the loan. A creditor shall determine the ability of the consumer to repay using a payment schedule that fully amortizes the loan over the term of the loan".[43] The same section further introduces a presump-tion of an 'ability-to-pay' if the loan at issue "is a qualified mortgage".

This is commonly known as the 'Ability to Repay (ATR)'/'Qualified Mortgage (QM)' Rule and it contains (as the name suggests) two components: an ability to pay requirement and a preferential treatment for so-called 'qualified mort-gages'. The principal requirements for a qualified mortgage are a residential mortgage loan for which the loan does not contain negative amortization, interest-only payments or balloon payments; for which the income and finan-cial resources of the obligors are verified and documented; for which the total points and fees payable in connection with the loan do not exceed 3 percent of the total loan amount; the term of the loan does not exceed 30 years; and it respects debt-to-income ratios below caps set by the Consumer Financial Protection Bureau.[44]

In 2013, the Consumer Financial Protection Bureau (CFPB) issued a Final Rule that further implements the Qualified Mortgage Rule. Indeed, the 'abil-ity to pay' standard, as laid down in the Dodd-Frank Act, leaves considerable discretion in its interpretation and can raise concerns over its lack of clarity; Section 1412 of the Dodd-Frank Act introduced the presumption that 'qualified

---

43   15 U.S.C. § 1639(c) – Dodd-Frank Act § 1411.

44   15 U.S.C. § 1639c(b) – Dodd-Frank Act § 1411. For certain other types of mortgages (enu-merated in the Title and as determined by the Federal Reserve Board), furthermore, there is a presumption of ability to repay (Dodd-Frank Act §1414). On the last require-ment (DTI caps) and on the impact that they may have on access to credit, see PA McCoy, SM Wachter, 'The Macroprudential Implications of the Qualified Mortgage Debate' (2020) 83 Law and Contemporary Problems 21.

mortgages' are compliant with the ability-to-repay requirements, without how-ever specifying whether the presumption creates a safe harbor or is rebuttable.

The Final Rule adopted by the CFPB clarifies the issue by distinguishing between loans that are 'higher-priced' (subprime) and loans that are not. For loans that meet with the requirements of a 'qualified mortgage' and are not higher-priced, there is the creation of a safe harbor from liability for lenders.[45] For 'higher-priced' mortgage loans, when these requirements are met, there is a – rebuttable– presumption that the loans are affordable.[46]

The grounds for rebutting the presumption for subprime qualified mort-gages are defined by the Final Rule adopted by the CFPB and provide that a consumer may rebut the presumption by showing that 'at the time the loan was originated, the consumer's income and debt obligations left insufficient residual income or assets to meet living expenses'. The Guidance on the rule also notes that the longer the consumer has demonstrated ability to repay (by making timely payments, without modification or accommodation for exam-ple), the harder it will be to demonstrate the rebuttal.

The Qualified Mortgage Rule and its presumption also mean that the assess-ment of the ability to repay of borrowers does not have to be conducted man-ually, as long as these standards are respected.[47] It has been noted that the introduction of qualified mortgages and the accompanying safe harbor also aimed at creating so-called 'plain vanilla' mortgage options, that lenders would want to originate because of the fewer regulatory and litigation risks they pose (and thus an indirect incentive of certain products over others).[48]

---

45 See Bureau of Consumer Financial Protection, 12 CFR Part 1026, 'Ability-to Repay and Qualified Mortgage Standards Under the Truth in Lending Act (Regulation Z); Final Rule' (January 30, 2013) 78 Federal Register No.20/*Rules and Regulations*; See MA Calabria, 'Mortgage Reform under the Dodd-Frank Act' (2014) Cato Working Paper 9.

46 See Bureau of Consumer Financial Protection, 12 CFR Part 1026 (n 45) 6409.

47 Dodd-Frank Act, section 1412. See Engel et al, *The Subprime Virus* (n 42) 229.

48 See D Reiss, 'Message in a Mortgage: What Dodd-Frank's 'Qualified Mortgage' Tells Us About Ourselves' (2011–2012) 31 Review of Banking & Financial Law 717, 723); a trend that seems confirmed by data on the types of mortgages issued in the five years follow-ing the adoption of the Dodd-Frank Act (See CK Odinet, 'The Unfinished Business of Dodd-Frank: Reforming the Mortgage Contract' (2016) 69 South Methodist University Law Review 653, 677–678).

A similar pattern (although for completely different purposes and for risky, rather than qualified, loans) can be seen with the Standardized Mortgage Form the was created in the 1970's by the GSEs (Fannie Mae and Freddie Mac) in the wake of the Emergency Home Finance Act of 1970 so as to favor, *inter alia*, the secondary mortgage market. See Odinet 661–663.

On the opposite risk, i.e. that depending on their definitions, the QM and QRM would not drive riskier mortgages out of the market, see AJ Levitin, AD Pavlov, SW Wachter,

The infringement of the duty to verify the ability-to-repay can lead to sanctions; in addition to actual damages and statutory damages up to a prescribed threshold, there are special statutory damages. Indeed, a violation of these minimum standards by a creditor can be used as a defense by a borrower to set off or recoup damages; the creditor will be liable for an amount equal to the sum of all finance charges and fees paid by the consumer, unless the creditor demonstrates that the failure to comply with these requirements is not material, and unless of course the borrower commits fraud in obtaining the mortgage.[49]

It has been highlighted that the introduction of the 'ability to pay' requirement in the mentioned terms, is not only an important break with past regulatory policies of consumer lending, but also with the defense of the principle of self-responsibility, or *caveat emptor*, in mortgage relationships, that has been upheld by courts right up to the outbreak of the financial crisis and according to which in a loan contract there is no fiduciary relationship between a commercial bank and its debtor, and the former does not have a duty to verify the borrower's repayment ability.[50]

The introduction of this requirement of preventive assessment of a borrower's capacity of repayment has naturally encountered both criticism and praise. It is first of all signaled as a shift towards a paternalist policy of lending regulation (justified, *inter alia*, by the findings of behavioral economics on the errors and irrational choices of consumers).[51] Concerns have been expressed

---

'The Dodd-Frank Act and Housing Finance: Can it Restore Private Risk Capital to the Securitization Market?', (2012) 29 Yale Journal on Regulation 155, 164 ff.

49   15 U.S.C. §1640 – Dodd-Frank Act §§ 1413,1417.

50   See Pottow (n 28) 177, and JD Wright 'Dodd-Frank's 'Abusive Standard': A Call for Certainty'(2011) 8 Berkeley Business Law Journal 164, 167–168 – both quoting the following cases: *Das v. Bank of America*, 186 Cal. App. 4th 727 (2010); *Renteria v. US*, 452 F. Supp. 2d 910 (D. Ariz. 2006); *Tenenbaum v. Gibbs*, 813 N.Y.S. 2d 155 (App. Div. 2006); *Nymark v. Heart Fed. Savs. & Loan*, 231 Cal. App. 3d 1089 (1991); *Wagner v. Benson* 101 Cal. App. 3d 27 (1980). See also FA Hirsch Jr., 'The Evolution of a Suitability Standard in the Mortgage Lending Industry: The Subprime Meltdown Fuels the Fires of Change' (2008) 12 North Carolina Banking Institute 21, 22 ff. On the difference between the *caveat emptor* rule governing mortgage relationships and the fiduciary relationship governing securities transactions (and on which further *infra*, especially in relation to the 'suitability duty'), see JR Macey, GP Miller, M O'Hara, GD Rosenberg, 'Helping Law Catch up to Markets: Applying Broker-Dealer Law To Subprime Mortgage' (2009) 34 The Journal of Corporation Law 789, 791 ff.

51   R Thaler, 'Towards a Positive Theory of Consumer Choice' (1980) 1 Journal of Economic Behavior and Organization 39. The works of Oren Bar-Gill and Elizabeth Warren (O Bar-Gill, E Warren 'Making Credit Safer', in 157 University of Pennsylvania Law Review 39, 2008), and Michael S Barr, Sendhil Mullainathan and Eldar Shafir (MS Barr,

on the impact of this shift on the cost and availability of credit, and on the (implicit) limit to freedom and flexibility of lenders in offering a variety of credit products to borrowers (with a corresponding restriction of the options for borrowers in accessing loans).

As for issues tied to policies of responsible credit, the scope of the 'Ability to Pay' Rule and its potential as a tool for lender liability was immediately compared with the 'suitability' duties that have long been a key principle in securities regulation and that raise important issues on the 'fiduciary' nature of such rules. Indeed, as will be seen (*infra*), the extension of a 'duty of suitability' for loans, whilst refused both by the US and the EU legislator, remains one of the potential tools envisaged by several scholars (and feared by the lending industry), for an expansive construction of rules for 'responsible lending', including the way in which duty of creditworthiness and/or ability to pay assessments should be interpreted.[52]

Another very relevant change introduced with the Dodd-Frank Act is the extension of the condemnation of 'unfair and deceptive practices' so as to include 'abusive practices' (for the first time in federal legislation on consumer protection) in connection with any transaction with a consumer for a consumer financial product or service[53] and the requirement that lenders make 'reasonable disclosures'.[54] This includes the power to "prescribe rules applicable to a covered person or service provider identifying as unlawful, unfair, deceptive or abusive acts or practices";[55] to prohibit or restrict consumer lending products; to require lenders to offer certain products that are designed by the CFPA and to require disclosures. The effects and potential of this new standard, as also the impact of its first years of implementation will be examined further *infra* (see par. 4.3.2).

S Mullainathan, E Shafir, 'Behaviourally Informed financial Services Regulation' (2008) New America Foundation) are, among others, recognized as providing the theoretical basis and advocacy for the policies adopted in the Dodd Frank Act, Title x (aka 'Consumer Financial Protection Act of 2010'). For a strong critical approach towards the paternalist shift at the basis of this reform, see DS Evans, JD Wright, 'The Effect of the Consumer Financial Protection Agency Act of 2009 on Consumer Credit' (2010) 22 Loyola Consumer Law Review 277, 309–316.

52   Pottow (n 28); Macey et al (n 50); OH Dombalagian, 'Investment Recommendations and the Essence of Duty' (2011) 60 American University Law Review 1265.

53   Dodd-Frank Act Section 1031, authorizing the Consumer Financial Protection Bureau to take action to prevent such behavior.

54   Dodd-Frank Act Section 1032.

55   Dodd-Frank Act Section 1031(b).

4.1.2   *The Duty of Creditworthiness Assessment in EU Law*

At the EU level a duty of creditworthiness assessment is framed, as already recalled, in various degrees and in different domains, including in capital requirements for credit institutions and investment firms, for credit rating agencies, providers of investment services, and, in the case of individual loan contracts, in consumer credit and mortgage credit contracts. The dimension of this duty clearly has distinct meanings and implications when considered in relation to its recipients and to the scope it intends to pursue.

These duties of assessment, especially in consumer credit and mortgage contracts, were elaborated *inter alia* with an intent of adopting policies of 'responsible credit' (visible for example in the recitals of both Directives, even though express duties of 'responsible lending' that were present in the draft proposals were discarded in the final versions approved and have only now been newly inserted in the Proposal for a new Directive on Consumer Credits – see *infra*); their actual implementation however deserves a few preliminary observations.

In the case of consumer credit, the provisions on responsible lending inserted in the 2002 draft proposal for the Directive were greatly 'diluted' in the final version adopted in 2008.[56] In the case of the Mortgage Credit Directive, on the contrary, the policy is more visible: its lengthy preparation lasted throughout the decisive years in which the financial crisis thrashed and if compared to the Consumer Credit Directive, the Market Credit Directive is quite markedly characterized by a stronger paternalist regulatory approach.[57] The approval of the Mortgage Credit Directive, in particular, was preceded by consultations of expert groups and preparatory documents, often under the aegis of the European Commission, in which concern for the effects of predatory lending practices and the financial turmoil of the crisis were clearly discernible.[58] More recently, analogous concerns and an express regard to

---

56   It is emblematic to compare for example the provisions on creditworthiness assessment in Article 9 ("Responsible lending") of the Draft Proposal for a Directive on credit for consumers (COM(2002) 443 final) with the final provision in Article 8 of Directive 2008/48/EC. See *infra*.

57   See Cherednychenko, 'Freedom of Contract in the Post-Crisis Era' (n 6) 394.

58   These included, *inter alia* the Report of the Mortgage Funding Expert Group of 2006 (European Commission, 22 December 2006); the White Paper on the Integration of EU Mortgage Credit Markets of 2007 (COM(2007) 807 final), the Special Report of the Centre for European Policy Studies 'A New Mortgage Credit Regime for Europe'(2011), many of which advocated the adoption of a common EU-wide legal framework for mortgage loans. See also T Josipović, 'Consumer Protection in EU Residential Mortgage Markets: Common EU Rules on Mortgage Credit in the Mortgage Credit Directive' (2014) 14

issues relating to responsible lending and borrowing also emerged from the consultations with stakeholders and from the evaluation on the implementation of the 2008 Consumer Credit Directive, which preceded the adoption of the Proposal for a new Directive on Consumer Credits.[59]

4.1.2.1   Creditworthiness Assessment in the Consumer Credit Directive
A first explicit formulation of a duty to asses creditworthiness for individual loan contracts in EU legislation is contained in Article 8 of the Consumer Credit Directive,[60] which imposes an obligation of creditworthiness assessment based on "sufficient information, where appropriate obtained from the consumer and, where necessary, on the basis of a consultation of the relevant database". The necessity in the latter hypothesis may stem from the need for financial institutions to consult relevant databases when this duty is imposed by law (typically for prudential reasons, which often include the duty for lenders to report past due and/or non-performing loans). The duty of creditworthiness assessment persists during the life of the contract in case there is a change in the amount of credit extended to the debtor after the conclusion of the credit agreement.

The extent of the duty of creditworthiness assessment as laid down in Article 8(1) of the Consumer Credit Directive is rather vague. The Article neither defines the actual content and meaning of 'creditworthiness' nor does it invest the Member States with the task of further detailing it.[61] When considering consumers, the parameters of creditworthiness clearly differ from those applicable when considering (the creditworthiness) of firms. In the latter case, the scope and use to which credit is put is normally examined along with other

---

Cambridge Yearbook of European Legal Studies 223, 228 and ff. reconstructing the phases of a 'Euromortgage' or 'Eurohypothek' project (aiming at the creation of a pan-European security right on immovable property) initially dating back to the mid 1960's.

59   (COM(2021)347 final). The Explanatory memorandum of the Proposal recalls the studies and reports on issues relating to responsible lending and borrowing relied upon by the Commission in drafting the proposal. These include the ICF study supporting the Directive's Impact Assessment (2021); the ICF study supporting the evaluation of the Consumer Credit Directive (2020); the LE Europe et al. Behavioural study on the digitalization of the marketing and distance selling of retail financial services (2019); the CIVIC study on measuring consumer detriment in the European Union (2017) and the CIVIC study on the over-indebtedness of European households (2013).

60   Directive 2008/48/EC.

61   Which is the case for precontractual information disclosure for example (Article 5, 6th comma, Directive 2008/48/EC). See Piepoli (n 19) 46.

factors; in the case of consumer credit, the scope is irrelevant, given the very nature of the credit request.[62]

The European Court of Justice has provided some indications in the *Consumer Finance* case according to which Article 8(1) of the Consumer Credit Directive "must be interpreted to the effect that, first, it does not preclude the consumer's creditworthiness assessment from being carried out solely on the basis of information supplied by the consumer, provided that that information is sufficient and that mere declarations by the consumer are also accompanied by supporting evidence and, secondly, that is does not require the creditor to carry out systematic checks of the veracity of the information supplied by the consumer".[63] The European Court of Justice has also, incidentally, clarified that the scope of the creditworthiness assessment is to "ensure the effective protection of consumers against the irresponsible granting of credit agreements which are beyond their financial capacities and which may bankrupt them",[64] tainting, according to some, the duty of creditworthiness not only as a public and prudential duty, but also as a 'private' obligation towards borrowers (see *infra*). This also sheds some light on the issue of the 'beneficiaries' of the creditworthiness assessment.

The clarification brought by the European Court of Justice reinforces the reading according to which the assessment of creditworthiness is functional to implementing 'responsible credit'. As such, it would not simply serve the needs of lenders who may have no interest in granting credit that will likely not be repaid, but it would be also oriented in favor of borrowers, so as to avoid that they undertake loans that may bring them to over-indebtedness.

This is closely tied to the issue of whether creditworthiness assessment as it is laid down in the EU legislation is a creditor-focused or a debtor-focused test. A distinction should be made at point between the assessment of creditworthiness as it is laid down in Article 8 of the Consumer Credit Directive, and as it is laid down in Articles 16 and following of the Mortgage Credit Directive. Whilst the highlighted vagueness of the wording of Article 8 of the Consumer Credit Directive has led to different standards of implementation in the Member States (including however two examples of national rules – in the UK and in the Netherlands – that have adopted a borrower-focused

---

62   M Gorgoni, 'Spigolature su luci (poche) e ombre (molte) della nuova disciplina dei contratti di credito ai consumatori', (2011) 76 Responsabilità civile e previdenza 755, 763. Note however, Article 18(4) and Recital 47 of the Proposal for a Consumer Credits Directive.

63   ECJ, Case C-449/13 *CA Consumer Finance SA* v. *Ingrid Bakkus et al* [2014] ECLI:EU: C:2014:2464, at par 39.

64   ECJ, Case C-565/12 *LCL Le Crédit Lyonnais SA* v. *Fesih Kalhan*, [2014] ECLI:EU:C:2014:190, at paras. 43 & 52.

approach), the test provided for in the Mortgage Credit Directive appears to be more borrower-focused.[65] A confirmation of the interpretation of the duty of creditworthiness assessment as implementing a policy of 'responsible lending' (and thus not only a tool for the interest of lenders and for the protection of the market) in the Directive on Mortgage Credit Agreements, can be seen from the circumstance that not only this duty is laid down in a much more detailed way (on which see *infra*) but it is also recommended in one of the recitals that the creditor's decision as to whether to grant the credit should not be influenced by "the capacity for the creditor to transfer part of the credit risk to a third party" thus leading him "to ignore the conclusions of the creditworthiness assessment by making a credit agreement available to a consumer who is likely not to be able to repay it".[66]

The 'vagueness' of Article 8 of the Consumer Credit Directive was one of the problems highlighted during the evaluation process (so-called REFIT evaluation) undertaken in view of its amendment. The new Article 18 adopted in the Proposal for the new Consumer Credits Directive, not surprisingly, is drafted much along the lines of the corresponding Article 16 of the Mortgage Credit Directive and confirms the reading of the Court of Justice of the creditworthiness assessment as a tool for the implementation of responsible lending and as a borrower-focused test: "That assessment [of the consumer's creditworthiness] shall be done in the interest of the consumer, to prevent irresponsible lending practices and over-indebtedness".[67] In the same view of implementing responsible credit policies the Proposal also marks a shift in the way in which the information paradigm is used (see *infra*) and introduces financial literacy provisions – with express reference to supporting "responsible borrowing and debt management".[68]

It is interesting to compare the provision on creditworthiness assessment as it is framed in the EU Consumer Credit Directive and in the Mortgage Credit Directive with the 'ability to pay' rule that is adopted by the Dodd-Frank Act in the United States. As noted previously, the 'ability to pay' rule contains specific indications of the basis for determination (i.e. which elements should be taken into consideration) on which the creditor should estimate if the borrower has a reasonable ability to repay the loan. It may seem on the one hand that this

---

65   Cherednychenko et al (n 5) 501–502.

66   See Recital 57, Directive 2014/17/EU.

67   Article 18 of the Proposal for a Directive on Consumer Credits (COM(2021)347 final); see also Recital 46 recalling the need for additional guidance to be issued by Member States "on additional criteria and methods to assess a consumer's creditworthiness, for example by setting limits on loan-to-value or loan-to-income ratios".

68   Article 34 of the Proposal for a Directive on Consumer Credits (COM(2021)347 final).

provision is less 'vague', than, for example, Article 8 of the Consumer Credit Directive (where however a different type of loan is at issue: consumer credit as opposed to mortgage loans in the case of the Dodd-Frank Act). Furthermore the 'ability to pay' appears to be a borrower-focused test. It should also be noted however, that through the introduction of standards of underwriting (the 'qualified mortgages') there is also a *favor creditoris* represented by the safe-harbor presumption that these loans ensure ability to repay. A presumption that simplifies (and standardizes) the actual assessment of the individual borrower.

It should also be noted that the Directive on Consumer Credit precedes the duty of creditworthiness assessment by a series of precontractual information duties that the lender has to provide the consumer.[69] It would thus seem that in the intentions of the European legislator, the creditworthiness assessment should be structured as a sort of 'bilateral' process, which requires input from both the lender (in an attempt to make the conditions of the loan contract – and burdens – conscionable for the borrower so as to enable him to take an informed decision), and from the consumer. The latter should be, according to the wording of the Directive, the preferential source of information for the lender.[70]

Article 8 of the Consumer Credit Directive leaves another issue unresolved: the issue of information sharing (except where there is a legislative duty to consult relevant databases). Indeed, it is not clear if and to what extent information should be shared or pooled between lenders.[71] One of the classical problems in data collection and credit reporting has always been, from the perspective of lenders, that of keeping the flow of information exclusive to those who developed the report (or subscribed for it) and avoiding free riding on behalf of third lenders; and from the perspective of regulators, that of ensuring competition and non-discriminatory access of creditors to databases (such as, in the case of the EU, databases developed in other Member States).

And indeed, immediately after imposing a duty to assess creditworthiness, there follows in the Directive a provision regulating database access (Article 9 CCD). This provision aims on the one hand at ensuring non-discrimination between national and cross-border lenders in the access to the relevant databases;[72] on the other hand, it concerns the right of the consumer

---

69   Articles 5 & 6, Directive 48/2008/EC.
70   Article 8, Directive 48/2008/EC.
71   F Ferretti, 'Credit Bureaus Between Risk-Management, Creditworthiness Assessment and Prudential Supervision' (2015) EUI Working Papers 20/2015, 3–4.
72   Article 9, Directive 48/2008: "Each Member State shall in the case of cross-border credit ensure access for creditors from other Member States to databases used in that Member

to be informed not only of the result of such a consultation, but also of the 'particulars of the database consulted'.[73]

4.1.2.2   Creditworthiness Assessment in the Mortgage Credit Directive

The Mortgage Credit Directive, in an effort to tackle more effectively the problems deriving from irresponsible lending practices (indeed, during the six-year interval between the two Directives the effects of the financial crisis had intensified), contains comparatively more extensive provisions on the duty of creditworthiness assessment and sets the minimum standard of harmonization, allowing Member States to maintain or introduce more stringent provisions.[74] As noted previously, the European Banking Authority enacted its Guidelines on Creditworthiness Assessment in 2015 precisely to ensure that the relevant provisions in the Mortgage Credit Directive be implemented consistently in all 28 EU Member States and has later adopted the Guidelines on loan origination and monitoring in 2020. An express reference to the latter for the assessment of creditworthiness of consumers is made by the 2021 Proposal for a Directive on Consumer Credits[75] with regard to the categories of data (indicated by the EBA guidelines) that may be used when personal data is processed for the scope of creditworthiness assessments. These include evidence of income or other sources of repayment, information on financial assets and liabilities and information on other financial commitments (other personal data, including data found on social media platforms, should not be used).

The obligation of assessing creditworthiness of the debtor is carried out by taking into 'appropriate account' the 'factors relevant to verifying the prospect

---

State for assessing the creditworthiness of consumers. The conditions for access shall be non-discriminatory".

73   It should be recalled that same Directive already states the right to be informed of the result of database consultation in the pre-contractual phase (duties of pre-contractual information) at article 5 (q) and article 6(j)). For the wider framework of data protection in credit reporting (and the use of databases), see Chapter 3.

74   Significantly enough, a full chapter of the Directive is devoted to 'Creditworthiness assessment', followed, rather consequently, by a section on 'Database Access'. See, respectively, Chapters 6 & 7 of Directive 2014/17/EU. These provisions (in line with the general system of the Directive), comprise both prudential and supervisory requirements for lenders and obligations and rights for borrowers.

It was precisely in view of the adoption of this Directive that the European Commission established, within the various expert committees following the Forum Group on Mortgage Credit, an Expert Group on Credit Histories to assist the Commission in preparing measures on credit data. The FSB Principles for Sound Underwriting Standards for Mortgages commissioned by the G20 were also taken into consideration (Directive 2014/17/EU, Recital (3)).

75   COM(2021)347 final, Recital (47).

of the consumer to meet his obligations under the credit agreement', and excluding that the assessment rely predominantly on the value of the residential immovable property (or on the assumption that the latter will increase in value).[76] This last specification implies a negative judgement on the common practice by lenders of basing creditworthiness on the sole assessment of the value of the immovable property (the regrettable consequences of which became visible with the subprime crisis).

As far as the factors to be taken into account for the assessment are concerned, (such as information on the consumer's income and expenses and other financial and economic circumstances that are 'necessary, sufficient and proportionate') they may first of all rely on information deriving from the consumer, which must be verified (if necessary with reference to independent documentation).[77]

The disclosure of information for the scope of assessing the creditworthiness of the borrowers is envisaged by the Mortgage Credit Directive as an interactive process between the lender and the consumer. Lenders must inform consumers clearly on what information is necessary and the timeframe within which it must be provided. They can seek clarifications from the consumers where needed and, must limit their request for information only to what is proportionate and necessary to conduct a proper assessment. Consumers on the other hand must be aware of the need to provide correct information in response to the request; lenders, prior to warning the consumers of this possibility, may refuse to extend credit if the creditworthiness assessment is impossible to carry out for want of information or verification that the consumer chose not to provide.

Whilst creditors are not allowed to terminate the credit agreement on the grounds that the information provided by the consumer was incomplete, they may do so when it is demonstrated that the consumer knowingly withheld or falsified the information.[78] This 'bilateral' process of information exchange can be considered as an attempt to introduce principles of 'responsible borrowing' for consumers, who are an active and co-responsible part in the assessment of their creditworthiness: the role of both contractual parties is necessary in order to implement 'responsible lending'.[79]

---

76 Article 18(1)(2), Directive 2014/17/EU.
77 Article 20, Directive 2014/47.
78 Article 20, Directive 2014/47.
79 See F Ferretti and C Livada, 'The over-indebtedness of European consumers under EU policy and law' in F Ferretti (ed), *Comparative Perspectives of Consumer Over-indebtedness – A View from the UK, Germany, Greece and Italy* (Eleven International Publishing 2016) 21–23.

The creditworthiness assessment may obviously also rely on external sources such as a consultation of databases. With regard to the consultation of databases, the Directive not only repeatedly makes a safeguard of the provisions of the legislation on data protection and requires that the consumer be informed in advance that a database is to be consulted; but it also introduces a relevant provision, if one considers the growing importance of automated credit scoring processes (Chapter 3). The creditor must first of all inform the consumer without delay in case the application is rejected; he must also inform him, where applicable, that the decision is based on automated processing of data. These provisions in Article 16 are followed by a safeguard clause on the applicability of the (then) Data Protection Directive, now abrogated by the General Data Protection Regulation. As seen previously, this entails that if the decision is a based on a 'solely automated decision making process' the right to explanation now laid down in Article 15 of the GDPR can be invoked (as can the other related safeguards recalled in several provisions of the Mortgage Credit Directive and the Consumer Credit Directive). And indeed a corresponding provision on use of profiling or other automated processing of personal data in creditworthiness assessment contained in the Proposal for the new Consumer Credit Directive not only expressly recognizes the right for the consumer to "obtain a clear explanation of the assessment of creditworthiness, including on the logic and risks involved in the automated processing of personal data as well as its significance and effects on the decision", but also to request and obtain human intervention to review the decision and to express his or her point of view and contest the assessment and decision.[80] Lastly, when the rejection is based on the result of database consultation, the lender has to inform the consumer of the result of such consultation and of the particulars of the database consulted.[81]

As already stated for consumer credit by the Consumer Credit Directive, in these cases access to databases (operated by private credit bureaus or credit reference agencies) and to public registers must be ensured in all Member States to all creditors on a non-discriminatory basis (article 21, Mortgage Credit Directive) for assessing creditworthiness of consumers and 'for the sole purpose of monitoring consumers' compliance with the credit obligations over the life of the credit agreement'. There are clearly concerns with competition

---

80   Article 18(6) Proposal for a Directive on Consumer Credits (COM(2021)347 final).
81   The Draft proposal of the Directive included a right for the consumer to have the decision reviewed manually. Article 14 (2) (f) Proposal for a Directive on credit agreements relating to residential property, COM(2011) 142 final, SEC(2011) 355 final SEC(2011) 356 final SEC(2011) 357 final.

in this provision (already expressed in the Recitals (60) of the Mortgage Credit Directive).

The effects of the outcome of the creditworthiness assessments deserve further analysis, especially given their relation (and impact on) contractual freedom. More specifically, when compared with the Directive on Consumer Credit, the creditworthiness assessment envisaged in the Mortgage Credit Directive has an increased relevance also with regard to a final provision, absent in the former. For credit agreements relating to mortgages, a positive result of a creditworthiness assessment is a prerequisite for the extension of credit.[82] This provision will be examined together with the other pre-contractual and contractual duties imposed onto the parties under the umbrella of implementing responsible credit policies.

4.2   Effects of the 'Responsible Lending' Provisions on Contract Law

After examining how the duty of creditworthiness is laid down, it is necessary to examine the impact of these provisions, largely guided by concerns of a prudential nature and of general systemic stability, on individual contractual relationships. More specifically, how these external obligations affect the loan agreement both in its pre-contractual phase and during its existence.

The effects on contract law and contract theory are particularly meaningful when considering consumer loans and mortgages. In analogy to what has already taken place in the last decades in consumer contract law, specific provisions of contractual governance often erode or derogate 'traditional' contract law, intervening with the goal of correcting market failures.[83]

Indeed, with the scope of implementing policies of consumer and investor protection, regulatory contract law and product regulation have been often used in the domains of consumer loans, mutual funds and insurance

---

82   Article 18(5) Directive 2014/17/EU. The Proposal for a new Directive on Consumer Credits is however now aligned to the provision contained in the Mortgage Credit Directive (see Article 18(4) of the Proposal).

83   The relationship between scope of contract and market regulation is neither new nor restricted to consumer law, as is the analysis of the trend of erosion of contractual rules by legislative intervention with the scope of pursuing goals of social, economic and political nature. A reconstruction of this historical development is, however, beyond the scope of the present analysis. For an interesting reconstruction with specific reference to banking and investment contracts see for example R Natoli, *Il contratto "adeguato"* (Giuffrè 2012) 25 ff.

policies.[84] One of the principal instruments employed to this end has been the use of mandatory contractual provisions that become regulatory standards, and thus impose what have been defined as 'hybrid duties'.[85] These duties are both contractual and administrative in nature, but their enforcement does not necessarily only rely on traditional contractual remedies; the latter will interact with the supervisory authorities (for example in financial markets) in different ways across jurisdictions, and rules of civil liability will find broader or stricter room for application according to the extent of competence of the supervisory authorities.[86] In the domain of loan contracts (both consumer credit and mortgage credit), an important example of a 'hybrid duty' concerns information disclosure, which is considered (not without criticisms)[87] a key tool for the reduction of opacity of access and complexity of certain products (typically financial products).[88]

Banks are traditionally subject to regulatory duties (other than regulatory supervision), such as fiscal duties and anti-money laundering obligations. However, the introduction of regulatory duties within the domain of loan contracts and the borrower-lender relationship is a rather recent phenomenon, that is in part due to the attempt, on behalf of legislators, to implement practices of 'responsible credit'. The impact on the contractual relationship between lenders and borrowers is quite pervasive.

4.2.1 _Precontractual Duties: Duties of Disclosure and Duty to Explain_

4.2.1.1   Duties of Disclosure

Starting the analysis along an ideal timeline that follows the genesis and duration of a loan contract, the first moment that will be examined is the precontractual phase.

As previously highlighted, an important tool of contract regulation that is widely used in several areas of consumer contract law (sometimes imposing 'hybrid duties' as defined above) concerns information disclosure. The US Truth in Lending Act (TILA) enacted in 1968[89] constitutes a prominent example

---

84   J Köndgen, 'Policy Responses to Credit Crises: Does the Law of Contract Provide an Answer?' in S Grundmann, YM Atamer (eds), _Financial Services, Financial Crisis and General European Contract Law_ (Wolters Kluwer 2011) 39.

85   Ibid 40, making the example of codes of conduct which have been adopted as standards in securities regulation.

86   Ibid 41.

87   For a strong criticism on the regulatory technique of mandated disclosure as a tool that purports improvement in decision making see O Ben Shahar, CE Schneider, 'The Failure of Mandated Disclosure' (2011) 159 University of Pennsylvania Law Review 647.

88   See Natoli (n 83) 12.

89   15 U.S.C. 1601 ff.

of the use of information disclosure in consumer financial protection. It is one of the most important pieces of federal consumer protection legislation due both to its extremely wide scope of application (covering almost every type of consumer credit transaction) and to the choice made by Congress to use disclosure, rather than substantive regulation of the market, as the main tool for furthering of its scope. This disclosure model long served as a template for legislation in different domains of consumer protection (not without criticism on its efficacy).[90]

The Truth in Lending Act was adopted under the neoclassical economic assumption that the informed use of credit, as a result of consumers' awareness, would ultimately enhance economic stability and competition among consumer credit providers. Thus, one of the scopes of the Truth in Lending Act is to promote the informed use of consumer credit and this is implemented by requiring a series of disclosure duties regarding the costs and terms of credit. Disclosure duties are also required for mortgage loans and the violation of these duties allow borrowers to rescind certain transactions secured by their homes.[91]

The information disclosure model of the Truth in Lending Act (based on mandatory disclosure and coordination of terms and conditions, and on a standardization of terms so as to enable consumers to more easily compare the offers of credit contracts and thus enhance competition) largely influenced the two Consumer Credit Directives in the EU.[92] Whereas information disclosure has long been used as a regulatory tool in contract governance for the protection of the 'weaker' parties, the duties of information disclosure contained in the two European Directives here examined (the Consumer Credit Directive and the Mortgage Credit Directive) are particularly meaningful for two reasons. First of all they highlight a gradual shift (visible, as previously noted, in the six years that separate their approval) from the adoption of the information paradigm as a 'soft' regulatory tool (still present in the Consumer

---

90   MA Edwards, 'Empirical and Behavioural Critiques of Mandatory Disclosure: Socio-Economics and the Quest for Truth in Lending' (2005) 14 Cornell Journal of Law and Public Policy 199, 203.

91   Bureau of Consumer Financial Protection, 12 CFR Part 1026, 'Ability-to Repay and Qualified Mortgage Standards Under the Truth in Lending Act (Regulation Z); Final Rule', 6412–6413. Enforcement of the Truth in Lending Act is divided among nine different Federal agencies led by the Federal Trade Commission; violations of the provisions of the TILA can lead both to civil liability (in the form of either actual or statutory damages) and to criminal sanctions for willful and knowing violations of the Statute. (See Edwards (n 90) 213).

92   Directive 87/102/EEC and Directive 2008/48/EC.

Credit Directive) to the more substantive and 'hard' provisions adopted in the Mortgage Credit Directive.[93]

In the second place, the duties of disclosure are framed within a wider set of pre-contractual information duties that comprise additional (and sometimes new) obligations for the parties, especially the credit providers; these include duties of explanation and duties of warning, and in some cases extend to ensuring 'suitability' of the product offered. The duty to provide advice, though adopted for other regulations on financial products (notoriously the MiFID I and MiFID II Directives), is not, however, a mandatory service for consumer credit and mortgage credit contracts.

The change in the type of information duties prescribed by regulators can be inserted within the more general modification in the approach towards disclosure. Given the proven insufficiency, inefficiency and sometimes failure of mandated disclosure as the tool for improved decision making and awareness on behalf of consumers, the more recent strategies of regulators (especially for so-called 'credence goods', of which financial and banking contracts constitute a very meaningful example) aim at gradually substituting mandated information with duties of 'assistance' or 'guidance' in the decision-making process, often through forms of (mandatory) cooperation.[94]

It has been observed that these information duties can be seen not only as part of a 'bilateral' or 'cooperative' process of decision-making; they can also be considered as tools that empower both parties, rather than limit their autonomy.[95]

The effectiveness of information disclosure in financial market legislation as an instrument aiming at making consumers conscionable of their rights and duties has long been discussed[96] and in the case of credit contracts (credit cards, consumer loans, mortgages), behavioral economics has widely provided

---

93   See Cherednychenko, 'Freedom of Contract in the Post-Crisis Era' (n 6) 394.

94   Natoli (n 83) 53–54 and the literature cited therein.

95   See S Pagliantini, 'Statuto dell'informazione e prestito responsabile nella direttiva 17/2014/ UE (sui contratti di credito ai consumatori relative a beni immobili residenziali)' in P Sirena (ed), *I mutui ipotecari nel diritto comparato ed europeo. Commentario alla direttiva 2014/17/UE*, I Quaderni della Fondazione Italiana del Notariato (il Sole 24 Ore 2016) 27, 28; G Comparato, I Domurath, 'Financialisation and Its Implications for Private Autonomy in Consumer Credit Law' (2015) *Osservatorio del diritto civile e commerciale* (1), 269, 282.

96   S Grundmann, W Kerber, S Weatherhill, 'Party Autonomy and the Role of Information in the Internal Market – an Overview', in S Grundmann, W Kerber, S Weatherhill, (eds), *Party Autonomy and the Role of Information in the Internal Market* (de Gruyter 2001) 3; I Ramsay, 'From Truth in Lending to Responsible Lending', in G Howells, A Janssen, R Schulze, *Information Rights and Obligations. A Challenge for Party Autonomy and Transactional Fairness* (Ashgate 2005) 47.

evidence of cognitive biases, bounded rationality and strategic trade behavior (herding) that (mis)guide borrowers even if the relevant information to make rational decisions is fully disclosed to them.[97] Another flaw in mere disclosure duties, which is signaled in general for consumer contracts but that is particularly relevant for credit contracts, is that information is useful only if consumers have choices: if there are no alternatives then understanding or receiving information only allows the consumer to decide whether or not to conclude that particular contract.[98] The case of low-income consumers of credit is emblematic.

Furthermore, it has been observed that mandated and standardized disclosure duties can have, from the point of view of lenders, the effect of reducing the variety of products that are offered to the public, with a negative impact on the overall position of the latter. Similar concerns have been for example expressed in relation to the adoption of substantive rules regulating not only the underwriting process, but also the content of mortgage loan contracts. This is the case of the so-called 'qualified mortgages' introduced by the Dodd-Frank Act in the United States.[99] For the same reasons, lenders may be induced to adopt anticompetitive behavior and functional aggregations so as to maximize the needs of certain categories of borrowers (to the detriment of others).[100]

When compared to this 'classic' tool of contract regulation used in consumer contracts, and based on the notion of disclosure as a means to correct information asymmetry,[101] the information disclosure duties set out for

---

97   *Ex multis*, see O Bar-Gill (n 17); E Avgouleas, 'The Global Financial Crisis, the Disclosure Paradigm, and European Financial Regulation: The Case for Reform'(2009) 6 European Company and Financial Law Review 440; Ben-Shahar, CE Schneider, 'The Failure of Mandated Disclosure' (2011) 159 University of Pennsylvania Law Review 647; TS Ulen, 'Information in the Market Economy – Cognitive Errors and Legal Correctives' in S Grundmann et al *Party Autonomy and the Role of Information in the Internal Market* (n 96) 98; Edwards (n 90).

98   See G Howells, C Twigg-Flesner, T Wilhelmsson, *Rethinking EU Consumer Law* (Routledge 2018) 35.

99   Reiss (n 48) 723 ff; Odinet (n 48) 676–677.

100   See Gorgoni (n 62) 760; A Mirone, 'L'evoluzione della disciplina sulla trasparenza bancaria in tempo di crisi: istruzioni di vigilanza, credito al consumo, commissioni di massimo scoperto' (2010) 63 Banca, borsa e titoli di credito 557, 558–559; and more generally on aggregations and the notion of consumer welfare, F Denozza, 'Aggregazioni arbitrarie v. 'tipi' protetti: la nozione di benessere del consumatore decostruita' (2009) 36 Giurisprudenza commerciale 1057.

101   On the different approaches to information disclosure and consumer policy proposed by different theoretical approaches of economics (economics of information, new institutional economics, behavioral economics) see F Rischkowsky, T Döring, 'Consumer Policy in a Market Economy: Considerations from the Perspective of the Economics of

consumer credit in the Consumer Credit Directive, though still based on the model of truth in lending and its information paradigm, are particularly extensive (though it should be noted that the proposed new Directive on Consumer Credits features a shift towards a reduction and simplification of the information to be disclosed during the pre-contractual phase).[102]

First of all, there is not only a detailed obligation of which information must be disclosed to the consumer/borrower (e.g. detailed information on the cost of credit and on the terms of the credit contract),[103] but also a prescription of the way in which the information must be disclosed, that is, through standardization. To this end, the two credit Directives have envisaged the Standard European Consumer Credit Information Form for consumer credit contracts[104] and the European Standardized Information Sheet (ESIS) for mortgage credit contracts.[105] These provisions have the dual scope both of making the terms and costs of the loan clearly intelligible (standardization aims at reducing the complexity of information), and of allowing an easy comparison between the contractual terms offered by other financial institutions.

Information, the New Institutional Economics as well as Behavioural Economics' (2008) 31 *Journal of Consumer Policy* 285.

102 See articles 8–9–10 of the Proposal for a Directive on Consumer Credits (COM(2021)347 final). The problem of information overload and the need to streamline the content of information given to consumers during the pre-contractual phase emerged as common demands made by all the stakeholders involved in the REFIT evaluation of the 2008 Consumer Credit Directive.

103 These include, *inter alia*: type of credit; total amount of credit and conditions governing the drawdown; duration of the credit agreement; borrowing rate and the conditions governing the application of the borrowing rate; annual percentage rate of charge and total amount payable by the consumer; amount, number and frequency of payments to be made by the consumer; the obligation, if any, to enter into an ancillary service contract relating to the credit agreement, in particular an insurance policy; interest rate applicable in the case of late payments; a warning regarding the consequences of missing payments; where applicable, the sureties required; existence or absence of a right of withdrawal; right of early repayment; consumer's right to be informed immediately and free of charge of the result of a database consultation carried out for the purposes of assessing his creditworthiness (See Article 5, Directive 2008/48/EC).

104 Article 5 and Annex II of the Directive 2008/48/EC. For a detailed reconstruction of the content and timeline with which information must be disclosed see CI Garcia Porras, WH Van Boom, 'Information disclosure in the EU Consumer Credit Directive: opportunities and limitations' in J Devenney, M Kenny (eds), *Consumer Credit, Debt and Investment in Europe* (Cambridge University Press 2012) 32–33.

105 Article 14 and Annex II of Directive 2014/17/EU. In the Truth in Lending Act in the United States the so-called "Schumer Box" (named after the Senator Charles Schumer who proposed this reform) provides a similar function in relation to credit card costs (See Regulation Z §226.5a(2)).

The scale of the disclosure duties becomes evident if one considers that legislation in some Member States sanctions the breach of this duty with a discharge for the borrower from the payment in whole or in part of the agreed interest rate[106] and courts in some cases have further recognized lenders as liable for breach of their disclosure duties.[107]

4.2.1.2 Duty to Explain

Another duty falling within information practices that is laid down in both EU Directives and that has a meaningful impact on private autonomy of the parties in the pre-contractual phase is the so-called 'duty to explain' for lenders. The duty comprises the provision on behalf of lenders of "adequate explanations to the consumer in order to place the consumer in a position enabling him to assess whether the proposed credit agreement is adapted to his needs and financial situation" and for him to understand *inter alia* the consequences of default in payment.[108] The exact contours of the duty to explain are not

---

106 The ECJ, in Case C-42/15 *Home Credit Slovakia a.s.* v. *Klára Bíróová* [2016] ECLI:EU:C: 2016:842, has ruled that this practice is not in contrast with Article 23 of the Directive: "Article 23 of Directive 2008/48 must be interpreted as not precluding a Member State from providing, under national law, that, where a credit agreement does not include all the information required under Article 10(2) of the Directive, the agreement is deemed to be interest-free and free of charges, provided that the information covers matters which, if not included, may compromise the ability of the consumer to assess the extent of his liability". See MR Maugeri, 'Precontractual Duties in Consumer Credit Contracts and Remedies for their Breach' (2018) Persona e Mercato (3), 189. More generally, on the judicial remedies for the infringement of pre-contractual duties see extensively MR Maugeri, S Pagliantini, *Il credito ai consumatori. I rimedi nella ricostruzione degli organi giudicanti* (Giuffré 2013) 22 ff. For example under Italian law (Article 215*bis* of the *Testo Unico Bancario* (Banking Law)), the non-disclosure of pre-contractual information can lead to either nullity of the contract (where the information that was not disclosed concerns the type of contract, the parties, or the total amount of the loan and the conditions of repayment) and restitution of the loan in instalments with no further costs, or statutory substitution of interest rates and the forgoing on behalf of the lender of any other payment, interest rate or commission (in case the omitted information regards costs that were not included in the annual percentage rate). Under German law, the failure to indicate the annual percentage rate or total amount payable by the borrower entails that the contractual interest rate will be reduced to the statutory rate of interest (see §494 (2) *BGB*).
107 The French *Cour de Cassation* has recognized that non-disclosure (in this case a failure of the duty to warn) can lead to liability for loss of a chance (i.e. not to conclude the contract). See *Cour de Cassation, Ch. Comm.*, 20 octobre 2009, n. 08–20274, *Recueil Dalloz*, 2009, 2607.
108 Article 5(6) of Directive 2008/48/EC. Article 16 of Directive 2014/17/EU is much on the same terms.

specified in the Directives and are left to the determination of domestic legislation. However, this duty clearly involves an active engagement on behalf of creditors: making sure that the borrower 'understands' is something more – and different – from making sure that the borrower 'has been informed'.[109]

A significant example is the English transposition of the duty to explain into national law,[110] which under the heading of "pre-contractual explanations", is emblematic of the new approach towards precontractual disclosure of information: the latter is once again constructed as a moment of exchange between the two parties that will lead to the decision. According to the UK Consumer Credit Act, the creditor has to provide an *adequate* explanation (emphasis added) which presupposes aiming at a standard (i.e. adequate enough so as to ensure comprehension). On the other hand, it is for the borrower to assess, on the basis of the explanation received, if the credit agreement is adapted to the needs. The duty of disclosure is thus conceived as an instrument that ought to enable the borrower to make not simply an 'informed' decision, but also a conscious one. It should be noted that this implies that the principle of self-responsibility is not completely wiped out with the adoption of 'responsible credit' policies; the ultimate decision is to be made by the consumer-borrower.

---

109   It should be noted that this does not extend, however, to a duty for lenders to 'give advice' to consumers-borrowers. The duty to give advice exists explicitly, for example in the MiFID – and is defined by Article 4(1)(4) as the 'provision of personal recommendations to a client, either upon its request or at the initiative of the investment firm, in respect of one or more transactions relating to financial instruments' (see also MiFID II, Directive 2014/65/EU of the Parliament and Council of 15 May 2014 on markets in financial instruments [2014] OJ L 173/349). On the duty of advice, see for example T Jørgensen, 'Credit Advice' (2012) 20 European Review of Private Law 961; A Lupoi, 'La Direttiva 17/2014, il mercato dei crediti immobiliari e la consulenza al credito' (2016) 69 Banca borsa e titoli di credito 234.

110   See article 55A of the UK Consumer Credit Act prescribing that before a regulated consumer credit agreement, the creditor provide the debtor with "an adequate explanation of the matters referred to in section (2) in order to place him in a position enabling him to assess whether the agreement is adapted to his needs and his financial situation". The matters referred to in the first section of the article include a) the features of the agreement which may make the credit to be provided under the agreement unsuitable for particular types of use; b) how much the debtor will have to pay periodically and, where the amount can be determined, in total under the agreement; c) the features of the agreement which may operate in a manner which would have significant adverse effect on the debtor in a way which the debtor is unlikely to foresee; d) the principal consequences for the debtor arising from a failure to make payments under the agreement at the times required [...] and e) the effect of the exercise of any rights to withdraw from the agreement and how and when this right may be exercised.

4.2.2   *Precontractual Duties: Duty to Warn*

In the case of mortgage credit, in addition to the 'duty to explain', lenders may have a 'duty to warn' on certain specific risks associated with credit agreements[111] and the further possibility for Member States to impose an obligation for creditors "to warn a consumer when, considering the consumer's financial situation, a credit agreement may induce a specific risk for the consumer".[112]

Whereas the duties to investigate (closely tied to the 'suitability' rule) and to warn have received wide judicial recognition with reference to investment contracts, where liability may arise either as a violation of principles of contract and tort law or as a violation of statutory provisions (at the EU level especially after the approval and transposition of the two MiFID Directives),[113] the scope of the duty to warn in loan contracts receives different judicial interpretations. Examples from the French, German and Austrian approaches can be indicative.

The duty to warn is considered for example in the French legal system as one of the principal duties falling on lenders, and it predates the Mortgage Credit Directive, since its origin lies in a judicial decision of 2005.[114] According to French law (so developed) the duty to warn concretely imposes onto the lender the duty to verify that the credit granted does not pose a risk for the borrower (namely the risk of missing timely payments), and that this leads to a risk of over-indebtedness of the borrower; in the presence of such a risk it imposes the duty to verify if the borrower is informed or not and, in the latter case, warn him of these risks before the agreement is concluded.

When compared to the duty to warn posed by Article 22(5) of the Mortgage Credit Directive (and transposed into French law by Article L 313-12 *Code de la Consommation*), it should be noted that the latter does not make the distinction between a borrower that is aware/informed or not (and it has been observed that to a certain extent there is an implicit assumption that a consumer is always 'unaware').[115] Courts have recognized that in such a case lia-

---

111   Article 11(6), Directive 2014/17/EU.
112   Article 22(5), Directive 2014/17/EU.
113   See D Busch, C van Dam, 'A Bank's Duty of Care. Perspectives from European and Comparative Law Part I' (2019) 30 European Business Law Review 117, 125–126.
114   Cass. 1er chambre civile du 12 juillet 2005, n. 03–10921, Bull.civ. i, n. 327; D. 2005, p.2276, obs. X. Delpech, Banque et Droit 2005, p.80; confirmed by Cass. Com. 3 mai 2006, n. 4–15517, 02–11211 et 04–19315 bull civ iv n. 101, 102, 103D. 2006, p.1618 note J. Francois; RTD civ 2007, p.103; and Cass. Ch. Mixte 29 juin 2007, n. 05–21104 et 06-11673.
115   See J Lasserre Capdeville, 'L'évaluation de la solvabilité de l'emprunteur et les devoirs d'explication et de mise en garde à la charge du prêteur', Gazette du Palais, 23–25 août 2015, Nos. 235–237, 2530–2531.

bility (and damages) arise limitedly to the loss of a chance of concluding the contract under better conditions.[116]

The German approach to recognizing liability for infringement of duties to warn in the case of loans has traditionally been much more restrictive, with courts rejecting liability of the lender regarding the viability of the loan.[117] An interesting intermediate position is the one adopted by the Austrian Supreme Court, which has recognized liability for failure to investigate and warn a borrower against the non-suitability of a foreign currency loan.[118]

The Mortgage Credit Directive furthermore imposes a duty to provide the consumer with 'personalized information' needed to compare the credits available on the market, assess their implications and make an informed decision on whether to conclude a credit agreement.[119] The provision of 'advice' is not mandatory according to the Directive, but it can be dispensed as an additional (possibly remunerated) service, with a series of standards and requirements for the providers.[120] The White Paper on the Integration of EU Mortgage Credit Markets of 2007, highlighted concerns on the possible effects of making extension of advice compulsory, including a negative impact on mortgage prices and a limit on the range of products that consumers could choose from (as mortgage lenders would naturally provide advice on their own range of products).[121]

4.2.3 Duty of Suitability

The so-called 'duty of suitability' (i.e. imposing that the lender assess whether the credit product that is being offered is 'suitable' for the consumer before deciding whether to conclude the transaction) is often considered as another of the foundational elements of responsible lending.[122]

---

116 Cass. Com., 20 oct. 2009, n. 08-20.274: JurisData n. 2009-049987; Cass. Com. 13 sept 2011, n. 10–20.644: JurisData n. 2011-018739.

117 Busch et al (n 113) 130–131 quoting considerable precedents from the German Federal Supreme Court (i.e., BGH, 29 October 1952 – II ZR 283/51; BGH 8 June 1978 – III ZR 136/76; BGH 28 February 1989 – IX ZR 130/88; BGH, 3 December 1991 – XI ZR 300/90; BGH 14 June 2004 – II ZR 393/02; BGH, 26 October 2004 – XI ZR 255/03; BGH, 16 May 2006).
   A similar reluctant approach is found in Irish case law (e.g. High Court of Ireland, *ACC Bank plc v. Deacon & anor*, [2013] IEHC 427) (Ibid).

118 *OGH*, 8 Ob 66/12g, EvBl, 2013, 922 (Cach). Busch et al (n 113) 130.

119 Article 14(1), Directive 2014/17/EU.

120 These are laid down in Article 22, Directive 2014/17/EU.

121 See Commission of the European Communities, 'White Paper on the Integration of EU Mortgage Credit Markets' COM (2007) 807 final, 7.

122 See for example Cherednychenko et al (n 5) 487.

'Suitability rules' (also known as 'Know-Your-Customer' rules) are rules that require businesses to make offers that take into consideration the specific characteristics and vulnerabilities of the consumers being targeted (such as the elderly, the disabled or young persons), principally regarding the knowledge, experience and capacity for making informed decisions.[123] They impose a 'duty to investigate', especially when considering the provisions of investment services. The duties to investigate, to disclose and to warn can also be considered as the different components of a wider notion of the 'duty of care' or of general duties of 'good faith' that credit providers (and banks more generally) owe their clients and that have been recognized as such by national courts.[124]

It has also been observed that making lenders responsible 'during all phases of the credit relationship' (as affirmed, for example, in Recital 26 of the Consumer Credit Directive) so as to find solutions that are best tailored for the individual needs of the borrower, adds a fiduciary element to loan contracts that traditionally is reserved to agency law and other fiduciary relationships.[125] This duty (also known as the 'suitability doctrine' already implemented in other areas of financial law and investor protection where, however, it also imposes a 'duty to warn' the client or potential client),[126] allegedly begins in the precontractual phase with disclosure obligations and the creditworthiness assessment of the borrower, and then continues throughout the life of the contract.

The obligation of 'suitability' of a loan is different both from the 'duty to explain', and from the assessment of creditworthiness,[127] even though some scholars have read the duty of suitability as the principle that guides the entire pre-contractual phase, where the assessment of creditworthiness is seen as functional to the offer of a 'suitable' credit product.[128] Even before the current EU legislation on consumer credit and mortgage credit and the MiFID

---

123   OECD, 'Report on OECD Member Countries' Approaches to Consumer Contracts', (2007) OECD Digital Economy Papers, No. 131, OECD Publishing, Paris, 7 <http://dx.doi .org/10.1787/230810708021> (accessed November 2019).

124   See Busch et al (n 113) 138–140, quoting case law from Italy, Germany, the Netherlands, France and the USA in which liability for failure to properly investigate the client's expertise when providing investment advice has been recognized by the courts.

125   Köndgen (n 84) 49.

126   See the Market in Financial Instruments Directive (MiFID), article 19(4) and (5); MIFID II; see Köndgen (n 84) 53.

127   F. Ferretti and D. Vandone, *Personal Debt in Europe* (Cambridge University Press 2019) 102.

128   Natoli (n 83) 149–150; or as part of a more general duty of (objective) good faith in pre-contractual dealings (AA Dolmetta, *Trasparenza dei prodotti bancari. Regole* (Zanichelli 2013) 124–125, 134).

were implemented, some authors considered that the duty to offer 'suitable' products in investment contracts (i.e. suitable to the patrimonial situation of the potential investor) could be considered as part of the wider duty of care imposed upon lenders to avoid granting 'abusive' credit to 'unworthy' borrowers or, seen otherwise, as the duty to grant them 'suitable' credit.[129]

The introduction of 'ability to pay' rules in the United States has similarly sparked debate on the relationship of this duty with the long known 'suitability rules' that are imposed in securities regulation as of the 1930's, with some authors identifying them as being "similarly spirited".[130]

Interestingly, both the draft proposal of the 2008 Consumer Credit Directive[131] and the draft proposal of the Mortgage Contract Directive imposed stricter rules on 'suitability', that were not, however, adopted in the final version. The suitability standard that in Europe has been famously laid down for investment services (especially in the MiFID I and MiFID II Directives) has not been extended to consumer loans. Within the wide umbrella of precontractual duties, creditors are obliged to explain, to warn, eventually to advise (as an additional service); but the final decision concerning the choice of the credit product lies with the consumer.

This reading was confirmed by the ECJ in the *Schyns v. Belfius Banque SA* case,[132] according to which "it follows that that directive [the Consumer Credit Directive] does not require Member States to provide for a general obligation on creditors to offer consumers the most suitable credit". This does not however preclude Member States from introducing national rules (as is the case of the Belgian law on consumer credit at issue) obliging creditors to provide 'additional assistance' for consumers (such as identifying, within the framework of the credit agreements usually offered, the type and amount of credit most suitable for the needs of the consumer, taking into account the consumer's financial situation) without prejudice to the other provisions of the Consumer Credit Directive and especially to the need to ensure harmonization in the credit market.

The same has occurred in the United States, where the Dodd-Frank Act in its final version did not extend the suitability rules and duties that are long found in securities regulation to mortgage lending, and only introduced the

---

129   See B Inzitari, 'La responsabilità della banca nell'esercizio del credito: abuso nella concessione e rottura del credito' (2001) 54 Banca borsa e titoli di credito 265, 295–296.

130   Pottow (n 28) 185–186.

131   Article 6 of the 2008 Consumer Credit Directive Draft Proposal.

132   ECJ Case C-58/18, *Michel Schyns v. Belfius Banque SA*, [2019] ECLI:EU:C:2019:467, n. 26, 35, 36.

'Ability-to pay' rule (notwithstanding political attempts and academic proposals to the contrary).[133]

4.2.4 *Precontractual Duties: Creditworthiness Assessment and the 'Duty to Deny'*

4.2.4.1 Nature of the Duty of Creditworthiness Assessment

Alongside typical duties of the pre-contractual phase such as information disclosure and good faith – in those legal traditions which impose it as a duty of conduct during negotiations and performance of the contract – probably the most meaningful precontractual and contractual duty (given that the creditworthiness must be monitored) from the point of view of responsible credit is the duty of creditworthiness assessment. The legislative and regulatory sources of this duty have been examined above. It is however not always easy to draw a clear distinction between the duty of creditworthiness assessment and the other pre-contractual duties aiming at the implementation of responsible credit policies. For example, a part of French scholarship has considered the 'duty to warn' the main (and only) duty arising as a consequence of a negative outcome of the creditworthiness assessment.[134]

Given the relevance of this duty, the entire pre-contractual phase is not simply a 'negotiation' or 'preparation' phase, nor a simple formal drill to be completed before the signature (as information disclosure has often grown into) but rather, creditworthiness assessment becomes a condition subsequent for the coming into existence of the contractual relationship. What is requested of the lender is a substantial duty of evaluation, verification, estimation of the probability of the positive outcome (repayment) of the transaction. Whilst as

---

133   See Pottow (n 28) 187–188, arguing however that even if the content of the 'ability-to-pay' rule is a constitutive factor of the 'suitability' duty, in the context of residential mortgage lending it encompasses the larger part of the assessment that the lender must carry out; thus *de facto* "much of the work of the suitability standard is already achieved through the ability to pay duty". See Macey et al (n 50) 836–837, arguing that the two duties are separate (ability to pay being "a necessary, but not sufficient, precondition for a determination of suitability"), but that suitability duties for securities trading should be extended and applied to subprime mortgages. See also, dating from before the crash of the subprime crisis, DS Ehrenberg, 'If the Loan Doesn't Fit, Don't Take It: Applying the Suitability Doctrine to the Mortgage Industry to Eliminate Predatory Lending' (2001) 10 Journal of Affordable Housing & Community Development Law 117; KC Engel, PA McCoy, 'A Tale of Three Markets: The Law and Economics of Predatory Lending' (2002) 80 Texas Law Review 1255.

134   For an argument against this thesis, R Vabres, 'Le devoir de ne pas contracter dans le secteur bancaire et financier' (2012) *La semaine juridique, éd. Générale*, n. 40, 1er octobre 2012, 1052.

observed earlier borrowers, who participate in the process, have a duty to provide truthful information: in case the consumer knowingly provides false or incorrect information, the creditor has the right to renounce the credit agreement. Within the *acquis* of consumer contracts this is not a common rule (nor is a preference for mandatory or restrictive substantive rules that interfere with private autonomy over disclosure duties usually expressed, in line with the 'information paradigm' that is traditionally adopted in financial services);[135] usually 'hybrid duties' are those laid in favor of consumers (i.e. right of withdrawal, anticipated discharge of the contract etc.).

It is interesting to note that in some legal systems an important issue that was raised concerns the nature (whether public or private) of the duty of creditworthiness assessment. The consequences are relevant both when taking into account the nature of the sanctions ensuing from the violation of the duty and when questioning whether a negative outcome of the assessment entails a duty to deny credit to the potential borrower.

The issue was much debated for example by German scholarship with reference to the German legal system (and had already been raised in the mid 1990's regarding, more generally, the duties of disclosure and information that providers of financial services owe consumers). The majority of opinions was initially oriented towards considering the duty as a public and prudential duty, given also that the creditworthiness assessment initially was only imposed on 'credit institutes'.[136] The implementation of the Mortgage Credit Directive and the introduction in the BGB of §§ 505a–505d extended the duty to a wider number of creditors and introduced civil law sanctions (§ 505d BGB) alongside public law sanctions in case of a violation of this obligation. The consensus now tends towards the qualification of the duty as a duty of private law, owed

---

135 See S Weatherhill, 'Justifying Limits to Party Autonomy in the Internal Market – EC Legislation in the Field of Consumer Protection', in Grundmann et al, *Party Autonomy* (n 96) 173; M Ebers, 'Information and Advising Requirements in the Financial Services Sector: Principles and Peculiarities in EC Law' (2004) 8.2 Electronic Journal of Comparative Law; on orientations of the ECJ on transparency as positive information obligation towards consumers, especially with reference to unfair terms, see for example HW Micklitz, N Reich, 'The Court and Sleeping Beauty: The Revival of the Unfair Contract Terms Directive (UCTD)' (2014) 51 Common Market Law Review 771; on the role that information intermediaries have in securities and insurance markets in allowing parties to make more informed decisions and reducing principal agent problems between sellers and buyers see for example S Grundmann, W Kerber, 'Information Intermediaries and Party Autonomy – The Example of Securities and Insurance Markets', in Grundmann et al, *Party Autonomy* (n 96) 264.

136 See *Kreditwesengesetz – KWG* (Banking Act), §18, subpar. 2.

by the creditor to the borrower (potentially entitling borrowers to damages in case this duty is breached).[137]

In Italy, the absence of a public sanction for the violation (when the assessment is not carried out) of the duty to assess creditworthiness laid down in article 124-*bis* of the *Testo Unico Bancario* (Banking Law, in which the Directive 2008/48/EC was transposed), has been interpreted as a confirmation of the private nature of the duty.[138]

The ECJ has contributed to the debate in the *LCL Le Crédit Lyonnais* case, where the affirmation that the obligation to assess the creditworthiness of borrowers responds to an objective of consumer protection against the irresponsible granting of credit agreements which are beyond their financial capacities, has been interpreted as a qualification of the duty of creditworthiness not only as a public duty but also as a private one that is owed to the borrower.[139]

The distinction becomes relevant when this duty is infringed: both in the hypothesis in which the creditworthiness assessment is omitted, and in the case in which legislation imposes limitations on the contractual freedom of the parties after the assessment has been carried out (more specifically, in those instances in which a lender is prevented by law to grant credit to a borrower whose assessment yields a negative outcome (see 4.2.4)). Closely related is also the debate on the nature (or rather, the prevailing nature) of the duty of creditworthiness assessment in the precontractual phase as either a prudential duty or as a duty aiming at inducing responsible conduct on the part of lenders. This is an issue that was for example raised in Italian law, especially in relation to the question of the so-called 'duty to deny' in case of a negative outcome of the assessment, which was not explicitly introduced into Italian law with the implementation of the Mortgage Credit Directive.[140]

---

137 See A Rank, M Schmidt-Kessel, 'Mortgage credit in Germany', (2017) 6 Journal of European Consumer and Market Law 176, 177–178; F Ferretti, R Salomone, H Sutschet, V Tsiafoutis, 'The regulatory framework of consumer over-indebtedness in the UK, Germany, Italy, and Greece: comparative profiles of responsible credit and personal insolvency law' (2016) 37 Business Law Review 64, 74 and the literature cited therein.

138 See Natoli (n 83) 141–142.

139 *LCL Le Crédit Lyonnais SA v. Fesih Kalhan*, (n 64) at paras. 43 & 52. See also Rank et al (n 137) 177; and Ferretti et al 'The regulatory framework of consumer over-indebtedness' (n 137) 96; HG Bamberger, H Roth, W Hau, R Poseck (eds), *Bürgerliches Gesetzbuch Kommentar* (4th ed CH Beck 2019) §505a, 184.

140 On the point see S Tommasi, *La tutela del consumatore nei contratti di credito immobiliare* (Edizioni scientifiche italiane 2018) 84; arguing in favour of a prudential duty see Mirone (n 100) 590; Gorgoni (n 62) 763; *contra* in favour of an interpretation as a contractual duty, L Modica, 'Concessione 'abusiva' di credito ai consumatori' (2012) 28 Contratto e impresa 492, 496.

An interesting example of the interplay between public regulation tools and private law tools in enforcing responsible lending duties (including the assessment of borrowers) is found in the English legislation in force before the reform introduced with the Mortgage Market Review. The original legislation on consumer credit (the Consumer Credit Act 1974) contained private law instruments allowing courts to sanction 'extortionate' credit bargains (see 4.3.2). This statute was amended by the Consumer Credit Act 2006, which although it did not lay down explicit requirements on responsible lending,[141] did however use 'irresponsible lending' practices as a fitness test under the Consumer Credit Act licensing provisions (at the time retained by the OFT), including the possibility of using disciplinary sanctions where the duty of creditworthiness assessment had been infringed.[142]

4.2.4.2   Infringement of the Duty of Assessment and the 'Duty to Deny'

Following the analysis of the procedure and the involvement of the parties (i.e. the prescribed cooperation between lenders and consumers in the disclosure

---

141   The OFT – Non-status Lending Guidelines (1997) were the first to mention responsible lending, providing that it should be exercised by taking into account a proper assessment of the borrower's ability to repay in underwriting decisions. Initially these Guidelines were limited to secured lending transactions to non-status borrowers. Later the principle of 'responsible lending' was adopted by industry codes (Finance and Leasing Association's Lending Code 2006, ss 1C.1 and 5; Banking Code 2005, ss. 10.9 and 13.1, (replaced by Lending Code in 2009)). See Fairweather (n 17) 91–92.

142   The OFT issued a Guidance in 2010, updated in 2011, containing indications – albeit not exhaustive – on the practices that might be considered 'irresponsible lending' under the fitness test (OFT Guidance, *Irresponsible lending – OFT guidance for creditors*, OFT1107, para 3.14 to 3.28). More specifically, the OFT could consider 'irresponsible lending practices' in determining whether the business practices of a lender are 'deceitful or oppressive or otherwise unfair or improper' (S.25 (2B) CCA 1974). *Inter alia* it drew a line between assessment of creditworthiness (a credit-focused test, as provided for by article 8 of the Consumer Credit Directive, transposed by the introduction of new s. 55B into the Consumer Credit Act 1974) and assessment of affordability (a borrower-focused test). The violation of the first duty (assessment of creditworthiness) could constitute an infringement of the provision of s.55B, Consumer Credit Act, and entail disciplinary consequences (which included licensing powers by the OFT). The regulatory layout was modified in 2014 following the Mortgage Market Review carried out by the Financial Services Authority (now replaced by the Financial Conduct Authority – FCA). The new regime is now contained in the FCA Handbook and in the Mortgage Conduct of Business Rules (MCOB), which include all types of secured credit. Under the new rules, as will be seen, stricter duties of responsible lending are imposed on lenders and the enforcement of these provisions lies with the FCA and consists in suspension or restriction of licenses or in penalties (FCA Decisions Procedure and Penalties Manual (DEPP)). See Fairweather (n 17) 88 ff.; V Mak, 'What is Responsible Lending? The EU Consumer Mortgage Credit Directive in the UK and the Netherlands' (2015) 38 Journal of Consumer Policy 411, 418–419.

of information relevant for the creditworthiness assessment) and the nature of the obligation, the consequences deriving from the infringement of this duty of assessment require further attention.

A first issue concerns the consequences in private law following from a violation of the duty to carry out the assessment. More specifically, what type of liability – if any – can be envisaged in case the assessment is not carried out at all.[143] As highlighted above, under the Dodd-Frank Act in the United States, the assessment of creditworthiness and affordability of mortgage loans is framed as a duty, and its violation (i.e. underwriting a loan without information on the borrower's creditworthiness) is illegal and is sanctioned.

A first divide is between rules that would make the agreement void (invalid) and rules that whilst maintaining the contract, would impose a form of liability (pre-contractual, contractual, or extracontractual). A proposed third option, could be a functional case-by-case evaluation that takes into account the balancing between the public interest and the need to protect the weaker party.[144]

The Italian Supreme Court for example, in an important judgement, distinguished "rules of conduct" from "rules of validity" and qualified duties of disclosure for financial intermediaries as belonging to the former (rules of conduct). As a consequence, according to the Italian Supreme Court, the type of liability (pre-contractual or contractual) will depend on the moment in which the duty of disclosure is infringed; the recoverable damages in case of precontractual liability (i.e. duty of disclosure infringed in the precontractual phase but the contract is concluded notwithstanding) can be calculated as the less favorable economic conditions or as the greater economic cost at which the

---

143   See ECJ, Case C-679/18 *OPR-Finance s.r.o. v GK* [2020], ECLI:EU:C:2020:167 holding that Articles 8 and 23 of the Consumer Credit Directive must be interpreted as an obligation on a national court to examine, of its own motion, whether there has been a failure to comply with the pre-contractual duty of creditworthiness assessment and to draw the consequences in case of failure of compliance. However, in such a case the failure cannot be penalized by nullity of the credit agreement (and an obligation for the consumer to return the principal sum under certain penalizing conditions). See also ECJ, Case C-303/20 *Ultimo Portfolio Investment (Luxembourg) SA v. KM*, [2021],ECLI:EU:C:2021:479, holding that the examination of the effectiveness of the penalties (provided for in Article 23 of the Directive) for failure to comply with the obligation to examine the creditworthiness of the consumer, must be carried out taking into account all the provisions of the national law at issue (not only those specifically adopted to transpose the Directive).

144   On the latter, see G Alpa, 'Gli obblighi informativi precontrattuali nei contratti di investimento finanziario. Per l'armonizzazione dei modelli regolatori e per l'uniformazione delle regole di diritto comune' (2008) 24 Contratto e impresa 889, 889; see also S Larocca, 'L'obbligo di verifica del merito creditizio del consumatore', in V Rizzo, E Caterini, L Di Nella, L Mezzasomma (eds), *La tutela del consumatore nelle posizioni di debito e credito* (Edizioni Scientifiche Italiane 2010) 231, 257.

contract was concluded (save for proof of further damage that is a direct consequence of the unlawful conduct).[145]

This in part also depends on the public/private nature understanding of the duty of assessment. In the first case, a sanction can be envisaged for the sole infringement of a prudential duty, regardless of the effects and of any damage eventually ensuing for debtors.

Under the second hypothesis, if the assessment is understood as a private law duty that is owed to the debtor, the first question is whether the creditor can be held responsible (and liable for damages) for the negative consequences suffered by a debtor that was not able to repay a debt that would probably never have been granted had the creditworthiness assessment been carried out. The borrower would have to prove, according to the rules of tortious liability, that there is a causal link between the loan and a worsening of his general economic and patrimonial condition; that the loan was 'unsustainable' from the very beginning (i.e. from the moment in which the loan was granted); and that this unsustainability was evident from the information provided from the borrower to the lender, or from the information that the latter should have obtained using professional diligence (save for a hypothesis of contributory negligence on behalf of the debtor in case of a partial omission of information).

If, furthermore, the 'improvident' extension of credit has led to a lowering of the borrower's credit score due to the difficulties in meeting payments in a timely manner, this could be a further potential head of damages, to be quantified for example in the loss of a chance to obtain credit in the future due to a negative credit history and more generally, in the injury to his reputation.[146]

The issue is distinct from the problem that has led to a specific hypothesis of so-called 'abusive granting of credit', that has been recognized for example both in the Italian and in the French legal systems as a form of liability aiming at protecting third parties (i.e. personal creditors of the borrower, and more generally, the market) against an 'artificial' sustenance of an insolvent firm through credit that lenders knew would not be repaid.[147] This hypothesis

---

145   Cass. ss. uu. 19.12.2007, n. 26724 and n. 26725, in (2008) Corriere giuridico 223.

146   See Natoli (n 83); G Biferali, *Credito al consumo e sovraindebitamento del consumatore* (Wolters Kluwer-Cedam 2019) 94; Gorgoni (n 62) 766.

147   On Italian law, see *ex multis* L Stanghellini, 'Il 'credito responsabile': dal credito all'impresa al credito al consumo' (2007) 26 Le società 395; Inzitari (n 129); B Inzitari, 'Concessione del credito: irregolarità del fido, false informazioni e danni conseguenti alla lesione dell'autonomia contrattuale' (1993) 7 Diritto della banca e del mercato finanziario 412; A Nigro, 'La responsabilità della banca per concessione 'abusiva' di credito', in G Portale (ed), *Le operazioni bancarie*, 1, (Giuffrè 1978) 301; and case law from the Italian supreme

has a 'public' taint to it (protection of third parties) that is absent in the characterization of creditworthiness assessment as a 'private' duty owed to consumer-debtors.

The second question would arise in the inverse hypothesis; namely, a credit denied because of a negligent creditworthiness assessment, yielding a negative result for the consumer (thus denied the loan or granted the loan at a higher cost), when a properly conducted assessment would have most likely led to authorizing the loan (or granting it at more favorable economic conditions for the borrower). Naturally, the issues highlighted earlier (Chapter 3) regarding inaccurate or erroneous data processing and the applicable remedies will be relevant where the decision to grant or deny the credit is based on credit scores and/or is an automated decision.

The hypothesis could be construed as a case of professional malpractice with a violation both of the standard of diligence owed to the borrower, and more generally, for those who consider the duty of creditworthiness assessment principally as a prudential, 'public' duty, of violation of prudential standards.[148] The damage could once again be envisioned as a loss of a chance, that would here materialize in the differential between the lower costs of credit potentially obtainable under a proper assessment, and the actual higher cost paid either on the regulated credit market or on the black market.

Furthermore, there have been cases decided by financial ombudsmen (for example by the Italian Banking and Financial Ombudsman – *Arbitro Bancario Finanziario*) that have also recognized a precontractual liability of the lender towards the borrower in case of prolonged negotiations, abrupt break off of negotiations, and detrimental reliance by the borrower on the conclusion of the contract (i.e. granting of the loan).[149] In this case, the recoverable damage (limited under Italian law to the so-called negative interest) includes both the costs borne during the prolonged negotiations and the loss of profit, which,

court (*Corte di Cassazione*, 13th January 1993, n. 343, in (1993) 7 Rivista della banca e del mercato finanziario, I, 399; *Corte di Cassazione*, 9th January 1997, n. 72, in (1997) 50 Banca borsa e titoli di credito 653; *Corte di Cassazione SS.UU.*, 28th March 2006, n. 7029, (in (2006) Il diritto fallimentare e delle società commerciali 323), n. 7030 (in (2006) Corriere giuridico 643), n. 7031 (in (2007) Il diritto fallimentare e delle società commerciali 195); *Corte di Cassazione*, 1st June 2010, n. 13413, in (2011) Giurisprudenza commerciale 1157; *Corte di Cassazione* 20th April 2017 n. 9983, in (2018) 71 Banca borsa e titoli di credito 162; *Corte di Cassazione* 5th July 2017, n. 11798, in (2017) Rivista dei dottori commercialisti 590); *Corte di Cassazione*, 14 May 2018, n. 11695. On French law A Brunet, 'La responsabilitè civile du banquier dispensateur de crédit' in (1998) 51 Banca borsa e titoli di credito 778.

148   See for example articles 5 and 127 of the *Testo Unico Bancario* imposing duties of "sound and prudent administration".

149   See Dolmetta (n 128) 94–95; Biferali (n 146) 95, both quoting decisions of the Italian Banking and Financial Ombudsman (*ABF*).

though much harder to prove, would entail the loss of a chance of concluding the contract with a third party.[150]

A second, different issue concerns the so-called 'duty to deny' credit that would arise where the creditworthiness assessment (conducted without negligence) yields a negative result. As previously highlighted for credit agreements relating to mortgages, credit will be granted only where there is a positive outcome of the creditworthiness assessment. Whilst a provision of this type is not found in the Consumer Credit Directive, it has nonetheless been applied to these contracts in the legislation of some Member States.[151] According to Article 18(5) of the Mortgage Credit Directive, Member States shall make sure that "the creditor only makes the credit available to the consumer where the result of the creditworthiness assessment indicates that the obligations resulting from the credit agreement are likely to be met in the manner required under that agreement".

This would imply a 'duty to deny' or 'duty to refuse' the loan where the outcome indicates that the obligations resulting from the credit agreement are unlikely to be met.

The Proposal for the new Consumer Credits Directive, in contrast to the 2008 Consumer Credit Directive, introduces an express provision on the point, bringing it into line with the prescription of the Mortgage Credit Directive and going even further. After stating in the same terms that credit shall only be made available where the outcome of the assessment indicates likely repayment, it allows the creditor or the provider to "exceptionally make credit available to the consumer in specific and well justified circumstances" (even when the assessment has yielded a negative result).[152] Recital 47 of the Proposal further clarifies these specific and justified circumstances in the existence of a long-standing relationship between the creditor and the consumer, or in case of loans to fund exceptional healthcare expenses, student loans or loans for consumers with disabilities. In these cases, account has to be taken of the amount and purpose of the credit and the likelihood that the obligations resulting from the agreement will be met.

In the 2011 draft Proposal of the Mortgage Credit Directive, the provisions on the point were far more stringent because they imposed not only a duty to deny/refuse credit in case of a negative outcome but also the obligation to

---

150   Biferali (n 146) 97.
151   This is the case in Germany, *ex* §505a(1), *BGB*, where the later implementation of the Mortgage Credit Directive extended some of its provision to all consumer loans (see *infra*).
152   Article 18(4) of the Proposal for a Consumer Credits Directive (COM(2021)347 final).

justify this denial[153] and they required credit providers to select products that were not 'unsuitable'.[154] It is interesting to note that whilst the proposed new Consumer Credits Directive introduces a much more extensive provision on creditworthiness assessment and expands on the alleged 'duty to deny' with an explicit orientation in favor of responsible lending, it has not however gone so far as retrieving these provisions that had circulated in the Mortgage Credit Directive Draft.

These provisions do not mean however, conversely, that a positive outcome of the assessment entails a 'right to obtain the loan' (Recital 57 of the Mortgage Credit Directive). Nor can a creditor subsequently cancel or alter the credit agreement to the detriment of the consumer on the grounds that the assessment of creditworthiness was incorrectly conducted (except, of course, in case of knowingly withheld or falsified information by the consumer).[155]

The Mortgage Credit Directive provides no further criteria nor any provisions on the legal consequences of a violation of this 'duty to deny'[156] and it is left to the Member States to do so. The ECJ confirmed that this domain remains a competence of the single Member States;[157] although in the case at issue it was referring to the introduction in the national law of a Member State (Belgium) of an 'obligation to refrain' from concluding a credit agreement in the domain of consumer credit, (and thus formally the issue was whether such a provision was in contrast with Article 5(6) and Article 8 of the Consumer Credit Directive), the ECJ however also recalled, in support of the thesis of the validity of such a national rule, the provision of Article 18(5)(a) of

---

153 "Member States shall ensure the following: a) where the assessment of the consumer's creditworthiness results in a negative prospect for his ability to repay the credit over the lifetime of the credit agreement, the creditor refuses the credit; b) where the credit application is rejected, the creditor informs the consumer immediately and without charge of the reasons for the rejection", Article 14(2) Proposal for a Directive of the European Parliament and of the Council on credit agreements relating to residential property, 31.3.2011, COM(2011) 142 final.

154 Article 14(4) Proposal for a Directive COM(2011) 142 final.: "Further to assessing a consumer's creditworthiness, Member States shall ensure that creditors and credit intermediaries obtain the necessary information regarding the consumer's personal and financial situation, his preferences and objective and consider a sufficiently large number of credit agreements that are not unsuitable for the consumer given his needs, financial situation and personal circumstances".

155 Article 18(4), Directive 2014/47.

156 I Domurath, 'A Map of Responsible Lending and Responsible Borrowing in the EU and Suggestions for a Stronger Legal Framework to Prevent Over-Indebtedness of European Consumers', in H-W Micklitz, I Domurath (eds), *Consumer Debt and Social Exclusion in Europe* (Routledge 2015) 163; Ferretti et al, *Personal Debt in Europe* (n 127) 99.

157 *Michel Schyns v. Belfius Banque SA* (n 132).

the Mortgage Credit Directive, even if it was not applicable *ratione temporis* or *ratione materiae*.[158]

Article 18(5)(a) is one of the most discussed provisions of the Mortgage Credit Directive, especially with regard to its impact on freedom of contract. In this sense, it embodies what may be deemed as the inherent challenge and risk in policies of responsible credit: excessive restriction of private autonomy with danger of barring access to credit for the most vulnerable categories of borrowers, and with the (paternalist) delegation of all decisions to the creditors, thus renouncing the principle of self-responsibility of borrowers (a principle that is for example also recalled by the ECJ).[159]

Striking a balance is a difficult task, which in the case of the EU legislation has furthermore been left to the implementation by Member States, with disparate results. Some interesting examples show a certain discrepancy between the literal provisions transposing the Directive and the interpretation given by scholarship and courts.

France for instance, which already had a duty to conduct a creditworthiness assessment before the Mortgage Credit Directive in its *Code de la Consommation*[160] has introduced a duty to deny in art. L 313-16(1) *Code de la consummation*.[161] Several authors have doubted that this imposes a binding duty to refuse credit, highlighting for example that the formulation in the French text is not as strict as the provision in Article 18(5) of the Directive.[162] This reading is based on the absence of an express provision limiting contractual freedom and on an analysis of the type of sanctions imposed by the same law in case a creditworthiness assessment is not conducted: article L 341-28 *Code de la Consommation* provides that the creditor who grants credit

---

158 *Michel Schyns v. Belfius Banque SA* (n 132) n 46–47.

159 See *Michel Schyns v. Belfius Banque SA* (n 132) n 47, confirming that an obligation to refrain from concluding the credit agreement does not "call into question the fundamental responsibility of the consumer to protect his own interests". This principle also calls however, for a consideration of the policies of 'responsible lending' recalled by the Court.

160 See article L 311-9 *Code de la Consommation*.

161 The Mortgage Credit Directive was transposed into French law by Ordinance n. 2016–351 of 25 March 2016.

162 According to Article 18(5) Directive 2014/17/EU "Member States shall ensure that the creditor *only* (emphasis added) makes the credit available to the consumer where the result of the creditworthiness assessment indicates that the obligations resulting from the credit agreement are likely to be met in the manner required under that agreement" whereas in the French provision the obligation is framed so that "the credit is not granted to the borrower unless the creditor has been *able to verify* that the obligations ensuing from the credit contract will *likely* be respected in conformity to what is stated in the contract" (emphasis added).

without conducting a creditworthiness assessment may lose his right to payment of interests in whole or in a proportion decided by a judge.[163] According to this argument, there is no express mention of a sanction in case the credit is granted notwithstanding a negative outcome of the assessment. It should be noted that in case the assessment is not conducted at all, in addition to the civil sanction seen above, there is a criminal fine of up to 30.000 euros and the threat of a possible interdiction from the activity of lending.[164] Another proposed interpretation is that the duty of creditworthiness assessment would be completed not by the 'duty to deny' whose binding effects are debated by French scholarship, but rather by the subsequent 'duty to warn' that is imposed onto the lender by the new article L 313.12 (see above 4.2.2).[165]

The case of the German implementation of the discipline on the pre-contractual duties is interesting because of the legislator's choice of unifying certain provisions on consumer credit and mortgage credit in the same new section of the civil code.[166] According to §505a (1) BGB if the creditworthiness

---

163   See previously article L 311-48 *Code de la Consommation* laying down the same type of sanctions.

164   Art. L 341-31-3, *Code de la Consommation*. See D Houtcieff, 'Les devoirs précontractuels d'information du prêteur', (2016) 17 Revue de droit bancaire et financier, n 5, 91, 95–96; and V Legrand, 'Le nouveau droit du crédit immobilier: enfin la consécration d'un crédit responsable?', Petites Affiches, 22 avril 2016, n 81; A Gourio, 'La réforme du crédit immobilier aux particuliers', (2016) La semaine juridique – entreprise et affaires (JCP E), 1362, 28; Legeais (n 18) 267. See, however, J Lasserre Capdeville, 'L'évaluation de la solvabilité de l'emprunteur et les devoirs d'explication et de mise en garde à la charge du prêteur', Gazette du Palais, 23–25 août 2015, nos 235–237, 2529 arguing (before the transposition of Directive 2014/17/EU into French law), that the textual provision of art.18(5) leaves no doubt as to the duty for the creditor to deny credit in case of a negative outcome of the creditworthiness assessment. French scholarship is divided on the point. See F Boucard "Le 'crédit responsable' vu par le Conseil d'État et la Cour de cassation" (2012) Revue de droit bancaire et financier (mars-avril 2012) 73, 74, arguing that the Supreme Courts (even though administrative and civil jurisdiction have had opposite orientations) have recognized a duty to refuse credit even before the approval of the Mortgage Credit Directive; such is the interpretation of the decision of the *Conseil d'Etat* 28 juillet 2011 n. 328655: JurisData n. 2011–015343 (competent on appeal against sanctioning decisions of the ACP, the Authority of Prudential Control) whereas the decisions of the *Cour de cassation* even on the duty to warn (see *supra*), especially after the first recognition in 2005 (Cass. 1er civ. 12 juill. 2005, n. 03–10.921, *cit.*) have been interpreted as placing the decision on whether to conclude the contract or not on the borrower, not on the lender. See also Vabres (n 134).

165   Legrand (n 164) 10. See also Boucard (n 164).

166   See §§505a–505e of the BGB, located in the Chapter on consumer credit agreements (§§ 491–513 of the BGB). Provisions implementing the Mortgage Credit Directive are also found in the Banking Act (*Gesetz über das Kreditwesen- KWG*), the Industrial Code (*Gewerbeordnung- GewO*), the Price Indication Ordinance (*Preisangabenverordnung- PAngV*) and the Introductory Act to the German Civil Code (*Einführungsgesetz zum*

assessment produces a negative result, the conclusion of the contract is forbidden for both the general consumer credit agreement and the immovable consumer credit agreement. However, there is a different threshold regarding the creditworthiness for general consumer credit agreements (which is positive when there are 'no significant doubts' about a repayment), and the stricter threshold for mortgage credit agreements (where the outcome is positive when 'payment is probable').[167] A violation of the lending prohibition in case of a negative creditworthiness assessment entails, as a sole consequence, a reduction of the agreed interest rate.[168] Nor can the lender assert any damages accruing from the credit agreement nevertheless concluded (notwithstanding a negative outcome of the assessment). The sanctions provided for under §505d, BGB have been interpreted as the only legal sanctions that follow a violation of the duty (§134 BGB on statutory prohibition which would result in the nullity of the credit agreement does not apply).[169] The sanctions are not applicable in case a proper creditworthiness assessment would have led to a positive outcome.

The transposition of Article 18 of the Mortgage Credit Directive into Italian law resulted in a provision (Article 120undecies of the *Testo Unico Bancario* (Banking Law)) that does not impose a duty to deny credit.[170] However, the debated issue of whether a duty to deny credit should nonetheless be recognized in the Italian system had already been raised with reference to consumer credit (even if the Consumer Credit Directive did not expressly lay down such

Bürgerlichen Gesetzbuch- EGBGB). See Rank et al (n 137) 176; D Krimphove, C Lüke, 'The Transformation of the Mortgage Credit Directive in German Law' in M Anderson, E Arroyo Amayuelas (eds), *The Impact of the Mortgage Credit Directive in Europe. Contrasting Views from Member States* (Europa Law Publishing 2017) 205, 217.

167 §505a (1), BGB. The interpretative doubts concerning these two different terms has yielded a certain flexibility for lenders (although the 'probability' of repayment required for mortgage credit agreements finds further criteria for its calculation in the Immovable Property Credit Rating Guidelines (*ImmoKWPLV*) based on §505e, BGB). See Bamberger et al (n 139), §505a.

168 §505d, BGB.

169 See the Draft Law Implementing the Mortgage Credit Directive, BT-Drs.18/5922, p. 98. See Bamberger et al (n 139), §505a; P Buck-Heeb, 'Rechtsfolgen fehlender oder fehlerhafter Kreditwürdigkeitsprüfung' (2016) 69 *Neue Juristische Wochenschrift*, H. 29, 2067.

170 The Banking Law, modified in 2016 (by d.lgs n. 72/2016, article 1(9)) has however recognized the possibility of administrative pecuniary sanctions in case of violations of a series of norms, including article 120decies that imposes the duty to assess creditworthiness for mortgage contracts (leaving out the analogous norm on creditworthiness assessment in case of consumer credit). The sanction refers to the hypothesis of omitted assessment (given that there is no express 'duty to deny' transposed into Italian law).

a provision).[171] The arguments previously advanced in favor of the recognition of this duty are re-proposed under the light of the Mortgage Credit Directive and its explicit provision of Article 18(5) by those who consider this duty to descend from the *ratio* and objectives of the legislation on consumer credit, by reasons of opportunity and fair dealing, and by a broad construction of information duties, such as to encompass duties of 'assistance' and sometimes even of 'advice' of the client (which includes, according to this interpretation, the assessment of creditworthiness).[172] Furthermore, if, according to some constructions, such a duty could be already envisaged for consumer credit contracts, this should be all the more the case for mortgage credit contracts, given that the Mortgage Credit Directive repeatedly refers to the specificity of these contracts and to the need to adopt a differentiated and stricter approach where creditworthiness assessment is concerned.[173]

Others, on the contrary, have highlighted that the absence of a duty to deny credit in case of a negative outcome (but also of an erroneous or incomplete or non-performed assessment) is confirmed by a comprehensive construction of the whole discipline; indeed, article 120*undecies*(3) of the Banking Law (transposing Article 18(4) of the Mortgage Credit Directive) implicitly confirms the validity of a credit agreement concluded after an incorrectly conducted creditworthiness assessment, by not allowing a creditor to subsequently cancel or

---

171   The absence of the explicit duty of abstention was not seen as an obstacle to its recognition both by those who recall the existence of 'virtual nullities' in the Italian legal system as a basis for invalidating the credit contract concluded in violation of this alleged 'duty to deny', and by those who recall the case law of the Italian Supreme Court (recalled *supra*) and of the ECJ (starting with Case C-453/99, *Courage v. Crehan* [2001] ECLI:EU:C:2001:465) which have both sanctioned conduct that takes advantage of the weaker party to conclude contracts that should not have been concluded with liability for breach of contractual duties. See for a reconstruction of the different positions Gorgoni (n 62) 767; see also G. De Cristofaro, 'La nuova disciplina comunitaria del credito al consumo: la direttiva 2008/48/CE e l'armonizzazione 'completa' delle disposizioni nazionali concernenti 'taluni aspetti' dei 'contratti di credito ai consumatori''(2008) 54 Rivista di diritto civile, 255, 274–275 contemplating that an infringement of the duty to deny could be qualified as an unfair commercial practice, if it be proved that this conduct is apt to distort the economic behavior of the consumer. Others, contesting the existence of such a duty, highlight that the law (article 124*bis* of the Banking Law) only imposes a duty to verify the creditworthiness and a duty to inform and to warn the consumer; it is the latter who will, ultimately, make an 'informed' decision and will thus be responsible for his credit (see for example Modica (n 140) 499–503).

172   Tommasi (n 140) 84; A. Nigro, 'Linee di tendenza delle nuove discipline di trasparenza. Dalla trasparenza alla "consulenza"?' (2011) 25 Diritto della banca e del mercato finanziario II, 17–19; Dolmetta (n 128) 135–136.

173   Recital 22, Directive 2014/17/EU, See Tommasi (n 140) 88–89.

alter the agreement on the grounds of the incorrect assessment.[174] The per-
plexities around the alleged duty to deny credit are also justified according
to other scholars by economic considerations: recognizing such a duty would
entail that any difficulties in repayment for the consumer could be transferred
onto the lender, with the consequence of not only eroding every element of
self-responsibility of the borrowers, but also of spreading the cost of this liability onto consumers who will encounter higher costs and limitations in access
to credit.[175]

In the Netherlands strict provisions aiming at responsible consumer
lending had already been introduced before the financial crisis, with the
Financial Supervision Act of 2006, and were strengthened in the post-crisis
era. Lenders are required to act as responsible creditors to prevent consumer
over-indebtedness both when providing consumer credit and when providing mortgage credit, and to this scope regulation requires that lenders obtain
information on the consumer's financial position in the best interests of the
consumer and that they assess whether entering into the credit agreement is
justified.[176] Furthermore, no credit contract is to be concluded (nor any substantial raise of the credit limit is to be granted) if this "would not be justified
with a view to overextension of credit to the consumer".[177] However, there have
been instances (before the Mortgage Credit Directive was approved) where

---

174   Falcone (n 26) 167.
175   Gorgoni (n 62) 766.
       An interesting and important provision has however been inserted in the latest reform
       of the consumer over-indebtedness procedure (d.lgs. 14/2019), where the creditor who
       has negligently determined or aggravated the over-indebtedness of the borrower, or that
       has violated the principles contained in article 124 of the *Testo Unico Bancario* (Banking
       Law) can suffer procedural sanctions (art.69) and the Organism for the Crisis Resolution
       (OCC) has to indicate in its report whether the lender took into account the creditworthi-
       ness of the debtor, assessed in relation to his disposable income, minus a sum sufficient
       to "maintain a dignified standard of living" (quantified in a sum lower than twice the
       measure of the ISEE index) (article 68, c.3, d.lgs 14/2019).
176   Financial Supervision Act 2006, (*Wet op het financieel toezicht*) art 4:34(1); See
       Cherednychenko (n 6) 413.
177   Financial Supervision Act 2006, (*Wet op het financieel toezicht*) art 4:34(2). The assess-
       ment of whether the granting of credit is justified is further detailed in ministerial reg-
       ulations and sector codes of conduct (for example the Code of Conduct for Mortgage
       Loans (*Gedragscode Hypothecaire Fincieringen – GHF*) that though voluntary in nature,
       is subscribed to by the majority of lenders). The latter for example examines, as a crite-
       rion that 'justifies' granting – responsible – credit, whether the borrower can repay his
       obligations and still be able to face his recurring expenses and basic needs. There are
       further parameters set out by the GHF so as to assess whether the mortgage loan would be
       'responsible', including, for example the LTI ratio (income of the borrower) and the LTV
       ratio (market value of the residence). These rules were later in part legally enshrined in

courts have refused to enforce this provision: they declined to impose an obligation on lenders to refuse granting credit to consumers where the creditworthiness assessment has produced a negative outcome. According to the courts, in such a case under Dutch contract law lenders only have a duty to advise the consumers not to enter the credit agreement.[178]

In the United Kingdom the regulation of consumer credit with the 2006 reform of the Consumer Credit Act of 1974 as seen previously had already introduced sanctions (then under the competence of the Office of Fair Trading, as of 2014 under competence of the Financial Conduct Authority) for 'irresponsible lending' practices, and provided that if the outcome of the 'affordability' assessment of the borrower suggests that the borrower is unlikely to be able to meet repayments in a sustainable manner the credit should not be made available for that amount and duration.[179] In the aftermath of the financial crisis the mortgage credit market also underwent reform starting with the Mortgage Market Review conducted in 2009, which has led to a revision of existing regulation and the adoption of new rules in 2014, contained in the FCA Handbook and more specifically in the part dealing with the Mortgage Conduct of Business Rules (MCOB) which include all types of secured credit.[180]

The provision according to which a loan should not be granted if the 'affordability' assessment yields a negative outcome (the consumer has no borrowing capacity or a negative borrowing capacity because their expenditure exceeds their income), was confirmed and extended to mortgage loans.[181] Under the new rules, stricter duties of responsible lending are imposed on lenders and they are articulated into separate duties, including *inter alia*, the assessment of affordability of the loan for the borrower[182] and a monitoring of the

---

the 2013 Temporary rules on mortgage credit (*Tijdelijke regeling hypothecair krediet*). See Cherednychenko (n 6) 414; Mak (n 142) 421–423.

178   See Cherednychenko (n 6) 420, quoting the Leeuwarden Court of Appeal, 7 February 2012, ECLI: NL:GHLEE:2012:BV3437.

179   Office of Fair Trading, 'Irresponsible Lending – OFT Guidance for Creditors', n. 4.8. The 'Irresponsible lending – OFT Guidance for Creditors' was published in 2010 so as to provide clarity to lenders as to the business practices that the OFT may consider to constitute irresponsible lending practices. It indicates "types of deceitful or oppressive or otherwise unfair or improper business practices which, if engaged in by a consumer credit business, could call into consideration its fitness to hold a consumer credit license". (OFT Guidance – Foreword). See also the OFT 'Non-Status Lending Guidelines' issued in 1997 which introduced the notion of responsible lending (although their application was limited to secured lending transactions to non-statues borrowers).

180   Mak (n 142) 417.

181   Financial Services Authority, Mortgage Market Review: Responsible Lending, 2.62.

182   Mortgages and Home Finance: Conduct of Business Sourcebook (MCOB), Rule 11.6.2R.

effectiveness of a firm's affordability assessments;[183] an interest stress test that takes into account the impact on the mortgage of market expectations of future increases in interest rates;[184] implementation of responsible lending or financing policy (through a written policy setting out the factors to be taken into account in assessing a customer's ability to pay sums due);[185] ensuring that the borrower has an acceptable repayment strategy (for interest-only mortgages);[186] record-keeping of the steps taken by a firm in compliance with duties on responsible lending laid down in the MCOB.[187]

It is also interesting to note which choices have been made by other legislators outside the EU (and before the Mortgage Credit Directive), where some countries had already introduced a 'duty to deny'.

In Switzerland, the Federal Law on Consumer Credit of 2001, in force as of 2003 (which is particularly interesting given its strong influence on the 2002 draft proposal of the Consumer Credit Directive) imposes this duty with sanctions in case of its substantive infringement. Interestingly, the introductory provision on the scope of conducting creditworthiness assessments expressly states that this is aimed at preventing excessive indebtedness a credit agreement could cause.[188] Creditworthiness is also defined in detail, as the financial capacity of the consumer to enter a credit agreement, which is considered positive if he can repay the credit without burdening the portion of revenue that cannot be seized according to specific provisions of the law on debt enforcement and bankruptcy.[189] If the creditor has neglected his duties in evaluating creditworthiness (as laid down in detail in articles 28–30 of the Law on Consumer Credit) he will lose the interest on the loan and the loan itself and the consumer can ask for the repayment of the amounts he has already paid according to the rules of the action for money had and received; if the creditor's violation is less serious (e.g. he has omitted to report to the Information Centre for Consumer Credit (established in Article 23 of the Law)) then he loses his claim for interest and expenses but he can demand repayment of the debt.[190]

---

183   MCOB Rule 11.6.22R.
184   MCOB Rules 11.6.5(4)R and 11.6.18R.
185   MCOB Rule 11.6.20R.
186   MCOB Rule 11.6.41R.
187   MCOB Rule 11.6.60R.
188   Article 22, [Swiss] Federal Law on Consumer Credit of 23 March 2001.
189   Article 93, (1) Federal Law of 11 April 1889 on Debt Enforcement and Bankruptcy. This portion of revenue is calculated by taking into account the effective rent due by the debtor, the income tax, the liabilities communicated to the Information Centre.
190   Article 32(1) and 32(2) [Swiss] Federal Law on Consumer Credit. See H Giger, *Key Problems of the new concept of the Swiss Consumer Credit Legislation* (Stæmpfli Publishers Ltd. 2003) 78–85; See also YM Atamer, 'Duty of Responsible Lending: Should the European

In Japan, the Law number 115 of 2006 on Moneylenders, has introduced specific provisions (applicable as of 2010) on responsible lending which not only affirm a duty of evaluation of consumers' ability to repay (article 13(1)), but also an express prohibition of excessive loans and a cap on the maximum amount of credit that can be granted (one-third of annual income, except for loans for acquisition of immovable property or vehicles). The violation of this duty is sanctioned by imprisonment (one-year sentence) or a monetary sanction of maximum 3 mln JPY.[191]

In South Africa, the South African National Credit Act of 2006 has a Chapter (Chapter 4, Part D) on "Over-indebtedness and reckless credit" which expressly defines (in section 80) "reckless" credit as an agreement for which the credit provider failed to conduct a creditworthiness assessment or, having conducted the assessment, entered into the credit agreement with the consumer despite the fact that the preponderance of information indicated that the consumer did not generally understand or appreciate the consumer's risks, costs or obligation, or that entering into that agreement would make the consumer over-indebted. The sanctions for reckless lending may include a court order setting aside all or part of the consumer's rights and obligations under that credit agreement, or the suspension of the force and effect of that agreement, and additionally there may be an administrative fine imposed onto the creditor who granted reckless credit and the risk of cancellation of its license to provide credit.[192]

4.2.5   *Some Additional Considerations on the 'Duty to Deny'*
Amongst the issues related to the effects of the 'duty to deny' credit on private autonomy, it may be useful to single a few emblematic points (which are obviously not exhaustive of the problems raised). First of all it may be questioned if

---

Union Take Action?', in S Grundmann, YM Atamer (eds), *Financial Services, Financial Crisis and General European Contract Law: Failure and Challenges of Contracting* (Kluwer Law International 2011) 192–193.

191   S Kozuka, L Nottage, 'The Myth of the Cautious Consumer: Law, Culture, Economics and Politics in the Rise and Partial Fall of Unsecured Lending in Japan', in J Niemi, I Ramsay, WC Whitford (eds), *Consumer Credit, Debt and Bankruptcy. Comparative and International Perspectives* (Hart Publishing 2009) 199, 203; S Kozuka, L Nottage, 'Re-regulating Unsecured Consumer Credit in Japan: Over-indebted Borrowers, the Supreme Court, and New Legislation', (2007) Sydney Law School, Legal Studies Research Paper n. 07/62, 26; Atamer (n 190) 194; AM Pardieck, 'Japan and the Moneylenders – Activist Courts and Substantive Justice' (2008) 17 *Pacific Rim Law & Policy Journal* 529, 579.

192   See C Van Heerden, S Renke, 'Perspectives on the South African Responsible Lending Regime and the Duty to Conduct Pre-agreement Assessment as a Responsible Lending Practice', (2015) 24 INSOL International Insolvency Review 67.

given the protective ratio of the rule, it should still find application if both parties (credit provider and consumer) are fully aware and understand the potential consequences of the negative outcome of the creditworthiness assessment and decide to conclude the credit agreement notwithstanding. Stated otherwise, how far should the 'paternalist' rule prevail over the free determination of the parties at the moment in which the contract is concluded? And are there third-party interests that may come into play in such a situation? The question could for example arise in the hypothesis that an interested third party, for example a spouse, an heir, a beneficiary of the credit contract may object to the granting of credit *after* the contract is concluded.

Answers in part depend (assuming a private law perspective of the duty) on the basic question of identifying in whose interest this rule was laid down and consequently towards whom a liability is owed. Liability could be envisaged differently according to whether one adopts the creditor-focused or the debtor-focused reading of the duty to assess creditworthiness.

If one adopts a creditor-oriented reading of the duty to conduct the creditworthiness assessment and to refuse credit if the outcome is negative, then it may be possible to envisage that the responsibility is not only towards the debtor/consumer/borrower. In such a case it could be relatively straightforward to envisage a liability of the lender towards his internal and external stakeholders (bank management, shareholders, equity holders). If a debtor-focused reading is adopted, then it seems that the discriminant would be whether the consumer-borrower properly understood the outcome of the assessment and its probable consequences (including the probability of over-indebtedness) and notwithstanding knowingly accepted to conclude the contract.

On a different note, in case both parties knowingly agree to the credit agreement that will unlikely be repaid and they do so for purposes that may not be defined as outright fraud or speculation but rather as taking a risk (i.e. the lender hopes to sell the loan or take out the collateral underlying the debt; the debtor hopes to sell his property on foreclosure) would the protective ratio of the norm still be invokable, and allow for example a request of annulation of the contract?

In the second place, it may be doubtful if the best solution for the borrower, in case the duty to deny has been infringed, is the invalidation of the contract (given that this would potentially cause the borrower hardship if he has to repay a sum that in the meantime has been used to buy the residential property); and indeed Article 18(4) of the Directive as previously recalled prohibits a creditor from subsequently canceling or altering the credit agreement to the detriment of the consumer on the grounds that the assessment of creditworthiness was *incorrectly conducted* (emphasis added).

It may be interesting to compare the alleged 'duty to deny' the extension of a loan with an alleged 'duty to refuse' to transact or advise a client on a risky investment, where the duties to investigate and to warn a client would suggest that the investment is not suitable for the customer (for example under MiFID rules). In such hypotheses, the predominant view in the jurisdictions that have been examined earlier is that freedom of contract should prevail, and the duties of suitability and warning do not extend to the point of imposing a prohibition on contracting.[193] It should be noted, nonetheless, that the protected interests at stake differ. In the case of investments, the duties aim at protecting the customer from a risk that may not have been fully understood and that would entail a pure economic loss. In the case of a loan, the rules aim at protecting the borrower from a situation of over-indebtedness, that can lead to personal insolvency and to loss of one's home.

Some have argued that such a restriction of contractual freedom would be, from a law and economics perspective, transaction-costs effective; given the non-transparency of the investment market, parties cannot properly exercise the cost-reducing functions of contractual freedom (i.e. negotiating the best contractual terms and selecting the most suitable and most cost-saving party and reducing the risk of contracting with an insolvent party, with a consequent reduction of the costs of law enforcement in case of insolvency).[194]

Even without considering the choice of implementing the 'stricter' version of the creditworthiness assessment as a tool for pursuing responsible lending, the 'minimum' harmonized rules posed by both EU Directives analyzed above already impact the relevant contract law meaningfully. Indeed, the burdening of the pre-contractual phase is not without consequences when taking into account the economic transaction as a whole.

On the one hand, the contractual freedom and party autonomy of deciding in favor of a risky transaction, with the possible acceptance of the risk of non-performance (which for any given reason the lender may be willing to run) but also with a prospective higher profit (such as that deriving first and foremost from higher interest rates charged) and of limitations of loss where there is underlying collateral, are greatly curtailed. It is true that this freedom of moral hazard was greatly abused of in the forerun to the financial crisis and is one of the main culprits for the consequences that derived for example from the default of the subprime market. It is equally true that there were and still are several devices developed by the financial markets themselves that allowed the affirmation/expansion of these abusive practices (e.g. securitization of

---

193   See Busch et al (n 113) 145.
194   See Krimphove et al (n 166) 206, 228–229.

risky loans). However, the substantial duty of a preventive assessment of the borrowers' creditworthiness (implying a positive outcome as a condition to grant the loan) restricts the pool of potential borrowers on the lender side, reducing the range of diversification in the loan portfolios, and prohibiting any compensatory instrument that allows lending to 'risky' borrowers.

On the borrower side of course, this makes access to credit for 'weak' borrowers much more problematic and can lead to financial exclusion and recourse to black markets for credit. From this point of view the new draft provision contained in the Proposal for the Consumer Credits Directive introduces, albeit as an exemplification in its recitals, specific hypotheses in which the alleged duty to deny can be derogated and which all relate to instances of credit that is required for access to essential goods and services (i.e. exceptional healthcare expenses, student loans or loans for consumers with disabilities).[195] One cannot but note that there is here an introduction of a 'hierarchy of scopes' for which credit is to be used; this would seem to move in the direction already undertaken with reference to the 'right to housing' as expressed in several judgements by the ECJ (on which see Chapter 5).

Furthermore, as previously observed, the breadth of the analysis required for the assessment of creditworthiness entails complex informational analysis that is either outsourced, as in the case of credit rating agencies for corporate borrowers or credit bureaus for consumers, or is developed in-house. In both cases this entails a higher cost for the processing of a loan application, which lenders then transfer onto the final cost of the product.

Questions have also been raised on the impact that this duty has on the contractual capacity of borrowers who are *not* creditworthy: the possibility for the latter to enter into contracts with delayed forms of payment is hampered, whilst it is not for those whose assessments yield a positive outcome.[196] This restriction of the access to consumer credit markets seems to find support in the prudential public interest of reducing NPLs in the context of consumer loans and of mitigating the risk of over-indebtedness, but it poses a fundamental problem of equality;[197] not to mention the impact that these duties

---

195   Recital 47 Proposal for a Consumer Credits Directive.

196   See V Zeno-Zencovich, "Smart Contracts', 'Granular Norms' and Non-Discrimination'", in C Busch, A De Franceschi, *Algorithmic Regulation and Personalized Law* (Hart 2020) 264, 272–273.

197   Ibid, quoting the Communication from the Commission to the European Parliament, the European Council and the European Central bank – Second Progress Report on the Reduction of Non-Performing Loans in Europe (14.3.2018, COM(2018)133 final, p.10); and the Communication from the Commission to the European Parliament, the Council and the European Central Bank, the European Economic and Social Committee and the

may have on the right to housing as a fundamental right. These latter aspects of the impact on access to credit and possible discrimination are examined in Chapter 5.

Even these brief remarks indicate that the adoption of measures of contract regulation in credit contracts are not mere declarations of intent. The question to be further posed is whether this impingement on contractual freedom is suited for the scope it should accomplish, which according to several political declarations is that of implementing practices of 'responsible lending'. The answer seems to be negative.

Indeed, it would appear that the task was only half completed. The duty of creditworthiness assessment whilst burdening the pre-contractual phase and private autonomy and weighing on the cost of taking out a loan, is not ultimately defined in such a way so as to provide the binding instruments that would serve as a protection in case of violation of these initial assessment duties. The divergence between the first draft of the second Consumer Credit Directive (2002) and the final version are well-known and have been widely discussed. Article 9 of the Draft proposal introduced the principle of 'responsible lending' according to which the creditor, when concluding a credit agreement or increasing the total amount of credit guaranteed is assumed to have previously assessed, by any means at his disposal whether the consumer can reasonably be expected to discharge his obligation; and the explanatory memorandum to the 2002 draft clarified that irresponsible credit (i.e. according to the memorandum "if on the basis of the information he [the creditor] obtained he ought to have decided not to grant new credit") could lead to the 'imposition of civil and trade sanctions' (proposal at 14). Article 31 of the Draft Directive further specified that penalties must be "effective, proportionate and must constitute a deterrent", and exemplified that they may provide for the loss of interest and charges by the creditor and continuation of the right of repayment in instalments by the consumer. These provisions on responsible lending were, as known, excluded from the final version of the Directive approved in 2008, which only maintained in its recitals recommendations for Member States to promote 'responsible practices during all phases of the credit relationship' and avoid that creditors engage in irresponsible lending or give out credit without prior assessment of creditworthiness.[198]

Committee of the Regions – Consumer Financial Services Action Plan: Better Products, More Choice (23.3.2017 COM(2017) 139 final, p.8).

198   On the history of the CCD see P Rott, 'Consumer credit', in N Reich et al (eds), *European Consumer Law* (Intersentia 2014) 197.

According to several observers, the removal of the explicit reference to 'responsible lending' from the Draft proposal of 2002 to the final version of the Directive on Consumer Credit in 2008 was due not only to the pressure exercised by lenders, but also to the consideration that this was a mere repetition of what was already the *de facto* practice of lenders; that it represented an excessive limitation to private autonomy; and that it would have had the effect of undermining the principle of self-responsibility of consumers.[199] It seems that the course now undertaken with the new proposed Consumer Credits Directive is steering away from the liberal approach of the 2008 Consumer Credit Directive in force and adopting a much more consumer-protective and paternalist approach that was already expressed by the Mortgage Credit Directive (and confirms that responsible lending policies are grounded on principles of protection).

In the Mortgage Credit Directive undoubtedly more detailed and articulated provisions aiming at promoting responsible credit were adopted; their effect requires appraisal. This is done in the following section, beginning with an analysis of enforcement.

4.3   Instruments for the Enforcement of 'Responsible Credit' Provisions

4.3.1   *Public Enforcement*
The last issue that requires analysis concerns the enforcement of the measures aiming at implementing responsible credit duties that have been examined above. Especially before the 2007–2008 financial crisis, in several legal systems there were measures of private enforcement, mostly of contractual nature, that could be referred to where loan agreements of various types contained elements that could be considered as 'unfair', or 'unconscionable', *et similia* and led to their termination or renegotiation *ex post*.

In the wake of the financial crisis the insufficiency of these instruments to face the large-scale effects of predatory and other irresponsible lending practices solicited public debate and action for the adoption of measures of public enforcement. The call for public enforcement inserted itself within a longstanding trend that had already highlighted the need of public intervention under the form of regulation, surveillance and sanctions for the scope of

---

199   For a reconstruction of the terms of the debate with regard to the last issue (self-responsibility of consumers), see S Tommasi (n 140) 76–77.

ensuring policies such as financial consumer protection and functioning of financial markets.[200]

Public enforcement is typically entrusted to public authorities that use administrative law tools; indeed in the field of European private law one openly speaks of 'regulatory' private law in which not only the enforcement is administrative, but there are also growing impositions on private autonomy that is substituted by 'regulated autonomy'.[201] In some areas of financial services (notably, the two MiFID Directives)[202] the EU legislator for example designed a supervisory framework which included contract-related conduct of business rules for which Member States should guarantee public enforcement.[203]

In the case of 'irresponsible lending' practices, the main difficulties encountered with public enforcement are twofold. The first, is that notwithstanding the existence of consumer protection legislation requiring Member States (but no centralized supervisory authority at the European level in this domain) to set up public authorities for the enforcement of the Consumer Credit Directive and the Mortgage Credit Directive (among others),[204] these authorities are

---

200   OO Cherednychenko, 'Public and Private Enforcement of European Private Law in the Financial Services Sector' (2015) 23 European Review of Private Law 621, 621. See also the G-20 High Level Principles developed by the Taskforce on Financial Consumer Protection of the OECD Committee on Financial Markets that several national authorities have implemented following the invitation of the G20 Finance Ministers and Central Bank Governors in 2011. For a reconstruction of the post-crisis regulatory landscape in the EU, see for example N Moloney, 'Resetting the Location of Regulatory and Supervisory Control over EU Financial Markets: Lessons from Five Years On', (2013) 62 International & Comparative Law Quarterly (2013), 955. See also OO Cherednychenko, M Andenas,(eds), *Financial Regulation and Civil Liability in European Law* (Elgar 2020) on the interplay between public regulation and civil liability in European financial law and on the regulatory and compensatory function of civil liability in the EU system of governance of financial markets.

201   See H-W Micklitz, 'Administrative Enforcement of European Private Law' in R Brownsword et al (eds), *The Foundations of European Private Law* (Hart Publishing 2011) 563; see also N Moloney, 'Resetting the Location of Regulatory and Supervisory Control Over EU Financial Markets: Lessons from Five Years On', (2013) 62 International and Comparative Law Quarterly 955; J Black, 'Paradoxes and Failures: 'New Governance' Techniques and the Financial Crisis' (2012) 75 Modern Law Review 1037.

202   Directive 2004/39/EC of 21 April 2004 on markets in financial instruments (MiFID I) [2004] OJ L 145/1; Directive 2014/65/EU of 15 May 2014 on markets in financial instruments (MiFID II) [2014] OJ L 173/349.

203   See MiFID I, Articles 19–24; MiFID II, Articles 24–30. See Cherednychenko, 'Public and Private Enforcement' (n 200) 623.

204   Regulation (EU) 2017/2394 of 12 December 2017 on cooperation between national authorities responsible for the enforcement of consumer protection laws and repealing Regulation (EC) No 2006/2004, [2017] OJ L 345/1.

called upon to enforce rules that are often open-ended or general. The case of the creditworthiness assessment is emblematic. The competent authorities therefore either may or may not engage in an activity of specification or formulation of standards of protection.[205]

A second problem concerns integrating financial consumer protection within the structure and activities of public authorities in charge of financial supervision.[206] Whereas the prudential supervisory approach leaves relatively more freedom in the governance and decision making process of financial institutions and in the freedom of contract of market participants and requires comparatively minor administrative interference in these processes (a significant example being the regulation of capital requirements for financial intermediaries, which also serves the function of balancing the interests of different participants in financial markets), the growing awareness of the limits of the prudential approach (which can for example be challenged by shadow financial institutions beyond the reach of the supervisor, or by endogenous risks that derive from the behavior of financial intermediaries or the offer of certain financial products), has prompted an expansion of 'the scope of institutions, products and contracting relationships that are of potential supervisory interest'.[207]

However, with reference to the two categories of loans (consumer credit contracts and mortgage loan contracts) examined above, there has been no harmonization at the EU level of the penalties and sanctions for the infringement of the provisions contained in the two Directives,[208] nor an imposition of enforcement through instruments of administrative law. The implementation of the measures of public enforcement, as long as the sanctions are effective, proportionate and dissuasive, have thus been left with the Member States (which have adopted a panoply of different penalties, ranging from

---

205   Cherednychenko et al (n 5) 508.
206   Ibid. See also Y Svetiev, A Ottow, 'Financial Supervision in the Interstices Between Private and Public Law' (2014) 10 European Review of Contract Law 496, 512–530 with examples from the Financial Market Authorities of the Netherlands (AFM), France (AMF), and especially Germany (BaFin).
207   Y. Svetiev, A. Ottow, "Financial Supervision in the Interstices Between Private and Public Law", cit., pgs. 498–499. This shift is also epitomized by the expansion of remedial tools of administrative nature (including punitive remedies) that are for example contained in the MiFID II (especially when compared with MiFID I). ID, pgs. 501–502.
208   See Directive 48/2008/EC, Article 23; Directive 17/2014/EU, Article 38. The Proposal for the Mortgage Credit Directive contained a provision aiming at harmonizing the public enforcement of conduct of business rules (Article 24, Proposal for a Directive on credit agreements relating to residential property, COM(2011) 142 final), but was discarded in the final version of the Directive that was enacted.

administrative to criminal sanctions).[209] The absence of harmonized measures of public enforcement at the EU level however does not mean that this legislation has only received private enforcement. On the contrary, at the level of the single Member States there has been a combination of instruments of enforcement adopted. In Germany for example, certain provisions of the Consumer Credit Directive (such as the duty of creditworthiness assessment) were initially of competence of the supervisory authority and only with the transposition of Mortgage Credit Directive were these provisions unified in the civil code. In the UK the transfer in 2014 of competences in regulation and enforcement of consumer credit from the Office of Fair Trading (competent under the Consumer Credit Act 1974) to the Financial Conduct Authority (FCA) has meant, on the contrary, involving an authority with wider powers of public supervision and enforcement.

Furthermore, the growing trend of public supervision over private relationships in regulated areas (for example through regulatory conduct of business rules that are subject to public enforcement) has led to the emergence of a body of law that whilst aiming at regulating the business-client relationship (thus, private law relationships), also concerns the relationship between the business and the administrative agencies that have supervisory and enforcement tasks and thus transcends contract law. It has been termed as "quasi-private" law and "European supervision private law"[210] yielding rules which govern the relationships between private parties that are subject to public supervision and enforcement.[211]

4.3.2 *Private Enforcement*

Private enforcement of consumer credit and mortgage credit legislation and of the norms identifiable as imposing policies of 'responsible credit' lies with

---

209 France has for example adopted criminal sanctions (monetary fees and interdiction from certain offices and professional activities) alongside civil sanctions for the violation of certain rules on consumer loans (See Articles L 341-16-L341-18 *Code de la consummation*). See Cherednychenko et al (n 5) 509. It is interesting to compare the choice of the EU legislator as far as public enforcement is concerned in the domain of loans and mortgages with the choice of full harmonization of enforcement measures for investor protection rules through administrative law contained in the MiFID I (Articles 48(2), 51) and MiFID II Directives (Articles 70–72). Ibid; and Cherednychenko, 'Public and Private Enforcement' (n 200) 623–624.
210 Ibid 632–633.
211 Ibid. This body of law is characterized by "a *regulatory* focus, predominantly *ex ante* norm-setting, particularly by supervisory authorities, developing *outside* national *private law* systems and being enforced by *public* bodies through *administrative* law means" (emphasis in the original).

civil courts and extra-judicial mechanisms and is traditionally a domain of national competence. This helps explain the scarce (if any) provisions relating to judicial enforcement in front of national civil courts in EU legislation on consumer loans (and more generally on investor protection: even the business conduct rules laid down in the two MiFID Directives have received varying consideration regarding their effect as standards for duty of care in private law disputes).[212]

It is interesting to note that without interfering directly with national procedural autonomy (through the imposition of harmonized rules that for example may facilitate the procedural position of consumers in litigation against lenders), the EU legislator however promotes the use of ADR as a means of private enforcement for consumer-borrowers. Indeed, as far as extra-judicial enforcement is concerned, both the Consumer Credit Directive (article 24) and Mortgage Credit Directive (article 39) oblige Member States to put in place adequate and effective out-of-court dispute resolution procedures for the settlement of consumer disputes on credit agreements.[213]

The efficacy of private enforcement (both judicial and extra-judicial) as a tool for the protection against irresponsible lending practices naturally depends on existing substantive rules of contract and tort and on procedural rules (including access to justice, costs, length of procedures, possibility of collective actions) that are in force in single legal systems.[214] Whereas instances of 'improvident' or 'unconscionable' lending have been raised decades before the financial crisis and in some systems also found support for example in legislation on consumer credit, it was the large-scale effects of the global financial crisis of 2007–2008 that raised the issues connected to claims of this type onto political agendas and in some cases induced legislative reforms or shifts in judicial practice.

Having examined certain aspects of the private enforcement of the duty of creditworthiness assessment and of duties of disclosure, including some important forms of liability – typically pre-contractual – related to the

---

212   Ibid 634–635, quoting examples of judicial practice from Luxembourg, Scotland, and the ECJ (Case C-604/11, *Genil* v. *Bankinter* [2013] ECLI:EU:C:2013:344).

213   See also Directive 2013/11/EU of 21 May 2013 on alternative dispute resolution for consumer disputes and amending Regulation (EC) N. 2006/2004 and Directive 2009/22/EC [2013] OJ L 165/63. It is interesting to note that procedures brought in front of national ombudsmen have dealt with, *inter alia*, issues of 'responsible lending', such as omitted or incorrect creditworthiness assessments and whether or not lenders have a specific duty to avoid that borrowers become overindebted. See for example the Italian ABF, *infra*.

214   On some of the procedural difficulties, including for a class action, surround a hypothetical imposition of liability for 'unsuitable' mortgages under US law, see Macey et al (n 50) 840–841.

infringement of these duties, it is now opportune to verify if and under which further legal vest 'irresponsible lending' behavior can be enforced under private law.

Put otherwise, it may be useful to question if there are some other forms of liability that have been or could be recognized as deriving from conduct of 'irresponsible lending' or 'irresponsible borrowing'.

This means questioning if there is for example either a general category in contract law or in tort law (given that the these are the most evident private law tools for sanctioning irresponsible conduct, although as always, the distinction between these two branches is more nuanced than what may appear *prima facie*), that could be referred to for example by national courts to ensure greater consumer protection.

Scholars, courts and legislators have, at a variance, made references to unfair terms, misrepresentation,[215] error or fraud,[216] 'abusive standards', the category of 'unconscionability' (especially in the common law tradition), or more generally to the duty of 'good faith', 'good morals' and 'professional diligence' (in civilian traditions). Under tort one could think of some form of 'duty of care', or, where there are specific rules in this sense, an action for damages for breach of a statutory duty.[217]

Following are a few examples of general categories of contract or tort law that have been proposed as potential tools for an *ex post* sanctioning of irresponsible lending (or borrowing) conduct.

Starting with national provisions, English law has provided interesting instruments, that are also emblematic of the interplay between private and public enforcement. Here, as also in US law, the doctrine of unconscionability has played a prominent role. It should be noted that whilst this instrument, that is not easily defined, has a judicial meaning in common law traditions, where it is sometimes also embedded in statutes,[218] the idea underlying 'unconsciona-

---

215   See V Mak, 'The 'Average Consumer' of EU Law in Domestic Litigation: Examples from Consumer Credit and Investment Cases', (2011) TISCO Working Paper Series on Banking, Finance and Services No. 003/2011, 16, recalling an important retail investment scheme case decided by the Dutch Supreme Court (HR, *De Treek v. Dexia*, 5 June 2009, LJN: BH2815) in which claims of liability for misleading advertising, misrepresentation and duty of care were addressed by the Court.

216   Busch et al (n 113) 119–121, 146–147, quoting case law in Spain and Austria in which disputes between customers and banks are resolved with reference to the doctrine of mistake or fraud.

217   As for example article 150 of the UK Financial Services and Markets Act (FSMA). See Mak (n 215) 12.

218   For example, in the United States and in Australia where the original equity doctrine is also found in statues; see the Uniform Commercial Code, § 2–302; the Australian

bility' or its equivalents has been used to invoke protection for the weak party in a contract (not only in a credit contract) in many legal systems, often under different names.[219]

In the example of English law, it is interesting to note that the 'broad discretionary jurisdiction' introduced with the Consumer Credit Act of 1974, that justified intervention in credit contracts on the grounds of unconscionability, was abandoned in favor of statutory provisions and regulatory responsibilities.[220] Indeed, under the original 1974 Consumer Credit Act, inspired by a neo-liberal approach based on the assumption that consumers were fully capable of managing their own financial affairs, were well-informed, and had to be guaranteed a competitive environment (all assumptions that have undergone strong criticism in the aftermath of the financial crisis), the system offered consumers protection both through public enforcement, by licensing of credit providers by the Director General of Fair Trading, and through private law as a potential tool *ex post* to sanction 'extortionate credit bargains'.[221]

The latter provisions were widely considered hard to satisfy (and proved to be) ineffective.[222] They were replaced with an 'unfair relationship' test in the Consumer Credit Act 2006[223] that is considered more debtor-friendly given, *inter alia*, that the requisite of 'unfairness' is less stringent than the 'extortionate' one and that 'unfairness' potentially encompasses both precontractual and post-contractual conduct (whereas an 'extortionate' credit bargain would only be the outcome of pre-contractual conduct). The test also introduces a presumption in favor of the borrower: it is the lender who must prove that a credit agreement is *not* unfair once unfairness is alleged.

Consumer Law, Part 2–2, Sections 20–22 and the previous section 51AA of the Trade Practices Act.

219   See M Kenny, J Devenney, L Fox O'Mahony, 'Introduction: conceptualizing unconscionability in Europe' in M Kenny, J Devenney, L Fox O'Mahony (eds), *Unconscionability in European Private Financial Transactions. Protecting the Vulnerable* (Cambridge University Press 2010) 1.

220   S Nield, 'Borrowers as consumers: new notions of unconscionability for domestic borrowers', in Kenny et al (n 219) 184.

221   Consumer Credit Act 1974, ss.137–140.

222   See Nield (n 220) 199 quoting the following cases: A. Ketley Ltd. v. Scott [1980] CCLR 37; Davies v. Direct Loans [1986] 1 WLR 823; Paragon Finance plc v Nash [2002] 1 WLR 685.

223   S.137(1)-140, CCA 1974. The CCA 2006 substituted the 'extortionate credit bargain' with the current 'unfair relationship' test. S.140(A) considers the relationship as potentially unfair because of one or more of the following: (a) any of the terms of the agreement or of any related agreement; (b) the way in which the creditor has exercised or enforced any of his rights under the agreement or any related agreement; (c) any other thing done (or not done) by, or on behalf of, the creditor (either before or after the making of the agreement or any related agreement).

It is worth noting, however, that the legal provisions in no way define (thus limiting) nor exemplify conduct that may be considered 'unfair' under the Act. This seems to have been a voluntary choice of the regulator in order not to circumscribe excessively freedom of action of the courts in sanctioning a behavior that may take different potential forms of 'unfairness'.[224] It is interesting furthermore that historically, the notion of 'unfairness' on which judicial intervention in private bargains is admitted refers to a procedural aspect; 'substantial unfairness' alone is not easily recognized as a basis for judicial interference with private autonomy. Typical examples of substantial unfairness in credit relationships may be those where there are exorbitant rates of interest and/or cases in which the unaffordability of the credit may be used as an argument for the unfairness of the credit contract.[225] As far as the redress is concerned, courts have different tools available, including reimbursement of sums paid by the borrower, the setting aside (either in whole or in part) of any duty imposed upon the borrower, and the alteration of the terms of the mortgage agreement.[226]

In the United States the doctrine of unconscionability was also invoked, especially by scholarship, before the more recent reforms in federal law (implemented with the Dodd-Frank Act) introduced statutory provisions recalling unfairness and abusive standards, both of which potentially legitimating the sanctioning of certain practices of irresponsible lending.

Years before the reform and before the collapse of the subprime market, during the 1960's, the idea of invoking unconscionability in credit contracts and of sanctioning practices of irresponsible lending had been proposed and

---

224 See also the Guidance issued by the OFT in 2003 on 'Enforcement of consumer protection legislation. Guidance on Part 8 of the Enterprise Act 2002'.

225 See Fairweather (n 17) 102–108, who analyzes case law on the two hypotheses and highlights unclear trends: the cases show varying attitudes in the willingness to recognize 'extortionate' rates of interest as giving rise to unfair relationships (see *Patel* v. *Patel* [2009] EWHC 3264, and a series of other cases decided by County Courts on so-called logbook loans) and on unaffordability of credit as a ground of unfairness (see *Khodari* v. *Tamimi*, [2008] EWHC 3065).

226 Article 140B CCA. See Fairweather (n 17) 84–85; 99–101, and the literature quoted therein; Nield (n 220) 198–200. More generally, remedies include bringing a claim for breach of statutory duty where the mortgage breaches the rules laid down by the FSMA (Financial Services and Markets Act 2000) and the Consumer Credit Act 1974) and the potential unenforceability of non-compliant CCA mortgages and the possibility of requesting the court to delay enforcement of lenders' right to enforce their security (under section 36 of the Administration of Justice Act 1970 and Pre-action Protocol for Possession Actions based upon Mortgage Arrears). Ibid 185.

widely discussed by American scholarship under different theories, one of the most famous being the so-called 'improvident extension of credit'.[227]

It was proposed that 'improvident credit extension' should be treated as an instance of unconscionability, to be used by bankruptcy courts in determining whether a consumer credit transaction is unconscionable. The extension of credit would accordingly qualify as 'improvident' when 'it cannot be reasonably expected that the debtor can repay the debt in full in view of the circumstances of the debtor as known to the creditor and of such circumstances as would have been revealed to him upon reasonable inquiry prior to the credit extension'.[228] This standard test (and notion) were also proposed to the Commission on the Bankruptcy Laws of the United States in 1972 while work for reform of the Bankruptcy Act was taking place (as it had already been to previous reform commissions on Bankruptcy); it was not, however, adopted.

It should be noted first of all, that recalling 'unconscionability' in credit contracts sets a stricter and different standard of sanctionable behavior that excludes merely 'negligent' lending.

As has been highlighted, the doctrine of unconscionability "regulates the scope of private lawmaking under contract law, but it does so using standards of objectivized behavior borrowed from tort".[229] 'Unconscionable' lending is thus by its very nature an instrument that is set at the borderline between contract and tort and the idea of using this doctrine in common law systems as the preferred private law tool to sanction intentional extension of credit that the lender knows will unlikely and with difficulty be repaid, signals the choice to provide a flexible tool that is not excessively confined into strict dogmatic boundaries. The idea of liability for reckless lending as a private liability was revived by scholarship more recently, with a proposal that contains a contractual version (with the consequence that a finding of reckless extension of credit would bar enforcement of the contract in collection proceedings) and can arrive (in its stricter version) to a tort allowing a claim for affirmative

---

227   See RL Hersbergen, 'The Improvident Extension of Credit as an Unconscionable Contract' (1974) 23 Drake Law Review 226; V Countryman, 'Improvident Credit Extension: A New Legal Concept Aborning?', (1975) 27 Maine Law Review 1.

228   See Countryman (n 227) 13 ff.

229   JAE Pottow, 'Private Liability for Reckless Consumer Lending' (2007) 1 University of Illinois Law Review 405, 429, highlighting how the standards of objectivized behavior taken from tort include "whether the bargain shocks the reasonable person's objective conscience, whether the superior party know or should have known of deficiencies of the inferior party, and so forth" (Ibid).

damages for causally linked harm.[230] The choice between the two options would depend on the different distribution of externalities.[231]

Yet another tool of private law proposed by American scholarship and that sets itself somewhere in the grey area between contract and tort is the construction of improvident/reckless lending as a tortious interference with contract: more precisely, the tort of 'negligent' interference with a credit contract, where the interference of an improvident lender is with the debtor's preexisting contractual lenders.[232] The proposed framing of a tort of 'negligent' interference with contract (that normally is not recognized)[233] is first of all limited to the hypothesis of credit contracts; secondly it only concerns those interferences with credit contracts that materialize through extension of excessive credit to a debtor; thirdly it provides a cause of action only for injured creditors (not debtors).[234] The construction of this 'new' tort was of course not a straightforward nor an easy attempt, in view, *inter alia*, of the difficulties in underpinning the elements of tort (causal link, 'negligence', other forms of misconduct, debtor's contributory negligence, etc.) into a pre-contractual conduct that only later leads to default.[235] The idea of sanctioning third party effects of a debtor's inability to repay a credit contract because of improvident lending is not new to those who consider a duty of responsible lending as a typical tool of contract governance.[236]

Still within the domain of proposed instruments of private law that can be used to sanction reckless lending, a further step down the scale of torts is taken by those who have theorized this behavior as the intentional tort of deceit (given the fraudulent business model of certain lenders);[237] or famously, the idea that credit products (mortgage loans, credit cards) should be treated as a

---

230 Pottow (n 229) *passim* and especially 425–428.

231 Ibid 456 ff.

232 LJ Long, 'An Uneasy Case for a Tort of Negligent Interference with Credit Contract', (2003–2004) 22 Quinnipiac Law Review 235.

233 I.e. Restatement (Second) of Torts: Intentional Interference with Performance of Contract by Third Party §766 (1965), §766C.

234 Long (n 232) 236. The proposed tort is constructed as a three-party tort, in which an injuring creditor, by extending additional credit to the debtor, interferes in the latter's economic relationship with his previous creditor (creditor-victim) by rendering the debtor's ability to repair the creditor-victim impossible or more burdensome.

235 Long (n 232) *passim* and 238 ff; Pottow (n 229) 441 ff.

236 See S Grundmann, F Möslein, K Riesenhuber, 'Contract Governance: Dimensions in Law and Interdisciplinary Research' in S Grundmann, F Möslein, K Riesenhuber, (eds), *Contract Governance. Dimensions in Law & Interdisciplinary Research* (Oxford University Press 2015) 2 ff. 2.

237 R Harris, E Albin, 'Bankruptcy Policy in Light of Manipulation in Credit Advertising' (2006) 7 Theoretical Inquiries in Law 431, 443–47.

dangerous product and require comprehensive safety regulation of consumer credit and the creation of a single regulatory body responsible for evaluating the safety of consumer credit products.[238]

The enactment of the Dodd-Frank Act in 2010 and the comprehensive reform that followed introduced a new potential tool that can be invoked to sanction, alongside elements of 'unfair and deceptive' practices, also 'abusive practices' in connection with any transaction with a consumer for a consumer financial product or service. As seen earlier, this included a series of powers of rulemaking and control that are attributed to the Consumer Financial Protection Bureau, which created a "Division of Supervision, Enforcement, and Fair Lending" (SEFL). Competences attributed to the CFPB include power to "prescribe rules applicable to a covered person or service provider identifying as unlawful, unfair, deceptive or abusive acts or practices";[239] to prohibit or restrict consumer lending products; to require lenders to offer certain products that are designed by the CFPA and to require disclosures.[240]

"Abusive behavior" is defined by the Dodd-Frank Act as an act or practice that "materially interferes with the ability of a consumer to understand a term or condition of a consumer financial product or service; or takes unreasonable advantage of a lack of understanding on the part of the consumer of the material risks, costs, or conditions of the product or service; or of the inability of the consumer to protect the interests of the consumer in selecting or using a consumer financial product or service; or of the reasonable reliance by the consumer on a covered person to act in the interests of the consumer".[241] The CFPB is empowered to seek not only appropriate legal or equitable relief (i.e. rescission, refunds, restitution, disgorgement, damages, public notification of violations, and limits on the activities of the defendant), but also to impose punitive civil money penalties.[242] The introduction of the 'abusive' standard raised strong debates regarding its potential to serve as a strong tool for the protection of consumers of financial products and, vice-versa, concerns on

---

238   Bar-Gill et al, 'Making Credit Safer' (n 51).

239   Dodd-Frank Act §1031(b).

240   See DS Evans, JD Wright, 'The Effect of the Consumer Financial Protection Agency Act of 2009 on Consumer Credit' (2010) 22 Loyola Consumer Law Review 277, 317–318; see also CL Peterson 'Consumer Financial Protection Bureau Law Enforcement: An Empirical Review' (2016) 90 Tulane Law Review 1058; LJ Kennedy, PA McCoy, E Bernstein, 'The Consumer Financial Protection Bureau: Financial Regulation for the Twenty-First Century', (2012) 97 Cornell Law Review 1141.

241   Dodd-Frank §1031(d).

242   For a detailed survey of the enforcement practices of the CFPB in its first years of operation see Peterson, 'Consumer Financial Protection Bureau Law Enforcement' (n 240); Kennedy et al (n 240).

the uncertainty surrounding the 'vagueness' of the term and potential for discretion accorded to the CFPB and the costs deriving from such a lack of definition.[243]

Beyond the general provisions quoted above, there is no further definition of the meaning of 'abusive standard' in the language used by Congress in the Dodd-Frank Act (a lack of definition acknowledged by the CFPB itself; following consultations, a Call for Evidence in 2018 and a Symposium in 2019 on abusive acts or standards (and on the need to clarify the abusiveness standard) the CFPB has published a Policy Statement in January 2020 on how it intends to interpret the abusiveness standard).[244] It seems as though at least in the first years of enforcement activity of the CFPB, the Bureau has proceeded cautiously and has exercised a quantitative restraint with regard to the number of proceedings alleging abusiveness.[245]

The abusiveness standard obviously does not fully meet the theoretical bases invoked in the past so as to sanction 'unconscionable' lending or borrowing practices. However, it will be interesting to see what type of construction the rule will receive in judicial interpretation and if it will be used as a basis to condemn practices that fall outside the standards laid down in the law (such as prohibited and qualified financial products, for example).

The concept of unconscionability however, as mentioned earlier, is not exclusive to the common law traditions and the development of theories in private law which aim to protect the weaker party against unconscionable bargains are common across European legal systems. An interesting example related to unconscionability in loan contracts can be found in the cases decided in Germany when a boom in the 1980's of overpriced lending to consumers led

---

243 *Ex multis*, see, on a very critical note, for example T Zwicki, 'The Consumer Financial Protection Bureau: Savior or Menace?' (2013) 81 The George Washington Law Review 857.

244 This includes three guidelines: 1) The Bureau will consider conduct as abusive if it concludes that "the harms to consumers from the conduct outweigh its benefits to consumers"; 2) the Bureau will "generally avoid challenging conduct as abusive that relies on all or nearly all of the same facts that the Bureau alleges are unfair or deceptive"; and 3) the Bureau "generally does not intend to seek certain types of monetary relief for abusiveness violations where the covered person was making a good-faith effort to comply with the abusiveness standard". See CFPB, 'Statement of Policy Regarding Prohibition on Abusive Acts or Practices', January 2020.

245 Peterson, 'Consumer Financial Protection Bureau Law Enforcement' (n 240) 1100 ff. As of fall 2019 there are a total of 32 enforcement actions that included an abusiveness claim, but of those 32, 30 enforcement actions also included an unfairness or deception claim, "and in many of these cases, the abusive claim arose from the same course of conduct as the unfairness or deception claim". See CFPB, 'Statement of Policy Regarding Prohibition on Abusive Acts or Practices', January 2020.

to (successful) claims of thousands of borrowers against their banks on the ground of usury and unconscionability.[246]

Interesting references instead to 'good faith' and 'irresponsible lending' practices emerge for example from some recent decisions of the Italian Banking and Financial Ombudsman (*ABF*) which, whilst mostly excluding (with some exceptions)[247] that there is a duty for the lender to avoid over-indebtedness of the borrower, recognizes that a liability could be envisaged only in the case of behavior that is 'self-evidently contrary to good faith'.[248]

In the domain of financial transactions, alongside traditional instruments of private law (from duties of good faith and/or good morals, to mistake), there has also been a growing influence of public law, such as can derive for example from the horizontal effect of fundamental rights on contract law.[249]

Furthermore, an important role is played at the EU level, with the introduction (albeit in the sector of investment services) of conduct of business rules that have been recalled as potential tools for the expansion of protective measures for weak parties in (other) transactions.[250]

The relationship between supervisory conduct of business rules and private law standards, as also the interaction between public and private law in this domain requires a much wider analysis than the few observations that are mentioned here. May it however suffice, for the purpose of these final notes, to recall a meaningful example, that also relates to the interaction between different duties (i.e. suitability, 'know your customer', advice, warning) that loan

---

[246] See Köndgen (n 84) 36, referring to Palandt/Ellenberger, Burgerliches Gestezbuch, (69th edition 2010) §138, n. 25 ff for relevant case law ("contracts were judged as unconscionable if they contained repressive clauses regarding late fees or easy termination by lenders"); see also U Reifner, J Kiesilainen, N Huls, H Springeneer, 'Consumer Overindebtedness and Consumer Law in the European Union', Final Report presented to the Commission of the European Communities, (2003) 100.

[247] See however ABF Collegio di Roma 20 agosto 2013 n. 4440, finding that lenders do have a precise duty to dissuade the consumer from concluding credit agreements that are inadequate to his or her financial situation and that could lead to his or her overindebtedness; in such a case there would be a pre-contractual liability of the lender.

[248] See *ex multis*, ABF, Collegio di Roma, Dec. n. 3134/2016; ABF, Collegio di Milano, Dec. n. 6419/2015; ABF, Collegio di Palermo, Dec. n. 1706/2019; ABF, Collegio di Napoli, Dec. 1067/2018.

[249] See OO Cherednychenko, 'Conceptualising unconscionability in the context of risky financial transactions: How to converge public and private law approaches?', Kenny et al (n 219) 247 ff, recalling the famous *Bürgschaft* case of the German Federal Constitutional Court (Bundesverfassungsgericht, 19 Ocotber 1993, *BVerfGE* 89, 214) as an indicative example. See also *infra* Chapter 5, par. 5.3.

[250] Ibid 266–268 on the impact that conduct of business rules have had in shaping private law standards, with examples from German, Dutch and English laws.

regulation borrows from the domain of investment services. More specifically, Article 24(1) of the MiFID II introduces a 'general conduct of business rule': an investment service provider is obliged to 'act honestly, fairly and professionally in accordance with the best interests of its clients'. This has been defined as an 'umbrella rule of conduct' that not only includes the duties laid down in the following articles of MiFID, but that also reflects a general rule of care that can be found in contract and tort laws of Member States.[251] One can question whether such a general rule could be applied or envisaged as a standard for general duties in the relationship between borrowers and lenders. This could be especially relevant for conduct that is not directly regulated by the existing legislation on consumer loans and mortgages but that can be qualified as 'irresponsible lending conduct' (examples include payday loans, high-cost credit, and credit cards).

The judicial construction of these duties and the impact that it could potentially have (so far such that it does not allow the identification of a strong trend in either direction), must be considered in the light of the wider implications of 'responsible lending' duties.

One of the most meaningful aspects, only briefly touched upon in the previous analysis, is the problem of access to credit. Not only the problem of the economic impact, in terms of costs, that policies of 'responsible lending' may have, but also the wider implications regarding fundamental rights, equality and non-discrimination. This is the object of the next chapter.

4.4   A Few Conclusive Comparative Remarks

It is now possible to draw some conclusions from a comparative perspective on the different regulatory choices expressed in the legal systems that have been analyzed.

First of all, from a general point of view, a first distinction that is necessary is between systems that have expressly introduced rules that recall some form of 'responsible credit' policy and systems where these policies can be outlined by a systemic and functional reconstruction of existing rules.

Here one can note first of all a convergence in intent that was either triggered or accelerated in the aftermath of the 2007–2008 financial crisis. Thus, legislative drafts, codes of conduct, guidelines have more or less openly spoken

---

251   M Kruithof, 'A Differentiated Approach to Client Protection: The Example of MiFID', in Grundmann et al (n 190) 105, 147 ff. See also Mak (n 215) 14.

of the need to pursuit 'responsible lending'. With very few exceptions, this did not directly translate into binding rules. Rather, both the United States and the European legislator chose to introduce specific precontractual duties that can be – at least in part – ascribed to this scope even if there is no explicit recognition. Rules like the 'ability to pay' under US law or the 'duty of creditworthiness assessment' under EU law are functional (also) to an implementation of responsible credit policies – and both examples comprise not only duties for lenders, but also for borrowers.

Second of all, from a regulatory point of view, it has been noted that the EU still relies on a regulatory model which 'prioritizes information over substantive regulation'.[252] Indeed if one compares the rules of the Dodd-Frank Act and of the two Directives on Consumer Credit and Mortgage lending quoted above, it is appreciable that the US regulation lays down rules that substantively qualify the loan products that are offered consumers; the EU approach on the contrary introduces procedural controls exemplified by a series of pre-contractual duties. It can be assumed that the stronger regulation of 'toxic products' in the US is due to the fact of having originated the 'subprime' crisis, whose impact imposed a reform of the entire system.

A second observation can be made within the system of the European Union. Here, as noted in part 2, the differences in implementation and interpretation of the provisions imposing pre-contractual duties (disclosure, explanation, creditworthiness assessment, duty to warn and the problematic 'duty to deny') have created diverging notions on the binding nature of these provisions, to the extent that, as seen, some systems seem to envisage restrictions to contractual freedom as the tradeoff for the implementation of 'responsible' or 'affordable' credit policies. In the absence of clear statutory indications on the efficacy of some of these duties (i.e. the effects of the duty to assess the creditworthiness of borrowers laid down in both of the European Directives examined), there have been different orientations regarding the nature of this duty (partly clarified by the ECJ), the mandatory effects of the outcome of the assessments, and the construction of the sanctions. It is also useful to recall that the one of the problematic aspects highlighted during the revision process of the EU Consumer Credit Directive revolved around the ambiguity of some of its provisions, including "a lack of clarity in the provisions on creditworthiness assessment resulting in insufficient protection for consumers"[253] and the persistence of irresponsible lending practices.

---

252   Howells et al, *Rethinking EU Consumer Law* (n 98) 7.

253   See the Explanatory Memorandum of the 2021 Proposal for a Consumer Credits Directive.

Finally, as even a very brief overview of some of the main issues surrounding the enforcement (public and private) of the duties laid down in the respective regulations in the United States and in the EU (duly transposed into national laws) has shown, the nature of responsible credit duties tends to be more easily framed within the contractual and pre-contractual, rather than the tortious, domain. The theoretical foundations (in the absence of a positive regulation) for this type of liability remain however multiple; not only within a trans-systemic divide between different legal families, but also within national legal systems whose scholarship and courts have offered numerous theses and doctrines. From the framing of the duties surrounding responsible credit and their enforcement, there follows the question of the impact on the lending market and the consequent availability of credit for borrowers.

Access to credit depends on a multiplicity of factors determined by the functioning of the credit markets, by public policies of promotion or restriction of 'democratization' of credit practices, by direct governmental interventions in times of emergencies (as the COVID-19 crisis has demonstrated); albeit to a lesser degree, it also depends on the pervasiveness, efficacity and stringency of responsible lending duties.

Access to Credit and Responsible Lending

Introduction

In the previous chapters the origin of the duty of assessing creditworthiness, its macro-economic implications, its transposition into law and its effect on contract law have been examined – all the while referring to the role that creditworthiness has in implementing 'responsible credit' (lending and borrowing) policies.

A fundamental question however that requires further consideration is whether the implementation of these duties and the embracing of a 'responsible credit' philosophy negatively impacts access to credit. The question naturally becomes particularly relevant when considering those categories of consumers that are most likely to suffer the consequences of financial (and social) exclusion.

The issue needs to be broken down into two aspects: the first is whether there is a 'right to (access) credit'; and the second is if responsible credit policies as they are currently framed and implemented infringe or jeopardize this right or rather promote it.

The discourse on access is tied to the one on inclusion, as the first is often a gateway to the second. Responsible credit, as will be seen, relates to the 'protective' dimension of access to credit (and inclusion).

The issue of access to credit is – and has been – foundational for multiple branches of social sciences, including economics, sociology, history, cultural studies, and of course, legal studies. Policies aiming at ensuring, regulating, promoting or restricting access to credit have characterized human history and the regulation of economic activities, spanning through different eras and different macro- and micro- economic (and legal) policies. If one restricts the analysis to the second half of the past century and the first two decades of the present-with a certain degree of over-simplification – there are two trends that can be discerned.

The first consists in a wave of policies promoting 'easy' credit, strongly tied to the so-called 'lending revolution' or 'democratization of credit', with policies emphasizing the inclusive effect of access to credit. This is followed by a more cautious approach emerging at the eve of the 2007–2008 financial crisis with the growing awareness of the effects in terms of consumer over-indebtedness, and fully affirming itself in the aftermath of the crisis and its ensuing credit crunch with the realization of the larger systemic impact of consumer debt on financial stability. Hence the introduction of several of the regulatory measures examined in the previous chapters and the rising importance of the concept of 'responsible credit'.

Finally, the 2020 COVID-19 pandemic has induced the adoption of important regulatory measures – typically authorized by national Central Banks and banking authorities of many systems as well as at the supranational level in the case of the EU – with the scope of ensuring that the restrictive orders affecting economic activities adopted in many States due to the health emergency, would not interrupt access to credit for businesses, SMEs and individual borrowers.[1]

Interestingly, interventions aiming at ensuring that credit flow would not be interrupted in the midst of an economic crisis due to a global pandemic have acted upon two fronts: uplifting or easing of the prudential capital requirements for lending institutions on the one side (allowing the strict parameters in terms of NPLS to be momentarily suspended); simplifying the processes of creditworthiness assessments for undertakings and individual borrowers on the other.

In order to understand how the politics of access to credit interact with the regulation of credit and the attempts at implementing duties of responsible credit, it is useful to examine the setting against which consumer credit and mortgage credit have developed over the past fifty years.

5.1   The 'Democratization of Credit'

Several of the policies and practices that have been analyzed in the previous chapters were originated by the so-called 'lending revolution' or 'democratization' of credit' (or in a wider sense, the process of 'democratization of finance'-i.e. the process through which individual citizens should be granted access to retail financial services, and of which access to credit constitutes an important – though not the only – feature).

This 'revolution', beginning in the late 1970's, was based on the promotion of financial liberalization, the deregulation of interest rates, the process of

---

1   See for example the EU Commission 'Temporary Framework for State aid measures to support the economy in the current COVID-19 outbreak' adopted of 19.3.2020 (C(2020) 1863 final) (and later amended) and the measures adopted within; or the US Federal Coronavirus Aid, Relief, and Economic Security (CARES) Act of 2020 and the Coronavirus Response and Consolidated Appropriations Act (2021).

securitization, the development and use of (computer-based) credit scoring, and the increase in use of all-purpose credit cards.[2] The lending revolution must naturally be inserted within a wider economic process which began in the early decades of the 20th century in the United States, in which different polices aiming at strengthening the demand of industrial goods by citizens, such as consumer lending, were adopted as a tool to fuel production of these commodities.[3] The process entailed a change of paradigm in the approach to money and debt, in which debt began to be perceived as having a positive role in the further development of the capitalist system, and personal indebtedness was no longer seen as a sign of financial recklessness and moral hazard.[4]

Where this type of policy was applied to the mortgage and housing market, allowing low income citizens to access private home-ownership, it was often associated with the idea not only of 'financial', but also of 'social' inclusion and was emblematically referred to, especially in the United States' context, as the 'democratization of finance and credit'.[5]

This process, which also concerned consumer credit, often under forms of unsecured credit (i.e. credit cards) affirmed itself in the last two decades of the 20th Century, and among other factors (such as the deregulation of consumer credit markets on the supply side) was, again, in the case of consumer credit also tied to the 'privatization' or reduction of the welfare state and the

---

2   I Ramsay, T Williams 'The Crash that launched a thousand fixes – Regulation of Consumer Credit after the Lending Revolution and the Credit Crunch', in A Kern, N Moloney, *Law Reform and Financial Markets* (Elgar 2011) 221; FDIC, 'Evaluating the Consumer Lending Revolution' (2003), 5 ff. https://www.fdic.gov/analysis/archived-research/fyi/091703fyi.pdf (accessed July 2021).

3   See TA Durkin, G Elliehausen, 'Consumer Lending', in AN Berger, P Molyneux, JOS Wilson, *The Oxford Handbook of Banking* (2d ed Oxford University Press 2015) 312, 313 on the role of consumer lending in contributing to the growth of durable goods industries.

4   See G Comparato, *The Financialisation of the Citizen* (Hart 2018) 38, recalling Max Weber's theories on the previous prevailing religious and ethical understanding of society, money, and debt and some of their critiques. See also D Burton, *Credit and Consumer Society* (Routledge 2008) 9 ff.

   Effects of this type have also been highlighted in the Neo-liberal model that between the 1980's and 1990's was introduced in several countries (especially in the US and UK economies) also defined as 'privatized Keynesianism', where private individuals, not the State, took out debt on the market to stimulate the economy (and where the growth of credit markets for poor and middle-income people, and of derivatives and futures markets among the wealthy "rescued the neo-liberal model from the instability that would otherwise have been its fate"). See C Crouch, 'Privatised Keynesianism: An Unacknowledged Policy Regime' (2009) 11 British Journal of Politics and International Relations 382, 390.

5   See Comparato (n 4) 41; see also, for a reconstruction, Burton (n 4).

need for citizens to take out debt to cover medical or educational expenses for example.[6]

A toll of the phenomenon – albeit not deriving solely from it – was an increase in consumer debt and in consumer over-indebtedness. Indeed, some have highlighted that democratization of finance has an "inherent contradiction": it needs to promote the access to financial products, and thus indebtedness, but on the other hand it has to avoid over-indebtedness.[7]

The ideology behind 'democratizing credit' was often understood as part of a wider movement and promise of social inclusion in which, through financialization, citizens would increase not only their welfare, but also their participation in the economic, and ultimately in the democratic, process.[8] Access to credit on a non-discriminatory basis emerged as a matter of justice: in consideration of its functional role in these models of access not only to basic consumption needs but also as a mechanism for achieving mobility and status and social inclusion, it has for example been linked, in the United States, to the discourse and fight for civil rights.[9]

More generally, the process of privatization of many services previously covered by the State posed the question of whether the "special responsibility towards the most disadvantaged citizens, as determined by the principle of compulsory provision of a service" could still be expected to some extent

---

6 For a reconstruction of 'democratisation of credit' see J Niemi – Kiesiläinen, I Ramsay, WC Whitford (eds), *Consumer Bankruptcy in Global Perspective* (Hart 2003) 4, also noting that "Democratisation of credit allowed for the privatisation of social insurance, in the form of credit availability, in societies where the public insurance provided by the welfare state has been reduced."

An acknowledgement of this type of policy was contained for example in the EU Commission White Paper on Financial Services Policy 2005–2010 (COM(2005) 629) which recognized the gradual withdrawal of the public sector from financing certain aspects of social systems and the need to promote 'good investment choices' (e.g. for pensions) and a direct involvement of citizens in financial issues (White Paper, 2.6).

7 Comparato (n 4) 72.

8 Ibid 42, reconstructing the ideologies of the 'promise of democratisation' of finance.

9 I Ramsay, 'Consumer Credit Law, Distributive Justice and the Welfare State' (1995) 15 Oxford Journal of Legal Studies 177, 177, 193 ff. See also AD Taibi, 'Banking, Finance, and Community Economic Empowerment: Structural Economic Theory, Procedural Civil Rights and Substantive Racial Justice' (1994) 107 Harvard Law Review 1465 for a community-empowerment perspective on legislation enacted in the United States, including the Equal Credit Opportunity Act (ECOA) and the Community Reinvestment Act (CRA), and the relationship between banking regulation and the discourse on civil rights.

after privatization and whether it could be upheld through principles of private law.[10]

As is counterintuitive, in these conditions, any policy acting upon availability of credit or introducing or allowing barriers in the access to credit, including different forms of discrimination, can entail not only financial, but also social exclusion.

Not surprisingly therefore, one of the principal concerns with the current widespread regulatory approach to consumer credit, which includes the pivotal tool of creditworthiness assessments, is related to the effects on access to credit (at affordable terms). This concern relates not only to the general public of consumers, but especially to the economically more vulnerable ones (see par. 5.2).

5.1.1   The Global Financial Crisis of 2007–2008

The pillars of the process of 'democratization of credit' were shaken strongly at their foundation by the 2007–2008 global financial crisis and the ensuing regulatory approach aiming at introducing corrective measures where the previous tenets proved to be particularly harmful for certain categories of borrowers (i.e. consumers) and, more generally for the markets. The combination of favorable economic conditions and the effects of the originate to distribute models (which freed lenders from the risk of non-performance) allowed expansive and 'easy credit' models to affirm themselves. Coupled with the growing privatization of the welfare state, the result at the individual level was a growth in consumer over-indebtedness.[11]

Not all the measures of the so-called 'neo-liberal' approach to consumer lending (largely supported by the World Bank for example), always proved effective in protecting consumers from predatory and mis-selling practices and from entering into spirals of debt.[12] This approach aims at facilitating access to

---

10   T Wilhelmsson, 'Services of general interests and European Private law,' in CE Rickett, TGW Telfer (eds), *International Perspectives on Consumers' Access to Justice* (Cambridge University Press 2003) 152.

11   In the EU this phenomenon hit particularly Member States in southern Europe and was fueled by an easier availability of consumer credit and mortgage credit which in turned was due, *inter alia*, to the lowering of nominal interest rates in many Member States following the completion of the EMU and the adoption of the Euro (as well as a long-term growth in real estate prices). See Comparato (n 4) 79–80, quoting studies on the housing markets from different Member States, including Ireland, Greece, Spain.

12   Ramsay et al 'The Crash that launched a thousand fixes' (n 1) 223–224; S Rutledge, N Annamalai, R Lester, R Symonds, 'Good practices for consumer protection and financial literacy in Europe and Central Asia: a diagnostic tool', (2010) Washington D.C., World Bank Group.

consumer credit (availability) and creating confidence in an expanding and competitive consumer credit market (safety), through promotion of the use of credit bureaus and positive credit reporting, truth in lending and product disclosures, financial literacy, financial ombudsmen, and prohibition of abusive business practices by financial service providers.[13] However, may it suffice to recall for example the problems of the exploitation of behavioral biases of borrowers, and the potentially discriminatory effects of risk based pricing made possible by large-scale credit scoring (and which can target more vulnerable borrowers with higher cost credit, for example in the credit card market); and more generally, the risks deriving from the structural asymmetries in digital consumer markets (including problems of fairness and discrimination deriving from personalized pricing and individualized marketing).[14]

With the 2007–2008 financial crisis, the problem of over-indebtedness and its relation to the politics of easy availability of credit became evident.[15] In this context, along with other policies such as financial product regulation, procedures to deal with consumer over-indebtedness, and financial literacy

---

See for example the results of the different Studies commissioned by the EU Parliament on the Mis-selling of Financial Products in the fields of subordinated debt and other junior liabilities (https://www.europarl.europa.eu/RegData/etudes/STUD/2018/618994/IPOL_STU(2018)618994_EN.pdf); mortgage credit and related products, including cross-currency loan (https://www.europarl.europa.eu/RegData/etudes/STUD/2018/618995/IPOL_STU(2018)618995_EN.pdf); marketing, distribution and sale of financial products regulated under MiFID, UCITS or AIMFD (https://www.europarl.europa.eu/RegData/etudes/STUD/2018/618996/IPOL_STU(2018)618996_EN.pdf); Consumer credit (https://www.europarl.europa.eu/RegData/etudes/STUD/2018/618997/IPOL_STU(2018)618997_EN.pdf); and a Case study on compensation of investors subject to mis-selling in Belgium (https://www.europarl.europa.eu/RegData/etudes/STUD/2018/618998/IPOL_STU(2018)618998_EN.pdf).

13 Ramsay et al 'The Crash that launched a thousand fixes' (n 4) 223.
14 See e.g. the joint report by N Helberger, O Lynskey, H-W Micklitz, P Rott, M Sax, J Strycharz, 'EU Consumer Protection 2.0. Structural asymmetries in digital consumer markets', (2021) BEUC, Brussels, March 2021, 94 and ff https://www.beuc.eu/publications/beuc-x-2021-018_eu_consumer_protection.0_0.pdf (accessed October 2021).
15 Indeed, see the recognition made by the Commission in its 2017 Consumer Financial Services Action Plan that "while the increased availability and easier access to consumer credit create opportunities for business and result in lower costs for borrowers, there is also an increased risk of irresponsible lending and borrowing causing over-indebtedness. This risk needs to be mitigated." (European Commission, Consumer Financial Services Action Plan: Better Products, More Choice, COM(2017)139 final, 2.6). See also the considerations of the Commission in the Europe 2020 Strategy for smart, sustainable inclusive growth (COM(2010) 2020 final), at p.8, on the relation between "availability of easy credit, short-termism and excessive risk-taking in financial markets around the world" and "speculative behavior, giving rise to bubble-driven growth and important imbalances".

programs, the notion of 'responsible credit' was revived as one of the instruments for achieving a balance between access to credit and protection from over-indebtedness.

This of course may imply a more cautious approach to 'easy access to credit' and may raise concerns with regards to consequences in terms of financial exclusion. These concerns derive from the observation that 'responsible lending' may become an instrument that is targeted more towards financial stability than towards consumer protection, and its invocation has not coincidentally occurred during a period of financial instability and credit crunch.[16] However, it is here purported that if responsible credit is conceived as having a wider scope of promoting 'suitable' and 'affordable' credit, tailored onto the specific needs of borrowers, it also encompasses a protective function (see Chapter 4 on the precontractual tools that can perform this function).

The financial crisis also brought to the fore a renewed attention to problems of financial exclusion and the need to implement inclusive policies (see par. 5.2). Financial and social exclusion are conceptually distinct phenomena, which are however often closely intertwined. The former can lead to the latter, and the latter can be further accentuated by the former.[17]

The case of access to mortgage credit is emblematic: it affects the right to housing and if loans are granted under particularly unfavorable terms it can jeopardize the probabilities of retaining a mortgaged dwelling over time. On the other hand, excessive protection (i.e. costly, lengthy, uncertain procedures for repossession of mortgaged property which neutralizes the security function of the mortgage) can lead to a restrictive approach to mortgage lending by lending institutions and thus hinder access.[18] A more debtor-defaulter friendly regime of foreclosure can for example induce lenders to require higher down payments, because of delay in repossession and the higher costs lenders face,

---

16   Comparato (n 4) 137.

17   See for example the Joint Report on Social Protection and Social Inclusion 2009 (COM(209)58 final and SEC(2009)141), 62, quoting the EU Commission 2008 Study on Financial Services Provision and Prevention of Financial Exclusion and highlighting how "groups facing poverty and/or exclusion encounter specific difficulties in accessing financial services, with negative consequences for their personal finance or ability to find a job. Denial of access to financial services on the mainstream market may lead people to turn to more costly and risky alternative financial products. On the other hand, for the general population, an improper use of financial services may, when combined with a critical life event, lead to over-indebtedness".

18   Comparato (n 4) 18–19.

and thwart access to credit.[19] The role of private and procedural law is fundamental for the outcome (and has also been questioned by courts).[20]

More generally, as highlighted previously, growth in credit supply (the willingness of lenders to extend credit on improved terms or to classes of borrowers previously excluded from credit markets) depends on a series of factors, such as technological advances, increased credit market competition, or government policies.[21] The increase in credit supply is not, however, without consequences on a systemic level and can impact financial stability.[22]

Whilst securitization increases credit supply, a misalignment of incentives can affect financial stability (see Chapter 2). Furthermore, an increase in access to credit involves growing numbers of subjects, some of which were previously excluded from credit. These however are the same subjects that are most fragile, that can be targets of forms of predatory lending, and that can be more easily affected by over-indebtedness; the financially fragile are often among the first to be touched by credit crunches that follow systemic crises.

When, as a consequence of crises having strong impacts (such as the global financial crisis of 2007–2008, or the COVID-19 pandemic crisis in 2020), there is a surge in non-performing loans, the credit supply is reduced unless external measures are taken, including for example measures to free lending institutions from the NPLS in their balance sheets and allow them to resume their lending activity. Unless and until this happens, crises can provoke a reduction in the overall capital available for loans which tends to exclude the most fragile borrowers.

---

19   See for a study in the early 2000's on the impact of different US State foreclosure laws on loan sizes, KM Pence, 'Foreclosing on Opportunity: State Laws and Mortgage Credit' (2006) 88 The Review of Economics and Statistics 177, finding that loan sizes are 3% to 7% smaller in defaulter-friendly states.

20   The analysis is beyond the scope of this work. See for example for a detailed and comparative analysis of the impact of different post-default debtor protection rules on the various credit and lending models, D Kennedy, 'Cost Benefit Analysis of Debtor Protection Rules in Subprime Market Default Situations', in E Belsky, N Retsinas (eds), *Building Assets, Building Credit: Creating Wealth in Low-Income Communities* (Brookings Institution Press 2005). For a comparison on data on evictions and repossession in Europe between the UK and Spain, see Comparato (n 4) 56–57.

    See *infra* on the role of the ECJ for example in questioning whether national laws governing mortgage enforcement procedures ensure effective judicial review of unfair terms in consumer contracts and confirming that mortgage proceedings fall within the scope of application of the EU Unfair Contract Terms Directive.

21   G Donadio, A Lehnert, 'Residential Mortgages', in Berger et al (n 3) 326, 346.

22   Ibid.

5.2   Access to Credit as a Policy for Consumers and the Problem of Financial Exclusion

Regulation of access to credit using the different instruments so far analyzed, has important impacts in terms of access to a series of fundamental rights and services for individuals (access to housing through mortgage debt; access to health or education where loans are taken out to pay for insurance or tuition fees, and so forth). The effectiveness of policies aiming at ensuring access to credit, as a means to access further rights, becomes of crucial standing. It is under this perspective that a negative and a positive dimension of access to credit can be envisioned; the negative dimension can be identified with policies against discrimination, whereas the positive dimension encompasses policies aiming at financial and social inclusion.

Antidiscrimination and financial inclusion, whilst pertaining to different aspects of access, are nonetheless closely connected not only by relations of cause and effect, but also by a concrete possibility that forms of 'economic discrimination' conceal discrimination based on other factors (i.e. race or gender). For these reasons, policies on access to credit are inevitably also tied to considerations regarding the social group(s) that are most affected by its denial: the 'economically and socially vulnerable' consumers.

There have been influential and extensive debates regarding who is to be considered a vulnerable (or disadvantaged) consumer and what makes a consumer in financial contracts 'vulnerable' (a term that itself is susceptible to various meanings, including subjects who are capable of suffering detriment in their consumption both due to personal reasons and those connected with the market).[23]

According to theories of classic economics, the vulnerability may depend on information asymmetry; on pressure (which can be especially relevant for consumers of financial services, not only due to the imbalance of power between the provider of the service and the consumers, but also to the frequent position of financial difficulty and/or indebtedness in which a consumer is when applying for a loan); on conditions of supply (lack of choice); on the impact of certain factors (i.e. in the case of financial services: poverty); and on the difficulty of obtaining redress (so-called redress vulnerability).[24] The

---

23   P Cartwright, 'Understanding and Protecting Vulnerable Financial Consumers', (2015) 38 Journal of Consumer Policy 119, 119–120, further proposing a taxonomy of vulnerability. See also, with reference to vulnerability in general in EU legislation and in case law of the ECJ, H-W Micklitz, *The Politics of Justice in European Private Law: Social Justice, Access Justice, Societal Justice*, (Cambridge University Press 2018) 318 ff.

24   Cartwright (n 23) 121–123.

latter type of vulnerability, which can depend on multiple factors, including lack of awareness, transaction and litigation costs, prevents consumers from exerting the market discipline that would otherwise, in a perfect market, hold providers accountable for unsatisfactory products and disincentivize them from improper conduct (such as mis-selling practices).[25]

Moreover, these vulnerable consumers are the customers/consumers who when they are not excluded, will typically only be able to access credit at much higher costs, further exacerbating the risk of defaulting or becoming overindebted and jeopardizing their chances of accessing credit in the future. The vicious circle effect is clear.

Different definitions of what constitutes 'financial inclusion' have also been proposed. Several authors stress that inclusion means not only a general access to 'mainstream financial services' (commonly intended as access to bank accounts, access to credit, and access to different forms of financial and investment contracts), but also includes the conditions under which this access becomes possible (namely access to 'appropriate', 'safe', 'fair', 'low cost' financial services), as well as the implementation both of policies aiming at financial literacy, and of those dealing with over-indebtedness.[26] Financial inclusion is thus intended in the broad significance which comprises not only the 'access' dimension, but which also includes the 'protective' dimension from financial and social risks.[27]

The financial inclusion discourse was originated in the United States and accompanied by a series of federal laws and subsidies for the provision of credit enacted as of the 1970s (the Community Reinvestment Act of 1977 constituting a famous – and much debated – example[28] as also the government sponsored entities Fannie Mae and Freddie Mac); it has also found an important place in the European agenda, where however regulatory measures and European private law have primarily dealt with 'market' inclusion, leaving social inclusion to the Member States.[29] This approach changed in part,

25   Cartwright (n 23) 124. See also I Ramsay, 'Consumer redress and access to justice' in Rickett et al (n 10).

26   For a reconstruction of some of the different definitions proposed by economic literature, Comparato (n 4) 18–19.

27   Comparato (n 4) 11; 18.

28   For a reconstruction of the CRA and other federal programs see MS Barr, 'Credit Where it Counts: The Community Reinvestment Act and Its Critics', (2005) 80 New York University Law Review 513; MS Barr, 'Modes of Credit Market Regulation' in Retsinas et al (n 20); LJ White, 'Focusing on Fannie and Freddie: The Dilemmas of Reforming Housing Finance', (2003) 23 Journal of Financial Services Research 43.

29   Comparato (n 4) 14; 72 ff.

with reference to certain financial services, after the financial crisis.[30] In its 2007–2013 Consumer Policy Strategy the EU Commission acknowledged the problem of the lack of access to bank accounts and recognized that 'affordable access to essential services for all is both essential for a modern and flexible economy but also for social inclusion';[31] however only in 2014 did this translate into the approval of the Payments Account Directive.[32]

More generally, in its 2009 Joint Report on Social Protection and Social Inclusion, the EU Commission identified the goals for regulatory responses to the problem of financial exclusion, including "effective, adequate and affordable access to basic banking services"; prevention (expressly requiring responsible borrowing and money management and responsible lending) and rehabilitation of over-indebtedness; "promotion of professional and personal microcredit" and policies for the "development of financial information and education for vulnerable consumers".[33]

The traditional focus on market inclusion as the principal tool for the promotion of financial inclusion falls in line with two phenomena that have been pinpointed in the development of European regulatory private law in the last decades: a changing paradigm of justice, identified with the move from 'social justice' to 'access justice', which is much closer to the idea of fairness of market access belonging to the Anglo-American tradition, rather than to the continental idea of social justice understood as distributive justice; and, as a second trend, the growing importance of the economic efficiency doctrine.[34]

---

30   The EU approach towards financial inclusion had begun changing in the mid 2000s and was later accelerated with the financial crisis. There had been previous acknowledgment on behalf of the Commission of the problem of access to financial services for low-income people (with the Commission Communication 'Financial services: enhancing consumer confidence', (COM(97) 309 final, 26.06.1997)) and previously in the Consumer Policy Action Plan 1999–2001 where there had been a push for the recognition of basic banking services and internet services as falling into the social and economic categories of services of general interest (at 15). This did not however lead to the adoption of concrete measures until much later.

31   COM (2007) 99 final, 9.

32   Directive 2014/92/EU of 23 July 2014 on the comparability of fees related to payment accounts, payment account switching and access to payment accounts with basic features, [2014] OJ L 257/214.

33   European Commission, 'Joint Report on Social Protection and Social Inclusion 2009', COM(209)58 final and SEC(2009)141, 62.

34   H-W Micklitz, 'The Visible Hand of European Regulatory Private Law. The Transformation of European Private Law from Autonomy to Functionalism in Competition and Regulation', (2008) EUI Law Working Paper, 2008/14, 9. Access justice is intended as a notion at the basis of EU regulatory private law including EU consumer law, discrimination law, telecommunication law, energy law, transport law, and it tends to 'include

The paradigm of 'access justice' is therefore a useful key in analyzing the discourse on financial inclusion and more specifically on access to credit from a comparative point of view.

Access justice is not limited to ensuring participation and access to the market for all participants, including consumers; it also requires that the position and rights of consumers and workers once they have accessed the market is guaranteed through judicial enforcement (i.e. Article 47 European Charter of Fundamental Rights).[35] The concept of access justice can once again be envisioned under a negative and a positive dimension: the negative dimension prohibits discrimination in the access to goods and services, whilst the positive dimension encompasses the rules actively allowing access to the rights and strengthening the position of consumers and workers.[36]

Applied to credit, on the negative dimension, one can recall first of all that specific non-discriminatory statutes for access to credit have been enacted for example in the United States in the mid 1970's, including the Equal Credit Opportunity Act[37] and the Fair Housing Act,[38] (prohibiting discrimination by direct providers of housing and by banks and other lending institutions); the Home Mortgage Disclosure Act[39] (requiring the disclosure of loan-level information about mortgages so as to allow, *inter alia*, the identification of lending patterns that could be discriminatory); and the Community Reinvestment Act[40] (encouraging lending activity by financial institutions in the communities in which they do business, including low-and moderate-income neighborhoods, and introducing *de facto* a social rating system on banks). In European private law the more general principles and fundamental rules on equality and non-discrimination contained in piecemeal legislation have been applied or interpreted as applying also to financial contracts[41] (and are now expressly

---

citizens as economic actors in newly liberalized markets', with a reduction in the scope of Member States' redistributive interventions to that of "providing a fair chance to benefit from the Internal Market". H-W Micklitz, 'Social Justice and Access Justice in Private Law', (2011) EUI Law Working Paper, 2011/02, 21.

35   Micklitz, 'Social Justice and Access Justice in Private Law' (n 34) 23.
36   Ibid 22.
37   15 U.S.C. 1691.
38   42 U.S.C. 3601.
39   12 U.S.C. 29.
40   12 U.S.C. 2901.
41   See for example the relevance of Directive 2004/113 implementing the principle of equal treatment between men and women in the access to supply of goods and services and the implications ensuing from the *Test-Achats* case of 2011 decided by the ECJ (Case C-236/09, *Association belge des Consommateurs Test-Achats ASBL v Conseil des ministres*, [2011], ECLI:EU:C:2011:100) (on which see Chapter 3).

recalled for loan contracts in the 2021 Proposal for a new Consumer Credits Directive).[42]

As seen previously (Chapter 3), this antidiscrimination legislation in its various forms identifies the elements (such as gender or ethnicity) that cannot be taken into account as a determinant in denying or granting credit. A problematic aspect however, that is not expressly considered, is the one relating to economic discrimination.[43] This can be identified as the crucial point in which the different perspectives so far examined on access, non-discrimination, responsible credit and financial inclusion intersect.

If access to credit has to respond to precise regulatory obligations (prudential duties and, where framed, responsible credit duties), with creditworthiness assessments as the principal tool used to comply with these duties, it is evident that the economic and financial situation of the applicant borrower becomes the determinant in the decision on whether to grant credit.

A denial of credit on the basis of insufficient guarantees of ability of repayment of a borrower is not unlawful (and notoriously also responds to precise prudential duties of lenders), but could be still be argued to constitute a hypothesis of economic discrimination and vice-versa: the economically more vulnerable are also often the subjects suffering from racial or gender discrimination. Economic discrimination could conceal (or be used to conceal), other forms of discrimination.[44]

If, however, access to credit were framed as a 'right', a decision of this type would infringe this right; or, stated differently, if a right to credit exists then credit should be granted regardless of the economic and financial situation of the applicant, with great relevance for vulnerable consumers.[45] The question

---

42   Article 6 of the Proposal for a Directive on Consumer Credits (COM(2021)347 final).

43   More generally on economic discrimination and contract law (also with reference to credit contracts), see T Wilhelmsson, *Social Contract Law and European Integration*, (Dartmouth 1995) 203–205; and T Wilhelmsson, 'Consumer Law and Social Justice', in I Ramsay (ed), *Consumer Law in the Global Economy*, (Ashgate-Dartmouth 1997) 225 ff.; D Caplovitz, *The Poor Pay More: Consumer Practices of Low-income Families* (Free Press 1967).

44   See I Ramsay, T Williams, 'Inequality, Market Discrimination, and Credit Markets', in Ramsay, *Consumer Law in the Global Economy* (n 43) 233–234, recalling the racial and racist assumptions that were used for example in US mortgage lending practices in the 1920's in the United States (where indeed, as previously recalled, specific antidiscrimination statutes for lending (i.e. the ECOA and the Fair Housing Act) were enacted) and questioning whether the incorporation of human rights law into regulation of credit services would serve as a protection for consumers against discrimination in credit markets.

45   See OO Cherednychenko, 'The EU Charter of Fundamental Rights and Consumer Credit: Towards Responsible Lending?', in H Collins (ed), *European Contract Law and the Charter*

is if and how a 'right to credit' could be framed and if such a right would be enforceable.

5.3   Access to Credit as a Right? Theorizing 'Due Process' in Access to Credit

References to a 'right to credit' are common in political and social discourse, especially in the analysis of policies aiming at reduction of poverty and at promotion of microcredit;[46] or with reference to credit as a means to access housing or other 'fundamental needs'.[47] How this however translates from a legal point of view into a binding and enforceable right is obviously a different – and much discussed – matter.[48]

There are two aspects under which a 'right to credit' could be examined. One relates to a basic dimension of universal access (in analogy to the way in which access to services such as education and health are framed and understood),

---

of Fundamental Rights (Intersentia 2017) 150; and Ramsay et al 'Inequality, Market Discrimination, and Credit Markets' (n 44) ibid.

46   Most notably M Yunus, *inter alia* in his speech 'Credit for Self-employment: A Fundamental Human Right', (Grameen Bank, 1987).

47   See for example the proposal in L Nogler, U Reifner (eds), *Life Time Contracts. Social·Long-Term Contracts in Labour, Tenancy and Consumer Credit Law* (Eleven International Publishing 2014) 3, Principle n. 8 "Access": "Providers of life time contracts must refrain from discrimination in terms of the personal and social characteristics of consumers at all stages of the contract, from access to termination, including discrimination in terms of the group of intended users of the contract, or individual members of that group. The importance of life time contracts in meeting the basic human needs of subsistence, employment and participation in economic life gives access to these goods, services and income opportunities the status of fundamental human right (distributive justice)" (where life time contracts here include labour, credit agreements, tenancy and supply), with credit being the contractual relation in which 'either income is allocated as and when it is needed (consumer credit, mortgage loans, private pension schemes, educational finance; bank account and payment services) or in which access to certain services like housing, transportation, water, heat and electricity are provided in the form of deferred payments or rent.' (Ibid *Introduction*, 1.2).

48   For a wider reflection on the meaning and potential 'dangers' of expanding the notion of fundamental rights, such as to lower the status of human rights, see J Gershman, J Morduch, 'Credit is not a right', in T Sorell, L Cabrera, *Microfinance, Rights and Global Justice*, (Cambridge University Press 2015) 22 ff. and the wide literature cited therein; see especially P Alston, 'Conjuring Up New Human Rights: A Proposal for Quality Control' (1984) 78 American Journal of International Law 607; on the ways in which a 'right to credit' is different from other human rights see M Hudon, 'Should Access to Credit be a Right?' (2009) 84 Journal of Business Ethics 17, 22.

and which, as seen, includes a 'negative' and a 'positive' dimension; and the other relating to a question of fair treatment and/or the quality of services (i.e. reference would be to price, duration, scale of access etc.).[49]

A potential construction of a 'right to credit', whichever dimension is examined, needs to find first of all a fundamental rights and/or constitutional basis for its defense. A fundamental rights basis of such a potential right can serve both as a ground for the 'access dimension' (especially considering that the conclusion of the contract is between private parties, therefore the question is if and to what extent there is a horizontal effect of this right), but also as a framework on which to build and define the duty of responsible credit.[50] The problem of the 'horizontal' effects extends beyond the European discourse and concerns more generally the obligations of 'non-state actors' in guaranteeing fundamental rights.[51]

The special nature of credit as a right deriving from a contractual relationship, which therefore involves a recognition and/or a duty on behalf of private parties, has immediately raised the principal objections towards this right: who should ensure its implementation, and how would this take place (without altering market forces for example)? From a libertarian perspective, the issue concerns the reconciliation of this obligation with the principle of contractual freedom.[52]

A first evident observation is that absent an explicit recognition or incorporation into legally binding charters, it becomes difficult to argue that a 'right to credit', in terms both of universal access and in terms of positive obligations is enforceable in any way, not even indirectly through a horizontal effect (i.e. in contracts between private parties).

Furthermore, even if it were recognized, the lack of two characteristics of other economic and social rights (namely a clear allocation of duties between parties responsible in ensuring the access to the right, and the extreme difficulty in meeting the demands of all potential right-holders), risks transforming a right to credit into a mere "manifesto right".[53] It has been observed that a right to credit would fall within economic, social and cultural rights characterized by 'progressive realization' (in the light of resource constraints that do not allow states to achieve these rights universally and for which rights citizens

49   See Gershman et al (n 48) 20.
50   See OO Cherednychenko, 'The EU Charter of Fundamental Rights and Consumer Credit' (n 45) 141,146.
51   See for example A Clapham, *Human Rights Obligations of Non-State Actors* (Oxford University Press 2006); and O O'Neill, 'Agents of Justice', (2001) 32 Metaphilosophy 180.
52   Hudon (n 48) 21.
53   Ibid 23–24.

have a right 'to the highest level attainable'); 'without urgency' attached to the right, and with the right framed in broad terms, there may be uncertainty as to the actual practical meaning of this right and it would end up as 'empty language'.[54] Others have thus proposed that a right to credit be recognized as a moral right in a goal-rights system.[55]

This does not entail however that a 'right of *access* to credit' does not find a legal recognition and protection indirectly, through other recognized constitutional rights. Even if a 'right to credit' does not exist as such, there are however other fundamental rights that are recognized at national and supranational (such as the EU) level; these rights include access in the terms that have been seen, a right to non-discrimination, and the principle of consumer protection.

It has been observed how from the point of view of reduction of discrimination, the indirect horizontal effect of fundamental rights as interpreted at national levels and to a certain extent in the case law of the ECJ has allowed to widen the array of basic interests that are juxtaposed in private contractual relationships; this has permitted a correction of an imbalance that tended to take into account certain rights (the economic freedom of banks for example) and ignore others (i.e. the self-determination of weaker contractual parties).[56]

This broadening of the panoply of rights taken into account and balanced in private law adjudication could serve as the ground for further adjustment and/ or for reinforcement of the position of weak or vulnerable contracting parties when 'fundamental' rights (for example housing) are at stake. As has been noted, courts in civil law cases play an important role in defining how, in the context of changing society "fundamental rights may affect the way in which the balance between self-reliance and protection is struck".[57]

---

54   Gershman et al (n 48) 22.

55   Hudon (n 48) 24, referring to the goal-rights system as described by Amartya Sen: "a moral system in which fulfilment and non-realization of the rights are included among the goals, incorporated in the evaluation of state of affairs, and then applied to the choice of actions through consequentialist links" (A Sen, 'Rights and Agency' (1982) 11 Philosophy & Public Affairs 3, 15).

56   See A Colombi Ciacchi, 'European Fundamental Rights, Private Law and Judicial Convergence' in H-W Micklitz (ed), *Constitutionalization of European Private Law* (Oxford University Press 2014) 126, 131–133. With reference to the horizontal effect of fundamental rights on contracts in four major legal systems in Europe (Germany, the Netherlands, Italy and England) see also C Mak, *Fundamental Rights in European Contract Law* (Kluwer Law International 2008), including important German case law recalled therein.

57   C Mak, 'Harmonising Effects of Fundamental Rights in European Contract Law' (2007) 1 Erasmus Law Review 59, 79.

Thus, even though they do not guarantee the substantive right to a loan, the rights that are recognized do guarantee a series of procedural and substantive safeguards with which the application for credit and its evaluation have to take place: one could speak of a 'due process in access to credit'. This construction implies the negative aspect concerning antidiscrimination, but it also encompasses the positive aspect by recalling the concept of 'responsible credit', when the latter is interpreted in its broad significance of ensuring 'protection' within the credit contract.

A 'due process in access to credit' translates into a series of duties, having a potential indirect horizontal effect, which relate creditworthiness assessments and responsible credit to each other, by ensuring a protective dimension for consumers.

The first duty, that of creditworthiness assessment, can and should adopt the 'affordability' standard insofar as it has a protective dimension. Furthermore, affordability, rather than credit*worthiness* eliminates any moral nuance tied to the instrument and helps to stress the inclusive, and not exclusive, meaning that this duty should pursue.

The second duty, that of responsible credit, allows for the implementation of both the negative aspect of access to credit (i.e. discrimination and predatory practices tailored towards the weaker/more vulnerable consumers) and the positive dimension of access to credit, namely through the duties of information and protection both in the pre-contractual phase and during the life of the credit contract (and in which duties of suitability are for example essential alongside other tools of assessment of borrowers). This also implies that responsible credit finds a basis in 'fundamental rights'.[58]

In this construction, the European paradigm of 'access justice' can once again serve as a useful framework to test the hypothesis. Access justice as defined above finds a recognition in the EU Charter of Fundamental Rights, whose Article 36 states that "[t]he Union recognizes and respects access to services of general economic interests as provided for in national laws and practices, in accordance with the Treaty establishing the European Union, in order to promote the social and territorial cohesion of the Union" (a provision which should be read together with the secondary legislation in the various categories of services falling under the notion of 'services of general economic interest' (i.e. telecommunication, postal services, electricity, gas and transport)

---

58   On the consumer protection in financial (and credit) contracts and its relationship with the fundamental rights dimension, see I Benhör, *EU Consumer Law and Human Rights* (Oxford University Press 2013), especially 109 ff.

so as to justify the existence of an enforceable right of access to services of general economic interest).[59]

Within the domain of private law, and of contract law more specifically, access justice translates into the conclusion of service contracts; whether access justice within this understanding also extends to financial services however (more specifically to the right to credit) has long been a debated issue,[60] all the more with reference to a credit contract.[61] Whilst at the EU level the Commission has for example recognized the importance of a bank account in order to participate in the modern economy, so that basic payment services and payment cards are considered 'essential services', this does not necessarily entail that credit falls within the category.[62]

It had previously been observed that even though these financial services are different from other essential services, in that citizens have not traditionally expected them to be provided by the public sector, they should nonetheless be included in discussions of necessary services. "In fact, the provision of means of payment (i.e. money) is undoubtedly considered a public task, and credit and bank cards are presently perhaps the most important means of payment".[63]

---

59   Micklitz, 'Social Justice and Access Justice in Private Law' (n 34) 25.
       In this context the question of what is comprised under 'services of general economic interest' is pivotal. This central and strongly debated issue is beyond the scope of this analysis. For a reconstruction of the debate with reference to some of the issues related to financial services see *inter alia* C Scott, 'Services of General Interest in EC Law: Matching Values to Regulatory Technique in the Public and Privatised Sectors' (2000) 6 European Law Journal 310; see also M Freedland, S Sciarra, *Public Services and Citizenship in European Law* (Oxford University Press 1998); and W Sauter, *Public Services in EU Law* (Cambridge University Press 2015); U Neergaard, E Szyszczak, JW van de Gronden, M Krajewski (eds), *Legal Issues of Services of General Interest* (TMC Asser Press-Springer 2013); P Rott, 'A New Social Contract Law for Public Services? Consequences from Regulation of Services of General Economic Interest in the EC' (2005) 1 European Review of Contract Law 323.

60   Micklitz, 'Social Justice and Access Justice in Private Law' (n 34) 26; Benhör (n 58) 125, recalling that financial services "are increasingly acknowledged in Member States as services of general interest".

61   According to Cherednychenko ('The EU Charter of Fundamental Rights and Consumer Credit' (n 45) 150–151), Article 36 of the European Charter of Fundamental Rights together with the principle of consumer protection enshrined in Article 38 of the Charter could serve as a legal basis for a fundamental right to credit; however, given major legal and regulatory problems (including objections on enforceability and the need to counterbalance this right with other fundamental rights of the lender such as the right to conduct a business), this recognition at the current state of affairs remains hypothetical.

62   Communication from the Commission 'A Quality Framework for Services of General Interest in Europe' COM (2011) 900 final 10.

63   Wilhelmsson, 'Services of general interest' (n 10) 154.

Proposals have also been advanced that the concept of vulnerability of consumers (that is relevant in universal services law), whilst not sufficiently protected under the current EU approach to consumer law, should be extended to the field of consumer credit and mortgage through an extension of the universal-service doctrine.[64] It is argued that the universal-service doctrine has for example already been extended to the retail financial services through the Payment Accounts Directive; given the importance of access to credit through private markets as a means of access to welfare (in consideration of the retreat of the welfare state), it could be equated to universal services. A final contention in favor of this extension is based on grounds of social inclusion for vulnerable consumers (which would otherwise predictably be excluded from access given the risk of market failure).[65]

Naturally and consequently, if access to certain financial services were to be considered as a 'service of general economic interest' under EU law, then this would entail that the different rules on general services (including, in the domain of contract law, consumer user and protection, choice and transparency, access, affordability, quality and continuity) would be applicable to financial service contracts. It has been observed how since the privatization of services of general economic interest, with private service providers that operate on a "more or less competitive market", "public law principles such as objectivity, equality, proportionality, neutrality or the compulsory provision of services that applied previously do not apply automatically anymore".[66] Indeed, financial services and information society have long been identified as examples of services "that run the 'risk' of becoming infected by the new principles developing in private law as a result of the privatization of public utilities".[67] These principles would also include a principle of legitimate

---

64   I Domurath, 'The Case for Vulnerability as the Normative Standard in European Consumer Credit and Mortgage Law – An Inquiry into the Paradigms of Consumer Law' (2013) 3 Journal of European Consumer and Market Law 124, 135. The universal-service doctrine, through a "human rights, or citizens' rights dimension" means "guaranteed access for everyone, whatever the economic, social, or geographical situation, to a service of a specified quality at an affordable price", and has been used in the EU policies in the field of services of general interest in combination with the so-called 'internal market approach' which aims at fostering competition through the opening of national markets. See P Rott, 'Consumers and services of general interest: Is EC consumer law the future?', (2007) 30 *Journal of Consumer Policy* 49, 53.

65   Domurath (n 64) 135–136; see also more generally on services of general interest, Rott 'Consumers and services of general interest' (n 64) 58.

66   See Rott, 'A New Social Contract Law for Public Services?' (n 59) 325.

67   Wilhelmsson, 'Services of general interest and European Private law' (n 10).

expectations,[68] even if it has been noted, that in financial services, as more generally in the law of regulated markets, this principle is not expressly referred to (as it is in previous "first-generation" consumer law where it is intended as the "right to a contract at fair conditions with enforceable remedies" which is to be balanced against the supplier's freedom of contract and freedom to do business). The reference in financial services is rather to "honesty" and "reasonableness" with regards to specific rights and obligations (such as the early repayment of mortgages, or fee for calculation of a mortgage, or the price of a bank account).[69]

Also included are the principles of non-discrimination and access to service, which are commonly questioned with regards to their 'impact' on contractual freedom. Indeed, whereas principles such as non-discrimination and of access to service should apply in all cases of services of general interest, in the case of access to credit (not simply access to a banking account or to availability of forms of payments such as credit cards (growingly "essential" in cashless societies)) they would govern application for loans.

However, a fundamental distinction between other banking services and access to credit needs to be made. A credit contract is first of all a private contractual relationship between a lender and a borrower. In the analysis of the respective positions, this would of course first of all impose a consideration of the well-known conflict between a 'right' to access credit of an applicant borrower and the contractual freedom and 'freedom to conduct a business' of the lender (also recognized for example by the EU Charter on Fundamental Rights at Article 16). Furthermore, as repeatedly recalled, granting a loan or mortgage credit also transcends the mere private contractual sphere of a debt and credit. Extension of credit depends on a previous assessment of the consumer's financial position (creditworthiness, ability to pay, adequacy, and so forth). The compliance with this requirement responds to two related functions: the observance of prudential requirements for lenders and the prevention over-indebtedness of borrowers.

It thus seems that whilst the access justice paradigm is insufficient for the recognition of a fundamental right dimension to obtain credit, it requires that the rules and rights governing access, including non-discrimination but also consumer protection, apply to the pre-contractual phase and to some extent to the substantive provisions of credit contracts. To answer the question initially posed, one can affirm that a 'right to credit' as such is not recognized and is of difficult recognition for the various reasons now recalled. In order to reduce

---

68   Ibid 155.

69   Micklitz, *The Politics of Justice in European Private Law* (n 23) 348.

economic discrimination, and to try and implement as far as possible a 'fair treatment' dimension of access to credit, it is here purported that one should regulate the 'process' of evaluation in such a way as to take account as far as possible of parameters of 'affordability', 'suitability' and 'fairness'. This can be referred to with the notion of 'due process in access to credit'.

5.4   Access to Credit and the Right to Housing

A more delicate and complex issue surrounding a hypothetical 'right to credit' is the one concerning the application for credit in order to purchase and cover essential needs: first and foremost, housing. The analysis of the scope and multiple social and economic dimensions of the right to housing is beyond the purview of these observations.[70] However one of these dimensions, the access to housing, becomes functional in questioning whether the multilevel constitutionalization of housing rights that has been observed across legal systems and at supranational level (for example via the ECHR and EU law) leads to a horizontal effect in private law relations, and more specifically in credit contracts (especially where there are policies promoting the 'ownership' of dwellings).[71] Put simply, does the right to housing imply that one has a 'right to credit' from a private lender when credit is sought to provide accommodation?

The process of growing privatization of the housing markets that has been registered in Europe in the last decades, has led to a retreat of public instruments of welfare aiming at guaranteeing public or social housing, and an increase in the relevance of private law relationships (rentals, but also mortgage

---

70   With no claim to completeness, see, under different profiles for example J Carbonnier (ed), *L'immeuble urbain à usage d'habitation* (LGDJ 1963); TC Grey, 'Property and Need: the Welfare State and Theories of Distributive Justice', in (1976) 28 Stanford Law Review 885; A Gambaro, *Proprietà privata e disciplina urbanistica* (Zanichelli 1977); M Partington, J Jowell (eds), *Welfare Law & Policy* (Pinter 1979); P Flora, AJ Heidenheimer (eds), *Lo sviluppo dello welfare state in Europa e in America*, Bologna, 1979; JB Cullingworth, *Essays on Housing Policy* (Allen and Unwin 1979); U Breccia, *Il diritto all'abitazione* (Giuffrè 1980); S Rodotà, *Il terribile diritto. Studi sulla proprietà privata* (Il Mulino 1981); G Tatarano (ed), *Diritto all'abitazione finanziamenti all'impresa, alla cooperazione, alla persona* (ESI 1986); A Heymann-Doat (ed), *L'Etat et le logement* (L'arbre verdoyant éditeur 1987); A De Vita 'Diritto alla casa in diritto comparato' *Digesto delle discipline privatistiche, sez civile*, (4th ed UTET 1990); U Mattei, *La proprietà immobiliare*, (Giappichelli 1993); MC Paglietti 'Percorsi evolutivi del diritto all'abitazione', (2008) 13 Rivista di diritto privato 1; J Hohmann, *The Right to Housing. Law, Concepts, Possibilities* (Hart Publishing 2013); A Arden, *Manual of Housing Law*, 11th ed (Legal Action Group 2020).

71   Article 47(2) of the Italian Constitution, promoting house ownership through the use of private savings, is emblematic; see n 73 and 74.

contracts) as the tools through which housing is accessed.[72] Indeed, there is an interaction between public and private law, with private law often intervening where the public machine of adjudication and the welfare state are insufficient or inefficient in responding to the requests of housing.[73] Whereas the right to housing is often emblematically listed within social and welfare rights in national constitutions[74] and/or in supranational charters,[75] this does not immediately translate into binding contractual obligations between private parties, unless specific legislation imposes terms and conditions with which this right is to be implemented and enforced.[76]

---

72   I Domurath, C Mak, 'Private Law and Housing Justice in Europe', in (2020) 83 Modern Law Review 1188, 1191, quoting for example the Study Housing Europe, 'The State of Housing in the EU 2017', Brussels, Housing Europe, European Federation of Public, Cooperative and Social Housing, 2017.

OECD data on housing tenure distribution from 2019 show that in the EU 51.7% of housing is owned outright; 20% is owned with a mortgage; 17,8% is rented at market price on private rental market; 5% is rented at reduced/subsidized price (the data of course differs widely between the Member States). The data on the UK is 34.3% outright ownership; 31% owned with a mortgage; 29.6% rented at market price on private rental market; 4.3% is rented at reduced/subsidized price; whilst for the United States the percentages are 24.5% outright ownership; 40% owned with a mortgage; 34.1% rented at market price on private rental market (with no instances of subsidized rent). See OECD, Affordable Housing, Compare your country <https://www.compareyourcountry.org/housing/en/0// default/> (accessed February 2022).

73   See, with ample comparative literature cited therein, A De Vita (n 70) 'Diritto alla casa in diritto comparato', *Digesto delle discipline privatistiche, sez civile*, (4th ed 1990). Ibid for a comparative analysis of the development of the right to housing as a social right object of specific legislation in the United States, in France, in Italy, in the UK and in Germany.

74   For an overview of examples of a direct and sometimes indirect constitutionalization of the right to housing in the Italian, Spanish, Portuguese, French, English and US experiences, see A De Vita (n 70). Examples include the Italian Constitution of 1947 (art 47, 2nd comma); the Portuguese Constitution of 1976 (Article 65, 1st comma); the Spanish Constitution of 1978 (Article 47); Article 1 of the French law n 82-526 of 22-6-1982 ('loi Quillot', recognizing housing as a fundamental right).

75   See eg Article 25(1) of the 1948 Universal Declaration of Human Rights; Article 11 of the 1966 International Covenant on Economic, Social and Cultural Rights; Article 34 EU Charter of Fundamental Rights.

76   Relevant examples are of course the case of tenancy laws and their constitutionality (on which there is ample constitutional case law across legal systems – beyond the purview of these observations), as well as the cases of subsidized rents. On these, see for example VA Judson, 'Defining Property Rights: the Constitutionality of Protecting Tenants from Condominium Conversion', (1983) 18 Harvard Civil Rights – Civil Liberties Law Review 179; EH Rabin, 'The Revolution in Landlord Tenant Law: Causes and Consequences', (1984) 69 Cornell Law Review 517; M Harloe, *Private Rented Housing in the United States and Europe* (Routledge 1985); A De Vita, *Il rapporto di locazione abitativa fra teoria e prassi* (Giuffrè 1985); MJ Radin, 'Residential Rent Control', (1986) 15 Philosophy & Public Affairs,

The complexity of the right to housing from the perspective of private law relationships derives from its dual nature of a social and economic good; this requires an exercise of balancing between the rights of the parties (i.e. owner and tenant; lender and borrower; mortgagee and mortgagor) which cannot merely be solved in terms of debtor-creditor relationships or of property rights, but also needs to take into account the social function (social inclusion, access to welfare, participation in community life) that housing embodies.[77]

The EU offers an emblematic example with the right to housing that is recognized in the EU Charter of Fundamental Rights in Articles 7 (right to respect for "private and family life, home and communications") and 34(3) (in order to combat social exclusion and poverty, recognition and respect of "the right to social and housing assistance so as to ensure a decent existence for all those who lack sufficient resources, in accordance with the rules laid down by Community law and national laws and practices"). Housing however does not fall within the scope of EU law; its effect on European private law has thus been considered indirectly, through the regulation of other areas of EU private law such as consumer credit, mortgage credit, and unfair contract terms.[78]

The 'right to housing' has indeed been invoked in case law of the ECJ dealing, not coincidentally, with mortgage enforcement proceedings, especially with reference to their compatibility with effective consumer protection under Directive 93/13 on unfair terms in consumer contracts (i.e. whether in

---

350; E Bargelli, *Proprietà e locazione* (Giappichelli 2004); see also the working papers of the Project on Tenancy Law at the EUI (2003) J Ziller 'The Constitutional Dimensions of Tenancy Law in the European Union' Background paper<https://www.eui.eu/Documents/DepartmentsCentres/Law/ResearchTeaching/ResearchThemes/EuropeanPrivateLaw/TenancyLawProject/TenancyLawZiller.pdf> (accessed October 2021); F Cafaggi 'Tenacy Law and European Contract Law' Working Paper <https://www.eui.eu/Documents/DepartmentsCentres/Law/ResearchTeaching/ResearchThemes/EuropeanPrivateLaw/TenancyLawProject/TenancyLawCafaggi.pdf> (accessed October 2021); CU Schmid 'General Report' Working Paper, <https://www.eui.eu/Documents/DepartmentsCentres/Law/ResearchTeaching/ResearchThemes/EuropeanPrivateLaw/TenancyLawProject/TenancyLawGeneralReport.pdf> (accessed October 2021).

77   I Domurath et al 'Private Law and Housing Justice in Europe' (n 72) 1192–1193. See also, on the relationship with the right to dignity, MR Marella 'Human Dignity in a Different Light: European Contract Law, Social Dignity and the Retreat of the Welfare State', in S Grundmann, *Constitutional Values and European Contract Law* (Kluwer Law International 2008) 123, 139–142; A Colombi Ciacchi, 'Social Rights, Human Dignity and European Contract Law', ibid; and E Eichenhofer, 'L'utilizzazione del diritto privato per scopi di politica sociale' in (1997) 43 Rivista di diritto civile 193; MW Hesselink, 'The Horizontal Effects of Social Rights in European Contract' (2003) 1, Europa e diritto privato 1.

78   Domurath et al 'Private Law and Housing Justice in Europe' (n 72) 1189.

mortgage eviction procedures consumers have effective procedural remedies and whether they can invoke the invalidity of certain terms of the underlying mortgage loan agreement).[79] In these cases the ECJ has operated a sometimes hidden (as in the famous *Aziz* judgement),[80] sometimes open (as in the *Sánchez Morcillo*[81] and *Kušionová*[82] judgements) constitutionalization of European contract law, and has recognized the "fundamental right to accommodation" under Article 7 of the EU Charter of Fundamental Rights.[83]

This however does not entail that there is also a right to obtain (mortgage) credit so as to purchase that accommodation, or more generally, a right to access housing through private contractual relationships. The importance of this case law rather lies in the fact that protection of the consumer as a debtor is recognized at a constitutional level as falling respectively under Articles 47 and 7 of the European Charter of Fundamental Rights, and in the recognition that the existence of effective procedural rights is deemed fundamental in both vertical and horizontal relations.[84]

These cases reach different results as to the way in which these rights are to be protected and recognized; this is especially true in the *Kušionová* judgement, in which notwithstanding the innovative recognition of the right to accommodation, the final outcome recognizes that the consumer is a normal debtor whose substantive and procedural rights are to be balanced against those of the creditor (whilst the *Sanchez Morcillo* case considers the consumer as a vulnerable subject who needs legal protection to exercise his rights against his contractual counterparty).[85] The ECJ does not ensure a 'right to housing' as such for consumers, nor does the right to housing (even if expressly recalled)

---

79   Other than in the first famous judgements the follow in the text, the issue was also posed by ECJ Case C-407/18 *Aleš Kuhar v. Addiko Bank d.d.*, [2019] ECLI:EU:C:2019:537 and ECJ Joined Cases C-70/17 and C-179/17, *Abanca Corporación Bancaria SA v. Alberto García Salamanca Santos* and *Bankia SA v. Alfonso Antonio Lau Mendoza* [2019] ECLI:EU:C:2019:250, confirming the Court's previous rulings.

80   ECJ Case C-415/11 *Mohamed Aziz v. Caixa d'Estalvis de Catalunya, Tarragona i Manresa (Catalunyacaixa)* [2013], ECLI:EU:C:2013:164.

81   ECJ Case C-169/14, *Juan Carlos Sánchez Morcillo and María del Carmen Abril García v. Banco Bilbao Vizcaya Argentaria SA.*, [2014] ECLI:EU:C:2014:2099.

82   ECJ Case C-34/13 *Monika Kušionová v SMART Capital*, [2014] ECLI:EU:C:2014:2189.

83   Cherednychenko 'The EU Charter of Fundamental Rights and Consumer Credit' (n 45) 161–162.

84   See F Della Negra, 'The uncertain development of the case law on consumer protection in mortgage enforcement proceedings: *Sánchez Morcillo* and *Kušionová*', (2015) 52 Common Market Law Review 1009, 1010; and Domurath et al 'Private Law and Housing Justice in Europe' (n 72) 1206 – further holding that the constitutionalization process that is operated by the ECJ through this case law is "proceduralised" (Ibid 1210).

85   Della Negra (n 84) 1011.

influence the outcome of the evaluation on the justice of the contract; however, the reference to the right to housing does influence the judgement on the proportionality of the remedy for the consumer where there is an unfair term in a mortgage contract. There is thus an indirect regulatory effect, which by aiming towards an open and inclusive market, also determines a specific effect of prevention of social 'imbalances'.[86] This line of cases of the ECJ has led to speak of the promotion of an indirect 'inclusive justice' for consumers and SMEs.[87]

The fundamental rights dimension of access to housing therefore does not extend horizontally onto private contractual relationships and confirms that even where the fundamental right of housing is at stake, there is no 'fundamental right to credit'. This is also confirmed for example by judgements of the European Court of Human Rights, which has dealt with the issue directly even if the ECHR does not explicitly recognize a 'right to housing' but rather, under Article 8, the respect of private life, family life and the 'home'.[88] Even the very 'right to housing' does not prevail over the contractual rights of private parties and its protection falls within the general umbrella of consumer rights and their protection.

However, with reference to the access dimension of housing through private contractual relationships, there is a further consideration that deserves attention: whilst there is no right to obtain housing on private markets – nor a corresponding obligation for private housing providers to provide housing –, what has been recognized by case law under the fundamental rights dimension, is the right to a non-discriminatory 'access right' to housing on private markets (whereas in the public law dimension a right to housing has received limited recognition).[89]

This confirms the conclusion submitted above regarding more generally the meaning of a 'right to credit': not a right to credit *per se* but rather a right to a 'due process' in the application for credit. A 'due process' which however is not limited to the pre-contractual phase: there is also a protection that is afforded

---

86   See E Navaretta, 'Principi dell'Unione europea, politiche economiche e diritto privato', (2020) Osservatorio del diritto civile e commerciale n. 2/2020, 409, 438.

87   Ibid 430 ff.

88   See for the relevant case law, Domurath et al 'Private Law and Housing Justice in Europe' (n 72) 1193 ff. See also, with reference to the UK, S Nield, 'Article 8 respect for the home: A human property right?', (2013) 24 King's Law Journal 147, and S Nield, N Hopkins, 'Human rights and mortgage repossession: beyond property law using Article 8', (2013) 33 Legal Studies 431.

89   Domurath et al 'Private Law and Housing Justice in Europe' (n 72) 1207.

to the substantive content of credit (and more specifically mortgage) contracts through remedies that are offered by the tool of unfair terms.

Whilst this does not mean that subjects that are excluded from accessing credit will be able to obtain credit through private contracts, it does enhance the protection of weaker and vulnerable borrowers from suffering the (potentially exclusionary) effects of unfair or unsustainable credit contracts they have already concluded.

5.5   Responsible Credit as a Protective Duty and a Tool for Inclusion

The relationship between financial (and social) inclusion and 'responsible lending and borrowing' is potentially problematic.

The principal concerns are tied to the consequences that ensue from an interpretation of responsible credit solely as an instrument to implement prudential standards and respond to macro-economic and systemic policies. Under this perspective, it is more likely to become a tool to deny credit rather than to promote access to 'suitable', 'adequate' and 'affordable' loans. Indeed, the discourse on a potential 'right to credit' previously recalled also encounters objections based on a potential contrast with responsible lending[90] and the risk of provoking over-indebtedness of consumers and of abusive financial practices by lenders.[91]

If however, 'responsible credit' (on the lender and on the borrower side) is interpreted and implemented as a protective policy – a policy in the interest of the consumer, as stated for example in declaratory provisions of EU law (or as propounded in behavioral studies that highlight the cognitive biases affecting borrowers)[92] – the perspective changes. It must then be understood and used as one of the tools which require the adoption of active measures, in terms of procedure (information, precontractual duties) but also in terms of the content of loan contracts, so as to promote the conclusion of 'sustainable' credit contracts. Under this perspective it can be read as an instrument that serves to protect borrowers (through policies of prevention and possibly of liability) whilst promoting access to credit. It responds to the call for a form of weak – but necessary – paternalism,[93] that to some degree already finds

---

90   Cherednychenko, 'The EU Charter of Fundamental Rights and Consumer Credit' (n 45) 151.

91   Hudon (n 48) 20.

92   The boundedly rational borrowing famously analyzed by CR Sunstein, 'Boundedly Rational Borrowing', (2006) 73 University of Chicago Law Review 249.

93   Propounded by Sunstein, Ibid.

place in existing regulation of credit contracts. In the query between balancing and ensuring policies that allow access to credit but at the same time 'protect' the most vulnerable consumers there are multiple considerations to be taken, the first and best known being precisely the argument on the desirability of 'paternalistic' policies and on their effects.

Even before the devastating impact of the global financial crisis of 2007–2008, arguments aiming at introducing considerations on the 'welfare' of borrowers (especially of fragile and/or low income borrowers often targeted by high cost credit) that lenders should take account of, have focused, *inter alia*, on competition (with requirements of transparency and rules preventing abuse of the most vulnerable consumers), market reorganization (introducing mechanisms which subordinate access of lenders to the credit market to compliance with rules on lending that are 'socially acceptable'), and the introduction of 'alternative institutions' onto the marketplace (i.e. social lending institutions).[94] Additionally, an unconscionability standard has been invoked, to be evaluated from the debtor's position (i.e. his or her true interest in the transaction) and not from a market position or from a purely formal analysis of the procedure leading to the conclusion of the contract.[95]

On the other hand, it is emblematic to note that evidences of this 'protective' approach are already visible in legislation – especially the more recent one. The provisions on creditworthiness assessment as framed in the Proposal for the new EU Consumer Credits Directive introduce a series of circumstances in which 'credit can be exceptionally granted' notwithstanding a negative outcome of the assessment (in derogation of a supposed 'duty to deny'). These circumstances correspond to specific uses for which the loans are taken out and it is hard not to observe first of all that there is an introduction of a hierarchy of scopes which justify – on the basis of a more impellent need – the assumption of a risky loan. If this type of provision seems most probably motivated by concerns of ensuring access to credit 'where it is most needed' (especially if and where there is no public or subsidized alternative to the provision of those services), on the other hand it shows a stricter/stronger (paternalist) approach to consumer credit for other – one may imagine, purely consumptive – goods and services. This position also confirms, *inter alia*, that the use of credit to access certain services that are deemed fundamental calls for specific protective provisions, such as already the case with housing.

---

94   See G Howells, 'Seeking Social Justice for Poor Consumers', in Ramsay (ed), *Consumer Law in the Global Economy* (n 43) 266 ff.

95   Ibid 275–276.

Finally, it should be noted that policies of protection (including, of interest here, responsible credit) do not exclusively focus on 'vulnerable' consumers. Indeed, responsible lending is invoked not only in cases where vulnerable borrowers are at risk of exclusion (where, alone, they prove insufficient to contrast certain market forces). Their relevance stretches across different categories of borrowers and includes consumers whose financial situation before concluding a credit or mortgage contract is not necessarily a fragile one. As studies on over-indebtedness have demonstrated abundantly,[96] difficulties of repayment are usually the consequence of life-affecting events (health issues, family issues, loss of employment) – cases in which for example the Nordic doctrine of 'social force majeure' has been invoked[97] (although while social force majeure is an 'interesting contractual tool for redistributive justice', it does not however reach those who have not been able to access credit in the first place).[98] In addition, even absent instances of hardship due to personal unforeseen events, borrowers may fall in arrears on repayment or find themselves in financial difficulties because of the structure of the loan contracts and/or because of their financial illiteracy and insufficient understanding of the type of contracts they have signed.

The protection of the weaker contractual party that is growingly entrusted to forms of regulatory law and supervisory standards (and not only private contractual law as in the past), especially in the field of financial services,[99] responds to needs that go beyond concerns with an individual consumer or with a category of contractual counterparties that require attention: as the 2008 financial crisis has demonstrated and as has been widely recounted in the

---

96   See already in the 1970's Caplovitz's study on consumers in the United States: D Caplovitz, *Consumers in Trouble*, (The Free Press 1974); and more recently ex multis, U Reifner, J Nieme-Kiesiläinen, N Huls, H Springeneer, *Overindebtedness in European Consumer Law*, (Books on Demand 2019); I Domurath, G Comparato, H-W Micklitz (eds), 'The Over-indebtedness of European Consumers: A View from Six Countries', (2014) EUI Law Working Paper n. 10/2014; H-W Micklitz, I Domurath (eds), *Consumer Debt and Social Exclusion in Europe*, (Routledge 2015); D. Vandone, F. Ferretti, *Personal Debt in Europe* (Cambridge University Press 2019).

97   See T Wilhelmsson, *Critical Studies in Private Law. A Treatise on Need-Rational Principles in Modern Law* (Kluwer Academic Publishers 1992), 181 ff. quoting studies of the 1990's from the United States, the UK, Germany.

98   Wilhelmsson, 'Consumer Law and Social Justice' (n 43) 226; Wilhelmsson, *Critical Studies in Private Law* (n 97) 176 ff.

99   The duties have been transposed into standards that are the object of financial supervision, in what has been defined as "European supervision private law". See OO Cherednychenko 'Public Supervision over Private Relationships: Towards European Supervision Private Law?' (2014) 22 European Review of Private Law 37.

previous chapters, the need to protect and avoid certain contractual models, especially in credit contracts, also responds to prudential and systemic concerns. Protection is thus, once again, a goal at different levels: protection of the individual borrower; protection of the lending institution (against the potentially destabilizing effects of non-repayment (NPLS and UPLS)); and above the individual level, protection of the credit markets and of the overall social welfare against the detrimental and destabilizing effects of over-indebtedness.

However, the paradigms invoked, starting from the access justice perspective, the focus on the information paradigm and on contractual freedom, may prove insufficient to ensure effective protection of weak or vulnerable consumers and more generally, of consumers in particular types of contracts – notably credit contracts and mortgage contracts. This is due, among other factors, to the consideration that there is no freedom of contract in consumer law; that as factual evidence has shown the normative standard of the 'average consumer' is detached from reality in consumer credit and mortgage credit and thus the information paradigm is limited; and that the access justice paradigm of EU law deprives consumers of possible higher protection standards in national legislation (at the expense of social justice).[100]

The responsible credit paradigm, though still not fully developed nor implemented, seems to provide a potential tool in reconciling the different needs that have so far been highlighted. As such it has to be interpreted as a flexible instrument, apt for the balancing of the juxtaposed interests at stake, especially when credit is the only tool to access certain fundamental rights and its denial is invoked – at least formally – as in the interest of the borrower, in a paternalist attempt to avoid future over-indebtedness. To avoid that responsible lending becomes a barrier to access affordable and fair credit through supervised channels (and thus lead to unregulated secondary markets of credit) with the risk of increasing – instead of avoiding – the road to over-indebtedness, the paradigm cannot ignore certain personal circumstances. From this point of view, the approach introduced with the new Consumer credits Directive proposal is to be welcomed. The growing availability of instruments based on data mining allowing the tailoring of personalized contracts to the needs of the single contractual parties is undoubtedly an important tool to this scope.

---

100 See Domurath, 'The Case for Vulnerability' (n 64) 133 ff.; I Domurath, *Consumer Vulnerability and Welfare in Mortgage Contracts*, (Oxford, Hart Publishing 2017). See also V. Mak, 'The "Average Consumer" of EU law in domestic litigation: Examples from consumer credit and investment cases', (2012) Tilburg Law School Legal Studies Research Paper Series n. 4.

More in general, the two global economic crises that have affected firms and households in the last fifteen years, namely the financial crisis of 2007–2008 and the crisis deriving from the COVID-19 pandemic, have both highlighted and accelerated a process of reform of financial services law and of credit contracts. The notion of responsible credit, originated in the first of the two emergencies and recalled during the second, is slowly finding its way in the ordinary regulation of lending and borrowing. The implementation that it will concretely find within the different legal traditions will determine whether it will be used as a tool for liability, feared by lenders, a tool barring access to credit, as feared by borrowers, or a tool for a fine tuning of credit contracts to the needs of both parties.

Bibliography

Abel RL, *The Politics of Informal Justice. Vol.2: Comparative Studies* (Academic Press 1981).

Adler B, Polak B, Schwartz A, 'Regulating Consumer Bankruptcy: A theoretical Inquiry', (2000) 29 Journal of Legal Studies 585.

Aggarwal N, 'The Norms of Algorithmic Credit Scoring' (2020), 3 <https://ssrn.com/abstract=3569083 or http://dx.doi.org/10.2139/ssrn.3569083> (accessed July 2020).

Ahrens C, *Persönlichkeitsrecht und Freiheit der Medienberichterstattung: Konflikt-situationen, Schutzansprüche, Verfahrensfragen* (Schmidt 2002).

Albareto G, Felici R, Sette E, 'Does credit scoring improve the selection of borrowers and credit quality?' (2016) Banca d'Italia Working Papers, n. 1090.

Alexander K, 'Tort Liability for Ratings of Structured Securities under English Law', (2015) University of Oslo Faculty of Law Legal Studies Research Paper Series No. 2015-06.

Alpa G, Bessone M, *Banche dati, telematica e diritti della persona* (Cedam 1984).

Alpa G, 'Aspetti della disciplina sui dati personali riguardanti gli enti e l'attività economica' (1998) 52 Rivista trimestrale di diritto e procedura civile 713.

Alpa G, 'Gli obblighi informativi precontrattuali nei contratti di investimento finanzi-ario. Per l'armonizzazione dei modelli regolatori e per l'uniformazione delle regole di diritto comune', (2008) 24 Contratto e impresa 889.

Alpa G, 'La responsabilità civile delle agenzie di rating. Alcuni rilievi sistematici' (2013) Rivista trimestrale di diritto dell'economia, n 2, 71.

Alston P, 'Conjuring Up New Human Rights: A Proposal for Quality Control' (1984) 78 American Journal of International Law 607.

Altunbas Y, Manganelli S, Marques-Ibanez, D, 'Bank Risk During the Financial Crisis. Do Business Models Matter?' (2014) ECB Working Paper Series n. 1394.

Ananny M, Crawford, K, 'Seeing Without Knowing: Limitations of the Transparency Ideal and Its Application to Algorithmic Accountability' (2016) 20 New Media & Society 973.

Arden A, *Manual of Housing Law*, 11th ed (Legal Action Group 2020).

Armour J, Awrey D, Davies P, Enriques L, Gordon JN, Mayer C, Payne J, *Principles of Financial Regulation* (Oxford University Press 2016).

Article 29 Data Protection Working Party 'Guidelines on Automated individual decision-making and profiling for the purposes of Regulation 2016/679' (3 October 2017).

Association of Consumer Credit Information Suppliers (ACCIS), '2017 Survey of Members. Analysis of Credit Reporting in Europe' (2018).

Atamer YM, 'Duty of Responsible Lending: Should the European Union Take Action?', in S Grundmann, YM Atamer (eds), *Financial Services, Financial Crisis and General*

European Contract Law: Failure and Challenges of Contracting (Kluwer Law International 2011).

Atik J, 'EU Implementation of Basel III in the Shadow of the Euro Crisis' (2014) 33 Review of Banking & Financial Law 287.

Audit M, 'Aspects internationaux de la responsabilité des agences de notation', (2011) 100 Revue critique de droit international privé 581.

Ausubel LM, 'Credit Card Defaults, Credit Card Profits, and Bankruptcy' (1997) 71 American Bankruptcy Law Journal 249.

Avgouleas E, 'The Global Financial Crisis, the Disclosure Paradigm, and European Financial Regulation: The Case for Reform' (2009) 6 European Company and Financial Law Review 440.

Bamberger HG, Roth H, Hau W, Poseck R (eds), *Bürgerliches Gesetzbuch Kommentar* (4th ed CH Beck 2019).

Bannier CE, Behr, P, Güttler A, 'Rating opaque borrowers: why are unsolicited ratings lower?' (2009) Frankfurt School-Working Paper Series, n. 133, Frankfurt School of Finance & Management.

Bar-Gill O, Warren E, 'Making Credit Safer' (2008) 157 University of Pennsylvania Law Review 39.

Bar-Gill O, 'The Law, Economics and Psychology of Subprime Mortgage Contracts' (2009) 94 Cornell Law Review 1073.

Bargelli E, *Proprietà e locazione* (Giappichelli 2004).

Barocas S, Selbst AD, 'Big Data's Disparate Impact' (2016) 104 California Law Review 671.

Barr MS, 'Credit Where it Counts: The Community Reinvestment Act and Its Critics', (2005) 80 New York University Law Review 513.

Barr MS, 'Modes of Credit Market Regulation' in N Retsinas, E Belsky (Eds), *Building Assets, Building Credit: Creating Wealth in Low-Income Communities* (Brookings Institution Press 2005).

Barr MS, Mullainathan S, Shafir E, 'Behaviourally Informed financial Services Regulation' (2008) New America Foundation.

Bartlett R, Morse A, Stanton R, Wallace N, 'Consumer lending discrimination in the Fintech era' (2019) UC Berkeley Public Law Research Paper <https://ssrn.com/abstract=3063448> (accessed July 2020).

Beaupré M, Kitamura I, De Groot GR, Herbots JH, Sacco R, 'La traduction juridique', (1987) 28 Les Cahiers de droit, 734.

Beddows S, McAteer M, 'Payday lending: fixing a broken market', Association of Chartered Certified Accountants (2014) <https://inclusioncentre.co.uk/wp-content/uploads/2014/08/Payday-lending-full-report.pdf> (accessed November 2019).

Ben Shahar O, Schneider CE, 'The Failure of Mandated Disclosure' (2011) 159 University of Pennsylvania Law Review 647.

Benhör I, *EU Consumer Law and Human Rights* (Oxford University Press 2013).

Bennett C, *Regulating Privacy-Data Protection and Public Policy in Europe and the United States*, (Cornell University Press 1992).

Berger AN, Udell GF, 'Small Business Credit Availability and Relationship Lending: The Importance of Bank Organisational Structure' (2002) 112 The Economic Journal 32.

Bergmans B, 'L'enseignement d'une terminologie juridique étrangère comme mode d'approche du droit comparé: l'exemple de l'allemand' (1987) 39 Revue internationale de droit comparé 89.

Berman HJ, *Law and Revolution* (Harvard University Press 1983).

Bertrand A, *Droit à la vie privée et droit à l'image* (LexisNexis-Litec 1999).

Bethel JE, Ferrell A, Hu G, 'Legal and Economic Issues in Litigation Arising from the 2007–2008 Credit Crisis', Harvard John M. Olin Discussion Paper Series, 2/2008.

Biferali G, 'Il social lending. Problemi di regolamentazione' (2017) Rivista trimestrale di diritto dell'economia 4/2017, 443.

Biferali G., '*Big Data* e valutazione del merito creditizio' (2018) 34 Diritto dell'informazione e dell'informatica, 487, 496–497.

Biferali G., *Credito al consumo e sovraindebitamento del consumatore* (Wolters Kluwer-Cedam, 2019).

Bignami F, Resta G, 'Transatlantic Privacy Regulation: Conflict and Cooperation', (2015) 78 Law and Contemporary Problems 231.

Bignami F, Zaring D (eds), *Comparative Law and Regulation. Understanding the Global Regulatory Process*, (Edward Elgar Publishing 2016).

Bix B, *Law, Language, and Legal Determinacy* (Oxford University Press, 1995).

Black J, 'Paradoxes and Failures: 'New Governance' Techniques and the Financial Crisis'(2012) 75 The Modern Law Review 1037.

Blair RD, Maurer V, 'Statute Law and Common Law: The Fair Credit Reporting Act' (1984) 49 Missouri Law Review 289.

Bloustein EJ, 'Privacy as an Aspect of Human Dignity: An Answer to Dean Prosser' (1964) 39 New York University Law Review 962.

Bocquet C, *La traduction juridique: Fondement et méthode* (De Boeck 2008).

Boucard F, 'Le 'crédit responsable' vu par le Conseil d'État et la Cour de cassation' (2012) Revue de droit bancaire et financier (mars-avril 2012) 73.

Bouteillé S, Coogan-Pushner D, *The Handbook of Credit Risk Management. Originating, Assessing, and Managing Credit Exposures* (J. Wiley & Sons Inc 2013).

Breccia U, *Il diritto all'abitazione* (Giuffrè 1980).

Brescia Morra C, 'Lending activity in the time of coronavirus' in WG Ringe, C Gortsos (eds), *Pandemic Crisis and Financial Stability* (EBI e-Book Series 2020) 391.

Bridges S, Disney R, 'Modelling Consumer Credit and Default: The Research Agenda', (2001) Experian Centre for Economic Modelling (ExCEM), University of Nottingham.

Brkan M, 'Do Algorithms Rule the World? Algorithmic Decision-Making in the Framework of the GDPR and Beyond' (2019) 27 International Journal of Law and Information Technology 91.

Brouwer E, *Digital Borders and Real Rights* (Brill 2007).

Brozzetti A, Cecchinato E, Martino E, 'Supervisione bancaria e Covid-19', in U Malvagna, A Sciarrone Alibrandi (eds), *Sistema produttivo e finanziario post Covid-19: dall'efficienza alla sostenibilità. Voci dal diritto dell'economia* (Pacini giuridica 2021).

Bruckner MA, 'The Promise and Perils of Algorithmic Lenders' Use of Big Data', (2018) 93 Chicago – Kent Law Review 3.

Brummer C, Yadav Y, 'Fintech and the Innovation Trilemma' (2019) 107 The Georgetown Law Journal 235.

Brunet A, 'La responsabilitè civile du banquier dispensateur de crédit' (1998) 51 Banca borsa e titoli di credito 778.

Buck-Heeb P, 'Rechtsfolgen fehlender oder fehlerhafter Kreditwürdigkeitsprüfung' (2016) 69 *Neue Juristische Wochenschrift*, H. 29, 2067.

Burrell J, 'How the machine 'thinks': Understanding opacity in machine learning algorithms' (2016) 3 Big Data & Society 1.

Burton D, *Credit and Consumer Society* (Routledge 2008).

Busch D, Van Dam C, 'A Bank's Duty of Care. Perspectives from European and Comparative Law – Part II', (2019) 30 European Business Law Review 367.

Bussani M, Palmer VV (eds), *Pure Economic Loss in Europe* (Cambridge University Press 2011).

Bussani M, 'Le agenzie di *rating* fra immunità e responsabilità', (2014) 60 Rivista di diritto civile 1337.

Bussani M, Infantino M, 'The many cultures of tort liability' in M Bussani, AJ Sebok (eds), *Comparative Tort Law. Global Perspectives* (Elgar 2015).

Bygrave LA, 'The Place of Privacy in Data Protection Law' (2001) 24 University of New South Wales Law Journal 277.

Bygrave LA, *Data Protection Law: Approaching Its Rationale, Logic and Limits* (Kluwer Law International 2002).

Cafaggi F, 'Tenacy Law and European Contract Law' Working Paper <https://www.eui .eu/Documents/DepartmentsCentres/Law/ResearchTeaching/ResearchThemes/ EuropeanPrivateLaw/TenancyLawProject/TenancyLawCafaggi.pdf> (accessed October 2021).

Calabresi G, *Ideals, Beliefs, Attitudes, and the Law. Private Law Perspectives on a Public Law Problem* (Syracuse University Press 1985).

Calabria MA, 'Mortgage Reform under the Dodd-Frank Act' (2014) Cato Working Paper 9.

Cane MB, Shamir A, Jodar T, 'Below Investment Grade and Above the Law: A Past, Present and Future Look at the Accountability of Credit Rating Agencies' (2012) 27 Fordham Journal of Corporate & Financial Law 1063.

Cao D, *Translating Law* (Multilingual Matters 2007).

Caplovitz D, *The Poor Pay More: Consumer Practices of Low-income Families* (Free Press 1967).

Caplovitz D, *Consumers in Trouble* (The Free Press 1974).

Carbonnier J (ed), *L'immeuble urbain à usage d'habitation*, (LGDJ 1963).

Cartwright P, 'Understanding and Protecting Vulnerable Financial Consumers', (2015) 38 Journal of Consumer Policy 119.

Cascione CM, 'L'accesso alle banche dati tra efficienza del mercato creditizio e tutela dei dati. Alla ricerca di un difficile equilibrio nel confronto con l'esperienza nordamericana' in Addante A, Bozzi L, *I contratti di credito immobiliare fra diritto europeo e attuazione nazionale* (Cacucci 2022).

Castaldo A, Palla L, *L'informazione nei mercati finanziari: il ruolo delle agenzie di rating* (Giappichelli 2016).

Castronovo C, *La nuova responsabilità civile* (Giuffrè 2006).

Casu B, Sarkisyan A, 'Securitization', in AN Berger, P Molyneux, JOS Wilson, *The Oxford Handbook of Banking* (2d ed Oxford University Press 2015) 354.

Cate FH, *Privacy in the Information Age* (Brookings Institution Press 1997).

CEPS-ECRI Task Force Report 'Towards Better Use of Credit Reporting in Europe', September 2013.

Chamberlain J, Reichel J, 'The Relationship Between Damages and Administrative Fines in the EU General Data Protection Regulation' (2020) Stockholm Faculty of Law Research Paper Series n. 72.

Chase O, *Law, Culture and Ritual. Disputing Systems in Cross-Cultural Context* (New York University Press 2005).

Cherednychenko OO, 'Conceptualising unconscionability in the context of risky financial transactions: How to converge public and private law approaches?', in M Kenny, J Devenney, L Fox O'Mahony (eds), *Unconscionability in European Private Financial Transactions* (Cambridge University Press 2010).

Cherednychenko OO, 'Freedom of contract in the post-crisis era: Quo Vadis?' (2014) 10 European Review of Contract Law 390.

Cherednychenko OO, 'Public Supervision over Private Relationships: Towards European Supervision Private Law?' (2014) 22 European Review of Private Law 37.

Cherednychenko OO, 'Public and Private Enforcement of European Private Law in the Financial Services Sector' (2015) 23 European Review of Private Law 621.

Cherednychenko OO, 'The EU Charter of Fundamental Rights and Consumer Credit: Towards Responsible Lending?', in H Collins (Ed), *European Contract Law and the Charter of Fundamental Rights* (Intersentia 2017).

Cherednychenko OO, Meindertsma JM, 'Irresponsible Lending in the Post-Crisis Era: Is the EU Consumer Credit Directive Fit for Its Purpose?' (2019) 42 Journal of Consumer Policy 483.

Cherednychenko OO, Andenas M (eds), *Financial Regulation and Civil Liability in European Law*, (Elgar 2020).

Choi SJ, 'Market Lessons for Gatekeepers', (1997–1998) 92 Northwestern University Law Review 916.

Choi SJ, 'A Framework for the Regulation of Securities Market Intermediaries' (2004) 1 Berkeley Business Law Journal 45.

Clapham A, *Human Rights Obligations of Non-State Actors* (Oxford University Press 2006).

Cochran RF, Ackerman RM, *Law and Community. The Case of Torts* (Rowman & Littlefield 2004).

Coffee JC Jr, 'Ratings Reform: The Good, the Bad, and the Ugly' (2011) 1 Harvard Business Law Review 231.

Colombi Ciacchi A, 'Social Rights, Human Dignity and European Contract Law', in S Grundmann, *Constitutional Values and European Contract Law* (Kluwer Law International 2008).

Colombi Ciacchi A, 'European Fundamental Rights, Private Law and Judicial Convergence' in H-W Micklitz (ed), *Constitutionalization of European Private Law* (Oxford University Press 2014) 126.

Comparato G, Domurath I, 'Financialisation and Its Implications for Private Autonomy in Consumer Credit Law' (2015) Osservatorio del diritto civile e commerciale 1/2015, 269.

Comparato G, *The Financialisation of the Citizen* (Hart 2018).

Cotterrell R, 'The Sociological Concept of Law' (1983) 10 Journal of Law and Society (1983), 241.

Cotterrell R, 'Comparative Law and Legal Culture' in Reimann, Zimmermann (eds) *The Oxford Handbook of Comparative Law* (Oxford University Press 2006) 709.

Countryman V, 'Improvident Credit Extension: A New Legal Concept Aborning?' (1975) 27 Maine Law Review 1.

Craig P, de Búrca G, *EU Law. Text, Cases and Materials* (6th ed Oxford University Press 2015).

Crawford K, 'The Hidden Biases in Big Data', (April 1, 2013) Harvard Business Review.

Crawford K, Schultz J, 'Big Data and Due Process: Towards a Framework to Redress Predictive Privacy Harms', (2014) 55 Boston College Law Review 93.

Crouch C, 'Privatised Keynesianism: An Unacknowledged Policy Regime' (2009) 11 British Journal of Politics and International Relations 382.

Cullingworth JB, *Essays on Housing Policy* (Allen and Unwin 1979).

Damia V, Israël JM, 'Standardised granular credit and credit risk data', (2014) Seventh IFC Conference on Indicators to support Monetary and Financial Stability Analysis: Data Sources and Statistical Methodologies.

Dannemann G, Ferreri S, Graziadei M, 'Language and terminology' in C Twigg Flessner (ed) *The Cambridge Companion to European Private Law* (Cambridge University Press 2010) 70.

De Armond ED, 'Frothy Chaos: Modern Data Warehousing and Old-Fashioned Defamation' (2007) 41 Valparaiso University Law Review 1059.

De Armond ED, 'A Dearth of Remedies' (2008) 113 Penn State Law Review 1.

de Búrca G, 'The Trajectories of European and American Antidiscrimination Law', (2012) 60 American Journal of Comparative Law 1.

De Cristofaro G, 'La nuova disciplina comunitaria del credito al consumo: la direttiva 2008/48/CE e l'armonizzazione "completa" delle disposizioni nazionali concernenti "taluni aspetti" dei "contratti di credito ai consumatori"' (2008) 54 Rivista di diritto civile 255.

de Haan J, Amtenbrink F, 'Credit Rating Agencies', 2011 DNB Working Paper, n. 278.

De Hert P, Gutwirth S, 'Data Protection in the Case Law of Strasbourg and Luxembourg: Constitutionalisation in Action', in S Gutwirth et al (eds), *Reinventing Data Protection* (Springer 2009).

de Janvry A, McIntosh C, Sadoulet E, 'The Supply and Demand Side Impacts of Credit Market Information' (2010) 93 Journal of Development Economics 173.

De Vita A, *Il rapporto di locazione abitativa fra teoria e prassi* (Giuffrè 1985).

De Vita A, 'Diritto alla casa in diritto comparato', *Digesto delle discipline privatistiche, sez civile,* (4th ed UTET 1990).

Deasai DR, Kroll JA, 'Trust But Verify: A Guide to Algorithms and the Law' (2017) 31 Harvard Journal of Law & Technology 1.

Deats C, 'Talk that isn't cheap: does the First Amendment protect credit rating agencies' faulty methodologies from regulation?' (2010) 110 Columbia Law Review 1818.

Deipenbrock G, 'Trying or Failing Better Next Time? – The European Legal Framework for Credit Rating Agencies after Its Second Reform' (2014) 25 European Business Law Review 207.

Della Negra F, 'The uncertain development of the case law on consumer protection in mortgage enforcement proceedings: *Sánchez Morcillo* and *Kušionová*' (2015) 52 Common Market Law Review 1009.

Denozza F, 'Aggregazioni arbitrarie v. 'tipi' protetti: la nozione di benessere del consumatore decostruita' (2009) 36 Giurisprudenza commerciale 1057.

Di Donna L, *La responsabilità civile delle agenzie di rating* (Cedam 2012).

Di Majo A, 'Il problema del danno al patrimonio', (1984) 2 Rivista critica di diritto privato 322.

Di Rienzo M, *Concessione del credito e tutela degli investimenti. Regole e principi in tema di responsabilità* (Giappichelli 2013).

Diamond DW, 'Financial Intermediation and Delegated Monitoring' (1984) LI Review of Economic Studies 393.

Djankov S, McLiesh C, Shleifer A, 'Private credit in 129 countries' (2007) 84 Journal of Financial Economics 299.

Dolmetta AA, *Trasparenza dei prodotti bancari. Regole* (Zanichelli 2013).

Dombalagian OH, 'Investment Recommendations and the Essence of Duty' (2011) 60 American University Law Review 1265.

Domurath I, 'The Case for Vulnerability as the Normative Standard in European Consumer Credit and Mortgage Law – An Inquiry into the Paradigms of Consumer Law', (2013) 3 Journal of European Consumer and Market Law 124.

Domurath I, Comparato G, Micklitz H-W (eds), 'The Over-indebtedness of European Consumers: A View from Six Countries', (2014) EUI Law Working Paper n. 10/2014.

Domurath I, 'A Map of Responsible Lending and Responsible Borrowing in the EU and Suggestions for a Stronger Legal Framework to Prevent Over-Indebtedness of European Consumers', in H-W Micklitz, I Domurath (eds), *Consumer Debt and Social Exclusion in Europe* (Routledge 2015).

Domurath I, *Consumer Vulnerability and Welfare in Mortgage Contracts* (Hart 2017).

Domurath I, Mak C, 'Private Law and Housing Justice in Europe' (2020) 83 Modern Law Review 1188.

Donadio G, Lehnert A, 'Residential Mortgages', in AN Berger, P Molyneux, JOS Wilson, *The Oxford Handbook of Banking* (2d ed Oxford University Press 2015).

Durkin TA, Elliehausen G, 'Consumer Lending', in AN Berger, P Molyneux, JOS Wilson, *The Oxford Handbook of Banking* (2d ed Oxford University Press 2015).

Eberle EJ, *Dignity and Liberty: Constitutional Visions in Germany and the United States* (Praeger 2002).

Ebers M, 'Information and Advising Requirements in the Financial Services Sector: Principles and Peculiarities in EC Law' (2004) 8.2 Electronic Journal of Comparative Law.

Edwards L, Veale M, 'Slave to the Algorithm? Why A 'Right to an Explanation' Is Probably Not the Remedy You Are Looking For' (2017) 16 Duke Law & Technology Review 18.

Edwards MA, 'Empirical and Behavioural Critiques of Mandatory Disclosure: Socio-Economics and the Quest for Truth in Lending' (2005) 14 Cornell Journal of Law and Public Policy 199.

Ehrenberg DS, 'If the Loan Doesn't Fit, Don't Take It: Applying the Suitability Doctrine to the Mortgage Industry to Eliminate Predatory Lending' (2001) 10 Journal of Affordable Housing & Community Development Law 117.

Eichenhofer E, 'L'utilizzazione del diritto privato per scopi di politica sociale' in (1997) 43 Rivista di diritto civile 193.

Electronic Privacy Information Center, *Credit Scoring*, 2016 <https://epic.org/privacy/creditscoring/> (accessed February 2020).

Ellickson RC, *Order without Law: How Neighbors Settle Disputes* (Harvard University Press 1999).

Ellis E, Watson P, *EU Anti-Discrimination Law* (2nd ed Oxford University Press 2012).

Engel DM, McCann M (eds), *Fault Lines. Tort Law as Cultural Practice* (Stanford University Press 2009).

Engel DM, 'Lumping as Default in Tort Cases: The Cultural Interpretation of Injury and Causation', (2010) 44 Loyola of Los Angeles Law Review 33.

Engel KC, McCoy PA, 'A Tale of Three Markets: The Law and Economics of Predatory Lending' (2002) 80 Texas Law Review 1255.

Engel KC, McCoy PA, *The Subprime Virus: Reckless Credit, Regulatory Failure and Next Steps*, (Oxford University Press 2011).

Erichsen H-U et al (eds), *Recht der Persönlichkeit* (Duncker & Humblot 1996).

European Commission Communication 'Financial services: enhancing consumer confidence', (COM(97) 309 final, 26.06.1997).

European Commission, Enterprise Directorate General, Best Project on Restructuring, Bankruptcy and a Fresh Start, Final Report of the Expert Group (2003), (available at https://www.iiiglobal.org/sites/default/files/EuropeanUnionProjecton RestructuringReportofExperts.pdf).

European Commission, 'Communication of the European Commission to the European Council of 4 March 2009 'Driving European Recovery" COM(2009) 114.

European Commission, 'Joint Report on Social Protection and Social Inclusion 2009', COM(209)58 final and SEC(2009)141.

European Commission, 'Public Consultation on Responsible Lending and Borrowing', 15 June 2009.

European Commission 'Communication from the Commission to the European Parliament, the Council and the European Central Bank, the European Economic and Social Committee and the Committee of the Regions 'Consumer Financial Services Action Plan: Better Products, More Choice" COM(2017) 139 final'.

European Council, J Niemi-Kiesiläinen, A. Henrikson, Bureau of the European Committee on Legal Co-Operation (CDCJ-BU), 'Report on Legal Solutions to Debt Problems In Credit Societies' (2005) <https://rm.coe.int/16807004bd> (accessed October 2019).

European Economic and Social Committee, 'Opinion of the Economic and Social Committee on 'Consumer protection and appropriate treatment of over-indebtedness to prevent social-exclusion' (Explanatory opinion)', INT/726 (2014).

Evans DS, Wright JD, 'The Effect of the Consumer Financial Protection Agency Act of 2009 on Consumer Credit' (2010) 22 Loyola Consumer Law Review 277.

Everhart Sickler AP, 'The (Un)Fair Credit Reporting Act' (2016) 28 Loyola Consumer Law Review 238.

Facci G, 'Le agenzie di rating e la responsabilità per informazioni inesatte' (2008) 24 Contratto e impresa 164.

Faillace S, *La responsabilità da contatto sociale* (Cedam 2004).

Fairweather K, 'The development of responsible lending in the UK consumer credit regime', in J Devenney, M Kenny (eds) *Consumer Credit, Debt and Investment in Europe* (Cambridge University Press 2012).

Falcone G, '"Prestito responsabile" e valutazione del merito creditizio', (2017) 44 Giurisprudenza commerciale, 147.

FCA, 'Preventing Financial Distress by Predicting Unaffordable Consumer Credit Agreements: An Applied Framework', (2017) FCA Occasional Paper 28.

FDIC 2019 Summary of Deposits Highlights, (2020) 14 FDIC Quarterly.

Feldman S, 'The Fair Credit Reporting Act – From the Regulators Vantage Point' (1971) 14 Santa Clara Lawyer 459.

Feldstein MS, 'Housing, Credit Markets and the Business Cycle', Nat'l Bureau of Econ Research, (2007) Working Paper No. 13471.

Felstiner WLF, Abel RL, Sarat A, 'The Emergence and Transformation of Disputes: Naming, Blaming, Claiming ...' (1980–1981) 15 Law & Society Review 631.

Ferretti F, 'The 'Credit Scoring Pandemic' and the European Vaccine: Making Sense of EU Data Protection Legislation' (2009) Journal of Information, Law & Technology 1.

Ferretti F, 'Credit Bureaus Between Risk-Management, Creditworthiness Assessment and Prudential Supervision', (2015) EUI Working Papers Law 2015/20.

Ferretti F (ed), *Comparative Perspectives of Consumer Over-indebtedness – A View from the UK, Germany, Greece and Italy* (Eleven International Publishing 2016).

Ferretti F, Salomone R, Sutschet H, Tsiafoutis V, 'The regulatory framework of consumer over-indebtedness in the UK, Germany, Italy, and Greece: comparative profiles of responsible credit and personal insolvency law' (2016) 37 Business Law Review 64.

Ferretti F, 'The Never-Ending European Credit Data Mess', (2017) Report for The European Consumer Organization.

Ferretti F, Vandone D, *Personal Debt in Europe. The EU Financial Market and Consumer Insolvency* (Cambridge University Press 2019).

Financial Stability Forum, 'Report of the Financial Stability Forum on Enhancing Market and Institutional Resilience', 2008.

Fischel DR, 'Use of Modern Finance Theory in Securities Fraud Cases Involving Actively Traded Securities' (1982) 38 Business Lawyer 11982.

Flora P, Heidenheimer AJ (eds), *Lo sviluppo dello welfare state in Europa e in America*, Bologna, 1979.

Freedland M, Sciarra S (eds), *Public Services and Citizenship in European Law* (Oxford University Press 1998).

Friedman B, Nissenbaum H, 'Bias in Computer Systems' (1996) 14 ACM Transactions on Information Systems 330.

Frigeni C, 'Segnalazioni presso le centrali rischi creditizi e tutela dell'interessato: profili evolutivi', (2013) 66 Banca borsa e titoli di credito 365.

Galanter M 'Real World Torts: An Antidote to Anecdote', (1996) 55 Maryland Law Review 1093.

Gambaro A, *Proprietà privata e disciplina urbanistica* (Zanichelli 1977).

Garcia Porras CI, Van Boom WH, 'Information disclosure in the EU Consumer Credit Directive: opportunities and limitations' in J Devenney, M Kenny (eds), *Consumer Credit, Debt and Investment in Europe* (Cambridge University Press 2012).

Gavison R, 'Privacy and the Limits of the Law', (1980) 89 Yale Law Journal 421.

Gellert R, De Vries K, De Hert P, Gutwirth S, 'A comparative analysis of anti-discrimination and data protection legislations' in B Custers et al (eds) *Discrimination and privacy in the information society. Data mining and profiling in large databases* (Springer 2021) 61.

Gémar J-C, *Langage du droit et traduction: essais de jurilinguistique* (Linguatech 1982).

Gershman J, Morduch J, 'Credit is not a right', in T Sorell, L Cabrera (eds), *Microfinance, Rights and Global Justice* (Cambridge University Press 2015).

Giger H, *Key Problems of the new concept of the Swiss Consumer Credit Legislation* (Stæmpfli Publishers Ltd 2003).

Giudici P, *La responsabilità civile nel diritto dei mercati finanziari*, (Giuffrè 2008).

Glenn PH, *Legal Traditions of the World: Sustainable Diversity in Law* (Oxford University Press 2000).

Goodman B, Flaxman S, 'European Union regulations on algorithmic decision-making and a 'right to explanation'', (2017) 38 AI Magazine 3.

Gordley J, 'The Functional Method' in PG Monateri (ed), *Methods of Comparative Law* (Edward Elgar 2012), 107.

Gorgoni M., 'Spigolature su luci (poche) e ombre (molte) della nuova disciplina dei contratti di credito ai consumatori', (2011) 76 Responsabilità civile e previdenza 755.

Gortsos CV, 'The response of the European Central Bank to the current pandemic crisis: monetary policy and prudential banking supervision decisions', (2020) EBI Working Paper Series n. 68/2020.

Gourio A, 'La réforme du crédit immobilier aux particuliers', (2016) La semaine juridique – entreprise et affaires (JCP E), 1362, 28.

Graziadei M, 'The functionalist heritage' in P Legrand, R Munday (eds), *Comparative Legal Studies: Traditions and Transitions* (Cambridge University Press 2003).

Grey TC, 'Property and Need: the Welfare State and Theories of Distributive Justice', in (1976) 28 Stanford Law Review 885.

Grundmann S, Kerber W, 'Information Intermediaries and Party Autonomy – The Example of Securities and Insurance Markets', in S Grundmann, W Kerver, S Weatherhill (eds), *Party Autonomy and the Role of Information in the Internal Market*, (de Gruyter 2001).

Grundmann S, Kerver W, Weatherhill S (eds), *Party Autonomy and the Role of Information in the Internal Market* (de Gruyter 2001).

Grundmann S, Möslein F, Riesenhuber K (eds), *Contract Governance. Dimensions in Law & Interdisciplinary Research* (Oxford University Press 2015).

Gutwirth S, *Privacy and the information age* (R Casert tr, Rowman & Littlefield 2002).

Haar B, 'Civil Liability of Credit Rating Agencies after CRA3 – Regulatory All-or-Nothing Approaches between Immunity and Over-Deterrence' (2014) 25 European Business Law Review 315.

Hacker P, 'Teaching fairness to artificial intelligence: Existing and novel strategies against algorithmic discrimination under EU law' (2018) 55 Common Market Law Review 1143.

Harloe M, *Private Rented Housing in the United States and Europe* (Routledge 1985).

Harris R, Albin E, 'Bankruptcy Policy in Light of Manipulation in Credit Advertising' (2006) 7 Theoretical Inquiries in Law 431.

Helberger N, Lynskey O, Micklitz H-W, Rott P, Sax M, Strycharz J, 'EU Consumer Protection 2.0. Structural asymmetries in digital consumer markets' (2021) BEUC, Brussels.

Hersbergen RL, 'The Improvident Extension of Credit as an Unconscionable Contract' (1974) 23 Drake Law Review 226.

Hesselink MW, 'The Horizontal Effects of Social Rights in European Contract' (2003) 1, Europa e diritto privato 1.

Heymann-Doat A (ed), *L'Etat et le logement* (L'arbre verdoyant éditeur 1987).

Hildebrandt M, 'Privacy and Identity', in E Claes, E Duff, S Gutwirth (eds), *Privacy and the Criminal Law* (Intersentia 2006) 43.

Hirsch Jr FA, 'The Evolution of a Suitability Standard in the Mortgage Lending Industry: The Subprime Meltdown Fuels the Fires of Change' (2008) 12 North Carolina Banking Institute 21.

Hohmann J, *The Right to Housing. Law, Concepts, Possibilities* (Hart 2013).

Houtcieff D, 'Les devoirs précontractuels d'information du prêteur' (2016) 17 Revue de droit bancaire et financier 91.

Howells G, 'Seeking Social Justice for Poor Consumers', in I Ramsay (ed), *Consumer Law in the Global Economy* (Ashgate 1997).

Howells G, Twigg-Flesner C, Wilhelmsson T, *Rethinking EU Consumer Law* (Routledge 2018).

Hudon M, 'Should Access to Credit be a Right?' (2009) 84 Journal of Business Ethics 17.

Huls N et al, *Overindebtedness of Consumers in the EC Member States: Facts and Search for Solutions*, (Story Scientia 1994).

Hurley M, Adebayo J, 'Credit Scoring in the Era of Big Data' (2016) 18 Yale Journal of Law & Technology 148.

Husa J, 'Farewell to Functionalism or Methodological Tolerance?' (2003) 67 Rabels Zeitschrift für ausländisches und internationales Privatrecht 419.

Husisian G, 'What Standard of Care Should Govern the World's Shortest Editorials?: An Analysis of Bond Rating Agency Liability' (1990) 75 Cornell Law Review 411.

Inness JC, *Privacy, Intimacy, and Isolation* (Oxford University Press 1992).

International Federation of Insolvency Professionals (INSOL), *Consumer Debt Report: Report of Findings and Recommendations*, 2001 <https://www.insol.org/_files/pdf/consdebt.pdf> (accessed November 2019).

Inzitari B, 'Concessione del credito: irregolarità del fido, false informazioni e danni conseguenti alla lesione dell'autonomia contrattuale' (1993) 7 Diritto della banca e del mercato finanziario 412.

Inzitari B, 'La responsabilità della banca nell'esercizio del credito: abuso nella concessione e rottura del credito', (2001) 54 Banca borsa e titoli di credito 265.

Jappelli T, Pagano M, 'Information Sharing in Credit Markets: The European Experience' (2000) *CSEF Working Paper* n. 35.

Jentzsch N, 'The Regulation of Financial Privacy: The United States vs. Europe', (2003) ECRI Research Report No.5.

Jones D, 'Emerging problems with the Basel Capital Accord: Regulatory capital arbitrage and related issues', (2000) 24 Journal of Banking & Finance 35.

Jørgensen T, 'Credit Advice' (2012) 20 European Review of Private Law 961.

Joseph C, *Advanced Credit Risk Analysis and Management* (Wiley 2013).

Josipović T, 'Consumer Protection in EU Residential Mortgage Markets: Common EU Rules on Mortgage Credit in the Mortgage Credit Directive' (2014) 14 Cambridge Yearbook of European Legal Studies 223.

Kaminski ME, 'The Right to Explanation, Explained' (2019) 34 Berkeley Technology Law Journal 189.

Keats Citron D, 'Reservoirs of Danger: The Evolution of Public and Private Law at the Dawn of the Information Age' (2007) 80 *South California Law Review* 241.

Keats Citron D, 'Technological Due Process' (2008) 85 *Washington University Law Review* 1249.

Keats Citron D, Pasquale F, 'The Scored Society: Due Process for Automated Predictions' (2014) 89 Washington Law Review 1.

Kennedy D, 'Cost Benefit Analysis of Debtor Protection Rules in Subprime Market Default Situations', in E Belsky, N Retsinas (eds), *Building Assets, Building Credit: Creating Wealth in Low-Income Communities* (Brookings Institution Press 2005).

Kennedy LJ, McCoy PA, Bernstein E, 'The Consumer Financial Protection Bureau: Financial Regulation for the Twenty-First Century' (2012) 97 Cornell Law Review 1141.

Kenny M, Devenney J, Fox O'Mahony L (eds), *Unconscionability in European Private Financial Transactions. Protecting the Vulnerable* (Cambridge University Press 2010).

Kilborn JJ, 'Expert Recommendations and the Evolution of European Best Practices for the Treatment of Overindebtedness, 1984–2010', 2010 <https://ssrn.com/abstract =1663108> (accessed October 2019).

Kim PT, 'Auditing Algorithms for Discrimination' (2017) 166 University of Pennsylvania Law Review Online 189.

Köndgen J, 'Policy Responses to Credit Crises: Does the Law of Contract Provide an Answer?' in S Grundmann, YM Atamer (eds), *Financial Services, Financial Crisis and General European Contract Law* (Wolters Kluwer 2011).

Kozuka S, Nottage L, 'Re-regulating Unsecured Consumer Credit in Japan: Over-indebted Borrowers, the Supreme Court, and New Legislation', (2007) Sydney Law School, Legal Studies Research Paper n. 07/62.

Kozuka S, Nottage L, 'The Myth of the Cautious Consumer: Law, Culture, Economics and Politics in the Rise and Partial Fall of Unsecured Lending in Japan', in J Niemi, I Ramsay, WC Whitford (eds), *Consumer Credit, Debt and Bankruptcy. Comparative and International Perspectives* (Hart 2009).

Krimphove D, Lüke D, 'The Transformation of the Mortgage Credit Directive in German Law' in M Anderson, E Arroyo Amayuelas (eds), *The Impact of the Mortgage Credit Directive in Europe. Contrasting Views from Member States* (Europa Law Publishing 2017).

Kroll JA, Huey J, Barocas S, Felten EW, Reidenberg JR, Robinson DG, Yu H, 'Accountable Algorithms' (2017) 165 University of Pennsylvania Law Review 633.

Kruithof M, 'A Differentiated Approach to Client Protection: The Example of MiFID', in S Grundmann, YM Atamer (eds), *Financial Services, Financial Crisis and General European Contract Law* (Wolters Kluwer 2011).

L Stanghellini, 'Il 'credito responsabile': dal credito all'impresa al credito al consumo' (2007) 26 Le società 395.

Lamandini M, Lusignani G, Muñoz DR, 'Does Europe Have What It Takes to Finish the Banking Union? Non-Performing Loans (NPLs) and Their Hard Choices, Non-Choices and Evolving Choices' (2017) EBI Working Paper.

Lambo L, 'Responsabilità civile e obblighi di protezione', (2008) 13 Danno e respon-sabilità, 129.

Lang F, Signore S, Gvetadze S, 'The role of cooperative banks and smaller institu-tions for the financing of SMEs and small midcaps in Europe' (2016) European Investment Fund Research & Market Analysis Working Paper 2016/36.

Larocca S, 'L'obbligo di verifica del merito creditizio del consumatore', in V Rizzo, E Caterini, L Di Nella, L Mezzasomma (eds), *La tutela del consumatore nelle posizioni di debito e credito* (Edizioni Scientifiche Italiane 2010).

Lasserre Capdeville J, 'L'évaluation de la solvabilité de l'emprunteur et les devoirs d'explication et de mise en garde à la charge du prêteur', Gazette du Palais, 23–25 août 2015, Nos. 235–237.

Lawless RM, 'The Paradox of Consumer Credit', (2007) 1 University of Illinois Law Review 347.

Legeais D, *Les Opérations de crédit* (LexisNexis 2015).

Legrand P, *Le droit compare* (3rd ed Presses Universitaires de France 2009).

Legrand V, 'Le nouveau droit du crédit immobilier: enfin la consécration d'un crédit responsable?', Petites Affiches, 22 avril 2016, n 81.

Levin A, Nicholson MJ, 'Privacy Law in the United States, the EU and Canada: The Allure of the Middle Ground' (2005) 2 University of Ottawa Law & Technology Journal 357.

Levitin AJ, Pavlov AD, Wachter SW, 'The Dodd-Frank Act and Housing Finance: Can it Restore Private Risk Capital to the Securitization Market?' (2012) 29 Yale Journal on Regulation 155.

Liberti JM, Peterson, MA, 'Information: Hard and Soft' (2019) 8 Review of Corporate Finance Studies 1.

Long, LJ 'An Uneasy Case for a Tort of Negligent Interference with Credit Contract', (2003–2004) 22 Quinnipiac Law Review 235.

Lubrano di Scorpaniello M, *Società di rating. Innovazioni di governance e tutela dell'affidamento* (Giuffrè 2016).

Lukacs, F, 'La responsabilità delle società di *rating* nei confronti dei soggetti valutati (per l'emissione di *solicited* o *unsolicited rating*) e nei confronti dei terzi', in A Principe (ed), *Le agenzie di rating* (Giuffrè 2014).

Lupoi A, 'La Direttiva 17/2014, il mercato dei crediti immobiliari e la consulenza al credito' (2016) 69 Banca borsa e titoli di credito 234.

Macey JR, Miller GP, O'Hara M, Rosenberg GD, 'Helping Law Catch up to Markets: Applying Broker-Dealer Law To Subprime Mortgage' (2009) 34 The Journal of Corporation Law 789, 791 ff.

Maculay S, 'Elegant Models, Empirical Pictures, and the Complexities of Contract', (1977) 11 Law & Society Review 507.

Maggiolino M, 'EU trade secrets law and algorithmic transparency' (2018) 27 AIDA Annali italiani del diritto d'autore, della cultura e dello spettacolo 199.

Mak C, 'Harmonising Effects of Fundamental Rights in European Contract Law' (2007) 1 Erasmus Law Review 59.

Mak C, *Fundamental Rights in European Contract Law* (Kluwer Law International 2008).

Mak V, 'The "Average Consumer" of EU law in domestic litigation: Examples from consumer credit and investment cases' (2012) Tilburg Law School Legal Studies Research Paper Series n. 4.

Mak V, 'What is Responsible Lending? The EU Consumer Mortgage Credit Directive in the UK and the Netherlands' (2015) 38 Journal of Consumer Policy 411.

Malgieri G, Comandé G, 'Why a Right to Legibility of Automated Decision-Making Exists in the General Data Protection Regulation' (2017) 7 International Data Privacy Law 243.

Malinconico A, *Il credit risk management del portafoglio prestiti. Da Basilea I a Basilea III* (Franco Angeli 2012).

Mann RJ, *Charging Ahead. The Growth and Regulation of Payment Card Markets around the World* (Cambridge University Press 2006).

Mann RJ, 'Credit Cards, Consumer Credit & Bankruptcy', (2006) University of Texas School of Law, Law and Economics Research Paper n. 44.

Mann RJ, 'Bankruptcy Reform and the "Sweat Box" of Credit Card Debt', [2007] University of Illinois Law Review 375.

Manns J, 'Rating Risk after the Subprime Mortgage Crisis: A User Fee Approach for Rating Agency Accountability' (2009) 87 North Carolina Law Review 1011.

Marchesi M, *Rating e trasparenza. Esperienze europee e nordamericane a confronto* (Giappichelli 2015).

Marella MR 'Human Dignity in a Different Light: European Contract Law, Social Dignity and the Retreat of the Welfare State', in S Grundmann, *Constitutional Values and European Contract Law* (Kluwer Law International 2008) 123.

Marsh TD, Norman JW, 'The Impact of Dodd-Frank on Community Banks' (2013) American Enterprise Institute, Wake Forest University Legal Studies Paper No.2302392.

Mattei U, *La proprietà immobiliare* (Giappichelli 1993).

Mattila HES, *Comparative Legal Linguistics. Language of Law, Latin and Modern Lingua Francas*, (2d. ed. Routledge 2016).

Maugeri MR, Pagliantini S, *Il credito ai consumatori. I rimedi nella ricostruzione degli organi giudicanti* (Giuffré 2013).

Maugeri MR, Pagliantini S, Las Casas A, 'Recent trends of the ECJ on consumer protection: *Aziz* and *Constructora Principado*', (2014) 10 European Review of Contract Law 444.

Maugeri MR, 'Precontractual Duties in Consumer Credit Contracts and Remedies for their Breach' (2018) *Persona e Mercato*, 2018/3, 189.

Maurer VG, Thomas RE, 'Getting Credit Where Credit Is Due: Proposed Changes in the Fair Credit Reporting Act' (1997) 34 American Business Law Journal 607.

McCoy PA, Wachter SM, 'The Macroprudential Implications of the Qualified Mortgage Debate' (2020) 83 *Law and Contemporary Problems* 21.

McNamara RM, 'The Fair Credit Reporting Act: A Legislative Overview' (1973) 22 Journal of Public Law 67.

McNamara RM, Piontek T, Metrick A, 'Basel III A: Regulatory History', (2014) Yale Program on Financial Stability Case Study 2014-1A-V1.

Mendoza I, Bygrave LA, 'The Right not to be Subject to Automated Decisions based on Profiling', in T Synodinou, P Jougleux, C Markou, T Prastitou, (eds), *EU Internet Law: Regulation and Enforcement* (Springer 2017).

Mengoni L, 'Sulla natura della responsabilità precontrattuale', (1956) 54 Rivista del diritto commerciale, 9–10, 360.

Mezzanotte F, 'Centrali rischi private e 'diritto di preavviso' della segnalazione' (2017) 33 La nuova giurisprudenza civile commentata, 303.

Mian A, Sufi A, 'The Consequences of Mortgage Credit Expansion: Evidence from the U.S. Mortgage Default Crisis', (2009) 124 Quarterly Journal of Economics 1449.

Michaels R, 'The Functional Method of Comparative Law', in M Reimann, R Zimmermann (eds), *The Oxford Handbook of Comparative Law* (Oxford University Press 2006) 339.

Micklitz H-W, 'The Visible Hand of European Regulatory Private Law. The Transformation of European Private Law from Autonomy to Functionalism in Competition and Regulation' (2008) EUI Law Working Paper 2008/14.

Micklitz H-W, 'Administrative Enforcement of European Private Law' in R Brownsword et al (eds), *The Foundations of European Private Law* (Hart Publishing 2011).

Micklitz H-W, 'Social Justice and Access Justice in Private Law', (2011) EUI Law Working Papers 2011/02.

Micklitz H-W, Reich N, 'The Court and Sleeping Beauty: The Revival of the Unfair Contract Terms Directive (UCTD)' (2014) 51 Common Market Law Review 771.

Micklitz H-W, Domurath I (eds), *Consumer Debt and Social Exclusion in Europe* (Routledge 2015).

Micklitz H-W, *The Politics of Justice in European Private Law: Social Justice, Access Justice, Societal Justice* (Cambridge University Press 2018).

Miglionico, A, *Enhancing the regulation of credit rating agencies, in search of a method*, Centre for Financial & Management Studies, SOAS (London 2012).

Miglionico, A., *The Governance of Credit Rating Agencies. Regulatory Regimes and Liability Issues*, (Elgar 2019).

Miller RE, Sarat A, 'Grievances, Claims, and Disputes: Assessing the Adversary Culture', (1980–1981) 15 Law & Society Review 525.

Minneci U, 'Erronea segnalazione alla centrale rischi: profili rimediali', (2004) 22 Rivista critica di diritto privato 89.

Mirone A, 'L'evoluzione della disciplina sulla trasparenza bancaria in tempo di crisi: istruzioni di vigilanza, credito al consumo, commissioni di massimo scoperto' (2010) 63 Banca, borsa e titoli di credito 557.

Modica L, 'Concessione 'abusiva' di credito ai consumatori' (2012) 28 Contratto e impresa 492.

Moloney N, 'Resetting the Location of Regulatory and Supervisory Control over EU Financial Markets: Lessons from Five Years On' (2013) 62 International & Comparative Law Quarterly 955.

Muldrew C, 'Interpreting the Market: The Ethics of Credit and Community Relations in Early Modern England' (1993) 18 Social History 163.

Nader L, *The Life of the Law. Anthropological Projects* (University of California Press 2002).

National Consumer Law Center, Yu et al, Big Data: A Big Disappointment for Scoring Consumer Credit Risk (2014) <https://www.nclc.org/images/pdf/pr-reports/report-big-data.pdf> (accessed July 2020).

Natoli R, *Il contratto"adeguato"* (Giuffrè 2012).

Navaretta E, 'Principi dell'Unione europea, politiche economiche e diritto privato', (2020) Osservatorio del diritto civile e commerciale n. 2/2020, 409.

Neergaard U, Szyszczak E, van de Gronden JW, Krajewski M (eds), *Legal Issues of Services of General Interest*, (TMC Asser Press-Springer 2013).

Nield S, Hopkins N, 'Human rights and mortgage repossession: beyond property law using Article 8' (2013) 33 Legal Studies 431.

Nield S, 'Borrowers as consumers: new notions of unconscionability for domestic borrowers', in M Kenny, J Devenney, L Fox O'Mahony (eds), *Unconscionability in European Private Financial Transactions. Protecting the Vulnerable* (Cambridge University Press 2010).

Nield S, 'Article 8 respect for the home: A human property right?', (2013) 24 *King's Law Journal* 147.

Niemi J, 'Personal Insolvency' in G Howells, I Ramsay, T Wilhelmsson, D Kraft (eds), *Handbook of Research on International Consumer Law* (Elgar 2010).

Niemi-Kiesiläinen J, Ramsay I, Whitford WC (eds), *Consumer Bankruptcy in Global Perspective* (Hart 2003).

Nigro A, 'La responsabilità della banca per concessione 'abusiva' di credito', in G Portale (ed), *Le operazioni bancarie*, (Giuffrè 1978).

Nigro A, 'Linee di tendenza delle nuove discipline di trasparenza. Dalla trasparenza alla "consulenza"?' (2011) 25 Diritto della banca e del mercato finanziario 11.

Nogler L, Reifner U, (eds), *Life Time Contracts. Social Long-Term Contracts in Labour, Tenancy and Consumer Credit Law* (Eleven International Publishing 2014).

O'Neill O, 'Agents of Justice', (2001) 32 Metaphilosophy 180.

OCC/FRB/FDIC 'Interagency Guidance on Leveraged Lending', (22 March 2013) 78 Federal Register 56.

Odinet CK, 'The Unfinished Business of Dodd-Frank: Reforming the Mortgage Contract' (2016) 69 South Methodist University Law Review 653.

Olegario R, *A Culture of Credit. Embedding Trust and Transparency in American Business* (Harvard University Press 2006).

Oliphant K, 'Culture of Tort Law in Europe' (2012) 3 Journal of European Tort Law 147.

Örücü E, Attwool E, Coyle S, *Studies in Legal Systems: Mixed and Mixing* (Kluwer Law International 1996).

Örücü E, 'Methodology of Comparative Law' in JM Smits (ed), *Elgar Encyclopedia of Comparative Law* (Edward Elgar 2012) 442.

Pacces AM, Romano A, 'A Strict Liability Regime for Rating Agencies', 2014 European Corporate Governance Institute Law Working Paper n. 245/2014.

Padilla JA, Pagano M, 'Sharing Default Information as a Borrower Discipline Device', (1999) CSEF Working Paper n 21.

Pagliantini S, 'Statuto dell'informazione e prestito responsabile nella direttiva 17/2014/ UE (sui contratti di credito ai consumatori relative a beni immobili residenziali)' in P Sirena (ed), *I mutui ipotecari nel diritto comparato ed europeo. Commentario alla direttiva 2014/17/UE*, I Quaderni della Fondazione Italiana del Notariato (il Sole 24 Ore 2016).

Paglietti MC 'Percorsi evolutivi del diritto all'abitazione', (2008) 13 Rivista di diritto privato 1.

Pardieck AM, 'Japan and the Moneylenders – Activist Courts and Substantive Justice' (2008) 17 Pacific Rim Law & Policy Journal 529.

Partington M, Jowell J (eds), *Welfare Law & Policy* (Pinter 1979).

Partnoy F, 'The Paradox of Credit Ratings', in RM Levich, G Majnoni, C Reinhart, (eds), *Ratings, Rating Agencies and the Global Financial System* (Springer Science+ Business Media 2002).

Partnoy F, 'How and Why Credit Rating Agencies Are Not Like Other Gatekeepers', in Y Fuchita, RE Litan (eds), *Financial Gatekeepers: Can they Protect Investors?* (Brookings Institution Press and the Nomura Institute of Capital Markets Research 2006).

Pasquale F, 'Restoring Transparency to Automated Authority' (2011) 9 Journal on Telecommunications & High Technology Law 235.

Pasquale F, *The Black Box Society: The Secret Algorithms That Control Money and Information* (Harvard University Press 2015).

Pence KM, 'Foreclosing on Opportunity: State Laws and Mortgage Credit' (2006) 88 The Review of Economics and Statistics 177.

Perrella A, Catz J, 'Interconnecting multiple granular datasets to evaluate credit risks. The ESCB experience', ECB, 17th International Conference on Credit Risk Evaluation Designed for Institutional Targeting in finance (2018) 7 <http://www .greta.it/credit/credit2018/PAPERS/Friday/poster/10_Perrella_Catz.pdf> (accessed July 2020).

Peterson CL, 'Truth, Understanding, and High-Cost Consumer Credit: The Historical Context of the Truth in Lending Act' (2003) 55 *Florida Law Review*, 808.

Peterson CL, 'Consumer Financial Protection Bureau Law Enforcement: An Empirical Review' (2016) 90 Tulane Law Review 1058.

Piepoli G, 'Sovraindebitamento e credito responsabile' (2013) 66 Banca borsa e titoli di credito 38.

Pincus LB, Johns R, 'Private Parts: A Global Analysis of Privacy Protection Schemes and a Proposed Innovation for Their Comparative Evaluation' (1997) 16 Journal of Business Ethics 1237.

Posner RA, 'The Right of Privacy' (9178) 12 Georgia Law Review 393.

Post RC, 'Three Concepts of Privacy' (2001) 89 Georgetown Law Journal 2087.

Pottow JAE, 'Private Liability for Reckless Consumer Lending' (2007) *University of Illinois Law Review* 405.

Pottow JAE, 'Ability to Pay', (2011) 8 Berkeley Business Law Journal 176.

Pozzo B (ed), *Ordinary Language and Legal Language* (Giuffrè, 2005).

Pozzo B, 'Comparative law and language' in M Bussani, U Mattei (eds) *The Cambridge Companion to Comparative Law* (Cambridge University Press 2012).

Pozzo B, *Lingua e diritto: oltre l'Europa* (Giuffrè 2014).

Rabin EH, 'The Revolution in Landlord Tenant Law: Causes and Consequences', in (1984) 69 Cornell Law Review 517.

Radin MJ, 'Residential Rent Control', in (1986) 15 Philosophy & Public Affairs, 350.

Ramsay I, 'Consumer Credit Law, Distributive Justice and the Welfare State', (1995) 15 Oxford Journal of Legal Studies 177.

Ramsay I, Williams T, 'Inequality, Market Discrimination, and Credit Markets', in I Ramsay (ed), *Consumer Law in the Global Economy* (Ashgate 1997).

Ramsay I, 'Consumer redress and access to justice' in CE Rickett, TGW Telfer (eds), *International Perspectives on Consumers' Access to Justice* (Cambridge University Press 2003).

Ramsay I, "From Truth in Lending to Responsible Lending", in G Howells, A Janssen, R Schulze (eds) *Information Rights and Obligations* (Ashgate 2005).

Ramsay I, Williams T, 'The Crash that launched a thousand fixes – Regulation of Consumer Credit after the Lending Revolution and the Credit Crunch', in A Kern, N Moloney, *Law Reform and Financial Markets* (Elgar 2011) 221.

Ramsay I, 'Consumer Credit Regulation after the Fall: International Dimensions' (2012) 1 Journal of European Consumer and Market Law, 24.

Rank A, Schmidt-Kessel M, 'Mortgage credit in Germany', (2017) 6 Journal of European Consumer and Market Law 176.

Reddix-Smalls B, 'Credit Scoring and Trade Secrecy: An Algorithmic Quagmire or How the Lack of Transparency in Complex Financial Models Scuttled the Finance Market' (2011) 12 U.C. Davis Business Law Journal 87.

Regan P, *Legislating Privacy*, (University of North Carolina Press 1995).

Reidenberg JR, 'Privacy in the Information Economy: A Fortress or Frontier for Individual Rights?' (1992) 44 Federal Communications Law Journal 195.

Reidenberg JR, Schwartz PM, *Data Privacy Law – A Study of United States Data Protection* (Michie 1996).

Reidenberg JR, 'Resolving Conflicting International Data Privacy Rules in Cyberspace' (1999–2000) 52 Stanford Law Review 1315.

Reifner U, Nieme-Kiesiläinen J, Huls N, Springeneer H, *Overindebtedness in European Consumer Law* (Books on Demand 2019).

Reiss D, 'Message in a Mortgage: What Dodd-Frank's 'Qualified Mortgage' Tells Us About Ourselves' (2011–2012) 31 Review of Banking & Financial Law 717.

Report of the Expert Group on Credit Histories, DG Internal Market and Services, 2009.

Resta G, *Autonomia privata e diritti della personalità* (Jovene 2005).

Richards NM, King JH, 'Three Paradoxes of Big Data' (2013) 66 Stanford Law Review Online 41.

Rigaux F, *La protection de la vie privée et des autres biens de la personnalité* (Bruylant 1990).

Rischkowsky F, Döring T, 'Consumer Policy in a Market Economy: Considerations from the Perspective of the Economics of Information, the New Institutional Economics as well as Behavioural Economics' (2008) 31 Journal of Consumer Policy 285.

Rodotà S, *Elaboratori elettronici e controllo sociale* (Il Mulino 1973).

Rodotà S, *Il terribile diritto. Studi sulla proprietà privata* (Il Mulino 1981).

Rodotà S, *Tecnologie e diritti* (Il Mulino 1995).

Rojas Elgueta G, The Economic Foundation of Debtor-Creditor Relations (Il Mulino 2018).

Rosenblatt E, *Credit Data and Scoring: The First Triumph of Big Data and Big Algorithms* (Elsevier 2020).

Rott P, 'A New Social Contract Law for Public Services? Consequences from Regulation of Services of General Economic Interest in the EC', (2005) European Review of Contract Law n. 3, 323.

Rott P, 'Consumers and services of general interest: Is EC consumer law the future?' (2007) 30 Journal of Consumer Policy 49.

Rott P, 'Consumer credit', in N Reich et al (eds), *European Consumer Law* (Intersentia 2014).

Rousseau, S, 'Regulating Credit Rating Agencies After the Financial Crisis: the Long and Winding Road Toward Accountability' (2009) Capital Markets Institute, Rotman School of Management, University of Toronto, 43.

Rouvroy A, Poullet Y, 'The Right to Informational Self-Determination and the Values of Self-Development: Reassessing the Value of Privacy for Democracy', in S Gutwirth (ed), *Reinventing Data Protection* (Springer 2009).

Rutledge S, Annamalai N, Lester R, Symonds R, 'Good practices for consumer protection and financial literacy in Europe and Central Asia: a diagnostic tool', (2010) Washington D.C., World Bank Group.

Sabato G, 'Credit Risk Scoring Models', 2010, 4 <https://ssrn.com/abstract=1546347> (accessed September 2019).

Sacco Ginevri A, 'Le società di rating nel regolamento CE n. 1060/2009: profili organizzativi dell'attività' (2010) 33 *Nuove leggi civili commentate* 291.

Sacco R, 'Legal Formants, A Dynamic Approach to Comparative Law I', (1991) 39 American Journal of Comparative Law 1.

Sacco R, 'Traduzione giuridica', in *Digesto delle discipline privatistiche, Aggiornamento,* (2000), 722.

Sacco R, *Antropologia giuridica. Contributo ad una macrostoria del diritto* (Il Mulino 2007).

Samuel G, *An Introduction to Comparative Law Theory and Method* (Hart 2014).

Sanna P, *La responsabilità civile delle agenzie di rating nei confronti degli investitori* (Edizioni scientifiche italiane 2011).

Šarčević S, *New Approach to Legal Translation* (Kluwer Law International 1997).

Saunders, A, Millon Cornett, M, *Financial Institutions Management. A risk management approach* (6th ed McGraw-Hill/Irwin 2008).

Saunders M, Cohen A, 'Federal Regulation of Consumer Credit: The Cause or the Cure for Predatory Lending?' (2004) Joint Center for Housing Studies, Harvard University, BABC 04-21, 10.

Sauter W, *Public Services in EU Law* (Cambridge University Press 2015).

Scaroni C, 'La responsabilità delle agenzie di rating nei confronti degli investitori' (2011) 27 Contratto e impresa 764.

Scarso A, 'The Liability of Credit Rating Agencies in a Comparative Perspective' (2013) 4 Journal of European Tort Law 163.

Schauer F, *Law and Language* (New York University Press 1993).

Schmid CU 'General Report' Working Paper, <https://www.eui.eu/Documents/Depart mentsCentres/Law/ResearchTeaching/ResearchThemes/EuropeanPrivateLaw/ TenancyLawProject/TenancyLawGeneralReport.pdf> (accessed October 2021).

Schramm-Strosser M, 'The 'Not So' Fair Credit Reporting Act: Federal Preemption, Injunctive Relief, and the Need to Return Remedies for Common Law Defamation to the States' (2012) 14 Duquesne Business Law Journal 165.

Schwarcz, SL, 'Private Ordering of Public Markets: the Rating Agency Paradox' (2002) 2 University of Illinois Law Review 12.

Schwarcz SL, 'Understanding the Subprime Financial Crisis' (2008–2009) 60 South Carolina Law Review 549.

Schwarcz SL, 'Macroprudential Regulation of Mortgage Lending', (2016) 69 South Methodist University Law Review 595.

Schwartz P, Solove D, 'The PII Problem: Privacy and a New Concept of Personally Identifiable Information', (2001) 86 New York University Law Review 1814.

Schwartz PM, 'The EU-U.S. Privacy Collision: a Turn to Institutions and Procedures' (2013) 126 Harvard Law Review 1966, 2013.

Sciarrone Alibrandi A, 'Centrali dei rischi creditizi e normativa di privacy: informazione e controlli dell'interessato' (2003) 49 Rivista di diritto civile 423.

Sciarrone Alibrandi A, 'Trasmissione dei dati alle centrali rischi: consenso e informazione dell'interessato', in A Sciarrone Alibrandi (ed) *Centrale dei rischi. Profili civilistici* (Giuffrè 2005).

Scognamiglio C, 'Il danno al patrimonio tra contratto e torto' (2007) 72 Responsabilità civile e previdenza 1255.

Scott C, 'Services of General Interest in EC Law: Matching Values to Regulatory Technique in the Public and Privatised Sectors' (2000) 6 European Law Journal 310.

Sen A, 'Rights and Agency' (1982) 11 Philosophy & Public Affairs 3.

Shapo MS, *Tort Law and Culture* (Carolina Academic Press 2003).

Shin HS, 'Securitisation and Financial Stability' (2009) 119 The Economic Journal 309.

Smith RE, *Ben Franklin's Web Site. Privacy and Curiosity from Plymouth Rock to the Internet*, (Privacy Journal Publisher 2004).

Solove DJ, 'Introduction: Privacy Self-Management and the Consent Dilemma' (2013) 126 Harvard Law Review 1880.

Steinbock DJ, 'Data Matching, Data Mining, and Due Process' (2005) 40 Georgia Law Review 1.

Stiglitz JE, Weiss A, 'Credit Rationing in Markets with Imperfect Information' (1981) 71 The American Economic Review 393.

Sullivan T, Warren E, Westbrook J, *The Fragile Middle Class: Americans in Debt* (Yale University Press 2000).

Sum K, *Post-Crisis Banking Regulation in the European Union. Opportunities and Threats* (Palgrave Macmillan 2016).

Sunstein CR, 'Boundedly Rational Borrowing' (2006) 73 University of Chicago Law Review 249.

Svetiev Y, Ottow A, 'Financial Supervision in the Interstices Between Private and Public Law' (2014) 10 European Review of Contract Law 496.

Sy ANR, 'Systemic Regulation of Credit Rating Agencies and Rated Markets', (2009) IMF Working Paper.

Taibi AD, 'Banking, Finance, and Community Economic Empowerment: Structural Economic Theory, Procedural Civil Rights and Substantive Racial Justice' (1994) 107 Harvard Law Review 1465.

Tatarano G (ed), *Diritto all'abitazione finanziamenti all'impresa, alla cooperazione, alla persona* (Edizioni Scientifiche Italiane 1986).

Thaler R, 'Towards a Positive Theory of Consumer Choice' (1980) 1 Journal of Economic Behavior and Organization 39.

Thomas LC, 'A survey of credit risk and behavioural scoring: forecasting financial risk of lending to consumers' (2000) 16 International Journal of Forecasting 149.

Thomas LC, *Consumer Credit Models: Pricing, Profit and Portfolios* (Oxford University Press 2009).

Thomas, LC, Edelman DB, Crook J, *Credit scoring and its applications* (2nd ed SIAM 2017).

Thomson J, 'The Right to Privacy' (1975) 4 Philosophy and Public Affairs 295.

Todeschini G, 'La banca e il ghetto. Una storia italiana (secoli XIV–XVI)' (Laterza 2016).

Tommasi S, *La tutela del consumatore nei contratti di credito immobiliare* (Edizioni scientifiche italiane 2018).

Truli E, 'The General Data Protection Regulation and Civil Liability', in M Bakhoum, M Conde Gallego, B Mackenrodt, et al, *Personal Data in Competition, Consumer Protection and Intellectual Property Law* (Springer 2018).

Tuch A, 'Multiple Gatekeepers' (2010) 96 Virginia Law Review 1583.

Turner MA, Walker PD, Chaudhuri S, Duncan J, Varghese R, 'Credit Impacts of More Comprehensive Credit Reporting in Australia and New Zealand' (2012) Policy & Economic Research Council, Durham.

Ulen TS, 'Information in the Market Economy – Cognitive Errors and Legal Correctives' in S Grundmann, W Kerver, S Weatherhill (eds), *Party Autonomy and the Role of Information in the Internal Market*, (de Gruyter 2001).

Vabres R, 'Le devoir de ne pas contracter dans le secteur bancaire et financier' (2012) *La semaine juridique, éd. Générale*, n. 40, 1er octobre 2012, 1052.

Valcke C, '"Droit": réflexions sur une définition aux fins de comparaison' in P Legrand, *Comparer les droits, résolument* (Presses Universitaires de France 2009) 99.

van Boom WH, Koziol H, Witting CA (eds), *Pure Economic Loss* (Springer 2004).

Van Heerden C, Renke S, 'Perspectives on the South African Responsible Lending Regime and the Duty to Conduct Pre-agreement Assessment as a Responsible Lending Practice', (2015) 24 INSOL International Insolvency Review 67.

van Hoecke M, Warrington M, 'Legal Cultures, Legal Paradigms and Legal Doctrine: Towards a New Model for Comparative Law' (1998) 47 International & Comparative Law Quarterly 495.

Van Roy P, 'Is there a difference between solicited and unsolicited bank ratings and if so, why?', National Bank of Belgium, (2006) Working Paper Research Series No.79.

Verdier R (ed), *La Vengeance: La vengeance dans les sociétés extra-occidentales* (Cujas 1980).

Wachter S, Mittelstadt B, Floridi L, 'Why a Right to Explanation of Automated Decision-Making Does Not Exist in the General Data Protection Regulation' (2017) 7 International Data Privacy Law 76.

Wacks R, 'The Poverty of Privacy', (1980) 96 Law Quarterly Review 73.

Warren SD, Brandeis LD, 'The Right to Privacy' (1980) 4 Harvard Law Review 195.

Weatherhill S, 'Justifying Limits to Party Autonomy in the Internal Market – EC Legislation in the Field of Consumer Protection', in S Grundmann, W Kerver, S Weatherhill (eds), *Party Autonomy and the Role of Information in the Internal Market*, (de Gruyter 2001).

Westin A, *Privacy and Freedom* (Atheneum 1967).

White LJ, 'Focusing on Fannie and Freddie: The Dilemmas of Reforming Housing Finance', (2003) 23 Journal of Financial Services Research 43.

Whitman JQ, 'The Two Western Cultures of Privacy: Dignity versus Liberty' (2004) 113 Yale Law Journal 1151.

Wilhelmsson T, *Critical Studies in Private Law. A Treatise on Need-Rational Principles in Modern Law* (Kluwer Academic Publishers 1992).

Wilhelmsson T, *Social Contract Law and European Integration* (Dartmouth 1995).

Wilhelmsson T, 'Consumer Law and Social Justice' in I Ramsay (ed), *Consumer Law in the Global Economy* (Ashgate-Dartmouth 1997).

Wilhelmsson T, 'Services of general interest and European Private law,' in CE Rickett, TGW Telfer (eds), *International Perspectives on Consumers' Access to Justice* (Cambridge University Press 2003).

Wilmarth AE Jr, 'The Dodd-Frank Act's Expansion of State Authority to Protect Consumers of Financial Services' (2011) 36 Journal of Corporation Law 893.

World Bank, 'General Principles for Credit Reporting', Financial Infrastructure Series, Credit Reporting Policy and Research (2011).

World Bank, 'Global Financial Development Report 2013: Rethinking the Role of State in Finance', Washington, DC (2012).

World Bank, 'Responsible Lending. Overview of Regulatory Tools' The World Bank, Washington D.C. (2013).

World Bank, 'Global Survey on Consumer Protection and Financial Literacy: Oversight Frameworks and Practices in 114 Economies', International Bank for Reconstruction and Development/The World Bank (2014).

Wright JD, 'Dodd-Frank's 'Abusive Standard': A Call for Certainty' (2011) 8 Berkeley Business Law Journal 164.

Wuermeling U, 'Scoring von Kreditrisiken' (2002) Neue Juristische Wochenschrift, 3508.

Wymeersch E, 'Corporate Governance of Banks According to the CRD IV' in P Gasós (ed) *Challenges in Securities Markets Regulation: Investor Protection and Corporate Governance, SUERF Study 2015/1*, (Larcier 2015) 67.

Zaring D, 'The emerging post-crisis paradigm for international financial regulation', in F Bignami, D Zaring (eds), *Comparative Law and Regulation. Understanding the Global Regulatory Process*, (Edward Elgar Publishing 2016).

Zarsky TZ, 'Transparent Predictions', (2013) University of Illinois Law Review 1503.

Zeno-Zencovich V, *Onore e reputazione nel sistema del diritto civile. Uno studio comparato* (Jovene 1985).

Zeno-Zencovich V, (ed) *Le banche dati in Italia* (Jovene 1985).

Zeno-Zencovich V, 'Privacy e informazioni a contenuto economico' in F Cardarelli, S Sica, V Zeno-Zencovich (eds) *Il codice dei dati personali. Temi e problemi* (Giuffrè 2004).

Zeno-Zencovich V, Giannone Codiglione G, 'Ten legal perspectives on the "big data revolution"' (2016) 23 Big Data e Concorrenza, Concorrenza e mercato numero speciale a.c. F. Di Porto, 33.

Zeno-Zencovich V, '"Smart Contracts', 'Granular Norms' and Non-Discrimination", in C Busch, A De Franceschi (ed), *Algorithmic Regulation and Personalized Law*, (Hart 2020) 264.

Ziller J, 'The Constitutional Dimensions of Tenancy Law in the European Union' Background paper <https://www.eui.eu/Documents/DepartmentsCentres/Law/ResearchTeaching/ResearchThemes/EuropeanPrivateLaw/TenancyLawProject/TenancyLawZiller.pdf> (accessed October 2021).

Zweigert K, Kötz H, *An Introduction to Comparative Law* (T Weir tr, 3rd ed, Oxford University Press 1998).

Zywicki TJ, Adamson JD 'The Law and Economics of Subprime Lending' (2009) 80 University of Colorado Law Review 1.

Zywicki TJ, 'The Consumer Financial Protection Bureau: Savior or Menace?' (2013) 81 The George Washington Law Review 857.

Index

Printed in the United States
by Baker & Taylor Publisher Services